# A Qualified Teacher in Every Classroom?

## Appraising Old Answers and New Ideas

*Edited by Frederick M. Hess,*
*Andrew J. Rotherham, and*
*Catherine B. Walsh*

HARVARD EDUCATION PRESS

# Contents

# Introduction

*Frederick M. Hess, Andrew J. Rotherham, and Catherine B. Walsh*

In recent years, the debate over teacher quality and preparation has gained new urgency. During that time, competing groups of partisans have dominated this debate, one seemingly eager to assail the nation's education schools and to suggest that there is an insufficiently defined body of professional teaching knowledge, and the other committed to advancing professionalism by ensuring that all teachers are prepared and licensed through a prescribed and formal training program. The conflict is suffusing research, confusing policymakers, and stifling potentially promising reforms.

Widespread teacher shortages in high-poverty schools and key academic areas, as well as impending mass retirements, have created a sense of urgency around teacher recruitment, preparation, and induction, and have rendered policy and practice ripe for rethinking.

Teachers are the key to making schools work. On this point there is agreement across the political spectrum, among educators and researchers, and within the policy community. The teacher-quality challenge is so daunting because so few schools have the teachers they need. Academically stronger college students tend to shun the teaching profession. Undergraduate education majors typically have lower SAT and ACT scores than other students, and teachers who leave the profession in their first few years have higher scores than those who remain in teaching. In addition, research shows that the lower the quality of the undergraduate institution one attends, the more likely they are to wind up in the teaching profession.

The result is that 44 percent of middle school students take at least one class with a teacher who doesn't have even a minor in the subject being taught. That figure is almost 25 percent for secondary school students, and it climbs to 32 percent in high-poverty schools. The problem is compounded because we need to hire about 200,000 new teachers a year just to fill the nation's classrooms at the same time new federal policies are raising the bar for teacher qualifications.

In other words, a confluence of events means that policymakers must take bold steps to meet this challenge. The needs are simply too great to rely on boutique efforts or changes at the margins.

The practical challenges of school staffing were codified into a statutory challenge by the sweeping federal No Child Left Behind (NCLB) legislation that was signed into law by President George W. Bush in January 2002. NCLB requires states to close the teacher-quality gap between high and low poverty schools and ensure that all teachers are "highly qualified" by 2005-06. However, while qualified teachers have long been identified by whether they had completed one of the nation's 1,300-plus teacher-preparation programs, NCLB was intentionally vague on this point. Instead, the law requires subject-matter expertise for middle and high school teachers and appropriate coursework for elementary school teachers. The law leaves it to states to decide what, beyond these core requirements, is required for certification and whether states choose to use a new metric for determining who is a qualified teacher.

NCLB forces states to confront the long-lamented fact that substantial numbers of their teachers, especially in urban schools, are neither licensed nor qualified to teach by almost any definition. Governors and state legislators are facing the question of how to find qualified teachers for these classrooms. In answering that challenge there are two very different courses of action consistent with the NCLB mandate.

In this volume, we seek to move beyond impassioned rhetoric by presenting fresh research on key elements of the teacher-quality challenge and by posing "next generation" models of reform. While the supply of quality teachers is certainly influenced by teacher salaries and school working environments, it is also shaped directly by state policies regarding teacher certification and by the quality of college and university teacher training programs. Despite the magnitude of this problem, promising innovations remain the exception, and traditional practices attract many heated critiques and defenses but little rigorous scrutiny.

## THE TEACHER-QUALITY DEBATE

From the early twentieth century until the 1980s the teacher-quality debate was largely shaped by two factors: a captive labor market for teachers and the lack of consensus about what constitutes good teaching and what characteristics teachers should have.

The teaching profession was long able to draw heavily from a captive labor force of talented women and African Americans for whom there were few other professional avenues available. This situation ensured a reasonably steady supply of women and minorities enrolling in local teacher-preparation programs and accepting jobs in schools reasonably proximate to where they were trained. These teachers also tended to remain in their schools for their entire careers.

At the same time there was little agreement about what teachers were supposed to teach and no systematic evaluation of their student's performance. Given an absence of clear standards, teachers were often expected to use their judgment about what to teach. Teachers working in such an environment likely benefited from a training program that exposed them to professional norms. Yet so long as schools did not collect and study data on student performance, it was not possible to systematically evaluate teacher performance once teachers were in the schools, or to infer what characteristics made some teachers more effective than others.

In this environment, state policymakers focused heavily on inputs [Author: OK?] and ensuring that truly weak teachers did not enter the profession. Little attention was paid to rethinking how to train or license teachers and whether the existing system was adequate.

During the 1980s, the context of the teacher-quality challenge changed. A series of high-profile state reform efforts were triggered by the 1983 *A Nation at Risk* report calling attention to problems in U. S. schools. Governors seeking to upgrade the teaching force confronted a grave challenge. By the mid-1970s the captive labor pool of women and African Americans had dissipated as college graduates found that neither race nor gender prohibited them any longer from entering medicine, law, engineering, or other professional fields. Meanwhile, rising enrollment and efforts to shrink class size had increased the size of the teacher work force by about 25 percent between 1970 and the mid-1980s.

Other education reforms in the 1980s created opportunities to rethink the traditional approach to teacher quality. A "standards movement" took shape in which states worked to develop and implement clear guidelines regarding the content that students were expected to learn. In the early 1990s, an accompanying "accountability" movement got its start in states like Texas, Massachusetts, and Virginia, as state governments devised assessments intended to make sure that students were mastering the material according to their standards.

Concerns about teacher quality and the changing environment gave birth to two distinct approaches to improving the teacher work force. Teacher educators and schools of education viewed concerns about teacher quality as reflecting a need to "professionalize" the field. The clearest statement of this philosophy was provided by the National Council on Teaching and America's Future (NCTAF) in its 1996 manifesto "What Matters Most? Teaching for America's Future." NCTAF called on states and schools of education to standardize their programs, to extend the number of years teaching candidates studied, to better integrate practice teaching with coursework, and to take steps to provide more money and support for the teaching profession. An important institutional byproduct of this reform effort was the National Board for Professional Teaching Standards (NBPTS), a body that established standards for teaching excellence and then created a process for determining whether veteran teachers met the standards. NBPTS received strong federal support with grants totaling $70 million over twelve years. Also during the 1990s, the National Council for the Accreditation of Teacher Education (NCATE) emerged from its formerly sleepy profile to shape the nation's teacher-preparation institutions. Within ten years, NCATE persuaded nearly 600 schools of education—and even more significantly the state education departments that must approve their programs—of the critical importance of the NCATE accreditation process.

A much smaller group of reformers worried that the time and cost of the preparation recommended in the NCTAF proposals would deter potentially effective teachers from entering the profession, particularly in urban communities, and would not appreciably improve the quality of teaching. Endorsing efforts to make it easier for nontraditional teachers to be considered for teaching positions, these reformers promoted "alternative certification" programs that would allow candidates to enter classrooms without completing the standard coursework and preparation programs. The first states to aggressively employ such "alternative" preparation programs were New Jersey, California, and Texas, which did so in the mid-1980s.

Such efforts, however, did not start to receive significant national notice until a young Princeton graduate named Wendy Kopp launched Teach For America (TFA) in 1990. TFA sought to entice graduates from elite colleges to take teaching jobs in troubled urban school systems after completing only an intensive summer preparatory "boot camp." Though the program was met with skepticism and heated criticism from the teacher-preparation community, it received enthusiastic acceptance from the business community and school districts desperate for teachers, and was soon placing hundreds of teachers a year.

By 2003, both TFA and the spin-off The New Teacher Project (TNTP) were annually swamped with applicants. In 2003, TFA had about 18,000 applicants for fewer than 2,000 spots—the vast majority from students at top universities. In fact, in 2002, 25 percent of the Yale graduating class applied to TFA.

During the 1990s the scope of alternative certification programs grew and the debate over their desirability intensified. By 2000, about one-sixth of Texas' teachers, one-fifth of New Jersey's, and 10 percent of California's teachers were entering the profession through alternate routes. Forty-five states had enacted alternative licensure and the federal government had provided funds to develop, study, and support these efforts. Still, alternative routes often existed only on paper, and teachers trained in alternative settings still constituted only a small minority of teachers entering the profession each year.

The debate gained more national attention in 1999 when the Thomas B. Fordham Foundation released a manifesto co-authored by Chester Finn, Jr., a noted education critic and former U.S. Assistant Secretary of Education. The Fordham manifesto essentially called for the abolition of certification. Criticism of current licensure schemes gained bipartisan traction in 2001 when the Progressive Policy Institute, a moderate Democratic think tank with strong ties to the administration of former President William J. Clinton, released a widely discussed critique of licensure. The report called for an overhaul of the licensing process so that it focused on teacher expertise in the subjects they would teach while leaving most decisions about hiring and training up to local school districts and schools.

Just as the push for enhanced licensure had earlier yielded the NBPTS, so the push for competitive certification led to the creation for the American Board for the Certification of Teaching Excellence (American Board). Seeking to give institutional form to the competitive certification philosophy, the American Board was launched in early 2001 to create a series of tests in content knowledge and professional teaching skills that could testify to a teacher's competence in lieu of traditional teacher preparation. With support from the U.S. Department of Education and $40 million in grants to date, the American Board worked to develop the necessary tests. In 2003, Pennsylvania became the first state to accept passage of the American Board exam as a permissible route to teacher licensure.

Still, major disagreements remained about how to design licensure policy and who should be able to seek a teaching job. This dispute was marked by an equally vigorous disagreement about what the research showed about various teacher-preparation alternatives.

## AMBIGUOUS EVIDENCE

Proponents of prescribed teacher licensure, most notably Stanford University professor Linda Darling-Hammond, had long argued that a preponderance of evidence clearly showed that certified teachers were more effective than their peers. Citing an extensive list of studies—ranging from sophisticated analyses to unpublished dissertations and case studies of the practices of a few teachers—into the late 1990s, Darling-Hammond argued that the research definitively showed the benefits of conventional licensure.

However, the emergence of systematic student achievement data and the collection of more extensive datasets on student outcomes made it possible for scholars to consider the evidence more thoroughly. Economists Dale Ballou, Mike Podgursky, Andrew Wayne, Peter Youngs, Dan Goldhaber, and Dominic Brewer authored various analyses between 1995 and 2003 that found no evidence that teacher-preparation coursework or a teaching license made a consistent difference in student performance. In 2001, the Maryland-based Abell Foundation published an extensive analysis that challenged the value and credibility of the list of the studies that Darling-Hammond had long cited in support of traditional teacher preparation.

A new body of scholarship on teaching and teachers also emerged. Hoover Institution scholar Margaret Raymond conducted a study of Teach For America recruits in Houston, which found that its new teachers appeared to perform at least as well as other teachers in terms of student achievement outcomes. At the same time, University of Pennsylvania education professor Richard Ingersoll produced influential research suggesting that the teacher shortage was largely due to the rate at which teachers left the profession early in their careers. The research suggested that teachers who had completed preparation programs were less likely to leave the profession than their peers, offering a new potential justification to proponents of traditional licensure

The continuing uncertainty over the value of teacher licensure or preparation was powerfully crystallized in 2003 when the Education Commission of the States (ECS), a nonpartisan partnership of governors and educators, released a report entitled *What Does Research Say About How to Prepare Quality Teachers?* After originally considering more than 500 scholarly studies conducted over twenty years, the ECS report found just ninety-two studies of teacher preparation that met the basic standard of reaching their conclusions on the basis of "systematic observation rather than . . . opinion."

After considering eight questions relating to licensure, the report concluded that the research evidence was nonexistent or inconclusive about seven of them. Perhaps the most significant finding was that there was little evidence that pedagogical coursework improved teacher effectiveness. The report did, however, conclude that there was reliable evidence for the intuitive notion that teachers with more content knowledge are more effective in the classroom.

In fact, the only traits that all researchers seem to agree are related to teacher quality are a teacher's knowledge of the content they will teach and their verbal ability. The fact that we know so little after decades of investment and research is one of the great obstacles confronting policymakers and practitioners trying to meet the teacher- quality challenge.

## THE AIMS OF THIS VOLUME

The inspiration for this volume arose after too many conversations with frustrated state, local, and federal officials seeking effective strategies for addressing the teacher-quality challenge. Amid the broader changes that have swept education in recent years, policymakers and practitioners have had their hands full trying to juggle practical and political challenges. They have had little time to reflect more deeply on the landscape, on new questions that need to be asked, or on broad models of structural reform.

As a result, for this volume we have gathered leading thinkers and scholars on teacher quality to provide a broad assessment of where we are and to pose a new agenda for research and reform. We have not attempted to tackle every facet of the teacher-quality challenge. Rather, we have assembled a team of authors to focus on the question of getting qualified teachers into the schools—how we should decide who to hire and who to keep out. There are other critical issues related to teacher performance and retention, such as teacher pay, mentoring and induction, and contractual requirements, but we think we have taken the prudent course in focusing on what seems to us a natural starting point and one where much policy activity has been concentrated.

The volume consists of three distinct sections. The first assesses the political, policy, and research landscape of teacher quality. The second poses new questions that can help extend the research beyond the long-running debate over the qualifications of licensed teachers and help us think more systematically about teacher preparation and teacher hiring. Finally, the third section proposes new models for how states might seek to ensure teacher quality.

## WHAT WE KNOW

The first group of authors offers a careful assessment of where matters stand in the teacher-quality debate. In chapter one, Andrew J. Rotherham and Sara Mead assess the history and status of teacher-quality efforts in the states and the politics of policymaking in this area. In chapter two, Heidi Ramírez shifts the focus to the federal role, explaining the minimal role that the federal government traditionally played in the issue of teacher quality and assessing the radically enhanced role it is playing due to the Higher Education Act of 1998 and to NCLB. In chapter three, Dan Goldhaber surveys the research to explain what it tells us about the benefits of teacher licensure, the track record of alternatively certified candidates, and what principles ought to guide researchers who are now able to use newly available data on student performance to analyze teacher performance in more systematic and sophisticated ways.

## NEW QUESTIONS

The second section tries to move beyond the traditional debates about teacher licensure and to ask more nuanced questions about what teacher preparation does and how prepared teachers wind up taking jobs in schools. The traditional approach to teacher licensure rests on three assumptions about how we can ensure a qualified teacher work force: that preparation programs provide teachers with essential knowledge and skills, that they keep unsuitable individuals from entering the profession and do not deter too many quality candidates from entering it, and that they provide an effective pipeline for getting teachers into schools.

In chapter four, David Leal undertakes the first systematic attempt to determine how effectively teacher-preparation programs are preventing unsuitable candidates from entering training or are weeding them out in the course of preparation. In chapter five, David Steiner conducts the first systematic inquiry into the materials being taught in teacher preparation courses in order to asses how focused these programs are on teaching professional skills and knowledge and in doing so in an intellectually balanced fashion. Susanna Loeb, James Wyckoff, and their colleagues, in chapter seven, use new data on New York teachers to examine how teacher-preparation graduates actually wind up making their way into the schools and what it means for efforts to promote teacher quality.

## NEW DIRECTIONS

In the final section, four influential education thinkers provide policy-makers with four very different models for addressing the teacher-quality challenge. Working from the presumption that states can choose to regulate teacher preparation programs with a lighter or heavier hand and can establish credentialing requirements that are more or less restrictive for individual teachers, the authors explain how states can use various combinations of candidate and program regulation to promote teacher quality.

In chapter seven, Gary Sykes, a frequent co-author with Linda Darling-Hammond, explains the merits of a "professionalism" model in which states aggressively regulate both which programs may train teachers and who may apply for a teaching position. In chapter eight, Bryan Hassel and Michele Sherburne explain the merits of a "portfolio of providers" strategy in which states are careful to cultivate and monitor a diverse portfolio of preparation programs. This means taking an output accountability rather than regulatory approach to ensure the quality of preparation programs without substantially regulating teacher candidates themselves. In chapter nine, Catherine Walsh makes the case for a "candidate-centered" model, in which the state holds individual prospective teachers accountable to demonstrate certain skills and knowledge, via a test or other assessment, but no longer regulates teacher-preparation programs nor requires teaching candidates to complete such a program. Finally, in chapter ten, Michael Podgursky explains the merits of a "deregulated" model in which the states permit schools and districts to hire as they see fit and does not regulate either teacher-preparation programs or who may teach.

## TOWARD A NEW DEBATE

It seems to us that much of the old debate about teacher licensure has been settled. Whatever the theoretical merits of licensure, the system as it is conceived has not worked to provide either the supply or the quality of teachers that we need. Confronted with a real, immediate challenge, neither parents nor policymakers have much use for continued partisan sparring over the merits of teacher licensure. What is needed are new research and new approaches to the problem that can inform our efforts and provide workable solutions. We hope that this volume can help us start down that course.

## CHAPTER 1

# Back to the Future

## The History and Politics of State Teacher Licensure and Certification

*Andrew J. Rotherham and Sara Mead*

### INTRODUCTION

Integral to thinking about any contemporary policy issue is understanding at least the broad contours of its history and the positions of major actors on significant points of consensus and dispute. That is particularly important in the case of teacher certification and licensure because there are substantial policy and political disagreements among major actors in the debate. Differences arise from varying interpretations of research evidence, competing policy prescriptions, and alternative philosophies about teaching and education.

Enormous amounts of money, time, and effort are devoted to positions on all sides, and every course of action carries costs, benefits, and policy trade-offs. As a rule, education policy changes that jeopardize adult interests or threaten to displace adults from positions of power and responsibility are the most controversial and hotly contested reforms. Moreover, many proposed changes to teacher training, certification, and licensure involve clearly visible costs to organized constituencies, while their benefits to the general public through improved education or, more immediately, to teachers and schools may be more difficult to discern. Substantial sums of public and private money are at stake. Hundreds of millions of dollars a year in tuition and professional development are directed to teacher-preparation programs. Under almost any reform option that is put forth, these funds would be reallocated.

To make sense of these politics and lay the foundation for discussions of policy and reform options, this chapter begins by describing the historical roots of the current debate about teacher certification. Many elements of contemporary discussion are clearly visible in past policy and political debates. We also analyze the political and policy landscapes that have been shaped by this history. We conclude by examining the politics of reform, discussing the positions of major actors, and hopefully helping readers understand why reform in this area faces such significant obstacles and entrenched opposition.

## WHAT DO STATE LICENSURE REQUIREMENTS LOOK LIKE?[1]

Every state in the country requires individuals hired to teach in its public schools to hold some form of license or certification, although these requirements are punctuated with loopholes. For example, some states exempt teachers in charter schools, and virtually every state has some form of "waiver" or emergency permit that allows individuals without licenses to teach if a certified individual cannot be found. In addition, forty-six states and the District of Columbia have some form of alternative certification that allows individuals who have not fulfilled all the requirements for traditional certification to teach while obtaining additional training.[2] This represents significant growth over the past twenty years. In 1983, when the report *A Nation at Risk* catalyzed debate about educational reform, only eight states had any sort of alternative route.[3] Although alternative certification has expanded rapidly since it emerged in the 1980s and accounts for roughly a quarter of new teachers, in some exceptional states (like New Jersey) and school districts, it is still a marginal reform.[4] Nationwide, only 200,000 individuals have been certified to teach through alternative routes; the vast majority of the nation's three million teachers continue to hold licenses obtained through traditional routes.[5] Moreover, in practice, many alternative programs exist only on paper or expect that teachers will eventually obtain the same coursework and other credentials mandated by traditional certification.

Traditional certification expects that teachers will have obtained the bulk of their preparation prior to entering the classroom, generally by completing an "approved teacher-preparation program" at an institution of higher education. Forty-five states require completion of a state-approved teacher-preparation program.[6]

## Standard Core, Diversity in Details

The basic outlines of initial teacher licensure requirements—a bachelor's degree, some training in pedagogy/professional education, subject-matter knowledge for at least secondary teachers, student teaching, and some form of tests—are fairly uniform across states.[7]

- Every state requires that teachers hold a bachelor's degree.[8]
- Every state requires some amount of training in pedagogy, either through specific coursework requirements or as part of an approved program route.[9]
- Forty-two states require secondary teachers to have training in the subjects they are certified to teach.[10]
- All but two states require student teaching.[11]
- Forty-six states and the District of Columbia require some form of testing, although eight test only basic skills.[12]
- Most states also require teachers to submit to fingerprinting and/or criminal background checks.[13]

Within these broad outlines there is significant variation. Some states set a minimum requirement for education courses that exceeds the maximum allowed in an approved program in other states. For example, Virginia does not allow more than eighteen credit hours of professional education for secondary and twenty-four hours for elementary and special education certification, and New Jersey does not allow more than thirty credits in professional pedagogy. In contrast, Louisiana requires thirty-nine semester hours professional education for certification to teach grades seven through twelve, forty-six hours for grades four through eight, and fifty-one hours for grades one through five. Missouri requires sixty credit hours of professional education for elementary and special education certification, fifty-three for middle school, and twenty-six for secondary. Rhode Island sets its minimum pedagogy coursework requirements at Virginia's maximum. Along the same lines, Idaho, Mississippi, North Dakota, South Dakota, and Wyoming require bachelor's degrees in education, while Texas has eliminated the bachelor's in education at all its public institutions of higher education, which prepare the majority of teachers for the state.

Specific subject-area coursework, student teaching and test requirements, and cut scores also vary. While most states require a major in the subject taught at the secondary level, at least nine also allow endorsements in areas where individuals possess only a minor. Michigan and Louisiana require secondary teachers to complete a major and a minor in order to be endorsed in two subject areas. Some states, for example Vermont, require elementary school teachers to have an arts and sciences major, while others, like Oklahoma, New York, Missouri, and Mississippi, require completion of a specific distribution of liberal arts courses. Michigan requires elementary education students to complete three academic minors. South Carolina requires only sixty days of student teaching, whereas several states require a full semester. Many states have unique requirements that do not fit into any of the conventional categories. For example, New York requires classes in school violence and child abuse prevention, Oklahoma requires foreign language skill at the novice level, Oregon requires a class and passage of a test in U.S. and Oregon civil rights laws, and South Dakota requires three semester hours in both Indian studies and human relations. A number of states also require a class in technology.

The specificity of state requirements varies greatly. Some states set very prescriptive requirements; others leave coursework and other requirements largely to the discretion of individual teacher-training programs. For example, Louisiana and many other states require a minimum number of hours of pedagogy coursework, while states like North Carolina and Indiana specify topics that must be covered or competencies that must be addressed, but leave specific coursework requirements to the individual program. Other states, like New York and New Mexico, set minimum credit hour requirements for pedagogy and specify that these must include a minimum number of hours of coursework in teaching of reading that meets specified criteria. Twenty-five states, primarily in the South, set minimum GPA requirements, while the rest leave this to the individual teacher-preparation program. Forty-eight states assert that they use standards of the National Council for Accreditation of Teacher Certification (NCATE) to approve teacher-preparation programs. NCATE standards focus on six areas: Candidate Knowledge, Skills, and Dispositions; Assessment; Field Experience; Diversity; Faculty Qualities; and Unit Governance and Resources. Under the first of these standards, programs are to show that graduates of their programs develop "the content, pedagogical, and professional knowledge, skills, and dispositions necessary to help all students learn" in a manner consistent with professional, state, and institutional standards. But teacher-preparation programs are given wide latitude in how to show this, and the standard does not translate into specific, concrete coursework or outcome requirements for what these programs ought to demand of students.[14]

## A Two-Step System in Many States

It is a common perception that traditional teacher certification requires teachers to obtain all their training before entering the classroom. But in thirty-five states, teacher certification is a multistep process.[15] Teachers receive an initial or provisional license upon completing an approved teacher-preparation program, and then must complete additional training or professional development requirements within the first several years of their careers in order to advance to a standard license. Those who do not advance to a standard license within a specified period of time may lose certification altogether. Requirements to progress to a standard or professional license vary greatly among these thirty-five states:

- Twenty-three states require new teachers to participate in some type of mentorship or induction program.
- Twelve states require teachers to complete additional coursework or earn a master's degree in the first several years in order to maintain certification.
- Five additional states require participation in some other form of professional development.
- Five states require additional tests or assessments.
- Several states require positive local evaluations or the recommendation of a local administrator.

Though their practical impact varies, several states are incorporating induction and mentorship (more commonly associated with alternative preparation, but increasingly viewed as something all new teachers need) into requirements for new teachers. Yet some requirements may be more a burden than a support. For example, Massachusetts, New York, and Washington recently increased or altered their requirements for progress to full licensure. New York now requires new teachers to complete a master's degree in three years (rather than five years, as previously required). Washington now requires fifteen hours of coursework in an individualized program coordinated through an institution of higher education in the first five years (previously, teachers were required to earn a master's degree in nine years). Massachusetts recently revised requirements for the master's degree teachers must earn in their first five years to include more coursework in the content area. Teachers who already have achieved professional licensure are "grandfathered" in and need not meet the revised requirements, but there is anecdotal evidence that some current provisionally licensed teachers are leaving rather than take the additional coursework.[16] Nationally, 61 percent of teachers under age thirty have taken college coursework in the past three years, spending an average of $4,726 on college courses out of pocket, not including the variety of local, state, and federal government subsidies that help offset coursework costs at public expense (in contrast to 46% for all teachers, at an average expenditure of $2,937).[17]

### Continuing and Professional Development Requirements

In addition to the requirement of thirty-five states that new teachers progress from an initial to a standard license, nearly all states also require teachers to complete additional coursework and professional development throughout their careers in order to renew standard certification. This typically amounts to about six semester hours of coursework (roughly two college courses) or equivalent professional development every five years. The specifics of what activities or courses may be used to meet these requirements vary.[18]

- New York is the only state that issues a lifelong certificate with no further renewal requirements. North Dakota does not require additional professional development, but does require individuals to renew their certificates.[19]
- Eleven states specifically require higher education coursework for renewal of certification.
- Twenty-six states require coursework or equivalent professional development activities, or a combination thereof.[20]
- Eight states require individualized professional development plans.
- At least six states require teaching experience during the period of the current certificate as a condition for renewal.

Nineteen states offer some form of optional advanced or master licensure for teachers who obtain an advanced degree (13 states)[21] or National Board for Professional Teaching Standards Certification (NBPTS; six states).[22] These certificates are often valid longer than standard certificates and may have other benefits that include fewer requirements for renewal, greater prestige, advancements on salary schedules, and other compensation benefits. State and district salary schedules typically reward teachers with compensation increases for coursework completion, and twenty-nine states provide some form of financial incentive for NBPTS-certified teachers, regardless of whether this is recognized with a special license. Texas and New Mexico also offer assessment- or competency- based advanced certifications to teachers who wish to serve as mentors or "instructional leaders."

Generally, states require similar core components, but the specifics can vary greatly from state to state throughout the process. Requirements to complete a state-approved preparation program and the variation in specific state requirements for coursework, tests, and student teaching can complicate teacher mobility from one state to another. To address this, most states have entered into reciprocity agreements. States that participate in such agreements allow teachers with certificates issued in other states to teach, although they generally require out-of-state certified teachers to take additional coursework or tests within a specified timeframe in order to satisfy all the requirements of their new state. Forty-one states and the District of Columbia are party to the National Association of State Directors of Teacher Education and Certification (NASDTEC) reciprocity agreement, and all but two other states participate in regional reciprocity agreements, the Northeast Regional Credential (NERC), and MOINKSA (Missouri, Oklahoma, Iowa, Nebraska, Kansas, South Dakota, and Arkansas) Agreement. Under NERC, individuals certified in any of the seven participating states (New York, Connecticut, Maine, Massachusetts, New Hampshire, Rhode Island, and Vermont) can apply for a regional credential valid to teach (with some subject restrictions in some states) in any of the seven states. In addition, some states accept individuals who complete NCATE-approved programs in another state as having completed a state-approved teacher-preparation program. The two states that do not participate in any reciprocity agreements (Alaska and Minnesota) allow teachers certified out-of-state to teach under a provisional certificate while meeting state requirements.

The variation in what "certification" means between states and among teacher-preparation programs within some states has important implications. The popular debate commonly equates certification with education coursework in pedagogy, but this oversimplifies the diversity of requirements and approaches currently in use around the country.

## HOW DID WE GET HERE?

Teacher licensure and certification systems are continuously evolving as a result of state-level political processes. Early in the history of public education, when most Americans were far less educated than today, local communities needed to identify individuals to teach and to equip potential teachers with needed education and skills. Over time, changes in teacher-certification policies have been driven not only by continued public interest in teacher quality but also by concerns about supply and demand for teachers and by power struggles between various interests competing for control of educational policy. These issues, which will be elaborated below, include state versus local control of education; "progressive" versus "liberal/classical" philosophies of education;[23] an "education establishment" consisting of professors and academics in schools of education, large district administrators, and bureaucrats in state and federal education agencies, as opposed to current classroom teachers;[24] different types of institutions competing for a share of (or control over) the teacher-preparation market; and various branches and agencies of state government seeking power over public education decision-making.

The immediate precursors to current teacher licensure and preparation schemes emerged with the common school movement in the nineteenth century. Dramatic expansion of public schooling created a demand for teachers, requiring systems both to produce an adequate supply of individuals educated to teach and to validate their qualifications. For example, between 1870 and 1890, public school enrollment in the United States grew from 7.6 million to 12.7 million; during the same period expenditures doubled from $69 million to $147 million.[25] As public education expanded, control over how and where American children would be educated shifted from private and religious authorities rooted in local communities to public control at the state level. The shape and control of teacher-certification systems largely paralleled these changes and evolved in roughly three phases over the course of the nineteenth and twentieth centuries:

- *Phase One*: Locally elected citizen school boards or superintendents issued local teaching licenses beginning with the establishment of public schools in the early nineteenth century. Though in some states this practice began to phase out following the Civil War, in others local licensure continued into the twentieth century.
- *Phase Two*: An "educational establishment" in university schools of education, state education departments, and urban school district administration created and controlled standardized state teacher licensure and certification systems beginning in the late 1800s through World War II.
- *Phase Three*: Classroom teachers and organizations representing their interests sought and gained increasing control following World War II, and they continue to dominate discussions of teacher licensure today.

Two themes emerge from this history and are particularly relevant to current politics and debates over teacher certification. First, the current debates are not new but the continuation of a much older debate between liberal/classical and progressive approaches to education in the United States. Second, an increasing number of public and private entities involved in teacher preparation and licensure continue to compete to control policy and practice.

## Local Citizen Control in the Nineteenth Century

In the nineteenth-century United States, locally elected citizens and boards of education, rather than professional educators, controlled public education. The responsibilities of the local boards included issuing teaching licenses. Most students did not pursue their education beyond an elementary level, and most public school teachers did not possess much more education themselves. Because formal education credentials were rare and not uniform, citizen board members and superintendents relied on examinations to assess teachers' qualifications and knowledge.

Different types of communities, particularly urban and rural communities, had different educational needs, resources, and labor-market conditions. As a result, several models of teacher preparation emerged to meet these needs. Some teacher-preparation models were specifically tailored to the needs of particular types of communities and schools.

Urban school districts had more resources and offered higher teacher salaries, more stable employment, and better working conditions that rural schools, and as a result were able to demand higher educational requirements of teachers. Many urban districts created high school-level programs to prepare teachers specifically for the district's schools, and some hired teachers only from graduates of these programs. This allowed urban school districts to control the quality of their teachers and, by restricting and expanding enrollment in these programs, to adjust the supply of teachers in response to labor-market conditions and enrollment demands.[26]

In rural areas, teacher-training institutes were created to provide a minimal level of additional academic education and practical teaching instruction for rural school teachers. These institutes were brief sessions offered during summers and school breaks to accommodate both prospective and working teachers. Since access to educational opportunities was limited in rural areas, institutes were often the only education rural teachers had beyond the elementary level. These institutes also held great appeal for individuals who did not intend to teach but who sought continuing-education opportunities.

During the second phase, as teacher preparation and certification became more centralized and teacher-education requirements were raised, these locally tailored preparation routes were phased out. However, three more generalized types of teacher-preparation programs in existence during Phase One adapted to new requirements throughout the second and third phases, and continue to form the backbone of teacher-preparation programs today. Liberal arts colleges had historically prepared young men to teach even before the emergence of widespread public schooling, but existing colleges lacked the capacity to prepare an adequate supply of teachers for expanding public school enrollment, and the level of education of their graduates exceeded the needs of most public schools. As a result, liberal arts colleges were not a dominant source of teachers but continued to play a key role in preparing high school teachers, particularly in New England, where liberal arts colleges were most common and established. "Chairs of pedagogy" originated as individual instructors in public universities who taught a few courses in education and pedagogy for university students seeking to teach.

As state requirements for teacher education rose in Phase Two to include a baccalaureate degree, including pedagogy coursework, demand for university courses in education also grew, and these chairs of pedagogy grew into university departments of education. This trend was strongest in the Midwest and West, where state land-grant universities were the main source of higher education. However, private and public universities throughout the country eventually established departments of education to train teachers and education professors, researchers, bureaucrats, and administrators. Normal schools, both public and private, were created specifically to prepare prospective teachers with a mix of additional academic and practical pedagogical training. While liberal arts colleges primarily prepared high school teachers, normal schools focused on preparing elementary school teachers, who were in greater demand because most students still did not continue their educations beyond elementary school. Normal schools placed a greater emphasis on pedagogy than liberal arts schools. Initially, normal school offerings were similar to a high school level; as teacher-certification requirements rose, normal schools transformed themselves into teachers' colleges and began to offer baccalaureate degrees. Some of today's largest public universities that produce teachers, such as Eastern Michigan University, originated as normal schools.

State and (in the case of land-grant institutions) federal funding and support to expand higher education supported the growth of these forms of teacher training and preparation. Indeed, the need to prepare public school teachers was one justification offered for state investments in public higher education. For example, as early as 1834, the State of New York began funding a normal school in Albany, and by 1849, graduates of this normal school were licensed to teach without further examination.[27] As chairs of pedagogy and normal schools became schools of education, they also became important fixtures of higher education and as they competed for market share with one another and with the liberal arts colleges, they were increasingly able to influence state teacher-certification policies in their favor.[28]

## Increased State and Education Establishment Control in the Progressive Era

Over the latter half of the nineteenth century, state officials and professional educators began to take control of teacher licensure and certification. Prompted by a new professional education establishment in state education departments, urban school districts, and emerging university departments and schools of education, a "progressive" education movement emerged in the early twentieth century. These progressives had a sweeping and ambitious agenda to reshape public education in ways they believed would make it more scientific and professional. Their agenda included changes to teacher preparation and certification. Specifically, they sought 1) higher education requirements and longer periods of formal training for teachers; 2) elimination of exam-based licensure in favor of training requirements; 3) increasingly specialized certificates; 4) standardized control of teacher licensure at the state level and elimination of local certificates; and 5) broad autonomy from state regulation for teacher-preparation programs.[29] These goals aligned with the ideology and the interests of administrative progressives in schools of education, state and federal bureaucracies, and large urban school district administration.

Higher training requirements for teachers bolstered demand for schools of education to prepare teachers, and more centralized state control required new state education bureaucracies to oversee teacher licensure. State control, with details of licensure delegated to state departments of education and broad autonomy for teacher-preparation programs, allowed administrative progressives to control entry to teaching and place the stamp of progressive ideas on future teachers with minimal outside interference. Because the progressives believed that professional administration and control would lead to educational improvements, gaining leverage over these issues was an essential part of their project.

As early as the 1830s, states began to standardize requirements by regulating locally used teacher-licensure exams and having a say on pass rates. Later, state officials offered statewide certificates as an alternative to local licensure and eventually required these state-issued teaching certificates. However, by 1898 only three states had fully state-controlled licensure systems, and most of the centralization of state control occurred between the turn of the century and World War II. By 1937, forty-one states had systems in which all teacher certificates were state issued. The earliest licensure was based on passing an exam, not completion of formal education requirements, and many teachers had less than the equivalent of today's high school diploma. Progressives in the late nineteenth and early twentieth century sought higher formal training requirements and attacked exam-based certification as a back door to teaching for untrained individuals. By 1937, twenty-eight of the forty-eight states had eliminated exams altogether, making professional training the only route to licensure.[30]

During the years between the Civil War and World War II, the progressive agenda overcame resistance from two key opponents: elected officials and liberal arts colleges. Local officials, particularly in rural areas, resisted both increased state control and higher requirements that made it more difficult to hire teachers for the rural schools. Elected state officials were unwilling to cede all control to unelected bureaucracies and continued to pass legislation addressing teacher preparation or licensure, infringing on the autonomy of state education agencies or education schools. Liberal arts colleges opposed increased education coursework requirements, which threatened their historic role in preparing teachers. This opposition also reflected a broader ideological schism between progressive educationists and proponents of classical and liberal arts traditions in education. This was an early manifestation of the debate over process and content.

But the progressive teacher-certification agenda was favored by the larger political context. Increased urbanization decreased the legislative clout of rural legislators. Meanwhile, broader political and economic changes meant that increased centralization, bureaucracy, and reliance on "experts" in government and business became more broadly accepted. This created a hospitable climate for the centralized and expertise-based teacher certification changes that the progressives sought, and helped them win allies in the broader progressive and business communities.

Despite teacher shortages in rural areas and rapidly expanding enrollments in urban areas, including shortages exacerbated by the world wars, general education and professional education coursework requirements for teachers rose substantially. By 1937, forty states required at least a high school diploma for initial licensure, thirty-four required at least some additional professional preparation beyond high school, and five required four years of college. Shortages and the continuing need to gain support from rural legislators resulted in the "phasing in" of many requirements, allowing teachers to be hired with minimal qualifications but requiring them to obtain additional training over the first several years of their careers.[31] Emergency certification was also widespread. Both approaches continue to be common in policy and practice today because school districts continue to face shortages and must have a teacher in front of a classroom.

By World War II, teacher certification was largely controlled by "education professionals" in state departments of higher education, large district administrators, and university schools of education. The more pluralistic approaches of the nineteenth century had been largely eliminated, and education professionals dictated teacher-certification policy with little input from classroom teachers.[37]

## World War II and After: Teachers and "Professional Standards"

From the late 1930s to early 1970s, teachers and their organizations sought control over teacher preparation, certification, and licensure as a way to restrict entry to the profession, to raise teacher pay, and to increase esteem for teachers and create a true profession. A new professional standards movement pursued an agenda that emphasized the unique knowledge and skills of teachers. This agenda included:

- continuing and building on the progressive push to raise formal education requirements for teacher certification, particularly coursework in pedagogy, ideally by making teacher education a graduate-level program, like law or medicine;
- granting primary responsibility for setting teacher-certification policy to organized practicing teachers, through creation of professional standards boards responsible for certification and licensure policy at the state level;
- seeking an "approved program" route to teacher certification, where states would approve higher education institutions' teacher-preparation programs and automatically certify graduates of these programs, rather than having specific coursework requirements for individuals;
- improving the quality and content in teacher-preparation programs;
- setting a uniform standard for the quality of teacher-preparation programs via a private, national accrediting body called the National Council for the Accreditation of Teacher Education (NCATE);
- streamlining the number and specificity of teacher certificates to a few broad categories, such as "elementary education," rather than the myriad of content- and age-specific certificates created by progressive bureaucracies;
- raising teacher salaries; and
- working toward a view of teaching as a "true profession" similar to medicine and law.

The goals and rhetoric of the professional standards movement in the 1950s will sound familiar to observers of current teacher-quality and certification discussions. However, in addition to its policy goals this movement focused on shifting control of teaching from policy elites into the hands of organized, practicing teachers. Organizations emerged to advance and support this agenda. The National Education Association (NEA), which was not yet a union (this was before collective bargaining in education) but a professional association that included education professors, administrators, and state and federal officials as well as teachers, led these efforts by establishing the National Commission on Teacher Education and Professional Standards (TEPS) in 1946. In 1952, TEPS, the National Association of State Directors of Teacher Education and Certification (NASDTEC), and the American Association of Colleges of Teacher Education (itself founded from the 1948 merger of several smaller associations of teacher colleges) founded NCATE to raise the prestige and quality of teacher preparation through national accreditation of teacher-preparation programs, which supporters hoped would supplant state-based approval. These groups sought to influence the content, quality, and control of teacher preparation.

The move to give teachers, rather than the education establishment, greater control over entry to teaching engendered opposition and met with limited success. During the 1950s, two-thirds of states undertook teacher-certification reforms, but a variety of issues drove reform efforts and many of the specific goals of the professional standards movement were not realized. Teacher control and autonomy were overwhelmed by debate about the quality of U.S. public education and progressive education ideology itself. Proponents of the liberal/classical approach that had lost out in Progressive Era reforms seized on post-Sputnik public concerns about education quality to attack the progressive approach, particularly schools of education and teacher preparation that emphasized the education process over content.

Congress reacted to concerns about America's ability to compete in the Cold War by passing the National Defense Education Act (NDEA) in 1958. NDEA expanded the federal role in education and specifically included incentives for students to become mathematics and science teachers. The salience of education as a national issue prompted both teachers and liberal/classical critics to criticize education elites and promote their agendas.[33]

In the end, some elements of the professional standards agenda—increased formal education requirements for teachers, some streamlining of certification categories, the "approved program" approach in most states— were adopted. However, those agenda items related to greater teacher control met with less success. All but six states established professional standards advisory commissions, but legislators and state bureaucracies were not willing to surrender control to independent, teacher-dominated bodies. NCATE accreditation progressed at a slow pace, with few schools earning accreditation. The slow pace of change along with disputes about control and emphasis (content versus pedagogy) meant that teaching did not gain the professional prestige of medicine or law.

The end of the mid-century professional standards movement in the 1970s was ultimately brought about by the economic self-interest of teachers themselves. Led by reformer Albert Shanker, the AFL-CIO-affiliated American Federation of Teachers (AFT) began organizing teachers, and the National Education Association responded to competitive pressure by also embracing collective bargaining. Adopting widescale unionism meant jettisoning the accoutrements of professionalism. Instead, the unions began to take collective bargaining stances traditionally associated with blue-collar workers, with the result that teacher professional organizations were recast as public sector employee unions. This approach proved highly effective at raising salaries and improving working conditions for teachers.[34] The political power of teachers unions was also ultimately more effective in achieving teacher control over education policy and the profession than previous efforts. In the 1980s and 1990s, the unions' enormous political clout allowed them to resurrect many of the items on the professionalization agenda and enjoy far greater success at incorporating them into state and national policy.

## TEACHER CERTIFICATION IN THE ERA OF STANDARDS: TWO SCHOOLS OF THOUGHT

The standards movement and renewed political and policy attention to improving public education beginning in the 1980s renewed concern about teacher quality. The standards movement was largely predicated on the notion that students should know and be able to do certain things at certain points in their schooling. A natural outgrowth of this emphasis was discussion about what teachers should know and be able to do as well. Today there is general agreement that teachers matter a great deal in student learning, but there are two divergent schools of thought about how to increase the supply of good teachers.[35] The two approaches can be labeled "teacher professionalism" and "competitive certification." The professionalism approach continues the emphasis on teaching as a profession like law and medicine. The competitive certification approach views teaching as more of a craft, such as journalism, policy analysis, or business management, and embraces a wider view of what constitutes a profession in today's society.

Teacher professionalism embraces much of the previous professional standards movement agenda, including:

- increased formal education and student teaching requirements;
- a preservice undergraduate or postbaccalaureate experience conducted, designed, or mediated by an institution of higher education;
- NCATE accreditation for teacher-preparation programs;
- increased professional development;
- restricting teachers to areas in which they are certified;
- control of the profession by professional educators who understand the unique knowledge and skills of teaching;
- professional certification of master teachers through NBPTS;
- higher teacher pay across the board; and[36]
- a broad view of effective teaching that is not limited to measured student performance.

Competitive certification advocates call for:

- reducing education coursework requirements where research evidence does not clearly link them with teacher effectiveness;
- lowering barriers wherever feasible, especially education coursework requirements, to expand the pool of prospective teachers;
- expanding alternative forms of teacher training and routes to licensure;
- greater emphasis on content knowledge relative to education coursework;
- greater flexibility for local administrators and schools in teacher hiring and other personnel matters;
- in terms of public policy, a more narrow view of teacher quality based on measured student performance; and
- pay increases based on differential or performance-based pay strategies to reward outstanding teachers and teachers with special or scarce skills, and to attract more teachers to subjects or communities where there are shortages.[37]

The debate does not always break down along clean binary lines, and many policy options fall under the category of competitive certification. Nonetheless, these general categories frame the broad outlines of this debate.

Debate over these approaches unfolds against a political and educational backdrop that has drawn public and policymaker attention to teacher quality which framed much of the debate. Three primary contextual factors are especially important. The standards movement has had an impact on the debate over teacher certification by increasing the emphasis on content and student achievement. Further, pronounced teacher shortages in some communities, particularly low-income communities, as well as shortages in some subjects like math, science, foreign languages, and special education have renewed attention to supply-and-demand issues in education. Finally, the increased attention to teacher certification has spawned new research into the effectiveness of current teacher-certification schemes, as well as some emerging alternatives such as Teach For America. Later sections examine the empirical evidence about existing approaches and some reform options.

## The Politics of Teacher Certification

Even the staunchest defenders of a regulated model of teacher certification find much to criticize in the current system. Thus, the debate is not between one side arguing for changes and the other resisting reform, but is, instead, a debate over competing ideas about change. Yet, given the substantial costs of the professionalism model and the lack of evidence of its effectiveness, resistance to substantial policy innovation at first appears to be a puzzle. But the explanation is fairly straightforward and lies in a set of political relationships, ideological beliefs, and education policymaking traps that together create an inhospitable environment for broad reform.

The debate centers on whether activities within the current framework (e.g., college-level teacher-preparation programs) need refinement or whether the framework itself should be reconsidered. However, this debate is severely constrained by special interests' influence and existing institutional arrangements. Teachers unions and related professional associations, institutions of higher education, and officials with a stake in current certification schemes present substantial barriers to those seeking to change the system. Notably, they exert overt and subtle pressure on state and federal legislators, who are in a position to drive change.

The rhetoric and agenda of teacher professionalism resurrects much of the language of the 1950s professional standards movement, but with two critical differences. First, instead of relatively weak professional associations promoting the standards movement, the professionalism approach enjoys powerful support. Higher education, organized by such groups as the American Association of Colleges of Teacher Education, the two politically powerful teachers unions, NEA and AFT, and a generally unified education establishment, including the "elites" who earlier resisted these reforms, are now all staunchly in favor.

The nexus between education schools and teachers unions is illustrated in collaboration on a third group of new organizations launched in the 1980s and 1990s to advance components of the professionalism agenda. These include the Interstate New Teacher Assessment and Support Consortium (INTASC) and NBPTS, both founded in 1987, as well as the National Commission on Teaching and America's Future (NCTAF), founded 1996. Moreover, the stakes of the debate between professionalism and competitive certification are higher because of the tremendous resources and political clout now invested in the current system.

## Teacher Professionalism Interests

### Institutions of Higher Education

Apart from any ideological motivations, higher education institutions have a substantial financial stake in certification because current policies based on completion of coursework ensure them a captive audience and revenue stream.

Graduate and undergraduate teacher preparation programs graduate roughly 200,000 students each year. Taking into account distribution and cost differentials among different types of teacher-preparation programs, the tuition costs of preparing these students are estimated to total $6.1 billion or more annually.[38] These costs are financed primarily by the students themselves and indirectly by taxpayers. Students are eligible for the same federal and state student aid as other students. In addition, federal programs such as the Perkins loan-cancellation program provide additional aid to students who teach in low-income schools or special education, and twenty-seven states currently offer college scholarships or loan-forgiveness programs to prospective teachers. In 1999, $81 million was budgeted nation-wide for these state programs.[39] Students are also eligible for institutional financial aid and private scholarships, some designated specifically for students preparing to become teachers, from a multitude of sources. Using tax dollars, states also subsidize public higher education institutions directly.

Expenditures on college coursework by current teachers are also substantial, although current research likely underestimates the true costs. Forty-six percent of teachers report having taken college courses in the previous three years, at a mean total expenditure of $2,937. With nearly three million public school teachers in the United States, this translates to about $1.35 billion in out-of-pocket expenditures on continuing education coursework by teachers annually, not including scholarships, financial aid, or district reimbursements.[40]

In addition, many schools and districts reimburse teachers for tuition expenditures, and teachers unions seek inclusion of this benefit in teacher contracts. This means that local property taxpayers also indirectly subsidize teacher training as well. More than 20 percent of teachers report receiving such support in the past year.[41] Quantifying the costs of this assistance is difficult. Even assuming a very modest average of $100 per teacher receiving a subsidy, that would represent a $60 million transfer from school districts to higher education annually.[42] Because of opaque school and district budgeting practices and a lack of national data collection, reliable information about professional development spending is scarce. Furthermore, the same coursework teachers take to maintain certification is generally rewarded with advancement on salary schedules, entailing substantial, although often ignored, costs to districts.

Colleges and universities generally pay lower average salaries to faculty in their schools of education and also use more lower cost adjunct faculty.[43] They also produce higher numbers of master's and doctoral degrees per faculty than other departments within institutions of higher education. The large numbers of practicing teachers seeking recertification credit in education graduate programs present less of a drain on university fixed resources (such as libraries, athletic facilities, computer infrastructure, and the like) and are less likely to qualify for or require institutional financial aid that other graduate programs provide to full-time graduate students.

Thus, teacher-education programs, with higher marginal revenues and lower marginal costs per student than many other departments, have been described as "cash cows" for universities,[44] a characterization that also reflects the fact that teacher-preparation programs serve a largely captive audience due to certification coursework requirements that protect the programs from competing approaches. In contrast to professions like journalism or business where employment is not conditioned on certifications and advanced degrees, most aspiring or current teachers have no option other than a college of education in order to maintain their eligibility to teach. This guaranteed enrollment, coupled with the relatively lucrative financial structure, is favorable for colleges and universities. In addition, specific coursework requirements for certification correlate with and preserve individual jobs and programs within schools of education. Discrete and proscribed requirements for certification or licensure create constituencies to defend them.[45]

At the same time, teacher-preparation programs have proven highly effective in seizing opportunities to expand, as in the case of alternative certification. Indeed, to the extent that alternative certification stimulates new philanthropic, state, federal, or school district spending, the growth of alternative certification programs provide a new source of revenue for higher education and a further transfer of public resources to higher education institutions. Many state and federal programs subsidize alternative certification. For example, the federal Transition to Teaching program provides grants to states, school districts, and partnerships to support alternative routes, including tuition and stipends for candidates. Washington State's Partnership Grant Program uses state appropriations and federal grant funds for mentored internships and forgivable tuition loans for interns. The Teach for Texas Alternative Certification Conditional Grant Program provides tuition grants to alternative route teachers in shortage fields and communities. Since these funds often come from budget categories devoted to improving elementary and secondary public education rather than postsecondary funding, they may come at the expense of alternative investments in public elementary and secondary education.[46] Furthermore, when these programs are based at universities, they may have an overhead cost structure that is higher than other settings, such as school districts or nonprofits.

Finally, public funding to support alternative certification coursework may displace discussions about paring down unnecessary coursework. Recent successful efforts by teacher professionalism and higher education advocates to "raise standards" for alternative routes (and protect their own market share) by imposing on candidates the same coursework requirements as traditional programs exacerbate this dynamic and public costs.

*Teachers Unions*

The most substantial political advantage the teacher professionalism movement has over contemporary proponents of competitive certification and the professional standards movement of the 1950s is the enormous political leverage of the two major teachers unions. Although public sector unionism and collective bargaining initially replaced professionalism as a model to improve teachers' welfare, in the 1990s teachers unions embraced the rhetoric of professionalism, in some cases integrating its goals into their political and collective bargaining agendas. While collective bargaining was effective in addressing working conditions and pay, teachers continued to seek the status accorded other professions.

Increased public acceptance of teacher unionism made the earlier conflict between teacher organizing and professionalism seem more compatible. Teacher professionalism provided a good public relations strategy for teachers unions in response to the standards movement's emphasis on content knowledge and accountability. Teacher professionalism allowed teachers unions to use the rhetoric of "higher standards" to advocate improving teacher quality in ways that were not a threat to their organizational goals, but rather advanced them. In addition, by gaining control over entry to the profession, unions hope to solidify broader control over education policy and practice and the conditions and incentives under which teachers work by influencing the supply, demand, and quality of the pool of prospective teachers and through the ideological gatekeeping function of teacher-preparation programs.

Teachers unions, particularly at the state and national level, view their role more broadly than traditional union activities and seek influence over a broad array of policies affecting education, not merely those that directly affect their members. Both the NEA and AFT are on record as supporting most key components of the professionalism agenda, including NCATE accreditation, NBPTS certification, elimination of emergency certification, tighter requirements for alternative routes, increased professional development, and, of course, higher teacher pay.[47] Both also promulgate notions of "new unionism" and argue that collective bargaining can and should be a tool for improving teacher quality. New unionism incorporates elements of the teacher professionalism agenda, such as mentoring, release time, and financial support for professional development, salary bonuses for National Board-certified teachers, and the like, into teachers' contracts. New unionism is also supposed to include provisions to increase professionalism, such as new evaluative practices and enhanced strategies for removing underperforming teachers. In practice, however, the agenda has resulted in many more carrots than sticks in collective bargaining agreements and has a mixed record of effectiveness.

Still, this approach now plays a prominent role in policymaking. The AFT resolutions adopted at its 1998 convention specifically address a professionalism agenda and were published in a booklet titled "Assuring Teacher Quality: It's Union Work."[48] The NEA has no explicit teacher-quality policy document comparable to AFT's, but at the national level it embraces many of the same policy prescriptions as AFT. The moniker "new unionism" is more associated with the NEA, yet in practice it is the AFT that has embraced new unionism approaches to a greater degree.

Teachers unions increasingly have a stake in higher education policy relating to teacher preparation.[49] Recent NEA lobbying on teacher-preparation issues in Title II of the Higher Education Act is illustrative. Not surprisingly, the NEA endorsed expanded teacher loan forgiveness, which directly benefits teachers. However, it is less obvious why the NEA would lobby to have higher education institutions (rather than school districts, states, or private or nonprofit organizations) serve as the fiscal agent for teacher-quality grants authorized under the legislation. A likely cause is the NEA's desire to keep control of these programs in more centralized institutions rather than allowing institutions or groups that may not share its goals to wield influence.[50]

Unions support the professionalism agenda through collective bargaining provisions rewarding teachers for coursework and professional development, providing financial bonuses and support for NBPTS certification, and reimbursing expenses for continuing coursework. Finally, teachers unions have helped create and support a variety of other organizations working to advance the professionalism agenda.

*Teacher Professionalism's Alphabet Soup: NCATE, NBPTS, NCTAF, INTASC, and AACTE*

In the 1980s and 1990s, a number of organizations emerged or stepped up their activities to advance the teacher professionalism movement. The major actors are described in this section.

NCATE, the National Council for the Accreditation of Teacher Education, was founded by TEPS and AACTE in 1950, but was largely ineffective until the 1990s. In the last decade, however, with support from teachers unions and AACTE, NCATE has substantially increased its activities, staff, funding, number of teacher-preparation programs accredited, and formal recognition in state policy. Today, 540 of the nation's 1,300 teacher training institutions are accredited by NCATE. These institutions prepare 70 percent of U.S. teachers. Eight states require their teacher-preparation programs to become NCATE accredited, and NCATE has formal partnerships with forty-six states for conducting joint reviews of schools of education. In 2002, *U.S. News & World Report* began to include NCATE accreditation in its ranking of the Best Graduate Schools in Education. NCATE's mission is to improve teacher quality and professionalism and the quality of teacher-preparation programs through performance-based professional accreditation. However, NCATE's critics assert that its accreditation process is too cumbersome and costly, reliant on institutional self-assessment and peer judgement rather than objective measures, and driven by input and process criteria rather than linked to demonstration of the skills and knowledge of teacher-preparation programs' graduates or their impact on student achievement. NCATE has recently sought to address some of these concerns, for example, partnering with the Educational Testing Service in efforts to establish a nationwide pass score on the Praxis teacher licensure exams.[51]

NBPTS, the National Board for Professional Teaching Standards, was created in 1987, in response to both the National Commission on Excellence in Education report *A Nation at Risk*,[52] published in 1983, and the 1986 Carnegie Forum on Education and the Economy's Task Force on Teaching as a Profession report, *A Nation Prepared: Teachers for the 21st Century.*[53] Its mission—to identify a set of professional teaching standards and establish voluntary, national certification of "master teachers" who meet the standards—was initially embraced by many education reform supporters. The notions of identifying a clear set of standards for what teachers must know and be able to do, breaking the state-level hold on certification, and identifying and rewarding exemplary teachers all have certain appeal for both teacher professionalism and competitive certification groups.

But the process of setting NBPTS standards was driven largely by the education associations that form the majority of its supporters and board, and competitive certification supporters rapidly became disenchanted.[54] Specifically, they criticize NBPTS standards as insufficiently concrete and focused on process, attitudes, and beliefs rather than measurable knowledge and skills. Critics also fault NBPTS for focusing on teacher behaviors rather than their students' achievement, and note that no major research study links NBPTS-certified teachers to improved student achievement.[55] To help address this, NBPTS is currently supporting a variety of research examining the effectiveness of its certified teachers, so more empirical evidence will be available in several years.

Nonetheless, many supporters, including elected state officials of both parties, continue to support NBPTS to raise the prestige of teaching and as a more politically palatable alternative to improve teacher compensation than across-the-board raises or merit pay. For example, governors Jeb Bush (R-FL) and Jim McGreevey (D-NJ), former governor Jim Hunt (D-NC), and U.S. Senator Lamar Alexander (R-TN) have all supported initiatives to encourage and reward NBPTS certification. Twenty-one states now offer a bonus or additional compensation to NBPTS-certified teachers. Many of these states, and a few others, also reimburse all or part of the $2,300 application fee to become NBPTS certified. School districts may also pay additional compensation to NBPTS-certified teachers pursuant to their teachers' contract. For example, Maryland pays up to 75 percent of the application fee for 500 teachers and will match up to $2,000 of any local stipend for NBPTS-certified teachers. Mississippi offers a $6,000 annual salary increase for NBPTS certification.

Some state officials initially saw these programs as a low-cost, token way to address teacher compensation. However, the number of NBPTS-certified teachers has grown in recent years, roughly doubling annually between 1997 and 2000 and rising from 177 in 1993 to 1,837 in 1998 to 23,935 today. Because the greatest growth is occurring in states with the strongest financial incentives, costs are also growing exponentially. For example, Georgia's annual 10 percent bonuses for NBPTS-certified teachers cost only $100,000 in 2002 but $3.5 million in 2003, and they are projected to cost $15.6 million in 2004—equivalent to a 1 percent raise for all Georgia teachers.[56] North Carolina's program, which pays the full application fee, gives teachers seeking NBPTS certification three days off to prepare, and provides a 12 percent salary increase, is perhaps the most generous and is estimated to cost an average $45,000 per teacher over the ten-year life of the NBPTS certificate. The annual cost of these bonuses to the state is $50 million. In addition to the challenge of meeting these promises during fiscal downturns, the distributional consequences also give some observers pause. An analysis of NBPTS-certified teachers in North Carolina found that they were significantly more likely to be in affluent schools than low-income schools. As a result, NBPTS subsidies effectively transfer state funds to more affluent schools.[57]

The National Commission on Teaching and America's Future (NCTAF) was launched in 1994 with funding from the Carnegie Corporation and strong support of the various teacher professionalism constituencies. Its chairman, former North Carolina governor Jim Hunt, and founding executive director, Linda Darling-Hammond, are among the foremost proponents of the teacher professionalism agenda. NCTAF's initial impact came with 1996 publication of its report, *What Matters Most: Teaching and America's Future*,[58] which was highly critical of the current state of teacher quality and preparation in the United States. Some of NCTAF's complaints, such as poor quality in schools of education and the prevalence of teachers teaching in subject areas where they do not have content knowledge, are shared by advocates of competitive certification. But the policy responses they recommend diverge from those of NCTAF's, where the emphasis is in line with the professionalism agenda. In addition to a strong emphasis on teacher certification and raising preservice requirements for prospective teachers, NCTAF's recommendations are also strongly supportive of NCATE and NBPTS, calling for states to require NCATE accreditation of all teacher-preparation programs and the creation of 100,000 NBPTS-certified teachers. Today, NCTAF works with a network of twenty "partner states"[59] on initiatives and policies to implement its recommendations, and is also a vocal advocate for the professionalism agenda at the national level. Though its focus has expanded to include teacher-quality issues, including professional development, retention, and improving teacher working conditions, NCTAF remains most strongly identified with defense of teacher certification and high preservice requirements to become a teacher.

The Interstate New Teacher Assessment and Support Consortium (INTASC) was created in 1987 under the umbrella of the Council of Chief State School Officers (CCSSO) as a consortium of state education agencies and national education groups, including NEA and AFT. Thirty-four states participate in INTASC,[60] which seeks to establish quality standards and assessments for teacher-preparation programs and prospective teachers, expand professional development, and make teacher licensure policies more compatible across states. INTASC has developed "model" standards, based largely on NBPTS standards, for teacher knowledge and skills in pedagogy and key subject areas, as well as quality principles for teacher-preparation programs.[61] Several participating states have or are in the process of incorporating various elements of INTASC standards into revisions of their certification and licensure systems,[62] and INTASC standards and principles are widely used by individual teacher-preparation programs. It has also developed a series of subject-specific portfolio assessments and initiated development of a new licensing exam in teaching skills, the "Test for Teaching Knowledge."

The American Association of Colleges of Teacher Education (AACTE), a membership association representing teacher-preparation institutions, was founded during the mid-century professional standards movement from the merger of a number of other groups representing teacher-training institutions. However, AACTE also actively supports and advocates for the teacher-professionalism agenda, both in the services and resources it provides its membership and the efforts of its state affiliates and the national organization in Washington, D.C.

The Association of Teacher Educators (ATE), founded in 1920, is an individual membership organization for both school-based and postsecondary teacher educators. It does not maintain a significant Washington presence and is less politically active than AACTE.

It would be a mistake to view these organizations as essentially independent and pursuing agendas that happen to overlap. To understand the politics of this issue it is important to understand the formal and informal relationships between these organizations, higher education, and the teachers unions.

NCATE is composed of thirty-three member organizations, including NEA, AFT, American Association of Colleges of Teacher Education (AACTE), the Association of Teacher Educators (which represents individuals), numerous "specialty" groups, and policymaker groups. Its bylaws specify that one-fifth of seats on its board are controlled by unions and another fifth by AACTE and ATE. Specialty groups and policymakers also each control one-fifth of seats, with the remainder held by an NBPTS representative and the chairs of NCATE's various governing boards. The presidents of AACTE, NBPTS, AFT, and NEA all serve on NCATE's board.[63]

NBPTS bylaws specify that a majority of its sixty-three board members be practicing teachers. Potential board members are selected by a nominating committee from the recommendations of NBPTS constituent organizations, which include NEA and AFT.[64] This in effect guarantees that unions control a majority of seats on the board. In addition, NEA and AFT presidents serve on NBPTS board, as do five other NCATE board members and NCTAF chair Jim Hunt, who was also the founding chairman of NBPTS.

NCTAF has twenty-nine commissioners, including the current AFT president, two past NEA presidents, the current and past presidents of NBPTS, and the president of NCATE.

The boards of AACTE and ATE are drawn from their memberships.[65] Of twenty AACTE board members, fifteen represent NCATE accredited institutions, as do all members of the AACTE Executive Committee.

In addition to these formal arrangements, there is also considerable cross-representation on the board of these groups. These organizations also receive substantial financial support from major philanthropic foundations. For example, NCATE has received more than $10 million in foundation funding since 1990, and NBPTS more than $80 million in foundation funding since its founding to 2001. The report generally credited with launching "teacher professionalism," *A Nation Prepared: Teacher for the 21st Century*, was the product of the Carnegie Forum on Education and the Economy's Task Force on Teaching as a Profession.[66] Since then, the Geraldine R. Dodge Foundation, the Lilly Endowment, the Ford Foundation, the Pew Charitable Trusts, the Rockefeller Foundation, the DeWitt-Readers Digest fund, and other foundations have joined the Carnegie Corporation of New York in providing financial support to teacher-professionalism organizations and initiatives. More than simply allowing these organizations to operate and expand, this philanthropic support builds the ally base and provides political and policy legitimacy for the teacher-professionalism agenda.[67]

### Competitive Certification Proponents

By contrast, the infrastructure supporting alternative and competitive certification is not nearly as well developed. In the academic community there are scholars, particularly economists and political scientists, who focus on the issue, and national organizations like Teach For America are predicated on a competitive approach. Dr. C. Emily Feistritzer, president and founder of the National Center for Education Information, tracks alternative certification in depth, and her work is frequently cited. However, few organizations work on alternative certification and competitive certification policy in depth, and these groups are not ideologically or politically homogenous.

Perhaps the best known of these groups is the Thomas B. Fordham Foundation, whose president, Chester E. Finn Jr., is a well-known conservative education critic and advocate of alternative certification. A 1999 Fordham Foundation "manifesto," *The Teachers We Need and How to Get More of Them*, is probably the earliest comprehensive articulation of many points of the competitive certification agenda.[68] This document has been endorsed by an array of elected officials, academics, and leaders of education reform organizations, as well as practicing teachers and other educators. However, not all signatories or all supporters of the competitive certification approach agree with every particular of the Fordham Foundation's approach to either teacher-quality issues or education reform more generally. Finn speaks and writes frequently on the issue, although Fordham's work encompasses a variety of other educational issues. The center-left think tank Progressive Policy Institute (PPI), which, like Fordham, works on a variety of educational issues, also supports competitive certification. In 2001, PPI released a paper by then-University of Virginia education professor Frederick Hess that called for "a radical overhaul of teacher certification."[69]

In 2001, the Fordham Foundation and the Education Leaders Council, a network of state officials supportive of education reform, founded the National Council on Teacher Quality (NCTQ) to serve as a unified voice and clearinghouse on these issues; it is the first prominent national group to focus on them exclusively. Under President George W. Bush, the U.S. Department of Education has supported new approaches to certification and specially directed funding to the American Board for Certification of Teacher Excellence (ABCTE). ABCTE is creating an examination for prospective teachers that will assess content and pedagogical knowledge and serve as an alternative credential for aspiring teachers in states that adopt it.

Proponents of alternative and competitive reform are not without a voice or influence in these debates. They are, however, much less organized than higher education, teachers unions, or the various groups that have emerged to support the professionalism agenda, and only a few organizations work on the issue full time. As a result, competitive certification proponents are substantially less likely to lobby at the state level, where much of this policy is decided and is often focused on a broader set of issues.

## IDEOLOGY

To be sure, established institutions and organizations have a vested political and economic interest as well as an ideological stake in preserving current teacher-certification structures. At the same time, the importance of ideology cannot be ignored.

Current debates over teacher certification are neither new nor simply a reinvigoration of the mid-century professional standards movement. They continue an ongoing debate about professional versus citizen control, bureaucracy versus flexibility, and progressive versus liberal/classical models in U.S. public education. Thus, the positions of these groups and their interrelationships are not merely the result of self-interested actors seeking to protect or enlarge their turf. Most key actors and supporters sincerely believe that the current approach is beneficial for students as well as teachers, and staunchly believe in the pedagogical traditions upon which it is based.

Advocates for teacher professionalism tend to ascribe to a philosophy of education broadly classified as progressivism and associated with the ideas of John Dewey, Jean Piaget, and other nineteenth- and early twentieth-century education reformers. This philosophy gained prominence along with the rapid expansion of public education in the United States and continues to hold considerable influence today. Progressives embrace curricular formalism, the belief that teaching students how to think critically, love learning, and be lifelong learners is more important than inculcating specific content knowledge. In terms of teaching practice, progressives advocate pedagogical naturalism, the idea that learning is a natural process when children are engaged in "relevant" activities, and argue that these practices are based in a science of how students learn that can be applied to teaching.

In contrast, most proponents of competitive certification tend to adhere to a more traditionalist view of education that sees student attainment of specified knowledge and skills as the primary purpose of education and, consequently, a grasp of subject matter as the most important requirement for qualified teachers. This view does not discount the importance of critical thinking, engaged learning, and active teaching, but it does rest on the notion that, for students and teachers alike, content knowledge is the foundation of these skills.

A 1997 Public Agenda study of professors of education demonstrates the extent to which Progressive views dominate in education schools and to which they are often at variance with those of the public at large. For example, nearly 90 percent of education professors said it is more important for students addressing a math or science problem to struggle with the process of finding the right answer than to arrive at the correct one.[70]

If one accepts the contention that education schools possess a scientific body of knowledge that supports progressive ideas that can inform teacher practice, it is then entirely reasonable that prospective teachers must be instructed in this science. In any case, many teachers, teacher educators, and teacher professionalism advocates believe strongly in a body of knowledge and attitudes about how to teach and in essential preparation for competent teaching, and this belief animates their support for teacher certification. Many teacher educators are deeply invested in this philosophy as well, and derive a sense of self-definition and the value of their work from identification with a professional science of education.

In addition to philosophical differences about the nature of education, partisans of teacher professionalism and of competitive certification also tend to disagree on the appropriate role of centralized governments in addressing social issues. Supporters of teacher professionalism in teachers unions and schools of education tend to be more liberal and support direct government action to address social issues, including teacher quality. Teacher professionalism supporters argue that by mandating crucial inputs and preparation for prospective teachers, such as course and high-quality clinical experience credits, and regulating teacher-preparation programs, state governments can ensure that these inputs produce quality teachers.

Supporters of competitive certification, who tend to be more centrist or conservative in their political leanings, note the failure of government mandates to achieve many important policy goals. They believe that deregulation, often accompanied by increased market competition (in this case, between teacher preparation programs and prospective teachers from different routes) is often a more promising policy option. Thus, they support local administrator flexibility and accountability for hiring quality teachers, and strong accountability and compensation incentives as better means to reach teacher-quality goals.

The claims on all sides are normatively and empirically debatable, but one cannot discount the extent to which ideological beliefs influence this debate.

## State-Level Actors

Balancing pressure from these competing points of view and answering the public demand for improved education are state-level agencies and actors.

As political entities, state education bureaucracies are responsive to constituent interests and subject to interest group pressure on governors and legislatures. In addition, professional standards boards established in many states often explicitly give teachers unions a role in formulating teacher-certification policy. Boards are typically comprised of public school teachers, administrators, and representatives of public teacher-preparation programs, selected from recommendations of the various constituent groups.[71] Thus, teachers unions have substantial influence over the significant share (and, in four states, a majority) of professional standards board seats designated for teachers, through political influence, practice, or (in several states) as a matter of statute.[72] While most of these boards are advisory with varying degrees of influence over teacher-certification policies adopted by state education boards and agencies, in sixteen states they operate autonomously with the power to set and even execute policy.[73]

In practice, this means that state officials who in theory should act independently and provide a check on the demands of special interests are often constrained by the very interests they should be regulating. Often, key actors are in a position to essentially regulate themselves.[74]

Increased attention to education in the 1980s and 1990s led to renewed attention to state policymaking arrangements. Many states had established professional standards boards in the 1950s, but since 1990, twenty-three revised or enacted professional standards board legislation. From 1999 to 2003, the Education Commission of the States records passage of thirteen laws in nine states to establish or alter the powers, composition, or selection of professional standards boards, which now exist in all but six states.[75] The political salience of education issues led to increased struggles between governors, legislatures, state boards, and state superintendents of instruction over control of education policymaking. Change in education governance structures also had an impact on the control of teacher certification in a number of states.

The tension is natural and obvious in a decentralized system. Governors naturally seek greater power over policymaking matters in their state, but are resisted by legislatures and semi-autonomous agencies and bodies. For example, in 1997, Governor John Engler (R-MI) issued an executive order stripping the state board of education of power over teacher-certification regulations, transferring it to the state schools chief. Engler was also planning to reorganize the state board of education, but members of his own party joined with Democrats to vote to block his order in the state's House of Representatives Education Committee. Eventually, a judge blocked Engler's order.[76]

More recently, in North Carolina, Governor Michael Easley (D) vetoed a teacher certification bill in June 2003.[77] The stated intent of the bill was to eliminate requirements that new teachers submit a portfolio for certification, but the real reason Easley vetoed the bill was a less publicized provision that would have shifted authority for setting teacher licensure requirements.[78]

These examples illustrate the struggles over who controls teacher-certification policy and other education policies, as well as efforts to increase accountability by vesting authority in fewer hands. For most state elected officials, however, teacher-certification issues have less to do with ideology or partisanship than with the realities of operating a system of schools and meeting public demand for quality teachers. For example, in his 2003 state of the state address, Governor Jeb Bush called for a "$27 million increase in funding... to mak[e] Florida lead the nation in the number of national board certified teachers," while Governor Jim Doyle (D-WI) specifically highlighted and praised alternative teacher-preparation programs in his state address.[79] The incentive driving policymakers is the knowledge that they will be held accountable for how they are perceived to have improved education. This reality and the fragmented nature of state certification systems creates an often confusing and contradictory policymaking environment. For example, states create or expand alternative routes to teaching while simultaneously raising requirements for the traditional routes these initiatives circumvent.

However, most state certification changes in either the professionalism or the competitive direction are on the margins, and substantial obstacles work against more substantial reforms.

Teacher preparation and certification are unusual among education issues in that both elementary/secondary and higher education systems, which generally have different governing authorities at the state level, play a crucial role. Thus, a wide array of government entities, each influenced by numerous interests, are involved in teacher preparation and certification, making broader reform difficult from an institutional perspective. These include governors, legislatures, state boards of education, state superintendents of instruction, state departments of education, professional standards boards, state higher education systems (which are responsible for preparing about three-quarters of teachers nationwide and often have their own dizzying array of boards and governance structures responsible for different segments of the state higher education system[80]), and regulatory agencies in some states responsible for private postsecondary education issues.

There is no single policy lever for reshaping teacher-preparation, certification, and licensure systems. Some state superintendents and boards of education are appointed; others are elected independently and may have very different agendas. The same holds true for higher education boards and agencies, which may have very different agendas than elementary and secondary agencies. Professional standards boards are often deliberately isolated from control by those who appoint them. In some states these boards have significant autonomy and control over policy, and many are dominated by representatives of the interests they regulate. The result is a lack of cohesive policy, practice, or planning among existing systems, and the multiplicity of entities thwarts reform by creating numerous opportunities to block significant changes.

Beyond politics and outside pressure, several other circumstances favor the teacher professionalism approach over the competitive certification approach. The rhetoric of teacher professionalism is appealing to parents and the public, who want quality teachers and accept the intuitive notion that existing certification is linked to quality. The current approach, with its defined preparation regimes, is perceived as carrying less bureaucratic and political risk. The "authorities" in academia who inform policymakers on certification issues have a vested interest in the professionalism agenda. A tremendous state-level infrastructure supports existing certification schemes.

The standards movement and associated demands for public accountability of policymakers are driving change in state education governance structures and systems. Governors in particular are seeking greater control over education in both K–12 and higher education. Still, in any state there are limits to what governors and administrative agencies can do without statutory change and the consent of the legislature.

Furthermore, many universities actively resist efforts to increase accountability. For example, teacher-preparation programs represented by AACTE and other higher education interest groups in Washington strongly resisted even the minimal accountability of the 1998 Higher Education Act Reauthorization's requirements that they report annually on the performance of their teacher-preparation program graduates on state certification exams, and have been accused of trying to undermine the goals of these provisions in their reporting.[81]

State-level policymakers responsible for education are rarely responsible for hiring teachers or addressing supply issues. Promising to "raise standards" by increasing teacher-certification requirements is politically popular with parents and powerful education interests in teachers unions and higher education. Policymakers also often face few costs in doing so. The actual costs of certification are borne mostly by prospective and practicing teachers and school districts. Emergency certification loopholes ensure that teaching positions will be filled, and, since there is actually a surplus of teachers who want to teach in suburban areas, the cost of shortages falls on low-income and minority communities that have the least political voice. Thus, incentives facing policymakers and barriers to change favor only minimal tweaking along lines most congenial to the teacher professionalism agenda. This suggests that substantial, rather than incremental or symbolic, reform may require outside stimulus, for example, directly or indirectly from the federal level.

## RECENT HISTORY AND THE ROAD AHEAD

In the 1990s, flush state budgets enabled many states to embrace costly initiatives advocated by the teacher professionalism agenda, such as salary increases, rewards for NBPTS-certified teachers, and investments in state teacher-preparation programs to meet NCATE input standards. The fate of these reforms in tighter budget circumstances that prevail in most states today remains unclear. Most states have sought to protect K–12 education, and teacher salaries and bonuses in particular. However, a forthcoming Economic Policy Institute study finds that Connecticut, Georgia, and Florida are trimming their teacher-incentive programs this year and suggests it is virtually inevitable that, barring dramatic tax increases or improvement in the economic conditions facing states, these programs will face greater scrutiny and cuts.[82] In the near future, state officials will need less costly approaches and reforms.

Between 1999 and August 2003, the Education Commission of the States records passage of nearly 150 state laws regarding teacher recruitment and retention, thirty-six regarding teacher preparation, eleven regarding alternative certification, fifteen regarding National Board certification, and nineteen regarding mentoring and induction.[83] However, this vastly understates the amount of activity around teacher-certification policy, as state legislatures continue to leave most details of teacher certification, professional development, and program approval requirements to state boards of education or independent professional standards boards, which enacted numerous changes throughout this period. Many changes that will have a significant impact on teacher certification and on both prospective and practicing teachers are the result not of state legislation, but of regulatory decisions of state boards and departments of education or more autonomous professional standards boards. For example, in 1998 Texas eliminated life certificates and began requiring teachers to meet continuing education requirements every five years to renew their certificates. This policy was highly controversial and opposed by teachers and teachers unions (in the face of this opposition, the State Board for Educator Certification eventually amended the proposal to allow current teachers who already had life certificates to be "grandfathered" out of these requirements). However, it required no legislation, only a regulatory change, and one made not by the elected State Board of Education but by the state's appointed professional standards board, the State Board for Educator Certification.[84]

The teacher professionalism agenda, particularly National Board Certification and NCATE accreditation, moved forward in many states. All but two states officially recognize NBPTS certification in some way, from credit toward continuing education and license renewal to substantial annual salary increases.[85] Twenty-nine states provide bonuses or salary increases for NBPTS-certified teachers, and thirty reimburse fees or provide other support.[86] Six offer advanced or "master" level teacher certification to NBPTS-certified teachers.[87] Forty-six states have formal partnerships with NCATE and eight require approved teacher-preparation programs to become NCATE-accredited.[88] States also adopted their own initiatives favored by professionalism advocates, including efforts to reduce emergency certification and out-of-field teaching, scholarships and loan forgiveness for students in teacher-preparation programs,[89] recognition of "excellent" teacher-preparation programs,[90] revamping standards for program approval, and redesigning teacher-preparation programs at state colleges and universities along professionalist models,[91] and expanding professional development support and requirements.[92] Flush budgets in the 1990s also enabled many states to raise teacher pay. Institutions of higher education also adopted professionalism reforms, like five-year teacher-preparation programs and full-year student teaching internships.

The competitive certification agenda advanced with the rapid spread of alternative certification, as forty-six states and the District of Columbia allowed the creation of alternative routes starting in the early 1980s.[93] Popular national initiatives like Teach For America and Troops to Teachers also advanced this agenda and highlighted demand for teaching opportunities among talented young people and individuals from other professions.[94] But in many states, alternative certification remains tightly regulated; it requires candidates to complete the same education coursework requirements as traditional program graduates and limits program size to produce few teachers. Alternative certification was increasingly co-opted by professionalism advocates and defined as a program of coursework and training, rather than alternative criteria by states as to individuals' fitness to teach. For example, in Nebraska, the state teachers union blocked an alternative certification program until union officials and the state board crafted a proposal that would require alternate route teachers to complete the same courses as traditionally trained teachers.[95]

In 2003, the New Jersey state board of education introduced new regulations, purportedly to standardize and raise teacher-certification require ments at the state's colleges, that some feared would also weaken the state's alternate route program, the oldest in the nation.[96] While well-intentioned, the U.S. Department of Education's No Child Left Behind (NCLB) guidelines specifying the characteristics alternative certification programs must have for candidates to be considered "highly qualified" may lend federal sanction to this trend.[97] Professionalism advocates pushed legislatures, state boards of education, and professional standards boards to require that alternate route teachers complete the same pedagogy coursework as for traditional certification, and as demand for alternative routes grew, education schools seized on a new market for their services.

## No Child Left Behind

The federal No Child Left Behind Act of 2001 significantly changes the dynamics of teacher-certification issues at the state level in ways that are only now beginning to emerge. NCLB requires that all teachers in core academic subjects be highly qualified by the 2005–2006 school year and defines in federal statute what it means for a teacher to be highly qualified. NCLB requires highly qualified teachers to 1) hold at least a bachelor's degree; 2) have full state certification as a teacher or have passed the state licensure exam and hold a license to teach; and 3) demonstrate competence in each academic subject in which the teacher teaches.[98]

At first glance, NCLB looks like a boon to the professionalism agenda, as it emphasizes the importance of teacher quality, raises teacher-quality requirements, and seeks to end the use of uncertified teachers by requiring certification based on state policies. However, advocates of competitive certification also see promise in the law, which places greater emphasis on subject knowledge while deferring to states regarding pedagogical training, presumably opening the door to streamlining requirements. In addition, NCLB prevents states from continuing to use emergency certification and waiver loopholes to fill teacher shortages while maintaining high barriers in standard certification. Competitive certification advocates hope this will encourage states to fundamentally rethink their teacher-certification systems along more competitive lines.

## Partisan Politics

As we have seen, the politics surrounding this issue stem from a variety of institutions, organizations, and beliefs. These are not explicitly partisan although they manifest themselves in partisan political debates.

At the state and national level, debate about teacher certification and licensure does not graft cleanly onto partisan political alignments, as though there are certainly some broad contours to the political debate. Overall, Republicans remain more friendly to policy alternatives such as alternative certification or competitive certification that challenge the status quo, although they tend to resist calls to increase spending on teacher preparation. Conversely, Democrats, who have stronger ties to teachers unions and many of the organizations championing the professionalism agenda, tend to favor more spending on teacher training but generally eschew policy options outside the traditional framework. However, prominent Democrats have challenged interest groups on key issues. For example, Representative George Miller (D-CA) championed federal standards to end out-of-field teaching, and Senator Jeff Bingaman (D-NM) and Miller have worked to increase accountability for schools of education. In addition, many Democrats support alternative certification.

## CONCLUSION

Starting from scratch, a modern professional agenda for teachers would probably include such elements as differential compensation based on knowledge, skills, and challenging assignments; some incorporation of performance into compensation; diffuse leadership structures that allow teachers to take on new responsibilities and grow in their careers while remaining in the classroom; and more fluid opportunities to shift between teaching and other professions over the course a career. In addition, preparation would likely be more flexible, dependent on local circumstances, and sequenced according to the needs of schools rather than statewide or national frameworks. Yet all these elements are at least in some way at odds with current certification schemes.

Changing existing policies is difficult because they are the result of years of accretion and have substantial stakeholder buy-in. In addition, powerful teacher professionalism interest groups, institutions of higher education, and teachers unions influence state-level policy actors to thwart change, as does an institutional structure that is not conducive to changes outside the existing policy and political framework. Those seeking reform outside the existing framework are a disparate group organizationally and ideologically, united neither by animating ideology nor unanimity about remedies. Not surprisingly, when a disorganized and fractured movement seeks changes resisted by an organized and focused movement, those changes face long odds.

Nonetheless, growing awareness that the current approach is failing to meet the needs of the nation's students along with changing societal contexts means this issue will continue to attract attention. It seems inevitable that emerging research, along with demographic changes that make the costs of the current system increasingly visible, will at some point make the status quo untenable and force more radical change.

The authors thank Amon Anderson, Karen Marshburn, and Alison Schary for their research assistance.

## CHAPTER 2

# The Shift from Hands-Off

## The Federal Role in Supporting and Defining Teacher Quality

*Heidi A. Ramírez*

The No Child Left Behind Act of 2001 (NCLB) is often described as a dramatic new direction in federal education law. NCLB ties federal aid to compliance with requirements for such things as the assurance of "highly qualified teachers" in every classroom, but this legislative direction is not an entirely new one. Rather, NCLB represents a continuation of many of the requirements initiated under the 1998 reauthorization of the Higher Education Act (HEA) and suggested by the last forty years of federal involvement in school reform.

Until the late 1950s, and particularly during President Johnson's mid-1960s pursuit of the Great Society, the federal government's reach into school matters was limited largely to land grants and financial supports for federally impacted areas. However, the 1958 passage of the National Defense Education Act and the 1965 Elementary and Secondary Education Act (ESEA) and Higher Education Act (HEA) began a new period of congressional interest in education improvement, an area that had long been regarded as strictly a state domain. Such congressional deference to the states (and, as a result, to the education institutions within their boundaries) continued to be a central theme in education policy, especially in policies related to teacher education, quality, and accountability, at least until the 1998 reauthorization of the HEA. Also central to federal efforts to improve teacher quality has been the debate over the importance and effectiveness of teacher-education programs.

This chapter describes the federal government's history of and emergent involvement in supporting, defining, and requiring accountability for teacher quality, as well as the political context that has framed it.

## FEDERAL POLICY IN AMERICAN EDUCATION: A HANDS-OFF APPROACH

> The powers not delegated to the United States by the Constitution, nor prohibited by it to the states, are reserved to the states respectively, or to the people.
>
> —U.S. Constitution, Amendment X

For more than 200 years, the notion that the federal government should keep its hands off education policy has been widely accepted. The Tenth Amendment to the Constitution has been the battle cry of both legislators and constituents opposing federal intervention in curriculum development, national testing, teacher licensure, and a host of other areas. This does not mean there has been no interest at the highest levels of government in the pursuit of educational improvement. Though the Tenth Amendment states clearly that any power not specifically delegated to the federal government is reserved to the states, Article I of the Constitution, which allows Congress the power to "lay and collect taxes... and provide for the common defense and general welfare of the United States," has, nearly from the nation's birth, been broadly interpreted as supporting a federal interest in education. George Washington included in his final message to Congress the unrealized goal of establishing a national university. Thomas Jefferson was well known for his advocacy of public education even before he became the nation's third president. Likewise, the pursuit of the general welfare of the nation (as described in Article I) was the rationale for passage of the Northwest Ordinances of 1785[1] and 1787. These acts provided communities, through the sale of public lands, land for the establishment of educational institutions.[2] Similarly, the Morrill Act, signed by President Lincoln in 1862, provided the states with public land grants for education, this time for agriculture and mechanical colleges. The second Morrill Act (1890) provided financial support for instruction in these institutions in the areas of agriculture, mechanical arts, and home economics, and provided grants to Black colleges for instruction in similarly specialized areas. The 1917 Smith-Hughes Act granted states funds for the planning of vocational education programs, specifying that some funding be allocated for teacher training.

From 1911 to 1920 the government continued its modest investment in education, focusing largely on vocational and rehabilitative education,[3] as well as veterans' support following each world war, including the 1944 Servicemen's Readjustment Act, also known as the GI Bill. And though the GI Bill helped hundreds of thousands of veterans become teachers,[4] with the exception of the 1946 National School Lunch Act, the 1954 School Milk Act, the establishment of the National Science Foundation (NSF) in 1950,[5] and acts authorizing statistics gathering (Educational Research Act and National Advisory Committee on Education Act), federal resources for education had been limited primarily to the provision of land,[6] military training,[7] and vocational and rehabilitative training. However, none of these efforts paid explicit attention to the quality of America's teachers, which was still seen as a responsibility of the states. In fact, during the ninety years following the 1867 establishment of the U.S. Department of Education, "the federal government had practically no policymaking role in elementary and secondary education in the United States. The U.S. Office of Education collected statistics; a few hundred districts received payments to offset the financial impact of nearby federal installations; and very small amounts of money were distributed to the states to further vocational education. But in the year-to-year development of local school policies, the federal government had no role."[8]

Even in the years after World War II, when questions about America's preparation for defense and further industrialization were common, federal involvement in education and teacher quality, though couched in the general welfare clause of the Constitution, remained limited. Those who might otherwise have been activists in this area were "thwarted by three obstacles: localism and resistance of federal control of educational policymaking; divided opinion (political and Constitutional) on aid to private, often church-related schools; and Southern resistance to desegregation requirements in postwar federal aid proposals."[9] Why, then, would the federal government get involved in the definition of teacher quality?

### Context for Federal Intervention:
### Historical Trends in Teacher Preparation

The long history of efforts to raise the bar for eligibility to teach in the United States begins with the issuing of licenses by colonial governors in the 1600s and continues with state funding of normal schools in the 1840s and locally administered teacher tests in the nineteenth and early twentieth centuries. This resulted in diverse state and local systems of licensure (see Rotherham & Mead, this volume), although with some effect in raising standards for the profession. By about 1910, most teachers had completed secondary school, and many had had some additional local training or earned a baccalaureate degree (though typically without much pedagogical training). A decade later, as normal schools evolved into state teachers' colleges and schools of education,[10] teacher licensure came to be based primarily on the candidate's graduation from a state-approved program. With this shift emerged a controversy about the nature of teacher education that remains today: the debate between those who believe that subject-matter knowledge suffices for good teaching and those who value professional knowledge, typically acquired through methods courses and teacher internships. Among the latter there exists the question of where such pedagogical knowledge is best developed: in the school of education, in the liberal arts college, or in classroom practice.

Aside from these debates, reviews of efforts to improve teacher quality are mixed. Continued increases in elementary enrollments[11] between 1900 and 1930, averaging nearly 14 percent per decade, exacerbated the demand for teachers[12] and resulted in less attention to teacher qualifications in local hiring decisions. By 1922, approximately one-fourth of primary school teachers still lacked a high school education, and fewer than half had completed two years of college. In 1931, only about one-tenth of elementary school teachers had a bachelor's degree and a quarter of secondary teachers lacked a four-year degree. Likewise, when teachers left their classrooms to serve in World War II, districts further relaxed their hiring standards, thus neglecting the already low standards many states had set for licensure. As a result, by the 1950s, although thirty-seven states required at least one and a half years of college for elementary school teachers, half of the nation's teachers still did not have a college degree,[13] and the value of such an education in preparing effective teachers was still being debated.

The Soviet launch of Sputnik I in 1957 and the resulting belief that America's schools were to blame for this defeat in the "space race" increased criticism of teacher-preparation programs. Despite efforts begun in 1946 by the Commission on Teacher Education to identify the necessary elements of teacher preparation,[14] teacher education controversies abounded. Preparation in the rigorous content necessary for American competitiveness, it was argued, was being overlooked in favor of meaningless pedagogical training. As one critic asserted at a 1959 conference on teacher education, elementary education curriculum represented "a dismal array of one-, two-, and three-hour courses in art for the artless, biology for babes, chemistry for kiddies, math and music for moppets, along with such academic fantasies as 'Creative Experiences with Materials'... cutting and pasting for college credit."[15]

Over the next two decades, such criticisms became increasingly common,[16] suggesting a need for significant change in teacher-education programs.[17] In 1983, the National Commission on Excellence report, *A Nation at Risk*, repeated this call, describing teacher-education programs as "weighted heavily with courses in 'educational methods' at the expense of courses of subjects to be taught." In response, a group of deans from leading schools of education formed the Holmes Group and endeavored to define long term reforms for teacher education and the profession itself. The group's report, *Tomorrow's Teachers*,[18] challenged the overly simplified "bright-person" models of good teaching and tried to define a program of professional studies in education that would meaningfully integrate content knowledge (liberal arts education) with pedagogical knowledge and skills, including the ability to reformulate content knowledge. However, this report, much like the Carnegie Foundation's *A Nation Prepared: Teachers for the 21st Century* (1986), while promoting the spread of professional development schools seemed to have little effect on the organization of teacher-education programs or their coordination with liberal arts colleges.

Many states thus developed more uniform requirements for licensure beyond years in college and local exams, specifying requisite college courses (e.g., in psychology, pedagogical theory, and classroom methodology). Licensing became firmly ensconced in state departments of education and dependent on completion of a bachelor's degree, often including state-mandated preparatory courses or credit hours. However, because most states historically invested little in meaningful program review processes[19] and, until recently, few states required their schools of education to be professionally accredited, schools of education experienced little program accountability.[20] Instead, reviews of teacher-education programs (e.g., in a process of program accreditation) typically included assessments of the teacher candidate's learning environment and program inputs (faculty-student ratio, course offerings, faculty qualifications, library specifications) rather than what he or she had actually learned or could do. As a result, "a critical check on quality that exists in other professions—a system for individual candidate assessment against some common standards of knowledge and skill—has been missing for many decades in teaching."[21]

In this landscape, where schools of education were held to few consistent, rigorous, or enforceable standards, the last twenty years of teacher-quality reform efforts continued to move toward tougher requirements for program entry. During this time, fifteen states set minimum grade point averages (GPAs) and nearly half the states enacted some form of testing as prerequisites for entry into teacher-education programs. Most teacher-education programs also set minimum grade requirements for admission, and more than half also required that students pass a proficiency test as a condition of program completion.[22] The majority of states also introduced the tests of minimal standards for initial teacher licensure that are now the norm, holding individuals, rather than the programs that train them, accountable for the quality of their teacher preparation.

The status quo in teacher education was thus well protected, even as higher standards for K–12 students were being advocated by national civil rights advocates, professional associations, and similar groups, as well as the federal government.

## FEDERAL GOVERNMENT AS EDUCATION REFORMER: THE NATIONAL DEFENSE EDUCATION ACT (NDEA)

By the mid-twentieth century, Congress' "hands-off" approach to schooling was changing dramatically. The failure of teacher education to reform itself, coupled with anxiety over the Sputnik defeat[23] and the resulting fears about the scientific and technological skills of American students, spurred federal lawmakers to get actively involved in K–12 education policy and, to a lesser extent, in teacher-quality policies, for the first time. President Eisenhower encouraged legislation to ensure that Americans had access to the training necessary to keep America competitive and secure.

In 1958, Congress passed the National Defense Education Act (NDEA), co-opting dozens of bills proposed that year dealing with education and reflecting the 85th Congress' anxiety about the Soviet Union's feat and America's failure. The legislation, which enjoyed bipartisan support,[24] represented a new federal commitment to improving education while making explicit states' primary authority in these matters:

> The Congress reaffirms the principle and declares that the States and local communities have and must retain control over and primary responsibility for public education. The national interest requires, however, that the Federal Government give assistance to education for programs which are important to our defense.... It is therefore the purpose of this Act to provide substantial assistance in various forms to individuals, and to States and their subdivisions, in order to insure trained manpower of sufficient quality and quantity to meet the national defense needs of the United States.[25]

To meet these national needs, the NDEA focused largely on vocational education and college scholarships, particularly in science and engineering, as well as research fellowships for prospective teacher educators.[26] At their height, Title IV programs provided approximately 6,000 new fellowships (at about $80 million) a year. Among many new programs,[27] the NDEA also authorized the deferment and forgiveness of college loans for students who trained to become teachers of math, science, or foreign languages, areas seen as central to national defense. Of particular note, Title III of the NDEA authorized financial assistance of $1 billion over four years for teacher training (e g , in-service summer institutes) and instruction in the target areas, though only $115 million was allocated in the program's first year.[28] Teacher-training centers at institutions of higher education (IHEs), much like the summer institutes funded by the NSF, were authorized under Titles V and VI. In 1964, the NDEA was amended to include Title XI and expand the reach of the law to teacher training in other content areas, including English, history, and geography. Title XI directed supports to teachers serving or preparing to serve disadvantaged youth, a group increasingly becoming the focus of federal education policy.

### Great Society Education Reforms

More federal action came as part of President Johnson's plan for the Great Society. President Kennedy's 1963 assassination created a wave of sympathy and public support that enabled President Johnson to promote many of the slain president's legislative proposals, including the Civil Rights Act of 1964, and to pursue his own vision for promoting equality, rebuilding cities, fighting poverty, and improving education.

In 1964, eight million American adults had fewer than five years of schooling; more than twenty million had not completed eight years; and almost a quarter of the nation's population, around fifty-four million people, hadn't finished high school.[29] Johnson urged Congress to consider how the United States could be expected to compete with the rest of the world when such a large proportion of its citizenry, particularly the poor and minorities, lacked academic resources. In 1965, under Johnson's leadership, Congress passed landmark legislation affecting both K–12 and postsecondary education.

*Elementary and Secondary Education Act*

In an effort to eliminate the gap in achievement between low-income students and their high-achieving peers in more affluent communities, the Elementary and Secondary Education Act (ESEA) provided the first federal dollars for pre-college education. In addition to the general supports for high-poverty schools authorized under Title I,[30] ESEA authorized financial support for the training of teachers already in the profession. For example, school districts (via the states) were given financial resources for in-service teacher training in math and science under the Title II Dwight D. Eisenhower National Program for Math and Science Education. It was the first significant investment in teacher preparation and the first time school districts without IHE partners would be awarded such funds.

Over time, reauthorizations of the ESEA added a variety of small programs that included funding for teacher training in specialized areas (e.g., National Writing Project, Javits Gifted and Talented Education, Character Education, Technology) and for specific student populations (e.g., migrant and American Indian students).

### Higher Education Act

The Higher Education Act of 1965 charged IHEs with helping to alleviate the disadvantages of poor and minority students. It provided a range of financial supports for college attendance, including scholarships, grants, and (later) work-study programs, and is often credited with providing access to higher education for many of the women and African Americans who entered the teaching profession in the 1970s. More specific to teacher education, though, the HEA authorized a series of new programs for the improved recruitment and training of teachers.

For example, the Teacher Corps program, based on the Cardozo (Washington, D.C.) Project in Urban Teaching,[31] was authorized to recruit and train K–12 teachers for "areas having concentrations of low-income families." Contrary to the desires of the IHEs and their representative organizations, the Teacher Corps encouraged a school/district site model and concrete teaching experiences, rather than requiring the allocation of resources to schools of education. To many, the Teacher Corps authorization signaled a federal effort to move supports for teacher training and development from the hands of IHEs to schools and districts. The Teacher Corps trained tens of thousands of teachers in schools across the country. Over time, though, as demand for teachers declined, the focus of the Teacher Corps shifted several times (e.g., from training inexperienced teachers to in-service training of existing teachers and teacher aides). Title V of HEA authorized graduate fellowships for K–12 teachers pursuing master's degrees via the Experienced Teacher Fellowship Program.

### Education Professions Development Act

Concerns about the quality of America's teachers raised by the Sputnik defeat and first addressed in the NDEA and HEA[32] were also central to the 1967 passage of the Education Professions Development Act (EPDA). The EPDA

(P.L. 90-35), far-reaching amendments to Title V of the HEA, brought together new and old programs, as well as support for personnel across subject
matter areas:

> To coordinate, broaden, and strengthen programs for the training and im-
> provement of the qualifications of teachers and other educational person-
> nel for all levels of the American educational system to provide a better
> foundation for meeting the critical needs of the Nation for personnel in
> those areas.

More specifically, and much to the dissatisfaction of the IHEs, the EPDA
awarded funds directly to schools and districts, made these available to
"other educational personnel" in addition to teachers, consolidated several
existing discretionary programs, focused less than the NDEA on supporting
the pursuit of Ph.D.s, extended the Teacher Corps, and created the Trainers
of Teacher Trainers program (Triple T) and the Career Opportunities (work-
study) Program (COP).[33] The COP funded recruitment of low-income community residents, Vietnam veterans, and some persons with disabilities to
serve as paraprofessionals in high-poverty schools while they trained to become licensed teachers. Triple T sought to revolutionize schools of
education.

Unlike prior federal programs that tinkered at the margins of teacher education by creating new courses or reducing class size in schools of education, Triple T was charged with improving the quality of teacher-education
faculty and coordinating school and community resources, as well as all departments in the IHE responsible for the education of future teachers. With
these daunting assignments, Triple T quickly became one of the largest and
most comprehensive federal programs in support of teacher quality, allocating $40 million over its short five-year life and engaging approximately
42,000 people, 12,000 of them elementary school teachers from a variety of
institutions across the country.[34]

The Nixon-Ford administration replaced the EPDA with teacher-training
block grants for vocational education in 1976. However, site-specific teacher
development continued to be supported via the Teachers Center Program
and the Teacher Corps, though the latter was redesigned to offer longer-
term demonstration projects for partnerships between districts, IHEs, and
local communities. Even before these changes, though, neither ESEA nor
the HEA demanded much of teacher preparation programs. ESEA focused resources on in-service teacher development, which, until recently, relied
largely on summer institutes and workshops separate from the school community, student needs, or a comprehensive improvement plan. HEA autho-

rized a variety of ever-evolving programs for teacher recruitment and training, but concentrated resources on IHEs, only later increasing supports for novel district and community efforts. But neither law required much of grantees beyond regular reports of the number of teachers or teacher candidates trained and the dollars spent. That is, despite the common dissatisfaction with the state of teacher-education programs, they were not held to account for efforts to improve their effectiveness in preparing teachers for the rigors of the classroom. Before such accountability would be addressed, the array of programs would be reconsidered.

### Program Consolidation: The 1970s

"By the end of 1976, the federal investment in professional preparation was substantial—over $500 million in grants, contracts, and other awards through some 40 separate Office of Education administered programs—with still more millions invested through a host of programs outside the Education Division" and spread across IHEs, districts, and state educations agencies.[35] In this environment, the new Carter administration began an examination of existing investments in teacher education to identify areas of concern. As a result, Assistant Commissioner for Policy Studies Marshall S. Smith[36] suggested the further coordination of federal teacher-training programs.[37] Commissioner Boyer also worked to coordinate teacher-preparation programs, establishing a task force on the issue that came to be known as the National Teacher Development Initiative (NTDI). In 1978, in preparation for the reauthorization of the HEA, a similar workgroup (headed by the same chair as the NTDI, former Commissioner William Smith, director of the Teacher Corps program) was established to make recommendations for Title V. While coordination of HEA teacher-development programs was being considered, the 1978 reauthorization of the ESEA was written to require that states coordinate their own professional development efforts.[38]

### 1980 HEA Reauthorization

The new attention to HEA's Title V programs and the effort in both K–12 and higher education to coordinate professional development programs presented real challenges for the 1980 HEA reauthorization process. The NEA wanted the Teacher Corps program abolished and its resources (approximately $30 million in 1980) allocated to the locally implemented Teacher Centers (funded at $14 million). In contrast, the American Association for Colleges of Teacher Education (AACTE) lobbied to require higher education-local district partnerships to ensure that IHEs stayed in the mix. The final HEA law (PL 96-374) dramatically rewrote the Teacher Corps program from support of teachers in Title I (high-poverty) schools to support for biomedical, scientific, and math teacher training. The reauthorization also included the Schools of Education Assistance Act,[39] creating what many described as "a long-awaited federal mandate"[40] for the redesign and reorientation of teacher-education institutions. Grants under this statute were to be used by schools and IHE teacher-education programs to develop model K–12 teacher-development programs and better train their higher education faculty to help meet the increasingly diverse needs of schools and society (e.g., in special education, adult education, gifted and talented education). In fact, conscious of the growing skepticism about teacher education represented in the Schools of Education Assistance Act, many within the higher education community (notably AACTE) became increasingly involved in education policy.[41]

### Call for Change: A Nation at Risk

By 1983 a new urgency in public education had emerged. The federally issued report *A Nation at Risk* argued that America's schools had fallen prey to a "rising tide of mediocrity," chastising schools for their failure to offer challenging courses and criticizing teachers for their inability to teach higher-level critical thinking skills, particularly in math and science. Schools of education were critiqued as the "cash cows" of universities (see Rotherham & Mead, this volume), allowed to exist without attention to rigorous academic content or to recruiting and training high-quality teacher candidates. Amid the Reagan administration's efforts to consolidate education programs and limit the reach of the federal government in school policy, *A Nation at Risk* created a nation of finger-pointing.

While elementary and secondary schools made curriculum changes, adding advanced courses in math and science, and raising requirements for graduation, schools of education were seen as complacent arbiters of educational malpractice failing to prepare teachers for such curricular changes. As one senator noted, the nation was experiencing disturbing trends with respect to teaching: teachers drawn from the bottom of academic ranks; teacher preparation curricula weighted with courses in educational methods; inadequate salaries; severe shortages in certain disciplines; and, in some cases, unqualified instructors.[42] As a result, despite AACTE's ongoing, federally sponsored study of teacher-education reforms, a 1984 Senate bill was introduced to establish an independent review of teacher preparation programs.[43] As stated in the bill's findings, Congress was increasingly concerned by what it perceived as the "poor quality of teacher education… [with] no national response" and "colleges of education [that were] not accountable to the public." Something, it was argued, needed to be done to improve the quality of teacher-education programs and the effectiveness of America's teachers.

This sentiment was still apparent in 1985 when the Senate held hearings on the American Defense Education Act (ADEA). Throughout, *A Nation at Risk* was repeatedly referenced, as were the National Science Foundation's findings that "for the 1982–1983 school year, 46 states reported a shortage of chemistry teachers, 45 reported a shortage of mathematics teachers, and 42 reported a shortage of physics teachers." Despite the ongoing anxiety, the ADEA embodied a much less aggressive approach to improving teaching and learning, suggesting that school districts develop programs to improve instruction and student achievement in math, science, technology, foreign language, and communications skills. With respect to higher education institutions and their role in improving teacher quality, the bill "encourage[d] institutions . . . to coordinate efforts with local school districts for the training and retraining of teachers through workshops, summer institutes, and in-service training." That is, while reports of teacher shortages in areas such as mathematics and physics were much cited, little was done beyond continuing investment in teacher in-service training to ensure that teachers had the skills and knowledge to meet the instructional challenges implicit in the reforms.

The elephant in the living room—preservice teacher education and institutional accountability—had again escaped legislative action. As Senator Gary Hart said, the federal role was still understood to serve "as a catalyst to encourage," not interfere in, "local action."[44] However, the federal government's hands-off approach to schooling, reinforced by Republican-led efforts to limit the powers of the U.S. Department of Education and consolidate programs in basic aid block grants, would soon be overlooked in favor of a proactive work on K–12 school reform.

### Goals 2000 and the Improving America's Schools Act

In 1989, in response to growing concerns about the state of American schooling raised by the nation's governors, President George H.W. Bush convened the National Education Summit in Charlottesville, Virginia. While reaffirming the states' authority in education, the governors pushed for federal support for comprehensive school reform. Months later, President Bush used his 1990 State of the Union address to announce six national education goals that would inspire considerable work by professional associations, including the National Council of Teachers of Mathematics to develop national (not federal) academic standards. Bush also proposed the controversial America 2000[45] program, which was soundly rejected by legislators.

Soon after taking office, President Bill Clinton[46] began pursuing his agenda for standards-based reform, building on the momentum started by the nation's governors and Bush's national goals. The standards-based reform movement envisioned the establishment of challenging academic standards that would inform the curriculum for all children within a state, regardless of race or socioeconomic status, and provide the focus for teachers' professional development, state assessments, and accountability systems. With the passage of the controversial Goals 2000: Educate America Act, Clinton not only expanded Bush's national goals, but also provided new grants to states, encouraged considerable spending on teacher in-service professional development, in the process prescribing an approach to systemic school reform under which states would submit plans to the Department of Education, with funding conditioned on a plan's approval by the secretary of education.

Despite concerns about the broad reach of the federal government and fears that the new legislation would lead to federally defined standards and curricula, an era in federal education policy arguably as dramatic as Johnson's Great Society had begun. Consistent with this new age, the Clinton administration reauthorized ESEA, continuing most of its existing programs and creating new programs for teacher development in the use of classroom technology,[47] while also creating new requirements for school and district accountability for the education of all children. The Improving America's Schools Act (IASA) sought to close the achievement gap between poor and minority children and their more affluent peers. It required that Title I schools be held to the same standards as others, and created assessment systems to ensure that schools were making adequate progress toward this goal.

By 2000, ESEA included more than sixty programs. Most grantees were encouraged, if not required, to invest in teacher learning. (Table 2 includes the recent budgets of teacher-quality-related ESEA programs.) But these programs, often the result of partnerships between IHEs and elementary and secondary schools, rarely included coordinated efforts to prepare new teachers. The federal hand in teacher recruitment was thus to be played in the Higher Education Act.

## ACCOUNTABILITY FOR TEACHER QUALITY: A NEW FEDERAL ARENA

In September 1996, while states were fast at work developing their Goals 2000 plans for standards-based reform, the National Commission on Teaching and America's Future (NCTAF)—a collaborative of governors, teachers and teacher educators, researchers, college presidents, business leaders, and union representatives—brought the challenges of classroom implementation of high standards to the forefront. In *What Matters Most: Teaching for America's Future,* NCTAF, with Linda Darling-Hammond's leadership, synthesized data on teacher preparation, licensure, out-of-field teaching, and in-service education to argue that America's educational goals could not be met without "a dramatic departure from the status quo"[48] in teacher preparation. The report offered a comprehensive plan intended to ensure that every child would have "access to competent, caring, qualified teaching" by 2006. It also identified several barriers to improved instructional practice, including low expectations for student performance, unenforced teacher standards, flawed teacher preparation, sloppy teacher recruitment, poor teacher induction, lack of professional development and rewards for knowledge and skill, and schools poorly structured for success.[49]

In 1998 President Clinton issued "A Call to Action for American Education in the 21st Century" and hosted the President's Summit on Teacher Quality,[50] proclaiming, "Every community should have a talented and dedicated teacher in every classroom. [We have] an enormous opportunity for ensuring teacher quality well into the 21st century, if we recruit promising people into teaching and give them the highest quality preparation and training."

Secretary of Education Richard Riley pursued this opportunity with the release of *Promising Practices: New Ways to Improve Teacher Quality,* which stressed the importance of teaching and highlighted model improvement efforts along the professional continuum of teacher recruitment, preparation, licensing and certification, and professional development. In speeches over the next two years, Riley, Clinton, and their surrogates emphasized the growing teacher shortage (then projected to reach 2.2 million by 2010) and the need for well-trained teachers to fill vacancies. In particular, they encouraged potential university-school partnerships (including professional development schools) as championed by the Holmes Group[51] and long supported by federal education policy, for example, in the definition of eligible grantees.[52] For the next several years the NCTAF report would serve as the battle cry for education reformers, Republican and Democratic lawmakers alike, particularly critics of the state of teacher education.

In his 1998 State of the Union address, trying to revitalize the reform momentum of his first term, President Clinton introduced a variety of education initiatives. Among these was a national effort to reduce class size in grades one through three. Over the next few months, the administration argued that the class-size-reduction initiative would "help make sure that every child receives personal attention, gets a solid foundation for further learning, and learns to read independently by the end of third grade."[53] The proposed funds, $7.3 billion over five years,[54] would be used to help districts hire and pay an additional 100,000 teachers to serve students in the early grades.

Class-size reduction was popular in the polls but faced considerable opposition in Congress. Opponents argued that, given the existing teacher shortage, the president's proposal would lead to dramatic increases in the hiring of unqualified teachers, especially in already hard-hit high-poverty schools and districts.[55] Senate Majority Leader Trent Lott (R-MS) charged that that the president had left teacher accountability out of the picture. Congressman Bill Goodling (R-PA) made a similar argument:

> We need quality in the classroom and we won't have it until our teachers are better trained in the subjects they teach. We should quickly put to rest this notion of President Clinton's that we should spend $12 billion to hire 100,000 new teachers in order to marginally reduce class size. The President's plan will do nothing but bring more poorly trained teachers into our nation's schools.[56]

Republicans, with the support of some moderate Democrats, proposed a series of block grants directly to local schools and districts, including the Better Opportunities for Our Kids and Schools (BOOKS) Act and the Teacher Empowerment Act, for teacher development, class-size reduction, and basic aid. These proposals signaled an increasing desire to increase localities' discretion to spend federal funds and respond to local needs. Even Clinton's class-size proposal allowed states to use a portion of the funds for activities as varied as teacher recruitment and training and the development of more rigorous professional knowledge and subject-matter tests.

In response to Republican concerns about accountability for federal funds, as well as pressure from civil rights advocates and Democratic members frustrated by disparities in teacher quality across high- and low-poverty communities, funded schools were also required to publish annual report cards to parents and the community describing student achievement, class size, and teacher qualifications. Secretary Riley said of the proposal in his annual State of American Education address:

> The success of any effort to reduce class size ultimately depends on the quality of the teachers and giving teachers the support, time, and tools to succeed.... States have to do their part as well and make a much more vigorous effort to raise their teacher standards.[57]

With the hard-fought class-size budget victory, the Clinton administration seemed comfortable leaving accountability for teacher quality to the continued discretion of the states. Several legislators were not.

### Federal Intervention in Teacher Quality: HEA 1998

Disturbed by the academic underachievement of students in his home state and the trend of hiring unqualified, emergency-credentialed teachers to ensure smaller class sizes, especially in underperforming, high-poverty schools, Congressman George Miller (D-CA) began to push measures to increase standards and accountability for teacher certification and licensure. With the reauthorization of the Higher Education Act (HEA) pending and several compromises on key student aid and other issues likely to be resolved early, the ranking Democrat saw HEA as a perfect legislative opportunity for challenging the status quo in teacher preparation.

Much as Darling-Hammond had become a voice on teacher quality, the children's advocacy organization The Education Trust, led by Katie Haycock, had become a trusted voice on ensuring parity in teacher quality across high- and low-poverty schools. As a result, Haycock, who championed strategies for narrowing the achievement gap by improving teacher quality in low-performing, high-poverty, and high-minority schools, gained the ear of Rep. Miller and other Democratic legislators. In early 1998, well before an administration proposal for the HEA, Rep. Miller, supported by The Education Trust, introduced the Teaching Excellence for All Children Act.[58] In the Senate, Jeff Bingaman (D-NM) introduced the Quality Teacher in Every Classroom Act.[59] Both proposals included a parental right to know (report card) on teacher qualifications, similar to those suggested by NCTAF[60] and several civil rights groups and included in the later class-size authorizing language, and proposed strict accountability standards. In addition, the bills would have required teacher-preparation programs to meet national accreditation standards in order to be eligible for federal dollars, set minimum standards for the percentage of an institution's teacher candidates who pass state licensure exams on their first attempt, and tied ESEA funds to the percentage of qualified teachers in K–12 classrooms. "We have some obligation to put accountability [in place]," Miller argued, given the federal government's investment of nearly $2 billion in teacher preparation.[61] Rep. Goodling, chair of the House Education and the Workforce Committee, seemed to agree with the intent, though not the approach. Goodling described such efforts at program accountability as "too arbitrary given that all states have different tests which they require for teacher licensure."[62] At the bill's committee markup,[63] the chairman offered an amendment to replace the many unfunded HEA Title V teacher-preparation programs with a single competitive block grant focused on teacher preparation, quality, and certification.

During this time, questions of teacher preparedness—measured largely by state tests for licensure—were raising increased concerns outside Washington. In April 1998, Massachusetts raised a firestorm of press criticism and public ridicule of teacher educators when only 41 percent of its 1,800 prospective teachers passed its first teacher licensing exam. As then chairman of the Massachusetts school board and the president of Boston University [WHO??] asserted, the state's reading and writing test "was an examination that a high school graduate ought to be able to pass. The idea that a college graduate can't pass it means that the college degree is fraudulent."[64] Despite little active support from the Clinton White House,[65] this heightened public concern, with little opposition from either the teachers unions (which were promoting teacher professionalism) or the relatively quiet higher education organizations (which were careful to not appear as protectionist obstacles to school reform), and helped many of the Miller Bingaman mandates find a place in the new HEA.

Reauthorized in October 1998, the law created two new Title II programs, Teacher Quality Enhancement Grants and Teacher Training Partnership Grants, replacing the previous array of Title V programs. More significantly, HEA also established new state and institutional reporting requirements, affirming a Congressional commitment to hold "institutions of higher education accountable for preparing teachers who have the necessary teaching skills and are highly competent in the academic content area in which the teachers plan to teach."[66] Departing dramatically from the hands-off approach to teacher preparation, Title II (sec. 207) of the law also called on states to become more active in ensuring the presence of qualified teachers in their schools. The law, closely based on The Education Trust's early proposals, required three annual reports to provide data toward this effort: 1) from institutions to states on their teacher-preparation programs and the pass rates of their teacher candidates on state licensure exams; 2) from states to the U.S. Secretary of Education on teacher-preparation programs and their pass rates, as well as the standards for state licensure, information on state assessments, qualifications of teachers within the state, the distribution of unqualified teachers across high- and low-poverty schools, state criteria for measuring program performance, and state efforts to improve teacher quality; and 3) reports synthesizing these data from the secretary to Congress and the public.

However, the very premises underlying the requirements evoked debate about whether institutions should be held accountable for the quality of teacher training; whether quality can be fairly evaluated on the basis of performances on state teacher-licensing tests; and whether teacher supply should be federally regulated.

*Institutional Accountability*

Throughout the legislative process, as well the two-year development of reporting guidelines, schools of education and the organizations that represent them—especially the American Council on Education (ACE), the American Association of Colleges for Teacher Education (AACTE), and the American Association of State Colleges and Universities (AASCU)—expressed concerns about the new mandates. Publicly they affirmed their commitment to improving teacher quality, but they argued that the requirements were unfair and too complex, burdensome, and costly to manage. They argued that, contrary to the law's requirements for reporting pass rates on all assessments required for licensure (including those of pedagogical and content knowledge, e.g., physics and algebra), schools of education should not be held accountable for the failings of the liberal arts colleges, which train teacher candidates in their subjects. Given this split responsibility, lobbyists argued, schools of education should at most be reporting on their candidates' knowledge of teaching, not content mastery.[67]

Others argued that tracking performance across so many different assessments (as many as 71 in some states[68]) would prove impractical. IHEs also complained that reporting requirements were unfair because teacher-training program completers take such tests at different times in their education (e.g., basic skills tests before admission to the program, assessments of pedagogy at the end of their formal training), have many opportunities to take and retake tests, and often take licensing tests in other states. IHEs thus built a solid reputation for obstructionism in the face of reform and accountability. The Education Trust reported:

> Congressional requirements that certain basic information be made public, and that states act to improve low performance, seem rather modest . . . [, but] you wouldn't have thought so when those provisions were first proposed. ... The organizations representing higher education fought vehemently against making these data public.[69]

Others criticized Title II for its approach to measuring accountability. Given the complexity of teaching, a single standardized test or even a battery of tests could not assess everything it takes to be a good teacher. It was argued that multiple measures of teacher knowledge and skills, including performance assessments, institutional/faculty recommendations, and feedback on teacher internships, would provide a richer picture of what teachers had learned in their preparation programs and could do in classrooms.[70] As the Department of Education summarized, Title II's critics:

> stressed the limitations of using pass rates on "paper and pencil examinations" and other required information to provide a good or complete picture of the quality of teacher preparation programs and state policies and activities in the area of teacher preparation, licensure, and certification.[71]

"We would certainly argue that state teacher-licensing exams are by no means good enough or rigorous enough," one HEA advocate asserted. "If schools of education can't get students to pass such a low bar, they have no business in the area of teacher preparation."[72]

*Disparate Impact*

Most school reform advocates agreed that higher standards and reporting requirements were good for teacher quality, but consensus was not perfect. Many higher education organizations representing the interests of racial and ethnic minorities raised specific concerns about the potential of the Title II law to discourage or prohibit badly needed would-be teachers from entering the profession. Because minority students have limited access to higher education and generally tend to score lower than their white peers on standardized tests,[73] including teacher assessments, they argued, IHEs that typically recruit and train high numbers of teachers from underrepresented groups would be disproportionately affected by reports of their students' initial pass rates. Many feared that to avoid the embarrassment and sanctions of low pass rates, more programs would begin to require passage of tests (e.g., of basic skills) as a prerequisite for admissions, threatening to further limit the number of future teachers from minority backgrounds.[74]

"One-third of K–12 students are black, Hispanic, or Asian, while 87% of teachers are white. [And n]early one-half of all schools do not have a single minority teacher."[75] In this environment, assessing program value and improving the quality and number of America's teachers while ensuring a diverse teaching force continues to pose a challenge.[76]

*Implications for the Teacher Supply*

In the early 1990s, more than one-third of states were already allowing existing teachers to teach "out of field" for some or all of the school day. Other states allowed college graduates with no professional teacher training to teach full time with "emergency certifications." Raising standards for entry into the profession thus struck critics as a path to exaggerating the problem of unqualified teachers and reducing the pool of people willing and able to teach.[77] Critics argued that smart, well-educated individuals, merely as a result of their high verbal ability and wide content knowledge, make good teachers, but are too frequently dissuaded from teaching by the extensive bureaucracy of teacher education.

This "bright person" model of good teaching has led many critics to insist that, instead of beefing up testing and reporting systems for initial teacher licensure, "states should de-emphasize traditional teacher education and instead open the profession to a large pool of talented and well-educated candidates."[78]

### Implementing Title II: Developing Guidelines

Title II of HEA also presented a variety of essential details for debate and resolution. To implement Title II and provide consistent data in the future, Congress deferred to the U.S. Department of Education to develop appropriate measures in consultation with the states, IHEs, and other relevant interest groups.[79] What measures were appropriate? After all, while Title II required institutions and states to report key data, such as the pass rates for "graduates" of their teacher-education programs and the percentage of teachers issued waivers of state licensure standards, the legislation did not furnish many of the definitions necessary to ensure timely and reliable data collection. In 2000, Secretary Riley released *The Initial Report of the Secretary on the Quality of Teacher Preparation* as required by law—for which states reported, according to their own definitions, whatever data they had at the time. The preliminary report highlighted the nearly impossible task of creating uniform reporting guidelines for the fifty states (plus Washington, D.C., Puerto Rico, and the territories) and more than 1,200 institutions.

The Department of Education was called on to develop implementation guidelines comprehensive enough to produce meaningful data, but not so extensive as to be unduly burdensome or exceed the letter of the law. Of particular concern to the IHEs was the submission of institutional and state pass rates[80] and how these would be synthesized in reports from the states and from the secretary of education to Congress.

### Program Completers

Even before the specifics of pass rates could be resolved, the class of persons for whom they would be reported needed clarification. The statute called for the rate for an institution's "graduates," but that seemed to include even alumni who had not received any teacher training at the institution. The final department guidelines thus established the term "program completer" to signify one who has "met all the requirements a state-a

*Pass Rates*

The statute also provides little guidance on the meaning of "pass rates." States require different numbers and types of tests for teacher licensure, including assessments of basic skills, professional knowledge and pedagogy, academic content, specialized instructional knowledge (e.g., special education, ESOL), and performance assessments. The final guidelines[82] require institutions and states to report three kinds of pass rates: 1) single-assessment pass rate (share of program completers who took the test who actually passed the test); 2) aggregate pass rates (share of program completers who passed all of the tests taken in each of six skill or knowledge areas); and 3) summary pass rates (share of program completers who passed all tests taken for their areas of specialization). The system would therefore count as failures those completers who, even if they had not completed the entire test battery, had failed at least one of the required assessments. Likewise, institutions could update data as their teacher candidates retook and successfully passed tests on repeated attempts.

The fact that teacher tests are taken at different points in one's training has implications for the reporting of pass rates as indicators of program quality. The Education Trust reports that "nearly half of the states that require teacher candidates to pass basic skills tests actually require those tests for program entry and/or prior to completion. In many other states, a large proportion of institutions have the same policy."[83] In these cases, as the Department of Education conceded, its "reporting system would have the[se] institutions report 100 percent pass rates for their program completers on these examinations, even though these data—while consistent with the requirements of the law—plainly say little about the relative performance or quality of the teacher preparation programs in that state."[84] This proved to be the case for five states (Alabama, Michigan, Montana, Oregon, and West Virginia) that posted 100percent pass rates in 2001.

*Waivers: Suspending Standards for Licensure*

Not only do states vary considerably in their standards (including tests and cut scores) required for entry into the profession, but efforts to enforce licensing standards also "vary radically from state to state."[85] The Consortium for Policy Research in Education (CPRE) reported in 1999 that, despite standards for initial teacher licensure, forty states allowed teachers without any training to be hired on temporary or emergency licenses, thus waiving the state standards. That is, while "some states do not allow districts to hire unqualified teachers," others, including Rep. Miller's home state of California, allowed the hiring of unqualified candidates. Similarly, in many states, schools and districts hire teachers certified in other subjects to teach other subjects for which they have not met state standards for licensure. This problem of out-of-field teaching is particularly acute in high-poverty schools, but it is common practice across the country. Nearly one in four middle and high school classes in core content areas is taught by a teacher who lacks even a minor in the subject being taught. That number reaches 35 percent for secondary mathematics classes, and jumps to 49 percent for such classes in high-poverty schools.[86]

Congress thus required that states report on the number and distribution of waivers across high- and low-poverty districts in the state. However, states had created many loopholes in the licensure process and many different terms (waivers, emergency certification and licenses, provisional licenses, long-term substitutes) to describe the approved hiring of unqualified teachers. Defining which data to report was nearly impossible; although the law required states to report the number of teachers lacking initial certification, collecting such data required clarity. For example, states like New York issue a provisional teaching license to candidates who have completed all program or coursework requirements and passed all necessary assessments; the unmet condition for full licensure is experience as a full-time classroom teacher. Several states, including Arizona, Connecticut, and New York, require a master's degree in addition to subject-matter training for a full professional license.[87] In still other states, provisional or probationary licenses are issued to those who have not yet met any of the requirements for initial licensure (e.g., college graduates with no teacher training who have not passed any required state assessments) to teach while working to meet the state's standards for teacher licensure.

The guidelines also asked states to distinguish between waivers granted to individuals who lacked both content and teaching knowledge, and those issued to content experts without pedagogical training. "Sufficient content knowledge" was used to indicate that a "teacher holds at least a bachelor's degree and demonstrates a high level of competency in all subject areas in which he or she teaches," as evidenced by having completed a college major or passing the state's assessment of subject-area knowledge in the area in which he teaches.[88] Such a distinction was especially important to highlight the value of hiring midcareer professionals with high levels of content expertise (such as retired engineers to teach math), rather than punish states for making the effort to fill vacancies with more than warm bodies. Likewise, the guidelines called on states to report the distribution of waivers across high- and low-poverty districts, data which, like waivers by subject area, were not readily available to most state education agencies.

## NCLB: Highly Qualified Teachers

Presidential candidates George W. Bush and Al Gore both campaigned on education issues in 2000, and both stressed the importance of good teachers and accountability, but they approached these in slightly different ways. In addition to plans for underperforming schools, Gore proposed a "Higher Standards/Higher Pay" initiative for pilot performance-based teacher pay projects; Bush proposed using student scores to inform state-developed differential pay systems. Both also proposed school report cards. Gore's proposal, like the Clinton administration's stalled proposal to reauthorize ESEA, included information on student achievement, attendance, and graduation rates, as well as class size, school safety, and teacher quality (similar to standards debated in the authorization of Goals 2000 and strongly supported by civil rights groups).[89] In contrast, the Bush campaign proposed report cards only for student achievement outcomes and school safety.[90]

However, when the bipartisan-supported No Child Left Behind Act (NCLB, P.L. 107-110) passed the Congress, it included reporting requirements and standards for qualified teachers much like those initially conceived by groups like The Education Trust, fought for by Rep. Miller, Senators Bingaman and Kennedy (in both HEA and ESEA debates), and signed into law in the 1998 HEA reauthorization. Whereas HEA Title II focused accountability efforts on institutions and states, NCLB endeavored to hold schools and districts accountable for their role in ensuring teacher quality. To the satisfaction of many civil rights and child advocacy groups and teachers unions, NCLB requires that all Title I schools hire only "highly qualified" teachers and ensure within four years that all beginning teachers are fully licensed, are assigned to teach in their field, and meet other criteria outlined in the law. (By 2006, all existing teachers are expected to meet the standards of the law, including teaching in the field for which they are licensed.)

NCLB's success depends on the terms *highly qualified* and *beginning teacher* to ensure that states with high numbers of unlicensed teachers won't be able to define themselves out of a teacher-quality problem (e.g., by calling teachers still en route to certification "qualified" or renaming emergency credentialed teachers "interns"). NCLB specified that a highly qualified teacher must have full state certification and/or pass the state's licensing examination,[91] suggesting that neither professional knowledge and skills nor completion of a teacher-preparation program were necessary. Here, as well as in the standards prescribed for the evaluation of existing teachers, the law relies heavily on state tests, assuming levels of rigor, alignment, and meaningful test content—a challenge, as described earlier, also inherent in the HEA reporting provisions.

NCLB attempts to address the out-of-field teaching problem, though the extent to which it closes state loopholes for hiring unlicensed teachers is still not clear. For example, California has attempted to redefine itself out of high waiver numbers by calling unqualified teachers "practicing teachers" or "teacher interns" as allowed under NCLB's definition of "beginning teacher."[92] Similarly, the new definition of "highly qualified teachers" can instantaneously transform unqualified teachers into qualified ones simply by disregarding elements of preparation that were previously required. Indeed, Secretary of Education Rod Paige's 2002 report proudly confirms that because "almost 50 percent of teachers on waivers . . . possess a major in their subject areas or have passed the state's content exams . . . Under a streamlined certification system [under NCLB] . . . these teachers would be considered highly qualified."[93]

## Changing the Yardstick: Federal Policy Looks for Alternatives to Schools of Education

The new law dramatically reinforced many other critics' lack of confidence in formal teacher-preparation programs and pleased many who were opposed to what they described as bureaucratic systems for teacher training and hiring. The Bush administration argues that the only "teacher attributes that relate directly to improved student achievement" are "high verbal ability and content knowledge."[94] As such, college coursework (measured in terms of baccalaureate majors and minors) and state assessments of content knowledge are considered particularly valuable indicators of teacher quality. Alternative routes to certification, namely Troops to Teachers and Teach For America, have become increasingly important to the Bush administration's discussions of teacher quality. For example, where the Clinton administration supported the National Board for Professional Teaching Standards (NBPTS) as a means of raising the standards for the profession by certifying master teachers (by assessing their content and pedagogical knowledge via portfolios, videotaped lessons, etc.), the Bush administration supports the emerging American Board for Certification of Teacher Excellence (ABCTE),[95] which is often criticized for offering college graduates a teaching license based on assessments of content knowledge with little attention to teaching skills.

### Impact of HEA Title II and NCLB Reporting Requirements

Limitations on available data make it impossible to measure accurately the success of the HEA legislation or predict the impact of NCLB. Consideration of a few key questions, however, may shed light on the early impact of these requirements. The questions include: Does the public have greater access to data on the quality of teacher preparation and the presence of qualified teachers? Are the data meaningful? Are institutions, districts, and states working to improve the quality of their teachers, and being held accountable for doing so?

The first step toward accountability is the collection and reporting of the required performance data. Both higher education institutions and states have significantly increased the dimensions along which they (not outside organizations) report information to the public. This was, however, an especially low benchmark for the IHEs to meet, given that almost none had regularly reported on the performance of the teachers they trained. As discussed earlier, quality had typically been reported and assessed in terms of program inputs. When outcomes were reported, most often in recruiting materials, these were typically limited to the number of teachers trained and hired. Whether or not program completers earned their licenses, the number of their attempts to pass the state assessments or their performances as teachers were rarely described.

Prior to HEA reauthorization, states had similarly reported more about what they required of their teachers (e.g., licensure requirements), typically only on state departmental websites, than on the qualifications of the existing teacher force. As such, standards for the profession were hardly part of the public consciousness. Table 1 below illustrates a sample of the categories for which increasing numbers of states are now reporting data. It is important to note, however, that this table does not address whether the data, of which there are more, are any more accurate or encouraging.[96]

Many states are publicly reporting legally accurate but not necessarily meaningful data. Other states, lacking either the resources or the will to collect, synthesize, and report data in compliance with the federal definitions, are reporting data that is both inaccurate and meaningless. As The Education Trust reports, even in cases where the law is clear, several states simply ignored the definitions of key terms like *waiver* or used their own definitions of *program completer.* In 2002, Georgia, South Dakota, Utah, West Virginia, Washington, D.C., and Ohio excluded long-term substitutes from their waiver counts.[104] Likewise, while Nevada issues provisional, nonrenewable licenses to individuals who have not completed their teacher-education

**TABLE 1   needs a title**

| Reported Data | Number of States Reporting Key Data on Teacher Quality | | |
|---|---|---|---|
| | 1998–1999[97] | 1999–2000[98] | 2000–2001[99] |
| Required major or minor in content area | | | 37** |
| Statewide testing for teacher licensure | 41[100] | N/A | 43 |
| Use of assessment of professional knowledge for licensure | 16 | 18 | |
| Use of assessment of content knowledge (math) for licensure** | 12 | 20 | 32[101] |
| Number of waivers*** | 43* | N/A | 48 |
| Number of waivers by SES, high-poverty schools | 34 | N/A | 45[102] |
| Number of waivers by subject area, math | 19 | N/A | 43[103] |
| Number of waivers by subject area, science | 19 | N/A | 43 |
| Number of "highly qualified" teachers (per NCLB) | 39 (Only reported in September 2003) | | |

*Washington, D.C., Iowa, and Ohio reported no teachers on waiver, and thus did not report waivers by subject.

\** Plus Puerto Rico; six states and Guam did not report

\*** In many cases, districts (not states) issue waivers and maintain information about these. As a result, some states do not have complete or accurate information.

program, it reported no waivers. Similarly, while states recently reported data on "highly qualified" teachers, many states provided information inconsistent with the federal definitions. For example, Utah counted veteran teachers as "highly qualified" even when they had not demonstrated content mastery (e.g., a major, minor, or license in the content area in which they teach) as required by law.[105] The vague definitions in NCLB, which seem to be both more rigorous and more flexible (in promoting "streamlined" processes that may cut mainstream programs out of the teacher-preparation process), need considerable clarification. Assuming that states will report the same data on qualified teachers for both HEA and ESEA, the quality of HEA data will likely depend heavily on both the guidelines for ESEA and the extent to which states are truly held accountable for the accuracy of their reports.

Beyond the gaming efforts by some states and institutions, the meaningfulness of the data depends on the standards for licensure in the states. Fewer than half of the states have teacher tests aligned to student standards. Most state licensure test content is benchmarked at high school levels.[106] Even then, most states set passing scores far below national averages; the majority set cut scores below the 50th percentile, and several set scores below the 25th percentile.[107] Pass rates on assessments of such little rigor tell us little about the quality of classroom teachers.

## Accountability and Improvement

Efforts to assess the extent to which IHEs are improving in response to the reporting mandates are hampered by insufficient data to assess institutional progress, and pass rates are limited proxies for program quality, especially when more than 90 percent of teacher candidates pass the necessary assessments for initial teacher licensure. However, intermediate indicators, largely anecdotal reports and assessments from the various program-accrediting organizations, suggest that some changes are occurring across teacher-education programs. Schools of education report new collaborations with the arts and sciences schools on their campuses and describe the Title II reporting requirements as a useful tool in leveraging institutional supports for improvements to the academic programs that provide their teacher candidates with their pedagogical and content training.[108] Schools and districts are not yet widely reporting noticeable changes in the skills or expertise in the pool of teachers now emerging from teacher-education programs. In fact, the only available evidence on program improvements shows a possible trend toward raising standards for program entry (e.g., required assessments, higher GPAs), rather than changes in the programs themselves.[109] Innovative programs implemented in large urban districts in New York City, Chicago, and Los Angeles for alternative certification and/or streamlined hiring processes do not yet represent widespread efforts and have not dramatically reduced the number of unqualified teachers, particularly in high-minority schools. (Certainly, some of these districts have seen dramatic differences in the rates of unqualified new hires.[110]) Although NCLB sets benchmarks for having a qualified teacher in every classroom, the Bush administration has yet to propose a plan for helping states reach them, outside of minor funding for alternative certification programs.

However, even if IHEs are successful in raising pass rates and states and districts decrease the number of unqualified teachers in their classrooms, progress in improving teacher quality might still be limited. That is, as NCES reports, only about one-third of teachers feel well prepared to implement curriculum and performance standards, and fewer than half feel very well prepared to implement new teaching methods. And despite the growing numbers of English-language learners in our schools, only about 20 percent

**TABLE 2   A Sample of Estimated Federal Spending on Programs in Support of Teacher Training**

| K–12 Program Supporting Teacher Quality | 2002 | 2003 | 2004 (Presidential Request) |
|---|---|---|---|
| TITLE I  (Under Title I, Part A districts must spend at least 5% of funds for teacher development, schools identified for improvement must spend at least 10%) | $10.35 billion | $11.68 billion | $12.35 billion |
| Eisenhower Professional Development Program  (pre-NCLB)/ Improving Teacher-Quality State Grants (ESEA, Title II, Part A) | $2.85 billion | $2.93 billion | $2.85 billion |
| Math and Science Partnership Program (ESEA, Title II, Part B) | $12.5 million (+$160 million through NSF) | $100.34 million | $12.5 million |
| Technology Literacy Challenge Fund (pre-NCLB)/Ed Tech State Grants (ESEA, Title II, part D) | $700.5 million | $695.9 million | $700.5 million |
| Goals 2000 State Grants | 0 | 0 | 0 |
| Preparing Tomorrow's Teachers to Use Technology (HEA) | $62.5 million | $62.09 million | 0 |
| Troops to Teachers (ESEA, Title II, Part C, Subpart 1) | $18 million | $28.81 million | $25 million |
| Transition to Teaching (ESEA, Title II, Part C, Subpart 1) | $35 million | $41.72 million | $49.4 million |

of teachers feel well prepared to meet their instructional needs or those of students with disabilities.[111] Many individuals are completing teacher-preparation programs, passing the required tests, earning licenses, and teaching in our schools, but still have considerable difficulty helping students meet high academic standards. Significant changes are still required.

### Interventions and Accountability

As described earlier, most states routinely approve nearly all their teacher-education programs, often with little review. HEA requires states to describe their processes and criteria for evaluating teacher-preparation programs and identifying low-performing institutions in the state, but states vary considerably in how they do this. In fact, many states failed to address questions

# Inclusive Ambiguity: Multicultural Conflict in an Era of Accountability

## FREDERICK M. HESS

*The expansion of high-stakes accountability in the past decades has created an unavoidable tension with contemporary efforts to promote multicultural curricula. Accountability requires that states establish common standards, a difficult task when there is disagreement about what content students should learn. Policy makers can adopt an "augmentative" strategy and add material to standards. This approach is less effective, however, in high-stakes systems where standards are expected to provide concrete guidance. At such times, negotiations become more nearly "zero sum"—something has to come out of the standards for each new item that goes in. Given the nature of the American system, conflicts are more often resolved by devising ambiguous and aspirational standards. Conflict is more common in the humanities and social sciences than in mathematics or science because the "soft" subjects are less able to appeal to a neutral authority and because additional content can be grafted onto them more readily.*

**Keywords:** *accountability; multicultural; politics; religion; social studies*

IN A PLURALIST NATION, debates about public norms inevitably tread fine lines of cultural and ideological disagreement. This is particularly true in American education, where the faith in schooling as a homogenizing influence has conflicted with a commitment to the right of families to maintain

AUTHOR'S NOTE: The author would like to thank Andrew Kelly and Brett Friedman for their invaluable assistance.

EDUCATIONAL POLICY, Vol. 18 No. 1, January and March 2004 95-115
DOI: 10.1177/0895904803260026
© 2004 Corwin Press

their cultural heritage. In this essay, I seek not to advance either normative claim but to understand how these tensions play out in efforts to address calls for multicultural curricular reform in an era of high-stakes accountability.

In education, this clash is familiar in the realm of choice-based reform (Macedo, 2000; Reich, 2002). Critics of school vouchers, in particular, have feared social fragmentation or that religious or ethnic groups will cluster in closed communities. Proponents have responded that a liberal state should not prohibit families from choosing a desired cultural milieu for their children.

Less frequently noted, but more substantively significant, has been the conflict between the majority and self-defined communities over curricular standards and school accountability (Hess, 2002, 2003). Although choice-based reforms currently enroll less than 2% of K-12 students, accountability systems and curricular standards affect all of America's public school students. Conflict over accountability addresses the question of what education the state will mandate for all students—whereas choice addresses the question of what kinds of exit options exist for some students.

The terms *standards* and *accountability* are often used interchangeably. That is a mistake. Although accountability systems are essentially intended to measure the degree to which standards are met, standards by themselves are simply a toothless aspiration. Educational standards alone are merely symbolic statements. Standards-based accountability, however, is a determination regarding what all children will be required to learn and how the performance of schools and educators will be assessed. The adoption of high-stakes accountability systems, with the implication that poorly performing students and educators will suffer tangible consequences, gives a new sense of urgency and import to conflicts about what standards should and should not include.

The allure of standards-based accountability is straightforward. It represents a public commitment that schools ought to ensure that all children be taught a discrete body of knowledge and skills to a specified level of mastery (Ravitch, 1995). This change comes at a price. High-stakes accountability systems require officials to make politically sensitive sets of decisions. They must designate a prescribed body of content and objectives to be tested, necessarily excluding and thus marginalizing some goals, objectives, and content. They must also impose assessments that gauge whether students have mastered the requisite skills and material. Both decisions tend to produce passionate opposition among those who feel that their interests, values, beliefs, or culture are being shortchanged (Kohn, 2000; McNeil, 2000; Meier, 2000; Ohanian, 1999).

The expansion of high-stakes accountability in the late 1990s and early 2000s has created an unavoidable tension with contemporary efforts to promote multiculturalism curricula and pedagogy. Since the 1980s, increasingly prominent efforts to promote multicultural education have emphasized the need to include schooling personages, content, and material that reflect a diverse array of cultures in K-12. In determining standards that students will be required to master, accountability requires agreement on a coherent set of learning objectives. Such an impulse runs counter to the multicultural imperative to broaden the curriculum. The tension has frequently resulted in clashes that have resulted in efforts to create all-embracing standards, ultimately yielding vague guidelines that are somewhat ambiguous as to just what students are expected to master.

The push for high-stakes accountability provokes conflict between the majority and those whose particular concerns are marginalized when school curricula are rendered more explicit. Teachers and instructional materials emphasize the content for which students are held responsible (Pedulla et al., 2003). If social studies test questions are based on 20th-century social movements rather than on the founding fathers, instruction will reflect that. Given sharp disagreement over the merits of various curricular and pedagogical approaches, efforts to impose statewide agreement inevitably offend some constituencies. Typically, the aggrieved protest while the broader public evinces limited interest.

The American political system is notoriously bad at pursuing collective goods, such as accountability, when it requires imposing concentrated costs on passionate, coherent constituencies. American government is highly permeable, making it relatively easy for passionate factions to block or soften adverse legislative or bureaucratic decisions (Chubb & Moe, 1990). Aggrieved groups can seek to block these programs by delaying the implementation of accountability programs—a tack that opponents have employed with a fair degree of success. If they cannot or do not wish to delay implementation of accountability, the aggrieved can seek to win the inclusion of their preferred material or can dilute the standards to the point that they are ambiguous enough that they no longer offend.

In practice, there is a balancing flywheel that governs efforts to make standards more inclusive along the dimensions of race, ethnicity, gender, and religion. The majoritarian perspective generally enjoys only vague, disinterested support, whereas the aggrieved interests are mobilized for particular concessions. When standards are drafted to reflect majoritarian beliefs, they often get watered down through a process of inclusion. On the other hand, when drafted "collaboratively," agreed-on standards are either so vague as to be both inoffensive and insignificant or counter-majoritarian enough to provoke traditionalists to the point that they demand revisions. Regardless, there is a tendency for the standards to successively teeter toward vague, watery compromises. For example, middle school students in New York are now expected to "know the social and economic characteristics, such as customs, traditions, child rearing practices, ways of making a living, education and socialization practices, gender roles, foods, and religious and spiritual beliefs that distinguish different cultures and civilizations" (New York State Education Department, 1996). Broad, airy guidelines like these offer little concrete direction as to what content teachers are expected to teach or students are expected to learn.

Efforts to develop common standards in any contested area tend to produce crowd-pleasing compromises that can be interpreted in many ways. The result is that the standards read impressively but are largely hollow and aspirational. Rather than being "standards-based," teaching winds up with little concrete guidance from the formal standards and teachers wind up taking more guidance from previous test questions or from personal instinct, just like before there were standards.

Another way to understand this dynamic is to recognize that policy makers have two available strategies for defusing opposition to standards. One approach is to add material to standards in response to particular complaints from critics. This "augmentative" strategy works reasonably well in an era of standards when there is no practical constraint on the amount of material that standards can include, but is much less effective under high-stakes accountability when standards are expected to provide concrete guidance. Under high-stakes accountability, where students are expected to master specifically enumerated material, the negotiations become more nearly "zero sum"—something has to come out of the standards for each new item that goes in. Given the political delicacy of these decisions, conflicts are more often resolved by compromising broad, ambiguous, and aspirational standards. These satisfy all parties by insisting on including relatively little concrete material, meaning that all parties can read the final standards as receptive to their concerns. Such compromises bear hidden costs in that they undermine the whole point of accountability testing. The lack of explicit direction grants undue influence to test makers, places students at the whims of their teacher's judgment, and leaves uncertain just what material students are expected to master.

## LITERATURE REVIEW

Little scholarship has addressed the tension between accountability and multiculturalism, and no systematic work has been pursued in this area. Much of the debate about multiculturalism in education, however, has been focused on the relative merits of seeking to modify standards or state curricula in accord with the precepts of multiculturalism. Stern (2001) noted the "curious dance" (p. 154) in which opponents and proponents of multiculturalism engage but said little about the effect of these polarizing forces on how standards are crafted. Ravitch (2003) examined the impact that multicultural interest groups have on American textbooks but did not detail their effect on accountability systems. The concept of *multiculturalism* itself, which has prompted much discussion in the past decade, is a relatively new addition to the vernacular. A Nexis search reveals that the term did not surface in the press until 1989, though the phrase has today become so politicized that it is hard to define it in a manner deemed unbiased and authoritative (Glazer, 1997).

American multiculturalism took root in the late 20th century when pluralism came to be explicitly championed as a "good and enriching" aspect of our way of life (Nicgorski, 1992, p. 15). Multiculturalists argued that the United States has been shaped by multiple ethnic, racial, and religious traditions and that the content taught in the nation's public schools has not reflected this pluralistic reality.

In education, there is widespread agreement that multiculturalism has triumphed over its critics and "has become something of a nationally institutionalized 'given' in new millennium school curricula" (Binder, 2002, p. 23). Glazer (1997) conceded the victory in his aptly titled *We Are All Multiculturalists Now* and observed,

Multiculturalism in education—so strongly denounced by so many powerful voices in American life . . . the occasion for so many battles in American education during the nineties, and so much at odds with the course of American culture, society, and education at least up until the 1960s—has, in a word, won. (p. 4)

Nonetheless, debate continues over the appropriate scope, balance, and meaning of multiculturalism in curricular standards.

The multicultural debates of the past decade, with their divisive rhetoric and emotionally charged arguments, have often hinted at James Hunter's (1990) foreboding and oft-cited *Culture Wars*. In fact, as with so many political debates, the multiculturalism dialogue is dominated by small, determined, and vocal minorities. Most Americans are of two minds, torn between respecting cultural differences and a commitment to a shared culture in the face of ethnic and racial particularism. Much of the popular writing on multicultural education embodies this ambivalence. As Ravitch (1990) has written,

Pluralism is a positive value, but it is also important that we preserve a sense of an American community—a society and a culture to which we all belong. If there is no overall community with an agreed-upon vision of liberty and justice, if all we have is a collection of racial and ethnic cultures, lacking any common bonds, . . . then each group will want to teach its own children in its own way, and public education ceases to exist. (p. 353)

Today, hardly any prominent educators or academics explicitly oppose the principle of diversity in the curriculum. Even general critics of multiculturalism such as E. D. Hirsch have taken pains to incorporate the accomplishments of minorities and women into recommended curricula. The debate is really about the appropriate extent of such efforts, with "cultural pluralists" such as Hirsch, Glazer, and Arthur Schlesinger arguing that diversity should have the ultimate purpose of encouraging participation by all groups in a "common American culture" (Schlesinger, 1998, p. 95).

In this belief, they are at odds with the proponents of "explicit multiculturalism," or particularism, who urge that we "celebrate" differences among cultures and extol the preservation of separate cultural identities. Proponents see particularism as essential to fostering participative democracy. Kenneth Howe (1997) has asserted that it is the responsibility of the public schools to eliminate all forms of oppression through the "virtue of recognition" embodied in a multicultural curriculum. It is not enough to promote tolerance and refrain from active repression of minorities, Howe argued that formalized measures mandating multiculturalism are needed to create a "just society" and "foster genuine democratic negotiation" (p. 70). Anne Norton (1998) has argued that multiculturalism "diminishes democratic vices" such as "primitive majoritarianism" whereas its enfranchisement of different groups is consistent with Madison's faith that a multiplicity of discrete groups deflate the "tyrannical potential of the majority" (p. 135). In an early defense of multiculturalism, Alan Singer (1993) praised the positive effects of multiculturalism and Afrocentrism for helping schools produce citizens committed to shared democratic values.

Critics dispute the benefits of particularism. Wilson Carey McWilliams (1998) has distinguished between cultural pluralism as an exercise "in the service of a generous, democratic end" and the particularistic approach as threatening the very fabric of majoritarian democracy by enshrining "a rival principle" that gives each distinct group a right to veto communal action (pp. 123, 126). James Ceaser (1998) has argued that the multicultural movement has dangerously placed much more emphasis on the culture at the expense of the individual, has made culture a matter of "government determination," and has often degenerated into culturalism based on biology and race (p. 155).

FREDERICK M. HESS 101

## THE POLITICAL FAULT LINES

Whatever the merits of the disputants in the larger debate, multicultural-ism has played a significant role in shaping the standards underlying account-ability, though not always in the intended fashion. The challenges have taken place along identifiable fault lines, the most prominent of these being race. Efforts to compensate for a history of slavery, Jim Crow, and the suppression of Black culture have led reformers to infuse public school history and litera-ture curricula with Black figures, writers, and perspectives. The more radical voices "claim that schools victimize students of color by not presenting accu-rate images of their ancestors" and that a curriculum of inclusion can help remedy the ravages of racism (Webster, 1997, p. 44).

A second fault line is ethnicity and national origin, as Latinos, Asians, and Native Americans, among others, have demanded that their heritage be woven into the fabric of required content. A third fault line centers on gender equity. Feminists call for greater inclusion of women in the literary canon and historical curricula, and this call has been echoed by advocates for gay and lesbian inclusion. A final area of contention is religion. Although religion has been largely removed from public education under the auspices of the First Amendment's "establishment" clause, religiously motivated debates about state standards have been among the most bitter.

These fault lines encompass some of the most politically sensitive terri-tory in modern American political discourse: religious belief, racism, sexual-ity, discrimination, and assimilation. The multicultural challengers of the early 1990s sought to add minority works and perspectives to the existing curriculum, an approach that public officials could pursue through a strategy of augmentation—simply adding some additional authors, books, content, or historic figures to existing standards. The advisory nature of standards allowed this dilution to be accomplished at little cost, because it neither required that officials remove any existing material nor necessitated any change in testing or teaching.

The ascendance of high-stakes accountability regimes have changed those rules and forced officials to wrestle with more of a zero-sum situation. The reliance on tests of discrete content, and the need to develop more focused curricula to accompany the tests, bolsters pressure to subtract some old content as new content is added and increases political tensions.

The fights over multicultural standards are bounded by three major sets of constraints: the nature of academic disciplines, constitutional stipulations, and the community's dominant sympathies.

## NATURE OF THE DISCIPLINES

The nature of the academic disciplines themselves shapes the multicultural tensions that emerge. Two dimensions are especially significant: the degree to which traditionalists can appeal to a neutral authority in resisting multicultural proposals and the ease with which curricular content can be modified or differences can be split.

Curricular fights are more common in the humanities and social sciences than in mathematics or science. Why have multiculturalists enjoyed greater success in the "soft" subjects? Literature and history are deemed negotiable because they lack the disembodied logic on which math and science ultimately rest. Fundamental mathematical laws and scientific facts are immutable; the area of a rectangle is always equal to its base times its height and the force of gravity always causes earthbound objects to fall at 9.8 meters per second squared. In 2002, reflecting a pattern that has been evident since at least the 1970s, more than 90% of Americans expressed a fair degree of trust in the scientific community—ranking scientists near the top of all professions (Davis & Smith, 2002). For instance, the perceived authority of science has undercut creationists' demand to include creationism in the science curriculum (Binder, 2002).

On the other hand, similarly absolute historical and literary truths are rare. Unlike the chemist or the mathematician, the historian or social studies instructor has a limited ability to appeal to neutral authority or abstract rules to justify particular assertions. The humanities instructor has almost no such ability. The merits of literature, the import of a renowned person, the lessons to be learned from a period of history—all of these are ultimately contested and uncertain.

Setting content standards in subjects such as math and the physical sciences is largely straightforward. Speaking generally, there is broad agreement on what students need to know and when they need to know it. For that reason, most conflict in subjects such as math, the physical sciences, and reading revolves more around how to teach than about what material is to be taught. The truth of the matter is that the famed math and reading "wars" are typically about pedagogy (i.e., whole language vs. phonics or "new math" vs. computation-based instruction) rather than content. The waters become murkier when it comes to social studies, literature, and history. Should the history curriculum give equal attention to the indigenous civilizations of pre-Columbian America and ancient Greece and Rome? Should children know more about Darwin in the Galapagos or the Book of Genesis? When standards are a question of which stories should be told and which should be left out, decisions become inherently political.

Math and the sciences do not readily lend themselves to such disputes because they are the mechanisms by which people convey abstract, externally defined, and largely apolitical concepts. They are based on verifiable laws and theories that are largely independent of social constructions. As a result, attempts to infuse these subjects with a multicultural perspective have typically embodied one of two strategies; reformers either pad around the edges by including historic anecdotes about minorities or more drastically, revise widely accepted scientific or mathematical truths to embody a multicultural perspective. The first of these strategies, which focuses on expanding the disciplinary boundaries toward the more readily contested realm of social studies and culture, tends to produce the successes that multicultural proponents do enjoy in the areas of math and the sciences. Although multiculturalists have succeeded in adding more sidebars about ancient Egyptian mathematicians or Latino physicists in textbooks, they have enjoyed little success at fundamentally reshaping curricula or content. Efforts to infuse math and science with more "diversity" have typically ended in failure and not infrequently, ridicule.

Take, for example, the Baseline Essays in Afrocentric Education developed in Portland, Oregon, in the early 1990s, which famously attempted to drive multiculturalism throughout the entire curriculum. Although the sections on art, language arts, and music "treat[ed] their African American sections accurately," (Martel, 1994) the science and math materials were filled with shocking examples of pseudoscience. They sought to trace all major discoveries in math, science, and technology back to Africa and promulgate scientifically dubious, non-Western theories such as "psi psychoenergetics," "precognition," and "psychokinesis." Children were to be taught that the ancient Egyptians built full-size gliders in 2000 B.C. and used these aircraft for travel and exploration (Martel, 1994). Irving Klotz (1993), a professor emeritus of chemistry at Northwestern University, was prompted to fume in *Phi Delta Kappan* that the materials had left him staggering "in incredulity" and that such "nonsense" would inculcate "an uncritical, superficial attitude toward science" in students (p. 266).

In some subjects, it is relatively simple to compromise or split differences without sacrificing the validity of the subject matter, whereas in others it is not. For instance, if women or Native Americans are not adequately represented in the history standards, state officials can add appropriate figures without having to fundamentally alter curriculum or assessments. Under standards-based accountability, splitting the difference no longer implies simply adding more content about different groups, a model that predominated in the mid-1990s. Today, additions generally imply subtractions from other content areas; in such an environment, states have been forced to find middle ground between ideologically polarized groups by either removing important content or settling for bland compromises.

Often, the infusion of additional materials or perspectives makes for obviously better history or humanities instruction. One cannot, for instance, fully consider the industrialization of America without referencing the experience of the European immigrants or the Black migration to the northern urban centers. The challenge is that historical and literary "truths" are both negotiable and inherently political. When politics enter the equation, standards revision is no longer a search for "better history" but an attempt to satisfy competing constituencies.

## CONSTITUTIONAL REGIME

At times, especially in the case of religion, multicultural conflict is framed by the constitutional regime. Clear demarcations as to what is and is not permissible can place some claimants in an untenable position by forcing them to challenge constitutional doctrine and by putting the points of contention beyond the control of compromise-minded legislators, public officials, or curriculum designers. The First Amendment's establishment clause has been interpreted to strictly regulate the role for religiosity in the public domain. In general, groups challenging curricula in response to religious concerns have found little success. The establishment clause was long read by the courts as erecting "a wall" between church and state, generally preventing religious concerns from playing a role in shaping curricula except in the most cursory sense (Levinson, 2001). Consequently, it is not surprising that religious curricular challenges have often failed to get off the ground.

In 1987, in *Edwards v. Aguillard*, the Supreme Court declared that it was unconstitutional even for states to require equal treatment of evolution and creationism. Even when creationist movements began to shift their emphasis from the spiritual aspect of creationism to the science of creationism, groups such as the American Civil Liberties Union, with the backing of the scientific community, threatened to bring civil rights suits against states or districts that mandated the teaching of creationism (Binder, 2002). No matter how much popular support they could garner, creationists faced a nearly insuperable opponent in the establishment clause and the barriers the courts imposed.

The more successful religious efforts to influence curricula, whether they be efforts to qualify the teaching of evolution or to increase attention to Islam, have shied away from religious rhetoric and appealed instead in the name of multicultural ideals such as "inclusion" and "multiple perspectives." After repeated defeats on religious grounds, some creationists have moved from "moralism to pluralism" in adopting an approach that invokes the principle of "equal time" in order to get creation science included alongside evolution in biology curricula (Zimmerman, 2002, p. 132). This new tactic avoids the establishment clause by renouncing any claims of theism, calling instead for diverse explanations of human origins as a matter of cultural fairness and respect (Nelson, 2002). Proponents of "intelligent design" (the notion that an unspecified intelligence" consciously designed the universe) have been surprisingly effective in recent years, in 1999 a group forced Kansas to drop evolution from its science standards for a time, and in 2002, Ohio adopted a compromise amendment that allowed teachers to discuss criticism of Darwin's theory (Warsmith, 2002). This approach has permitted intelligent-design proponents to make their case on constitutionally feasible ground.

## DOMINANT NORMS AND VALUES

As noted, disciplinary and constitutional issues bound multicultural conflicts over curricula. Most battles occur in social studies, history, and the humanities on issues that do not run afoul of constitutional doctrine. This is the contested terrain in the multicultural-inspired conflicts under accountability.

Within these parameters, groups considered legitimate or mainstream by the majority are far more effective than are more marginal or controversial groups. Ceasar (1998) explained that although the political debates that surround multiculturalism are complex, the movement's proponents have been able to simplify the schematic to a battle between the "hegemon and the other" (p. 141). In this system, opposition to the "other" implies a tacit acceptance of oppression. This rhetorical environment makes simple hostility to multiculturalism an untenable position and encourages members of the majority to seek compromise with sympathetic out groups—even as they resist the demands of more marginal groups.

Take, for example, the recent controversy that surrounded the National Education Association's attempt to ratify a statement on gay and lesbian–friendly curriculum. In 2001, the National Education Association tabled a resolution encouraging teachers and schools to include curricular materials dealing with the struggles of gay, lesbian, bisexual, and transgender people after conservative state lawmakers and Christian groups launched an outraged letter-writing campaign to local union representatives (Associated Press, 2001). At the other end of the political spectrum, the Sons of Confederate Veterans Virginia Regiment and the Heritage Preservation Society were unsuccessful in their 2001 attempt to convince state officials to include more about Virginia's role in the Confederate war in the state history standards (Wermers, 2001d). These failures contrast with the evident success of less controversial groups that can appeal to the mainstream values of inclusion and pluralism. The Latino community in Texas, for example, has reportedly been effective in convincing authorities to include Latino authors, artists, and historical figures in many district curricula (Caballero & De Leon, 2002).

## TEETERING TOWARD AMBIGUITY

In social studies, history, and literature, multicultural proponents typically advocate increasing attention to minority and female personages and accomplishment; emphasizing more pre-Columbian, African, Asian, Latin American, and social history; and reading more literary works authored by minorities, non-Americans, and women. Traditionalists respond by challenging such revisions for devaluing American history and the Western tradition, diluting curricula, and mounting thinly disguised attacks on the United States and its culture. Seeking to please sympathetic and active minorities without alienating traditionalists or provoking backlash, public officials pursue compromise, ultimately winding up with standards that are acceptable to all parties due to their elasticity. The progression from angry minority demands for inclusion to majoritarian backlash to hollow political compromise has played out repeatedly in recent years. Perhaps the classic example was the 1994 effort by the National Center for History in the Schools to craft national history standards.

In 1992, in conjunction with the National Endowment for the Humanities and the Office of Educational Research and Innovation of the Department of Education, the National Center for History in the Schools created the National Council for History Standards to oversee the process. Appointed with input from prominent traditionalists such as Lynne Cheney and Diane Ravitch, the Council's membership was hailed for including an ideologically balanced mix of history scholars, educators, and advocates (Gitlin, 1995). The real work of fashioning the standards, however, fell to the various historical and educational organizations, professional historians, and veteran teachers that the Council consulted. These groups included the American Historical Association, the National Alliance for Black Education, the National Association for Asian and Pacific American Education, and the League of United Latin American Citizens (National Center for History in the Schools, 1994). The standards produced by these groups, released in three volumes at the end of 1994, emphasized the history of preliterate African and Mexican societies and asserted that children should be able to discuss gender roles in the early agricultural communities of the Fertile Crescent (Glazer, 1997). At the same time, the new standards did not include historical figures such as Paul Revere, Thomas Edison, or the Wright Brothers, instead focusing on

America's warts. McCarthyism was mentioned 19 times and the Great Depression 25 times, and the Ku Klux Klan was featured prominently (Cheney, 1995). Shortly after the standards were released, the Senate rejected them on a 99 to 1 vote, sending them back for revision.

The revision of the standards, largely based on the "valuable recommendations" of the conservative Council for Basic Education, was undertaken by a new group of scholars who were less friendly to the tenets of multiculturalism (Nash, 1997). Stephen Thernstrom, David Hollinger, and Maris Vinovskis joined Ravitch and others on the new panel. The new guidelines simply did away with the teaching examples, the section that had drawn the most ire from conservatives. When released, however, the revised standards were still criticized by conservatives for "[attacking] our heritage" (Cheney, 1996) and "[getting] it wrong again" (Diggins, 1996). The standards were criticized not only for ideological bias but also for being unrealistically ambitious and nebulous. Students were asked to compare the "tribal rituals and food gathering" of 15th century Native American and West African societies, though even African and Native American history experts have limited concrete knowledge of how such societies operated (Diggins, 1996).

The revised standards were also attacked by multiculturalists who felt that the revisions went too far in the opposite direction. Joyce Appleby, a professor of history at the University of California, Los Angeles and future president of the American Historical Association, asserted, "I was very pleased with the original one. Lynne Cheney is not a professional historian. You couldn't name more than five historians who would criticize [the original standards]" (Thomas, 1996). Particularly troubling to some multiculturalists was the fact that the revisions had reduced the prevalence of female historical figures and had "defeminized" the guidelines. For instance, the initial guidelines mentioned Harriet Tubman six times and asked children to discuss gender roles in almost every civilization and society that the standards dealt with, elements that were missing in the second draft. An article in *The History Teacher* complained that it was "disturbing that women as a part of history were singled out for such an extensive revision" (Keller, 1997, p. 336).

Despite the political criticism by both sides, the directors of the national standards project were satisfied. As Gary Nash (1997), codirector of the standards project, asserted, "I am satisfied that the standards reflect this genera tion's scholarship in a form and at a level appropriate to precollegiate education" (p. 600). Former critics also accepted the revisions: Ravitch and Schlesinger praised the new standards, as did George Will, who found them "purged of partisanship" (Keller, 1997, p. 320). In reaching this happy agreement, however, the Council had largely denuded the standards of meaning, settling instead for watery banalities.

Two independent panels that were commissioned by the Council for Basic Education to appraise the revised standards asserted that the lack of specifics had succeeded in "[eliminating] many of the problems related to the absence or presence of individual names, since the standards themselves name relatively few historical figures" (Thomas, 1996). The panels went on to note that

the teaching of history within the general frame proposed by the standards will necessarily include examples of individuals with varying degrees of influence on the events of their own time. . . . But it is not the job of the standards to provide a list. (Thomas, 1996)

Thus, the panels placed their stamp of approval on hundreds of vacuous standards, largely devoid of specific historical terms, figures, or places.

The final product's dominant theme was ambiguity: "The postwar extension of the New Deal" became the catchall "domestic policies after World War II"; the charge that students "demonstrate understanding of Nixon's domestic agenda and the Watergate affair" became the suggestion that "the student understands domestic politics from Nixon to Carter"; and the mandate for "examining the 'red scare' and Palmer raids as a reaction to Bolshevism" became the vague "assess the state and federal government reactions to the growth of radical political movements" (Keller, 1997, pp. 312-317).

No one much cared that the standards were nebulous: minority constituencies and traditionalists could read their preferences into these broad guidelines, the general public was little interested in this arcane dispute, and nothing of consequence would be done with the standards. It did not matter if children learned the material listed in the standards or not, as they would not be tested or evaluated on their mastery. The standards themselves were intended to be nothing more than suggested guidelines for the states. As one close observer bluntly observed, "Since the standards are guidelines, those who find the changes offensive can re-edit the revised standards or insert the original versions" (Keller, 1997, p. 336). Under voluntary standards, educators can take away what they like and discard the rest. It would be left up to the teacher to define which individuals were important enough to be included in his or her lesson plans. Even in this case of relatively low stakes, concise and meaningful standards proved elusive.

The easy compromises available to those composing guidelines start to impose more significant costs after the introduction of meaningful accountability. In such a world, the delegation of responsibility for curriculum to the classroom teacher is no longer inconsequential. Standards-based accountability transforms curricular standards from voluntary suggestions to high-stakes mandates. Because students will now be asked to master specific material, ambiguous standards mean that teachers and students are responsible for a somewhat ill-defined body of content, undermining the very purpose of standards and the value and legitimacy of accountability.

As the stakes rise, and the costs of ambiguity increase, the unfortunate fact is that the pressure to resolve clashes by resorting to studied ambiguity grows more intense. Consider the fight over the high-stakes Virginia history standards that took place in 2001. In November 2000, the board of education revised the state's history and social science standards. Both conservatives and liberals criticized the revisions for eliminating specifics. The liberal grassroots group Parents Across Virginia United to Reform SOLs asserted that the standards were characterized by "the elimination of as many controversial or unpleasant things as possible" (Wermers, 2001a). John Fonte, head of the conservative Hudon Institute's Center for American Common Culture, attacked the elimination of specific historic figures and events; David Warren Saxe, a professor of education at Pennsylvania State noted that of the 95 historical figures previously listed, 59 had been cut or moved from their original placements in the new standards and 14 had been added, reducing the total count to 54 (Wermers, 2001a). In all, 62% of the figures listed in the 1995 standards had been eliminated. Prominent cuts in the early grades included traditional Civil War figures such as Stonewall Jackson and Robert E. Lee. The previous standards asked that students discuss "the economic and philosophical differences between North and South, as exemplified by such men as Daniel Webster and John C. Calhoun," whereas the revised standards stripped the names from the question (Wermers, 2001c, p. B5).

In response to these criticisms, the committee making the revisions offered to remove all names from the standards and list them instead in the teaching guide. Fonte observed in response, "The vaguer you get, the more problems you have" (Wermers, 2001c). Stuck between irate traditionalists and reformers, the official line, voiced by state Senator Benjamin Lambert III, was that the standards should not force students to "go over every fine detail" and that teachers were free to supplement the guidelines if they wished to go more in-depth (Wermers, 2001d).

Consider the challenge from determined Armenian Americans who demanded that the Armenian Genocide of 1915 to 1923 be included in the new standards. Twenty-six Armenians asked the state board of education to recognize the 1.5 million Christian Armenians that were killed under the Ottoman Empire between 1915 and 1923 in the new version of the standards. Despite their small numbers, the Armenians enjoyed some initial success due to their disciplined lobbying. The board of education agreed to include the "mass deportations and massacres of the Armenians" in the World War I standard, though the board stopped short of labeling the event a *genocide* (Wermers, 2001b). Shortly, though, the board of education came under fire from the more established Turkish community and finally decided to strike any specific reference to ethnic violence in the Ottoman Empire during or after World War I. The revised standard now asked students to explain "the genocide of Armenians and deportations and massacres of Turks, Kurds, and other ethnic groups" (Wermers, 2001e, p. A1). Armenians were furious at the compromise, arguing that there had been no massacres of Turks and that they objected to "including a lie" about Turkish suffering (Wermers, 2001e). The board of education nonetheless settled on this vague and inclusive, if inaccurate, compromise.

Take the case of New Jersey, which revised its history standards in early 2002. The revised standards added new references to the evils of slavery, obscure slavery opponents Sarah Grimke and Theodore Dwight Weld, the Holocaust, and present-day Iraq. To make room for this material, the standards sought to drop older material, including references to George Washington, Thomas Jefferson, and Benjamin Franklin, the pilgrims of Massachusetts Bay, and the Mayflower. When attacked for excluding founding figures, the head of New Jersey's Division of Academic and Career Standards responded, "We don't intentionally exclude names. But how long should the list of names be? Who do we include or not include?" (Sorokin, 2002a). That decision, it seems, was to be left up to each individual teacher, effectively derailing the original mission of content standards. After an outcry from traditionalists, the founding fathers were added to the revised standards, as were Abraham Lincoln, Franklin Roosevelt, Martin Luther King, and Lyndon Johnson, all of who had been omitted in the original version (Sorokin, 2002b).

## CONCLUSION

The most conspicuous result of successful multicultural efforts—those launched by "mainstream" minorities on safe constitutional ground in the areas of social science and the humanities—has been to encourage policy makers to adopt a studied ambiguity when crafting standards for high-stakes accountability. Ravitch (2003) has concluded that only 14 states have strong U.S. history standards, whereas more than half have weak standards or no standards at all. We wind up with history and literary standards that have no obvious meaning, besides a sense of grandiose ambition, even in states with standards widely regarded as exemplary. A simple comparison of history standards to math standards in various states helps to make clear just how relatively vague history standards often are. Take, for example, Pennsylvania's Grade 6 history standard: "Identify and explain how individuals and groups made significant political and cultural contributions to world history (for Africa, Asia, Europe, the Americas)" (Pennsylvania Department of Education, 2002). Or consider New York's Grades 1 through 5 standard: "Students should know the roots of American culture, its development from many different traditions, and the ways many people from a variety of groups and backgrounds played a role in creating it" (New York State Education Department, 1996). It is not clear what these statements mean, what teachers are expected to teach, or what students are expected to know. The standards are vacuous aspirations carefully shorn of substantive significance.

Such ambiguity is the norm rather than the exception. Even in states with acclaimed history standards, close examination reveals the same tendency toward vague, all-inclusive, and grandiose standards. In Texas, widely regarded as a national exemplar for its standards, students in Grades 9 through 12 are to understand "how people from various groups, including racial, ethnic, and religious groups, adapt to life in the United States and contribute to our national identity" (Texas Education Agency, 1998). Sixth graders in Oklahoma, another state hailed for its standards, are asked to "analyze selected cultures which have affected our history" with the corollary that they should be able to "compare and contrast common characteristics of culture, such as language, customs, shelter, diet, traditional occupations, belief systems, and folk traditions" (Oklahoma Department of Education, 2002).[1]

This is not to say that there are no states with clear, specific, and meaningful standards. Indiana and Kansas, for instance, have been commended for the clarity and general excellence of their content requirements.[2] It is worth noting, however, that both states are more than 85% White and among the most racially homogeneous states in the nation (U.S. Census Bureau, 2000). The multicultural tensions that exist elsewhere are milder in states like these. The reduced influence of minority groups enables public officials to more readily stand by specific standards without fearing they are courting trouble.

The politics of multicultural conflict under accountability are straightforward. The majority discourse enjoys only vague support, whereas the discrete ethnic, religious, and racial interests are mobilized and advocate for particular concessions. If the original document is majoritarian, it gets watered down. If done in a collaborative fashion, it comes out watery or with too much objectionable material—in which case it can trigger a majority backlash. The process eventually teeters toward a vague, fence-straddling compromise. The result is that efforts in contested areas tend to produce hollow standards that sound promising but that can be interpreted in many ways. The result is that the standards wind up getting driven by the particular test questions that get adopted or by the preferences of teachers, just as if the standards were not in place.

This ambiguity undermines test validity, leaves much of the substance of what students need to know to the whims of test designers, and undermines the notion that standards provide clear direction as to what students are expected to master. This disadvantages those students from poor families who have fewer resources at home and must depend more heavily on classroom instruction for knowledge. This development may also undercut public faith in the tests in the areas of history, social studies, and literature. Consequently, it becomes increasingly easy for public officials to focus testing on the relatively uncontroversial areas of reading, mathematics, and science while marginalizing the role of testing in subjects such as history and literature. This process has the potential to become cyclical, with reduced testing leading to a reduction in emphasis on the humanities and social sciences.

The challenge for policy makers is that high-stakes accountability requires tough-minded choices regarding what students will be expected to master. Useful curricular guidelines must be coherent, reasonable, and concrete. However, the checks and balances of the American system, with its plentiful veto points and permeable democracy, tend to promote grandiose ambiguity. Faced with intensely concerned particular constituencies and a largely apathetic public, policy makers tend to seek compromise when faced with sympathetic demands. Policy makers add material to the standards to placate irate constituencies or make standards vague enough to alleviate complainant concerns that their preferred content is being marginalized. Public officials find it easy to face down such pressure only when the complainants lack legitimacy, make demands that contradict authoritative scholarly principles, or run afoul of the constitutional regime.

## NOTES

1. Even traditionalist critics such as the Thomas B. Fordham Foundation (2000) have ranked Texas and Oklahoma's history standards as among the 10 best in the nation (Ravitch 2003).
2. Ravitch (2003) and the Thomas B. Fordham Foundation (2000) have ranked Kansas and Indiana's history standards in the top third nationally.

## REFERENCES

Associated Press. (2001, July 8). *Lawmaker hails teachers' union scrapping of gay curriculum.* Associated Press State & Local Wire. Retrieved from LexisNexis database.

Binder, A. (2002). *Contentious curriculum.* Princeton, NJ: Princeton University Press.

Caballero, P., & DeLeon, J. (2002, September 15). Changing the face of education: School districts must do more to teach students about Hispanics' contributions to the U.S. *Fort Worth Star-Telegram*, p. 1.

Ceaser, J. W. (1998). Multiculturalism and American liberal democracy. In A. M. Meltzer, J. Weinberger, & R. Zinman (Eds.), *Multiculturalism and American democracy* (pp. 139-156). Lawrence: University of Kansas Press.

Cheney, L. (1995). *Telling the truth*. New York: Touchstone.

Cheney, L. (1996, May 2). New history standards still attack our heritage. *Wall Street Journal*, p. A14.

Chubb, J., & Moe, T. (1990). *Politics, markets, and American schools*. Washington, DC: Brookings Institution.

Davis, J. A., & Smith, T. W. (2002). *General social survey*. Chicago: National Opinion Research Center.

Diggins, J. P. (1996, May 15). History standards get it wrong again. *The New York Times*, p. A21.

Edwards v. Aguillard, 482 U.S. 578 (1987).

Thomas B. Fordham Foundation. (2000). *The state of state standards*. Washington, DC: Author.

Gitlin, T. (1995). *The twilight of common dreams: Why America is wracked by culture wars*. New York: Metropolitan Books.

Glazer, N. (1997). *We are all multiculturalists now*. Cambridge, MA: Harvard University Press.

Hess, F. M. (2002). Reform, resistance, . . . retreat? The predictable politics of accountability in Virginia. In D. Ravitch (Ed.), *Brookings papers on education policy 2002*. Washington DC: Brookings Institution.

Hess, F. M. (2003). Refining or retreating? High-stakes accountability in the states. In P. Peterson & M. West (Eds.), *Taking account of accountability* (pp. 69-122). Washington DC: Brookings Institution.

Howe, K. R. (1997). *Understanding equal educational opportunity: Social justice, democracy, and schooling*. New York: Teachers College Press.

Hunter, J. (1990). *Culture wars: The struggle to define America*. New York: Basic Books.

Keller, C. W. (1997). Comparing the original and revised standards for history. *The History Teacher, 30*(1), 306-338.

Klotz, I. (1993). Multicultural perspectives in science education: One prescription for failure. *Phi Delta Kappan, /5*(3), 266-269.

Kohn, A. (2000). *The case against standardized testing*. Portsmouth, NH: Heinemann.

Levinson, S. V. (2001). Promoting diversity in the public schools. In S. A. Barber & R. P. George (Eds.), *Constitutional politics* (pp. 193-222). Princeton, NJ: Princeton University Press.

Macedo, S. (2000). *Diversity and distrust: Civic education in a multicultural democracy*. Cambridge, MA: Harvard University Press.

Martel, E. (1994, February 20). The Egyptian illusion: Fatal flaws in one popular Afrocentric text. *The Washington Post*, p. C3.

McNeil, L. (2000). *Contradictions of school reform: Educational costs of standardized testing*. New York: Routledge Kegan Paul.

McWilliams, W. C. (1998). Democratic multiculturalism. In A. M. Meltzer, J. Weinberger, & R. Zinman (Eds.), *Multiculturalism and American democracy* (pp. 120-129). Lawrence: University of Kansas Press.

Meier, D. (2000). *Will standards save public education?* East Sussex, UK: Beacon.

Nash, G. B. (1997). Early American history and the national history standards. *William and Mary Quarterly, 54*(3), 579-600.

National Center for History in the Schools. (1994). *National standards for world history: Exploring paths to the present, expanded edition* (G. Nash & C. Crabtree, Eds.). Los Angeles: Author.

Nelson, B. (2002, March 11). Creation vs. evolution. *Newsday*, p. B6.

New York State Education Department. (1996). *Learning standards for social studies*. Retrieved on June 11, 2003, from http://usny.nysed.gov/teachers/nyslearningstandards.html

Nicgorski, W. (1992). American pluralism: A condition or a goal? In D. Lapsley & C. Power (Eds.), *The challenge of pluralism: Education, politics and values* (pp. 15-37). Notre Dame, Indiana: University of Notre Dame Press.

Norton, A. (1998). The virtues of multiculturalism. In A. M. Meltzer, J. Weinberger, & R. Zinman (Eds.), *Multiculturalism and American democracy* (pp. 130-138). Lawrence: University of Kansas Press.

Ohanian, S. (1999). *One size fits few: The folly of educational standards*. Portsmouth, NH: Heinemann.

Oklahoma Department of Education. (2002). *Priority academic student skills: Social studies*. Retrieved on June 11, 2003, from http://sde.state.ok.us/acrob/pass/socialstudies.pdf

Pedulla, J. J., Abrams, L., Madaus, G., Russel, M., Ramos, M., & Miao, J. (2003). *Perceived effects of state-mandated testing programs on teaching and learning: Findings from a national survey of teachers*. Boston: National Board on Educational Testing and Public Policy.

Pennsylvania Department of Education. (2002). *Academic standards for history*. Retrieved on June 11, 2003, from http://www.pde.state.pa.us/stateboard_ed/cwp/view.asp?a=3&Q=76716&stateboard_edNav=|5467|&pde_internetNav=|

Ravitch, D. (1990). Multiculturalism: E Pluribus Plures. *The American Scholar, 59*(3), 337-354.

Ravitch, D. (1995). *National standards in American education*. Washington, DC: Brookings Institution.

Ravitch, D. (2003). *The language police: How pressure groups restrict what students learn*. New York: Knopf.

Reich, R. (2002). *Bridging liberalism and multiculturalism in American education*. Chicago: University of Chicago Press.

Schlesinger, A. (1998). *The disuniting of America: Reflections on a multicultural society*. New York: Norton.

Singer, A. (1993, October). Multiculturalism and Afrocentricity: How they influence teaching U.S. History. *Social Education*, (57), 283-286.

Sorokin, E. (2002a, January 28). No founding fathers? That's our new history: Overkill on political correctness seen. *The Washington Times*, p. A1.

Sorokin, E. (2002b, February 2). Founding fathers given new life in New Jersey: Draft left them out of history books. *The Washington Times*, p. A1.

Stern, S. (2001). Why the battle over history standards? In S. Stotsky (Ed.), *What's at stake in the K-12 standards wars: A primer for education policy makers* (pp. 149-168). New York: Peter Lang.

Texas Education Agency. (1998). *Texas essential knowledge and skills for social studies: Subchapter C, high school*. Retrieved on June 11, 2003, from http://www.tea.state.tx.us/rules/tac/chapter113/ch113c.html#113.31

Thomas, J. (1996, April 3). Revised history standards disarm the explosive issues. *New York Times*, p. B8.

U.S. Census Bureau. (2000). *State and county quick facts*. Retrieved on June 1, 2003, from http://quickfacts.census.gov/qfd/states/

Warsmith, S. (2002, December 8). Theory of evolution will face test in vote. *Akron Beacon Journal*, p. A1.

Webster, Y. (1997). *Against the multicultural agenda: A critical thinking alternative*. Westport, CT: Praeger.

Wermers, J. (2001a, January 22). Educators struggle to revise standards: What to include in history, social sciences stirs trouble. *Richmond Times Dispatch*, p. B1.

Wermers, J. (2001b, March 2). Panel suggests revision: Proposal adds Armenian genocide. *Richmond Times Dispatch*, p. A1.

Wermers, J. (2001c, March 12). Revised standards criticized: History changes rapped by second group. *Richmond Times Dispatch*, p. B5.

Wermers, J. (2001d, March 22). Critics say SOLs slight Civil War. *Richmond Times Dispatch*, p. B1.

Wermers, J. (2001e, March 24). SOL genocide plank deleted: Revised history standards OK'd. *Richmond Times Dispatch*, p. A1.

Zimmerman, J. (2002) *Whose America? Culture wars in the public schools.* Cambridge, MA: Harvard University Press.

*Frederick M. Hess is a resident scholar at the American Enterprise Institute. His books include* Bringing the Social Sciences Alive *(Allyn & Bacon, 1999),* Spinning Wheels *(Brookings Institution, 1999),* Revolution at the Margins *(Brookings Institution, 2002), and the forthcoming* Common Sense School Reform *(Palgrave, in press). His work has appeared in scholarly journals including* Social Science Quarterly, American Politics Quarterly, Urban Affairs Review, *and* Teachers College Record. *He is a former high school social studies teacher.*

# A Sound Education for All:
# Multicultural Issues in Music Education

## BOB L. JOHNSON JR.

*Establishing the legitimacy of the arts within the larger school curriculum is a defining issue in arts education. Within the context of this perennial challenge, this article examines two multicultural issues in music education: equal music education opportunity and the idiomatic hegemony of the Western classical tradition. Discussions of the essence of music, the current state of music education practice, competing demands within the field, and of the educational benefits associated with the study of music provide the context for this examination. No student, it is argued, should be denied access to the arts based on the property wealth of his or her district, household, or cultural background. If music is to remain a viable curricular option, music educators must adapt both curricula and methods to the cultural backgrounds and needs of a changing student population.*

***Keywords:*** *music education; music education practice; music education policy; arts education policy; multicultural issues in music education*

A REVIEW OF THE HISTORY of arts education in the United States reveals a perennial struggle encountered by arts advocates: the challenge of establishing the legitimacy of the arts within the larger school curriculum (Birge, 1988; Keene, 1982; Leonhard, 1999; Mark & Gary, 1992; Smith, 1992; Werner, 2001). From an advocacy standpoint, the tone of this debate has been notably defensive. Rather than establishing the case for the study of music, art, theater, or dance as ends in themselves, advocates have sought to justify the study of the arts in terms of the means they provide to more legitimate and

EDUCATIONAL POLICY, Vol. 18 No. 1, January and March 2004 116-141
DOI: 10.1177/0895904803260028
© 2004 Corwin Press

| | | | |
|---|---|---|---|
| English Language Acquisition (ELA) Act National Professional Development Program (ESEA, Title III) (Pre-NCLB ESEA, Title VII included several discretionary programs for teacher preparation, including instructional Services and Professional Development Grants. These programs were not reauthorized, and thus funding includes payments on existing discretionary grants to districts and IHEs.)* | $37.5 million  *National Activities* $209.6 million | $37.5 million (2003 Presidential request)  *National Activities* $133.4 million (2003 Presidential request) | $37.5 million  *National Activities* $83.7 million |
| ELA State Grants (ESEA, Title III)* | $411.6 million | $466.4 million (2003 Presidential request) | $538.1 million |
| Teacher Quality Enhancement (HEA, Title II, part A) | $90 million | $89.42 million | $90 million |

U.S. Department of Education budget documents now report only a single ELA allocation for all Title III programs and expenses. This includes $664.27 million appropriated for 2002, $685.52 million for 2003, and a 2004 presidential request of $665 million.pproved teacher preparation program."81 This too raised concern, as it presented institutions with a new opportunity to game the system by requiring students to pass state assessments as a prerequisite for program completion (much like requiring a specific course). Institutions may thus limit the number of teacher candidates about whom they must report to the successful test-takers.

about low performance or reported very general criteria in their submissions to Secretary Paige. For example, Washington, D.C., will not even begin to identify schools as low performing until 2012, and fifteen states failed to provide any timeline for identifying and intervening in low-performing programs. Three states did not report any of the required information about state systems for improving the quality of teacher-preparation programs.

As early signs of state commitments to improving teacher preparation, these examples are not encouraging. Likewise, if the Department of Education continues to accept incomplete and inaccurate data without sanction or intervention, then the possibility that HEA and NCLB will be catalysts for teacher improvement is dim. For example, will millions of Title I dollars really be refused to states when they fail to report complete and accurate data on highly qualified teachers? Will states be held responsible for building coherent, rigorous systems for teacher recruitment, preparation, placement, and ongoing professional development?

## CONCLUSION: HIGH-QUALITY PROGRAMS
## AND HIGHLY QUALIFIED TEACHERS

In only a few years, the federal government has moved from vocal opposition to opportunity-to-learn standards (e.g., in Goals 2000) and a hands-off approach to teacher preparation to a legislative commitment to guarantee the quality of teachers in America's schools. Unfortunately, implementation of ESEA and HEA requirements is plagued by the challenges of working with more than fifty different state systems for teacher licensure, hundreds of systems for hiring and placing teachers, and more than a thousand approaches to teacher preparation. Most troublesome is the difficulty of creating "gaming-proof" uniform definitions and reporting procedures and reliance on state assessments whose value has been questioned.

The effectiveness of these new teacher-quality laws will rely on the honesty and commitment of states, districts, and IHEs, and the willingness of the U.S. Department of Education to hold feet to the fire when parties fail to comply with the laws and provide necessary supports when they struggle to meet federal standards. Likewise, members of Congress will need to fight the urge to lower standards and pressures for accountability to placate dissatisfied constituent institutions. Success will, therefore, rely on policymakers' adherence to a coherent vision of teacher quality that considers the full continuum of the teaching profession and the ways in which policies and practices must align to ensure that states are teaching, testing, and reporting the things that really matter in the nation's classrooms.

Can the effort to streamline teacher hiring coexist with the effort to raise teacher quality, and can the continuing debates about the effectiveness of teacher-education programs actually lead to institutional changes? Will the federal government stay involved (hands-on) long enough not only to define requirements but also to provide supports for necessary change? Through all the careful crafting of legislative language, across the fragmented educational landscape, important questions remain: Will our children—especially our poor, minority, and language-minority children—be able to reach high academic standards? Can the shift that occurred from hands-off to active federal support and accountability for *teacher* quality now evolve into meaningful discourse and supports for improving *teaching* quality?

## CHAPTER 3

# Why Do We License Teachers?

*Dan D. Goldhaber*

## INTRODUCTION

States use teacher licensure to regulate who may enter the teaching profession. Debate over the efficacy of licensure has grown in recent years with the advent of alternative licensure, a pathway into the classroom for those who have not completed all of the requirements associated with a state's traditional licensure program. This pathway emerged in the 1980s and 1990s as a policy response to difficulties in staffing schools, particularly those in high-poverty urban areas, and concerns about the quality of the teacher labor force.[1] The degree to which policymakers and the public view the supply (or lack) of teachers as a crisis tends to vary with the overall health of the economy: in general, it is more difficult to staff schools when the economy is growing at a rapid pace and the labor market is tight. Regardless of the state of the labor market, school systems—particularly those in urban, high-needs communities—face difficulties hiring enough high-quality teachers.

Irrespective of the immediacy of the supply and quality problems, there are two compelling reasons to focus on the efficacy of different teacher licensure policies: 1) teacher quality can have a tremendous impact on student achievement, and 2) our aging teacher labor force will produce significant future retirements and, thus, an opportunity to greatly influence the nation's teacher work force.[2]

* The views expressed here are solely those of the author and do not necessarily reflect those of the University of Washington or the Urban Institute.

In this paper I focus on the debate about various licensure policies, review some evidence on the efficacy of these policies, and suggest how we might learn more about key licensure policy issues. First, I review the arguments for and against alternative teacher licensure and posit that the generic "for or against" debate is largely unhelpful in informing policy-making. Next, I demonstrate the potential relationship between licensure requirements, the teacher applicant pool, and the quality of teachers who are in the classroom. Third, I examine empirical evidence that bears on this debate and discusses why it cannot yield answers to some key policy questions. Fourth, I focus on what questions policymakers ought to ask when considering various licensure options and how new sources of data may be used to answer these questions.

## SHOULD (ALTERNATIVE) LICENSURE EXIST?

Should alternative licensure exist? I would argue that the question, so phrased, makes no sense. Because alternative licensure policies differ significantly from one state to the next, it is not useful to think of "alternative licensure" as a single policy.

Alternative licensure programs are based on the premise that it is possible to get more quality teachers by allowing them to bypass or postpone some of the requirements (particularly education-specific coursework) associated with traditional licensure programs. In general, these alternative programs share the requirements that applicants have a baccalaureate degree, pass a licensure test, and receive additional supervision (mentoring) and on-the-job training. The on-the-job training often involves satisfying the pedagogical coursework requirements consistent with traditional licensure programs, and this is the major area where state policies diverge from one another. Some of the forty-six jurisdictions with alternative programs use them to encourage recruitment of individuals from other professions into teaching, and their pedagogical requirements are designed to further this purpose. In other states, the alternative program is designed primarily to allow localities facing "emergency" teacher shortages to hire for one year applicants who haven't yet satisfied all the traditional pedagogical requirements. After one year, however, if these requirements have not been satisfied, the emergency hires are no longer eligible to teach.[3] These differences in program design reflect the major disparities in states' use of alternative licensure as a source of teacher supply.

Texas and New Jersey have relied on alternative programs as a major source of teachers; 16 percent and 22 percent, respectively, of their new teachers have an alternative credential.[4] Most states, however, rely very little on alternative programs when hiring new teachers. The major difference among states with alternative programs is the way education coursework requirements are handled. Embedded in the overarching question of whether alternative licensure should exist at all are more nuanced issues of the value added by required education courses and the degree to which requiring new teachers to pass these courses up front dissuades potential high-quality teachers from attempting to teach.

Since there is no single alternative licensure policy, generic comparisons between alternative and traditional licensure do not make sense. Both traditional and alternative licensure policies have significant state-to-state variation in terms of the prescribed college majors, coursework, licensure exam, and student-teaching requirements.[5]

The better question to ask is: What is the proper regulatory role for states in the teacher labor market?[6] At one end of the spectrum is the argument that it's unnecessary and undesirable to regulate entry into the teaching profession, because it distorts free market equilibria and restricts the ability of localities to hire whom they wish. At the other end is the contention that teaching is a precise science best learned through a prescribed training program. Of course, many policies and proposals reflect points of view between the poles defining this spectrum.

The validity of the arguments over state regulation of the teacher labor market depends in part on what one hopes this regulation will accomplish. Many voices on both sides of this regulatory debate believe the dispute is one about the effects of regulation on teacher quality. However, the specified purpose of teacher licensure is to guarantee a *minimum* standard of quality of public school teachers by avoiding the possibility that poor local hiring decisions result in the employment of unsuitable teachers.[7] Therefore, the quality debate may be only tangential to the intended objectives of this regulation. (It is conceivable that regulation could serve to lower the *average* quality of the teacher work force while simultaneously preventing the *lowest-quality* teachers from entering the classroom.)

The arguments for and against state regulation of the teacher labor market, and alternative licensure programs in particular, should revolve around two complicated questions: 1) Which teachers would be hired? 2) How effective would these individuals be, and for how long, if licensure policies were different? These questions cannot be answered directly, because we cannot observe the teachers who would be in classrooms if policies were different. Thus, policymaking must be informed by answers to a related set of questions: 1) What essential preparation and skills should individuals have before entering the classroom, and how are these skills acquired? 2) Do school systems make good hiring decisions when given more freedom to make them? 3) How do licensure requirements, and in particular the existence of alternative licensure, affect the teacher applicant pool?

Though policymakers have some evidence about teacher effectiveness to consult when designing regulatory policies, on the whole existing research does not come close to answering any of the questions posed above.[8] It is clear, however, that advocates of alternative licensure and less regulation of the teacher labor market have very different views about what the answers might be from advocates of stricter licensure standards and greater regulation.[9]

Advocates of alternative licensure policies believe the skills necessary to be an effective teacher may be acquired in a variety of settings, and therefore entry into the teaching profession should not be restricted to those who have completed a traditional teacher-preparation program. (Alternative licensure does not represent the total deregulation of the teacher labor market envisioned by some free market advocates, but it does represent a reduction of state-level regulation.) From this perspective, alternative licensure is a tool for enticing "large numbers of highly qualified, talented, and enthusiastic individuals" into the profession who otherwise might have judged the time and expense of more traditional teacher-preparation programs to be too high in comparison to other career opportunities.[10] Alternative licensure proponents argue that judgments about teacher qualifications and quality are best left to local officials, often school principals, who are better able to evaluate which applicants would best fit individual schools' needs.

Alternative licensure opponents, by contrast, contend that allowing individuals to enter teaching without conventional training downgrades teaching as a profession and is potentially harmful to children. Their concern is that individuals becoming teachers through these routes are of poorer quality and lack the training necessary to teach competently in many settings.[11] This is problematic if school systems, for good or ill reasons, hire these incompetent individuals as teachers. Some would also argue that alternative licensure is simply a policy response to tight teacher labor markets, and as such deflects policymakers from the real teacher-quality issue: low teacher salaries.

## LICENSURE REQUIREMENTS, THE TEACHER APPLICANT POOL, AND TEACHER QUALITY

It is conceivable that teacher licensure policies could protect the public from very low-quality teachers while simultaneously lowering the overall

**FIGURE 1    needs a title**

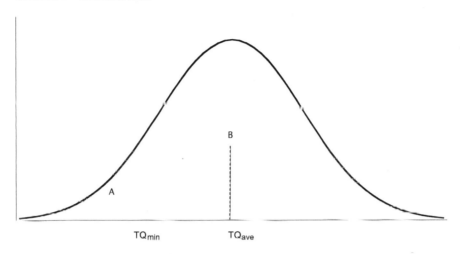

quality of the teacher work force. It is also plausible that licensure policies might have a very different impact on schools and school districts operating in different environments. Nonetheless, the goal of licensure policy is to create a teacher work force of higher overall quality than would exist in its absence. While the following discussion does not deal directly with alternative licensure, one might think of alternative licensure as a relaxation of the existing hurdles associated with entry into teaching.

The effects of a licensure policy on people who are hired as teachers depends on 1) the strength of the relationship between observable teacher attributes and student outcomes; 2) how specific licensure provisions impact individuals' labor market decisions; and 3) local school system selection of teachers through existing recruitment, screening, and hiring processes. These factors are illustrated graphically by the figures in the Appendix.

Imagine that teacher quality (TQ) falls along a continuum and that the distribution of teacher quality in the population is bell-shaped. Figure 1 depicts this hypothetical bell-shaped distribution of TQ for potential teachers in the population *in the absence of teacher licensure*.[12] The horizontal axis shows the level of TQ and the vertical axis shows the number of individuals in the population of that quality level. The average quality in the population of potential teachers is depicted as $TQ_{ave}$.

Were it possible to directly observe TQ, we might wish to prohibit individuals who fall below some quality level (call it $TQ_{min}$) from employment as teachers. In that case, the individuals in Area A of the figure, who fall below the socially desirable minimum quality level, are excluded from the teacher labor market, and school systems can hire only applicants in Area B of the figure.

It is not possible to observe a teacher's quality before he or she is actually teaching. Therefore, licensure requirements are established based on a set of observable characteristics (e.g., whether an individual holds a baccalaureate degree or has passed a specified exam) that are believed to be proxies for teacher quality. Most states have adopted a common set of core requirements for those wishing to be licensed to teach in the state. In 2002, for instance, all states required prospective teachers to have a bachelor's degree and at least some coursework in pedagogy, and most require at least some subject-matter study.[13] Most states also require prospective teachers to have a minimum grade point average and to pass some type of standardized test before either teacher training or licensure.[14]

The underlying assumption is that teacher candidates who fail to meet the minimum standards defined by these requirements will tend to be of worse quality than those who do meet the standards, and may be of such low quality that they are unsuitable for the classroom. The potential problem here is that the relationship between specific observable teacher characteristics (e.g., whether they have graduated from a teacher-training program or passed a basic skills test) and what schools want (teacher quality) may be quite weak.

Issues raised by a weak correlation between teacher quality and observable characteristics are depicted in Figure 2, which shows a hypothetical bivariate relationship between TQ and some measure used to screen teachers (in our example, performance on a licensure exam). If we assume that TQ follows a bell-shaped distribution and that the scores on the licensure tests also follow a bell-shaped distribution, then the joint distribution will be a bell-shaped mound. The total area represented by Quadrants A and B in Figure 2 (which corresponds with Section A in Figure 1) represents prospective teachers who fall below a set standard of quality ($TQ_{min}$). However, we do not directly observe TQ. Instead, we observe a teacher standard (TS): performance on licensure exams. We can prohibit prospective teachers who score below a given standard ($TS_{min}$) from participating in the teacher labor market; however, this results in what might be called false positives and false negatives. The individuals in Quadrant A (who do well on the test but are low-quality teachers) are the false positives. They are allowed into the teacher labor market despite their low TQ. Those individuals in Quadrant C (who do poorly on the test but would be high-quality teachers) represent false negatives. They are excluded from the teacher labor market despite

**FIGURE 2**   needs a title

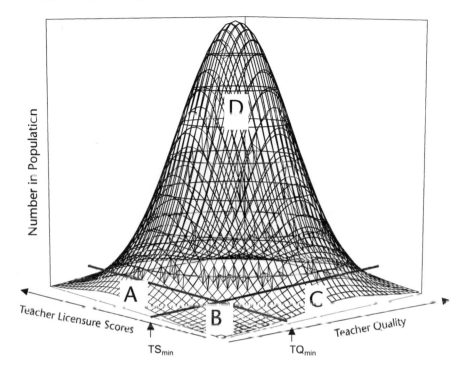

their high quality. Individuals in Quadrants B and D represent true negatives and true positives, respectively: individuals that we wish to (and do) exclude from the labor market, and individuals that we wish to (and do) include in the labor market. The existence of such standards will always result in some number of false positives and false negatives; policymakers should strive to establish a standard that will minimize the occurrence of both.

The height of the mound in Figure 2 corresponds to the number of people with a given TQ who have a particular licensure score, and the exact shape of the mound depends on how closely TQ correlates with licensure test performance.[15] Because it is difficult to display three-dimensional graphs on paper, it is often helpful to examine the mound as it would appear looking straight down from above, as if it were a topographical map. The height of the mound is represented by the ellipses in the diagram, as shown in Figures 3 and 4 (whose four quadrants correspond exactly with those in Figure 2), with the smaller ellipses representing higher points on the mound. Figure 3 depicts a situation where the licensure test score is strongly associated with TQ, and Figure 4 depicts a weak association.

**FIGURE 3    needs a title**

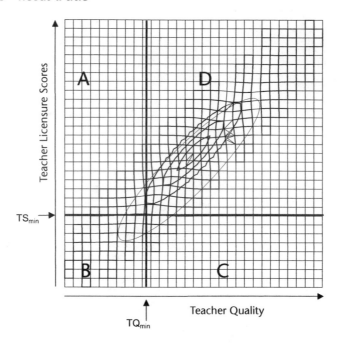

The strength of the relationship between TQ and performance on licensure exams (or other criteria used to regulate entry into the teacher labor market) will help determine how effective a licensure policy is. If there is a strong relationship between the two, as depicted by Figure 3, there will be relatively few false positives and false negatives. If there is a weak relationship, as depicted by Figure 4, there will be many more false negatives and false positives.

The number of false positives and false negatives will also be affected by both the difficulty of the hurdle (in this case, the passing score set for the licensure exam) and the number of hurdles. Higher hurdles will result in more false negatives but fewer false positives.

Another consequence of licensure policies is that they may influence who chooses to enter the teacher labor market. Figure 1 shows the hypothetical distribution of TQ in the population. Occupational licensure policies, however, will likely have an impact on who opts to teach and, consequently, the distribution of TQ among those eligible to be hired by school systems. The short-run labor economics of teacher licensure are relatively

**FIGURE 4   needs a title**

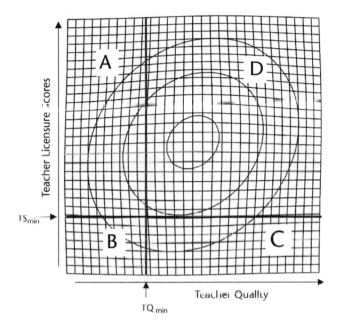

simple: imposing more requirements to enter an occupation will screen out more potential participants from that occupation's labor market.[16]

The longer-run implications of licensure for who opts to pursue a career in teaching are more complicated. Because licensure requirements drive up wages in an occupation by restricting the supply of labor, these requirements may change the public's perception of the occupation.[17] Thus, stricter licensure policies might cause more prestige to be associated with employment in an occupation.[18] However, to the degree that licensure policies dissuade talented individuals from entering the profession, such policies could lower the prestige of being a teacher.[19] Either of these effects could have a longer-term impact on the number or type of individuals who wish to enter the occupation. Thus, the distribution of TQ among those eligible to be hired by school systems could either rise or fall as a result of licensure.

There is no direct evidence of how licensure affects the teacher applicant pool, but we know that teachers tend to be drawn from the lower end of the distribution of academic proficiency. Some might argue that this is due, at least in part, to licensure policies that dissuade more academically talented students from considering teaching.[20] Unfortunately, we know virtually nothing about the people who never enter the teacher applicant pools due to real or perceived hurdles associated with becoming a teacher.

While states' traditional and alternative licensure policies determine who is eligible to teach, the quality of the teacher work force will ultimately be determined by the effectiveness of local school systems in selecting and hiring teachers. A primary argument for state-level governance of entry into the teaching profession is the belief that local school districts, left to their own devices, would hire ill-qualified teachers at great cost to students.[21] This could occur if local districts (the consumers of teachers' services) either lack the expertise to judge the quality of services they are buying from prospective teachers or purposely hire poor teachers for other reasons, such as nepotism. In the absence of licensure requirements, local systems might opt to hire many teachers from the lower end of the TQ distribution (e.g., those in Area A of Figure 1), leading to an average TQ that falls below $TQ_{min}$. Imposition of a licensure requirement would preclude the hiring of teachers below $TQ_{min}$, so even if local systems made very poor decisions, the minimum quality of the teacher work force would be $TQ_{min}$.

What does research tell us about the ways in which licensure policies or the relaxation of strict licensure requirements as represented by alternative licensure might affect teacher quality? As I describe below, the answer is "relatively little."

## EMPIRICAL EVIDENCE

As the previous section illustrates, it is not possible on theoretical grounds to determine whether teacher licensure as currently designed (or occupational licensure in general) will increase or decrease the quality of service provided.[22] However, a licensure policy is more likely to be effective if it is based on a strong relationship between teacher quality and observable teacher attributes.

What preparation and skills should individuals have before they enter the classroom? A significant body of research has investigated the extent to which teacher attributes such as degree(s) earned and experience levels affect both teaching strategies and student outcomes. There is disagreement, due to an uncertain relationship between pedagogical approaches and student outcomes, over the appropriateness of any particular teaching technique, so I will concentrate on those studies focusing on student outcomes.[23]

The literature linking teachers and students shows that teacher quality plays a relatively large role in influencing student outcomes. In fact, it is likely the most important schooling factor, with a much larger impact than other commonly measured school attributes such as class size.[24] However, there does not appear to be a strong link between many readily quantifiable teacher attributes (such as teacher subject specialty, degree level, licensure type, or years of teaching experience) and teacher quality. A much smaller body of research exists on the relationship between academic proficiency and student outcomes, but is more definitive in showing a relationship between measures of academic proficiency and teacher quality. It is, therefore, difficult to determine whether aspiring teachers (following either traditional or alternative routes) should be subject to any specific requirements.

Degree and experience levels are the teacher attributes used most commonly in educational production function studies, largely because they are easy to measure and widely available. Several meta-analyses have reached different conclusions regarding the relationships between these teacher attributes and student outcomes.[25] A 1986 study, for example, concludes that "the results are startlingly consistent in finding no strong evidence that teacher-student ratios, teacher education, or teachers' years of experience have an expected positive effect on student achievement."[26] A 1996 study reaches a very different conclusion: "[V]ariables like teacher academic ability, teacher education, and teacher experience show very strong relations with student achievement."[27]

These differences can be explained by the selection of relevant studies and the methodology researchers use to synthesize their findings. A more nuanced picture emerges when looking at individual teacher attributes or teaching context, such as the grade level or subject area taught or the particular point in a teacher's career. For example, a teacher's degree level has been found to have an impact on student achievement only for math and science degrees held by teachers who teach those subjects. Likewise, teaching experience gained in the early years of a career has a greater impact than experience gained toward the end of a career.

There appears to be greater consensus in the literature that teachers with higher levels of academic proficiency are more effective;[28] this can support a more compelling argument for licensure examinations. A number of aggregate-level studies that include at least some controls for students' backgrounds find a positive relationship between measures of teachers' academic proficiency and student achievement.[29] Several of these studies focus specifically on the relationship between teacher performance on licensure exams and student achievement.

Research at the individual student level that includes background controls also finds a positive relationship between a teacher's academic proficiency and student outcomes.[30] However, because there is so little of this type of research, it is difficult to come to any strong conclusions.[31] This paucity of information on the relationship between academic proficiency and student achievement is noteworthy, because most states require teacher candidates to achieve a specified score on a licensure examination for both traditional and alternative licensure. A recent publication by the National Research Council, *Testing Teacher Candidates*, highlights the scarcity of good information relating teacher performance on licensure exams to student outcomes; one of their panels was unable to find any evidence relating licensure exams used in 2001 to student achievement.[32] Furthermore, we have virtually no information about the degree to which exams or other hurdles associated with obtaining a license screen out high-quality individuals from the teacher labor market or dissuade them from attempting to become teachers.

It is entirely possible for restrictive licensure policies to make for good public policy even if the relationship between specific teacher attributes and student achievement is weak, if both of the following are true: 1) individuals in the course of achieving a traditional license learn teaching skills that are crucial but not easily quantified; and 2) local school systems, when left to their own devices (i.e., operating in a less restrictive regulatory regime), opt to hire individuals who do not have these important skills.

If it were true that individuals acquired crucial teaching skills primarily through traditional teacher-preparation programs, we might expect to see significant differences in teacher effectiveness between traditionally licensed teachers and those with alternative credentials. As we found with research on teacher attributes in general, research on this issue is sparse and often methodologically flawed, and therefore too weak to support strong conclusions.

A widely cited 1985 review of thirteen studies reported that, of the eleven studies that found fully licensed teachers to be more effective, only two (one unpublished dissertation and one that does not separate the impact of licensure from that of teacher experience) are based on student outcomes. The review's authors note that much research on teacher education "is often of dubious scientific merit" and the findings reported in the paper do "not add up to a defense of teacher preparation as it exists in most institutions." Nonetheless, the authors conclude that fully licensed teachers tend to be more effective than those who have not completed the requirements for full licensure.[33]

A more recent review of roughly 150 studies (most of which do not focus exclusively on student outcomes) of teacher licensure concludes that there is little evidence linking traditional licensure to teacher effectiveness.[34] This review resulted in a heated debate over which studies are of high enough quality to inform questions on teacher licensure and how to interpret the findings of the studies included in the report.[35]

Many of the studies included in these meta-analyses do not meet accepted standards of academic rigor. For instance, failure to account for differences in student backgrounds is problematic, because teachers are not randomly distributed across schools and students: teachers with additional experience and credentials are more likely to be teaching higher-achieving students from more affluent, educated families. This point is particularly important when evaluating different licensure policies. Because of pressure on schools to hire "fully licensed" personnel, schools that employ teachers with an alternative or emergency license are likely doing so only because they find it difficult to hire teachers who have satisfied all their state's traditional licensure requirements. These are the same school systems most likely to serve students who are struggling academically.

This failure to account adequately for students' backgrounds might lead researchers to misinterpret a correlational relationship between lack of full licensure and low student achievement as a causal relationship. There are very few studies (a 2003 review finds only two) focusing on the licensure-achievement relationship that control adequately for students' backgrounds.[36] One of these illustrates the need to account for students' backgrounds;[37] it found that students taught by fully licensed teachers tend to have higher levels of performance in math and science. But when measuring growth, the study found few differences in student achievement between students taught by teachers with standard state certification and those with emergency certification.[38]

The mixed findings of teacher licensure research are not surprising, given the variation in states' requirements for both traditional and alternative licensure. This raises the question of whether schools make good decisions when they have more flexibility in hiring, as they do in some states, an issue that goes to the heart of the debate over alternative licensure and to the role of state regulation in general. If localities always made optimal hiring decisions, there would be very little reason for licensure. On the other hand, the need to protect students from at least some poor local hiring decisions makes the case for regulating licensure.

Relaxing licensure requirements does not *guarantee* employment for individuals who are consequently allowed to teach. Rather, it *permits* the employment of some individuals who otherwise would not have been eligible to teach. It also has no impact on the value of teacher (or pedagogical) training, which likely has considerable variation in quality.

State regulation of the teacher labor market has a positive impact on teacher quality if, in its absence, localities hire teachers from Area A in Figure 1. If, on the other hand, localities adequately screen their applicants, state-level regulation of the teacher labor market would be unnecessary and could even lead to a lower-quality teacher work force. The care localities exercise in their hiring practices would, of course, depend on variables such as the capacity of their human resource departments or the amount of pressure they feel to improve students' academic achievement. It is at least conceivable that licensure has no impact whatsoever on whom school districts hire to teach; they might hire exactly the same teachers regardless of licensure requirements.

The slight evidence on school system hiring provides little proof that teacher quality is a major factor in their hiring decisions. Several recent studies suggest that systems do not hire from a large geographic region. A 1998 study, for instance, found that only 25 percent of Pennsylvania school districts advertised open teaching positions outside the state, and most districts do not advertise or seek teacher candidates outside their local labor markets.[39]

Given this, it is perhaps not surprising that 60 percent of newly hired teachers in the Strauss et al. study were hired from teacher-preparation institutions no more than seventy miles away from the school district where they found employment. These findings are confirmed in a 2002 study, which found that teachers in New York are twice as likely to work at a school within five miles of their home town (more precisely, where they graduated from high school) than to work at one within twenty miles of their home town.[40]

It is not clear whether these findings are a result of school systems' hiring preferences or of teachers' preferences for working close to their hometowns, but they suggest that systems are not casting a wide net when recruiting new teachers.[41] This does not necessarily mean they ought to be casting a wider net, but there is some research showing that school systems do not highly value measures of academic proficiency, the very characteristic that appears to be most highly correlated with student outcomes.[42] Teacher applicants who attended above-average colleges were significantly less likely to be hired than applicants who had attended below-average colleges, and attributes such as undergraduate GPA and subject specialties were found to have only a small effect on an applicant's probability of being hired. In fact, recent evidence suggests that districts rely more on interviews and teacher credentials than on classroom observations of teachers in making hiring decisions.[43]

We have little evidence on the hiring practices of districts, and even less on the ways in which teacher licensure affects the teacher applicant pool. The argument of alternative licensure proponents—that legions of highly qualified individuals are waiting to teach if they could enter the classroom without having to satisfy so many requirements—is, though plausible, mere speculation. The number of applicants to major alternative teacher programs such as Teach For America (TFA) typically exceeds available slots, but they represent only a small percentage of the number of teachers that are hired nationally each year. For instance, in 2003, TFA had 16,000 applicants for 1,800 available slots.[44]

Research on licensure exams finds pass rates between 70 percent and 90 percent in different states, as well as an indication that these tests tend to screen out a disproportionate number of minority teacher applicants.[45] Whether one sees this disparate impact as a problem depends, in part, on one view of the importance of bringing traditionally underrepresented groups into the profession and creating a culturally diverse teacher labor force, but also on whether minority teachers may be more effective in educating minority students, as is often suggested.[46] More importantly, there appears to be no research examining whether hurdles associated with entry into the teacher labor market (e.g., prescribed coursework, passing a licensure exam, etc.) discourage some individuals from even attempting to become teachers. This is doubtless the most difficult of the three questions (repeated in the next paragraph) to get a handle on.

## HOW TO ANSWER THE QUESTIONS THAT SHOULD BE ASKED

What do we know about licensure and its effects? Not very much, and certainly not enough to make sound policy judgments. This does not preclude us from learning a great deal and beginning to answer these policy questions: 1) What preparation and skills should individuals have before entering the classroom, and how are these skills acquired? 2) Do school systems make good decisions when given more freedom over whom they may hire? 3) How do licensure requirements affect the teacher applicant pool?

Large-scale national datasets collected for the U.S. Department of Education—the National Educational Longitudinal Survey (NELS) of 1988, the Schools and Staffing Survey (SASS), and the Baccalaureate and Beyond Longitudinal Study (B&B)—have been used to study some teacher licensure questions. Each of these datasets has certain features that can be used to help answer key licensure questions posed by this paper.

The National Educational Longitudinal Survey of 1988 allows researchers to link teachers to students and estimate value-added models of student achievement. However, there are several limitations on most national datasets that include measures of student outcomes. First, the descriptions of teacher credentials (particularly licensure) they report are somewhat vague, with teachers self-identifying their licensure status. NELS reports no category that perfectly corresponds to the definition of "alternative" used by policymakers and academics. Additionally, there is no standard among the states for categorizing different types of licenses (e.g., an "emergency license" in one state might be equivalent to "not licensed in subject" in another), making comparisons between traditionally and alternatively licensed teachers very challenging.

NELS data do not include information on when and where teachers received their credentials, making it impossible to link state licensure policies to particular teachers. Finally, in most cases the small sample size of teachers in any one state means that statistical estimates of state effects (e.g., of a state's licensure policies) are likely to be imprecise.

The Schools and Staffing Survey is a large comprehensive survey with detailed information on teacher attributes, including licensure. Its data have allowed researchers to identify the attributes of teachers entering the profession through alternative routes as opposed to traditional ones. Unfortunately, SASS lacks information on student outcomes, making it impossible to determine the relationship between licensure and student achievement— the relationship of most interest to many policymakers. Furthermore, SASS data include information on school personnel but not on aspiring teachers, so it cannot be used to infer how licensure policies influence those who might think of becoming teachers.

One can learn more about who chooses to teach by examining the Baccalaureate and Beyond Longitudinal Study, a sample of individuals who graduated from college in academic year 1992–1993 and subsequently entered the labor market. However, like NELS, the sample sizes are relatively small for any single state and, like SASS, there is no direct link to students. Thus, B&B is not very useful for inferring how state policies affect career decisions, or for any student outcome analyses.

Discussion of licensure is further complicated by the fact that the quality and content of teacher-training programs vary greatly. Much of the variation in teacher preparation is due to differing educational philosophies at the institutional level, which means researchers who wish to study the effectiveness of particular types of teacher preparation must worry not only about interstate variation in policies, but also about intrastate variation in training models.[47]

Despite the difficulties associated with making comparisons between traditionally and alternatively licensed individuals and the study of licensure in general, there is still much we can learn. With the right type of data and properly designed studies, we can infer some information based on variations in existing policies. Furthermore, the No Child Left Behind (NCLB) Act's data collection requirements may provide new opportunities for gathering the type of data researchers currently lack. A crucial data element is the ability to link teachers to their students and track them both over time; as states begin to test students in grades three through eight and track them in order to comply with NCLB, at least some of these necessary data will become available.

For certain types of studies, information available in some state databases is already superior to that found in comparable national databases. North Carolina's dataset, for instance, includes some information about students' backgrounds (socio-economic status, special education status, etc.) and also makes it possible to link students to their teachers. Such a link permits researchers to use sophisticated statistical models to compare traditionally licensed teachers to those with alternative licenses and to judge the relative effectiveness of these teachers based on how well their students perform.[48] The major advantage of using a state dataset over a national survey is that the former's large samples of students and teachers are all subject to the same set of state policies, with no ambiguity about what different licensure categories mean.[49]

Studies of alternative versus traditional licensure *within* states allow for some assessment of the relative effectiveness of alternatively licensed individuals under a particular set of state policies. Given the considerable variation in curricular emphasis and quality among teacher licensing programs, analysis could be taken further were it possible to obtain information about the institution where teachers received their degree. In theory, this would allow for research on the quality of teacher-training institutions and provide better information about the effectiveness of different pedagogical approaches.

When conducting studies that compare student outcomes under teachers with different backgrounds, it is essential to consider the relevant alternatives for local school systems. School districts and individual schools differ in their needs for particular teaching skills and their abilities to attract and retain teachers. Many school systems, primarily suburban systems serving more advantaged students, have far more applicants than teaching slots and might not alter their hiring decisions if licensure requirements were relaxed. Others, primarily urban systems serving more disadvantaged students, report enormous difficulty attracting enough teachers to meet their teaching needs, and they likely would use the greater hiring flexibility that an alternative licensure option would provide.

Unattractive salary levels and working conditions force many systems to staff some positions with long-term substitutes, even under licensure requirements strengthened by the closure of alternative "loopholes." The relevant question for these systems may not be whether to hire a traditionally *versus* alternatively licensed teacher; instead, it might be whether to hire teachers with alternative licenses or to staff positions with long-term substitutes.[50] It is conceivable for alternatively licensed teachers to be of lower quality than those with traditional licensure, but at the same time to have alternative licensure policies that benefit disadvantaged school systems.

Researchers might assess the relevant alternatives that school systems face by studying school systems in similar labor markets but in different states with different licensure policies, in order to analyze the efficacy of systems' processes for selecting teachers. This may be addressed to some degree by analyzing data on new graduates and looking at the likelihood that individuals with particular characteristics are hired and what salaries they are offered.[51] Unfortunately, this method is less than ideal, since teacher quality is at best weakly correlated with easily observable teacher characteristics, and information on the candidates that school systems did not hire is not available.[52] In order to address questions of which teachers from an applicant pool are hired by school systems, one would ideally have information not only on who is hired, but also on applicants who are not hired. To my knowledge, such data are not available.

A final and very important issue for policymakers is how the existence of alternative licensure and licensure requirements in general affect the public's interest in pursuing teaching as a career, and the characteristics of the resulting teacher applicant pool. Researchers might explore this issue by exploiting variation in states' traditional and alternative licensure policies and, more specifically, by comparing similar individuals seeking employment in similar labor markets but living in different states. This could be done using a number of large-scale national datasets and linking the data to states' licensure policies. Comparisons of hiring decisions in public schools with hiring decisions in charter and private schools may be useful in this regard, because they reflect both the types of individuals who may wish to teach without having to satisfy licensure requirements and the hiring preferences of school officials in a more relaxed regulatory environment.[53]

## CONCLUSIONS

Ultimately, it is hoped, licensure policies lead to a high-quality work force and, at the very least, help ensure that teachers at the bottom of the quality distribution do not find their way into the classroom. The danger with any regulation not well conceived is that it may do more harm than good. The primary concern with teacher licensure policies is that they may result in false positives (letting in undesirable teachers) and false negatives (screening out suitable teachers). Additionally, regulations may exclude good teachers indirectly by discouraging individuals who would be effective teachers from considering the teaching profession. We do not yet know much about some of these issues.

Studying the ramifications of traditional and alternative licensure policies is difficult because few existing datasets can support methodologically rigorous research on this issue. Sadly, much of the debate and rhetoric surrounding licensure issues provide more heat than light, and may in fact be counterproductive by encouraging a focus on "traditional" *versus* "alternative," rather than more thoughtful reflection on what specific policies might encourage individuals who would make high-quality teachers to enter the teacher labor market.

Fortunately, data do exist that offer the opportunity to answer questions that would help inform sound licensure policies. The importance of teachers' influence on student outcomes and the likely wave of teacher retirements in the near future mean that now the right time to learn what licensure policies would be most effective for the next generation of teachers and students.

Teacher quality may well take significant time and investment to develop. This investment can occur up front in the form of preservice training, or over time in the form of in-service development. Issues of licensure focus on the satisfaction of preservice requirements, but teacher quality will ultimately depend on a broad range of policies that affect teachers throughout their careers. Policy deliberations that focus on reconceptualizing licensure must also consider mentoring and training opportunities, to ensure that both work in tandem to produce quality teachers.

## CHAPTER 4

# Assessing Traditional Teacher Preparation

## Evidence from a Survey of Graduate and Undergraduate Programs

*David L. Leal*

### INTRODUCTION

Research shows that the most important influence on a child's educational success, after family background and involvement, is the teacher. Given the No Child Left Behind (NCLB) Act's mandates for teacher quality, the need to investigate the dynamics of teacher preparation is more pressing than ever.

There are three points where schools, colleges, and departments of education (collectively, SCDEs) can help ensure that qualified individuals become K–12 teachers. The first is by maintaining high standards in the admission decision, the second is through effective instruction, and the third is by weeding out teacher candidates who are perceived as likely to fail in the classroom. More attention has been paid to the first two points than to the third. The project presented here is an effort to contribute to our understanding of the first and third points.[1]

This paper reports an investigation into the standards of admission, the academic performance of students, and the instructional philosophies of both graduate and undergraduate programs of teacher education. In particular, this paper's focus is whether such programs serve to "weed out" inadequate teacher candidates or, instead, allow the candidates themselves and K–12 schools to decide if they are fit to teach.

The contemporary system for bringing teachers into public school class-rooms depends largely on the traditional licensure approach. Ideally, this re-quires SCDEs to teach essential skills and knowledge and to screen out un-suitable candidates before they reach the public schools. The latter function is particularly important because some proponents of traditional teacher preparation argue that only in the context of student teaching and campus-based preparation can we judge the aptitude of candidates for classroom work. This paper is the first effort to empirically assess whether and to what degree SCDEs exercise quality control at the point of admission and before graduation, particularly at the student teaching stage.

One of the difficulties in evaluating the contribution of teacher-prepara-tion programs is a lack of data. Only limited information is currently avail-able, such as the pass rates for state licensing exams, the SAT and GRE scores of entering education students, and the comparative GPAs of education and non-education students.

There are few systematic and national studies, however, of the educa-tional philosophies of SCDEs on larger questions. For instance, is the proper role of an SCDE to set high admission standards that lead to many rejected applications, or to focus on teaching those who wish to work in the class-room? Should the responsibility of screening out inadequate teachers be left to school districts? What is the nature of admissions criteria to teacher-prep-aration programs? What do SCDE leaders themselves say about the aca-demic quality of their students in terms of grades and test scores? Do under-graduate and graduate programs provide different answers to these questions?

The basis of this paper is a confidential survey conducted of the leaders of the largest SCDEs in the United States. The survey instrument is discussed in detail in the next section. We received 122 completed questionnaires from a wide range of undergraduate and graduate educational institutions. The re-sponse rate was approximately 28 percent for the former and 17 percent for the latter. While this rate is lower than ideal, it is reasonable in light of the somewhat controversial questions, the completely voluntary nature of the effort, and the busy schedules of those surveyed.

While the survey responses are by no means the final word on this com-plex topic, they provide new and useful data on contemporary teacher edu-cation. This study is therefore best seen as an initial effort to break ground in a subject area that has received little quantitative attention. Future stud-ies, it is hoped, will expand on this effort and explore more deeply the dy-namics of quality control in teacher preparation programs.

## THE SURVEYS

In order to better understand how the teachers of tomorrow are prepared for the classroom, I mailed a questionnaire in early August 2003 to approximately 275 of the largest programs (in terms of students graduated) of both undergraduate and graduate SCDEs. Approximately 550 surveys were therefore mailed to the deans, chairs, and directors of such programs.

In order to facilitate responses, the surveys were not mailed to individuals by name but to the holder of the position. For instance, the first line in the address of a typical letter would read "Dean, Graduate School of Education" instead of "Dr. Roberto Chavez, Dean of the Graduate School of Education." The questionnaire, as well as the accompanying letter, also stated clearly that the identities of all respondents would be completely confidential.

Each mailer contained four pieces: a cover letter explaining the purpose of the questionnaire, a one-page description of the conference at which the paper would be presented, a stamped self-addressed envelope, and the questionnaire itself. The cover letters, questionnaires, and conference description can be found on the book's website [OK?].

I received seventy-six undergraduate questionnaires and forty-six graduate questionnaires (response rates of approximately 28% and 17%, respectively). While a higher response rate would have been desirable, there was no easy way to increase cooperation. School officials were under no obligation to answer the survey. These individuals are typically busy, and some may have been concerned about confidentiality. In addition, some administrators may have felt that the American Enterprise Institute's cosponsorship of the conference indicated a research project at odds with their own ideological perspectives. Nevertheless, I decided that full disclosure about the conference was necessary.

In addition, the nature of the questions may have discouraged responses from those programs that did not perform well according to admission and performance measures. Programs with minimal entry requirements that make little attempt to weed out underperforming students, for example, may have felt little incentive to reveal these facts to researchers.

There is, therefore, the possibility of sample bias, meaning that the people responding to the survey could hold fundamentally different opinions about the questions from those who did not respond. However, this would be a concern even if the response rate were much higher. For instance, if 80 percent of education schools were opposed to the aggressive weeding out of inadequate students and 20 percent were in favor of doing so, an 80 percent response rate would be problematic if the respondents consisted entirely of members of the former group.

Nevertheless, the survey is still useful because few scholars have systematically examined the opinions of a national sample of education schools on student admission and teacher preparation issues. Any dataset containing over 120 such observations is a unique research resource, and at the very least it stands as a baseline of comparison for future studies. It is hoped this study will encourage other academics, and perhaps government agencies such as the U.S. Department of Education, to pursue these important questions.

The questions were organized into three sections in each questionnaire: "Your Program," "Characteristics of Students," and "Student Teaching (The Practicum)." The order of the questions was chosen to maximize the response rate. "Your Program" questions are factual and less controversial and therefore best to include at the beginning. The "Student Teaching" questions are more controversial, as they ask about issues such as the weeding out of inadequate students. These questions were therefore placed last, as their placement at the beginning might deter the respondents. The hope was that respondents would be encouraged to start the survey by the easy, factual questions at the beginning and that a certain momentum would carry them through the more controversial questions.

The questions asked in the three sections vary somewhat on the undergraduate and graduate surveys, but only in minor ways. The first section asked about the admission requirements to the program or major. For example, does the program have a minimum GPA requirement or require interviews for admission? The second section asked about the performance of students in the degree program. Questions included what percentage of students graduate, and how student grades in education classes compare with student grades in non-education classes.

Third, the questionnaire asked about the student teaching (practicum) component of the program. What are the completion rates, for example, and when students withdrew, who made the final decision? A number of questions also ask about the philosophy of the program concerning the sensitive issue of weeding out students who might not make effective teachers. There is little information in the literature about this aspect of the teacher-preparation experience, and these questions provide the first systematic evidence of how education schools define their role.

Some respondents indicated either suspicion of or enthusiasm for the project through marginal notes, as well as in email and voice-mail messages. Negative comments were more common than positive. A few seem to have assumed that the project had a specific normative orientation. According to one respondent, "I have the feeling you already know the answers you want to get – this survey is not very well-designed, in my view." Another person wrote, "I trust this survey won't be the last word. I can just hear the presentations." This person likely felt that the conference would be an exercise in what some call "teacher bashing."

Some respondents, however, indicated that they had been thinking about the issues raised by the questionnaire. Others went further and stated that their program had changed in recent years in order to raise the quality of the student body and the value of their teacher-preparation program. A few others more generally noted their awareness that quality and standards were important concerns that schools of education could not ignore. Some wrote words of encouragement or expressed an interest in attending the conference.

A few comments were made in response to the final question, in which I asked respondents whether there were any questions I should have asked but did not, and what their answers might have been. These comments generally indicated that the goal of increasing the effectiveness of teacher-preparation programs had been noted and pursued. One person wrote, "Is your program more effective now than it was 10 years ago? Very much so." Another respondent wrote in this section, "And I DO think that some schools of education need more rigor, but let's not eliminate those, like us, that do!"

## FINDINGS

### Your Program

*Undergraduate*

The first question on the survey for undergraduate programs was: "Are there any criteria for admission to the Education major beyond admission to the overall university?" Respondents were asked to check yes or no; if they checked yes, they were asked to list the requirements.

Most programs (91%) indicated some type of extra admissions criteria, although they vary widely and are not easy to assess systematically. Some require the taking of standardized tests, including Praxis, various state exams, the ACT, and PPST; others noted a minimum score required for admission to their college or program. Some reported minimum GPAs in other college courses that ranged from 2.0 to 3.0, with most requirements around 2.5.

Other requirements included completion of all or a specific number of university general education requirements; criminal background checks on applicants; the creation of a portfolio; taking at least one English and one math class; taking another combination of specific classes; a personal statement; a writing sample from a general education class; a speech and hearing test; evidence of technological literacy; or prior experience working with children or youth. One school reported extra requirements only for transfer students.

Taken together, this wide range of requirements suggests the need for more research on best practices in this area. Is there any evidence that any one of these specific criteria is associated with better teacher candidates, and therefore better teachers?

The next set of questions inquires about the standards used in the admissions process. Almost all programs (99%) reported a minimum GPA requirement for admission into the teacher-preparation program. A lower figure (87%) reported a requirement for a minimum standardized test score, such as the SAT or ACT.

The next questions asked whether recommendations and interviews were required as part of the application process. Approximately 68 percent of programs reported that recommendations were necessary, and interviews were required at 43 percent of schools. Further research might be usefully done about the nature of the recommendations, specifically about what admissions committees look for in the letters. Do the letters typically address the potential of the applicant to teach, for example, or do they just discuss the applicant's academic record as an undergraduate? A similar effort might be made to understand the dynamics of the interview process, specifically what statements the committees believe indicate positive or negative potential for teaching.

The survey also asked in what year students are allowed to enter the teacher preparation program. The average answer is 2.4, which suggests that the typical program allows for entry between the sophomore and junior year. An important question is whether there are benefits for earlier entry. Some might suggest that experience in the classroom cannot begin too soon, while others could argue that students should first take a number of pedagogical and methodological classes.

*Graduate*

The first questions ask about the admission of students into the graduate program. We see that the average program admits approximately 78 percent of all students. This is far from qualifying as highly selective, but it does not indicate that education programs are accepting all comers. Almost one-quarter of all applicants are rejected, although the meaning of this figure depends upon the quality of the applicant pool. An education school that is part of an elite educational institution might admit three-quarters of applicants and nevertheless field a competent class. This may not necessarily be the case for small, regional institutions that may field fewer strong applicants. Nevertheless, this figure should give pause to anyone who assumes that SCDEs have open admissions and are unwilling to conduct any sorting or assessment at this initial stage.

The remaining four questions in this section were also asked in the undergraduate questionnaire. The respondents reported that 98 percent of programs have a minimum GPA,[2] 62 percent require some minimum score on a standardized test,[3] 85 percent ask for personal recommendations for entry into the program, and 59 percent require interviews.

The requirements for admission to a graduate program are therefore both more and less demanding than those for undergraduate programs. It would seem that undergraduate programs are more focused on test scores, while graduate programs are more likely to incorporate interviews and personal recommendations. Researchers might ask whether these differences are based on research into the teacher-preparation process, or whether they have evolved for practical reasons (undergraduates likely have fewer life and classroom experiences and, therefore, fewer potential writers of relevant letters of recommendation) or some other reason.

### Characteristics of Students in the Teacher-Training[4] *Program*

*Undergraduate*

Fifty programs provided data on the average SAT or ACT scores of students. The average score was 996 for the former and 21 for the latter. The number of responses for each is too low to draw any clear conclusions, however.

Seventy-six percent of students who declare an education major graduate with that degree. This indicates that just over one-fourth did not finish, but we cannot conclude from this that programs are weeding people out. Large numbers of undergraduate students drop out every year, often for financial or other reasons that are unrelated to the policies of their major. One would need to compare the dropout rates of education majors versus students with declared majors in other subjects. Nevertheless, the 76 percent figure indicates that, for whatever reason, many of those who intend to become teachers do not complete the first hurdle. Coincidentally, this percentage is similar to the average rate of admissions for graduate education programs (78%).

The questionnaire asked respondents to estimate student GPAs in education and non-education classes. The former is generally higher than the latter, although grades were reported as equal in nine cases, and education grades were reported as lower in two cases. The reported education GPA was 3.1, while the average non-education GPA was 2.8. Some respondents indicated that comparisons were not possible because students did not take any non-education classes. For the question that asked respondents to compare the GPAs of their students in education and non-education classes, on a 1 (lower) to 3 (higher) scale, the respondents provided an average answer of 2.7.

There are varying ways to interpret these results. One respondent noted this point, writing in the margins of the questionnaire that researchers are too quick to draw negative conclusions and rarely look for alternative explanations.[5] While the surface evidence is that education classes are less demanding, it might be useful to compare the grades received by students in their major and nonmajor classes in different departments and schools in universities. In addition, future studies would be well advised to examine the content of the classes taken by students, not only the grades received. Would an A average in tangential courses reflect better preparation of students for the classroom than a C average in relevant coursework?

The next question asked about the percentage of students who passed the state certification exam. The pass rate for state certification exams was high (although some programs reported that their state had no certification exam), as 95 percent of undergraduates reportedly passed the exam. This suggests that either teacher candidates are remarkably well prepared for the classroom or that the exams are remarkably easy. Such high pass rates are well known by observers, however, and this survey item serves as confirmation.

These exams are difficult to compare with those required by other professional occupations, notably law and medicine. Similar pass rates, for instance, could have very different meanings. A high pass rate could reflect either difficult exams and highly qualified applicants, or easy tests and more modestly qualified applicants.

Nevertheless, the 2002 overall pass rate for state bar examinations was 63 percent,[6] which is significantly lower than the corresponding figure for state education licensing exams. Education schools have sometimes aspired to professional status, and teachers have often sought recognition by society as professionals, but these data may help explain why such recognition has not always been received.

Lastly, I inquired about the jobs taken by graduating students. The overwhelmingly popular choice was public school teacher (75%), followed by private school teacher (9%). This suggests that almost all the people in teacher-preparation programs enter the classroom after graduation, so the overall statistics reported in this paper about student achievement largely apply to those who become teachers. If a much larger percentage were headed for non-education jobs, then we might wonder how the statistics differentially applied to teachers and nonteachers.

*Graduate*

In addition to the question from the first section about whether test scores are required, we asked about the average GRE scores of students in the teacher-preparation program. Of those programs that responded to this question (only 12), the average score was 1,079. Given the low response, in part explained by the lack of GRE requirements, we should not put too much faith in this figure. In addition, this average score likely includes only the verbal and math scores of the GRE and not the analytical score. If all three were included, it would suggest that education students average about 360 on each section, which would be very low.

For the comparative grade point average questions, keep in mind that the respondents from undergraduate programs indicated a 0.3 difference (3.1 versus 2.8). For graduate programs, we found approximately a 0.2 difference (3.1 in education courses, 2.9 in other courses). For the comparative GPA question, the respondents provided an average answer of 2.4.

We also asked about the percentage of graduate education students who passed the state certification exam. The average reported pass rate was just over 96 percent, which indicates that these exams prevent very few people from entering the teaching profession. Some respondents noted in the margins that they reported the average pass rate for each sitting, but that failing students would retake the exam and all would eventually pass. Others noted that passing the exam is a requirement for graduation, and others reported that no such exam existed in their state. This again indicates either a remarkable level of preparation or a lack of standards in the exam.

## Student Teaching (The Practicum)

The undergraduate and graduate answers to the practicum questions are discussed together in this section. As it is important to reproduce the wording of some of the questions, reporting the combined results reduces repetition.

*Program Completion*

First, we inquired about the percentage of students who successfully completed the student teaching experience. While the practicum is intended to impart knowledge and experience that will make the candidate more effective in the classroom, it might also weed out those candidates who exhibit poor potential for teaching. It is not easy to determine who will make a good teacher from test scores and other application materials. Watching candidates in front of a classroom over time, however, should arguably provide educators and professors with some indication of their ability. If this weeding out does not take place, then there is one less argument in favor of traditional teacher education over alternative certification plans.

Respondents indicated that almost all who began the student teaching (practicum) phase successfully completed it. The undergraduate figure was 95 percent, and only one program reported a pass rate below 90 percent. For graduate programs, the respondents replied that 96 percent of candidates completed the program. Only six programs reported a rate below 95 percent.

There are two explanations for why so many student teachers complete the practicum. The first is that the students who enter the program are well prepared, either through coursework or a rigorous screening of candidates. Some respondents noted in the margins that the latter was the case. According to one, "We have extremely high admission standards. The students who are admitted to the program are bright, articulate, and committed to teaching. We have little/no need to weed out unfit candidates."

Others agreed that it is too late to sort candidates at the student teaching stage, and that decisions about ability must be made sooner. According to one person, "Our students DO NOT get to that point [being weeded out] because of our evaluations of pre-student teaching experiences . . . by the time a candidate reaches the student teacher stage, we have evidence of not only their content knowledge but of the strength of their pedagogy." Another indicated, "We identify and screen them out BEFORE they are allowed to student teach." One person wrote, "We prefer to be rigorous upon admission and then work with students to become effective teachers."

The second possibility is that the program is not very rigorous. Some programs may mistakenly believe that unskilled student teachers are in fact adequate to the task. Some supervisors may believe it is not their job to exclude those who want to teach from the classroom. Others may hope that poor performers will eventually improve their skills, perhaps through later on-the-job experience. Another possible explanation is that a teacher shortage encourages education schools to graduate almost all their students.

It is not possible to be certain which factor is at work, and it is possible that both could be at work in different programs. These marginal comments suggest that teacher-preparation programs may be sensitive to these issues and are taking steps at an early point to deter those without aptitude.

To better understand whether education programs weed out those with little potential, we asked respondents to indicate why people did not complete the student teaching phase over the last few years. There were three options: voluntary withdrawal, withdrawal "due to the judgment of mentor teachers, education school professors, or other supervisory personnel," and "other reasons."

The results indicate that approximately 40 percent of undergraduate students withdrew voluntarily, 48 percent withdrew due to the judgment of those who supervised the programs, and 10 percent withdrew for other reasons.[7] The respective graduate figures were 40 percent, 47 percent, and 11 percent. One caveat is that some respondents wrote in the margins that it was difficult to assign percentages because only a small number of candidates failed to complete the program in recent years. While almost half of such candidates therefore withdrew because of supervisory evaluations, it is important to keep in mind that only a very few withdrew for any reason.

Lastly, we asked programs what percentage of teacher candidates were engaged in student teaching during the previous (2002–2003) academic year. A low percentage of students occupied with such training suggests that education schools may not be adequately preparing students for the classroom. Part of the argument for lengthy teacher-preparation programs is that they impart knowledge and experience that would be difficult to replicate in other settings, such as a summer session in an alternate certification program designed to move individuals into the classroom with only minimum preparation. An important question, therefore, is how much practical classroom experience are candidates receiving?

We did not assess the value of such experience or whether alternative pedagogies might be equally effective. Nor did we ask how many hours constituted completion of student teaching. A program might indicate that 100 percent of students were involved in this component, but students might not spend much time in the classroom, and the experience might not be guided by best practices.

The respondents indicated that 56 percent of graduate teacher candidates and 43 percent of undergraduate candidates were so engaged. Whether this is too high or too low a figure is debatable, but at least it indicates that about half of potential teachers spent some time in K–12 classrooms in the previous year.

*Evaluative Questions*

Respondents were asked to indicate how much their student teachers love teaching. If programs believe that their candidates love to teach, this might help explain why so few are asked to leave the program. Love of teaching is not necessarily correlated with the ability to teach, but a certain level of enthusiasm and excitement is useful for this demanding career. On a one-to-four scale (one indicating the least agreement, four indicating the most agreement), the average level of agreement was 3.8 for undergraduate and 3.7 for graduate programs, and no school gave an evaluation lower than 3.0. This suggests that programs see almost all of their students as very devoted to becoming teachers.

We also inquired about the commitment of programs to training teachers from diverse backgrounds. The average answer was 3.8 for both types of programs, which indicates that almost all expressed the highest level of enthusiasm for this goal. Some respondents noted in the margins that their support of this goal was somewhat hypothetical, insofar as their institutions were located in states and regions of only limited diversity, and their programs consequently did not have a very diverse student body.

The survey then asked the respondents to indicate their agreement or disagreement with several statements that directly involve the issue of weeding out inadequate student teachers. As mentioned previously, these questions were placed at the end of the survey because of their potential for controversy. Respondents might have reacted defensively if they were placed at the beginning of the survey, and my hope was that people who had already completed the less controversial first two segments of the questionnaire would be motivated to finish the third segment.

One person may have indicated this uneasiness when he or she wrote in the margins, "These are 'somewhat' loaded questions and how you interpret the responses will be highly subjective." I agree that interpretation is key and hope the discussion in the following section does not advance too far beyond the evidence provided by the respondents.

Let us first examine two questions from the survey, reproduced below, intended to gauge the attitude of the program toward inadequate students. These statements were written to suggest a strong interest in "weeding out" inadequate students:

> "An important function of student teaching is that it permits us to identify ineffective candidates and ensure that they are not certified."

> "Our job is to determine who is equipped to teach, and we aggressively seek to deter candidates we deem unfit from becoming certified to teach."

The respondents indicated a generally high level of agreement with these statements. On the one-to-four agreement scale, the figures for the graduate programs were 3.0 and 3.3; figures for undergraduate programs were 2.6 and 3.1. It is not clear why the former gave somewhat more supportive answers than the latter, but in both cases the answers are close to 3.0. This suggests that schools of education take seriously their gatekeeping role and work to prevent inadequate candidates from reaching the classroom. This does not reflect the stereotypical view of education schools, which are rarely associated with high standards and rigor by much of the academic world (e.g., see Shen).[8] As one person wrote, while "this is very late in the program to make this decision, and it rarely happens, we do see this as a function of the experience."

Two statements worded to indicate opposition to the proactive weeding out of students were also presented. These statements are reproduced below:

"It is our job to provide training to those who wish to teach, not to deter potential teachers based on their academic performance."

"It is not always easy to be sure who will become an effective teacher. A more aggressive 'weeding out' of teacher candidates might reduce the number of future teachers while providing no guarantee that ineffective teachers are kept away from the classroom."

The level of agreement with these statements was not very high. For the first question, the average undergraduate program response was 2.1 and the average graduate response was 2.4. For the second questions, the respective average answers were 2.5 and 2.6. These answers are generally in the middle of the four-point scale, indicating a reluctance to clearly support or oppose the stated opinions. Common stereotypes of education schools might lead some to expect that respondents would strongly support students who wish to teach, regardless of ability, and would believe that weeding out students might have negative side effects. The respondents in this sample, which may or may not be representative of all SCDEs, provided mixed opinions.

Another statement asked about the use of grades and test scores as indicators of teaching potential. The use of standardized testing is dramatically growing in K–12 education due to NCLB mandates, and many in schools of education have been critical of this trend. This survey item, therefore, checks whether those who administer teacher-preparation programs believe that test scores and grades are not useful indicators of teaching potential. The statement is:

"We do not think that test scores or grade point averages are very useful in judging who will be an effective teacher."

The average level of agreement with this statement is 2.5 for undergraduate program respondents and 2.8 for graduate respondents. Common stereotypes of education programs might suggest that numerical indicators would be less favored than the case-by-case judgment of professors. Nevertheless, the respondents were on average only slightly more inclined to agree than to disagree, which suggests a middle position that gives scores and grades some legitimate standing in teacher-preparation programs.[9]

The last statement asked whether teacher preparation programs should devolve the task of weeding out to others:

> "The 'weeding out' of ineffective teachers is a task best done at the schools themselves by principals and other school leaders, not in teacher training programs such as ours."

Relatively few respondents agreed with this statement; it in fact received the lowest agreement level of any question in this section. The average rating was 1.7 by undergraduate program respondents and 1.8 by graduate respondents. Such answers are between "not very much" and "not at all," albeit closer to the former than the latter.

## CONCLUSIONS

Traditional licensure systems produce the teachers who educate the great majority of America's children. The trust placed in these systems is based on the argument that SCDEs teach essential skills and knowledge and prevent unsuitable candidates from reaching the classroom. The screening function is particularly important because many proponents of teacher education argue that only in the context of student teaching and school-based preparation can we judge the aptitude of candidates for classroom work. This paper is the first effort to assess empirically whether and to what degree SCDEs are screening out unsuitable candidates at the admissions stage and weeding out poor teaching prospects, particularly at the student teaching stage.

This survey of many of the largest graduate and undergraduate teacher-preparation programs garnered much information about the admission and training of teacher candidates. The data include details about admissions standards, the achievement of the student body in the classroom and in student teaching settings, and the views of administrators about weeding out inadequate candidates. Such questions touch on many of the key issues in the contemporary debate about traditional teacher licensure programs.

What patterns and conclusions emerge from this exercise? Let us start at the beginning of the teacher-preparation process: admissions. According to the information provided by the respondents, education programs do have admissions criteria and are slightly selective in the students they admit. For instance, the average responding graduate program accepted 78 percent of all students; all programs but two required a minimum GPA between a B and B-minus average; 62 percent required a minimum score on the GRE or some other standardized test, and large numbers required recommendations and interviews. Whether these standards are high or low is debatable, and it is unclear whether the programs that responded to the survey constitute a representative sample. Nevertheless, it cannot be claimed that traditional licensure programs admit all applicants regardless of standard indicators of academic aptitude.

A similar story is told at the undergraduate level: 76 percent of those who declare an education major eventually graduate with an education degree; 91 percent of programs indicated some type of admissions criteria beyond admission to the overall college or university; almost all have a minimum GPA and standardized test requirement; and many require recommendations or interviews.

Some concerns emerged in the section regarding characteristics of students in the teacher-training programs. We ascertained that the GPA of graduate and undergraduate education students is from 0.2 to 0.3 points higher (on the traditional zero-to-four scale) in education classes than in non-education classes. One possible explanation is that education courses are less challenging, although there are other explanations for this frequently discussed phenomenon.

We might also be concerned that the reported graduate and undergraduate pass rates on state certification exams were about 95 percent. This suggests that either the exams were unchallenging or that contemporary education students are very highly skilled. The average pass rate for state bar exams in 2002, by contrast, was 63 percent.

The student teaching (practicum) questions indicate that about 95 percent of those who begin the experience successfully complete it. As with the state exams figure, it represents either a very talented group of candidates or a relatively undemanding experience. A number of respondents wrote in the margins of the questionnaire that they prevented inadequate students from reaching this point, so that those who experienced the practicum were well prepared. To confirm this claim would require research into the proportion and the nature of those students who were dissuaded from the practicum.

Is it possible that the practicum can simultaneously be a valuable and rigorous experience and that almost all students can pass it? Education programs might argue that the knowledge learned in this setting is essential for teacher candidates yet not particularly difficult to acquire. If this is the case, some might suggest that the practicum be eliminated and this knowledge learned instead on the job in K-12 classrooms. This would shorten the teacher-preparation program and thereby provide less of a deterrent to those who want to teach but do not want to spend a large amount of time and money undergoing the traditional preparation experience. Whether the students in those K-12 classrooms would suffer educationally while their teachers learned "on the job" would depend upon how quickly this knowledge could be acquired and applied.

Respondents from both graduate and undergraduate programs reported that, of those who did not complete the practicum, just under half withdrew because of the judgment of supervisory personnel. This does indicate some willingness on the part of education programs to sift students, although this must be interpreted in light of the very few students who fail to complete the program.

The evaluation of statements about weeding out inadequate students is also revealing. On the one-to-four scale, respondents on average expressed agreement in the low 3s that "an important function of student teaching is that it permits us to identify ineffective candidates and ensure that they are not certified" and that "our job is to determine who is equipped to teach, and we aggressively seek to deter candidates we deem unfit from becoming certified to teach."

Respondents also provided only lukewarm support (in the mid-2s) for statements indicating that education programs should focus on instruction and not deterrence, and that aggressive weeding out of students might have negative consequences. In addition, respondents provided the least support (1.8 and 1.7) for the suggestion that the weeding out of students is best done at the school level by principals and other school leaders, not by teacher-preparation programs.

While there are some differences in the answers provided by graduate and undergraduate programs, they point in contradictory directions and are substantively small. Taken together, it appears that neither program is more or less inclined to weed out students along the dimensions asked by the survey.

Overall, this paper reports evidence for both sides of the debate over traditional teacher-preparation programs. Those who see low standards and general inadequacies in such programs will find some data to support their cause. Those who wish to defend the traditional path to licensure will be able to point to other data indicating that issues of quality control in the entry and training phases are not ignored. Education schools can therefore be neither roundly condemned nor enthusiastically praised. In addition, the imprecise nature of some of the questions and responses, as well as questions about how accurately the data represent the universe of large graduate and undergraduate teacher-preparation programs, should temper the impulse for simple (and probably wrong) conclusions.

This study cannot be the final word on the complicated debate over traditional teacher licensure programs. It does provide some tentative findings and points to subjects that need further research. For instance, not only should we examine the content of education courses, but we also should investigate whether the difference between GPAs in education and non-education classes is meaningful. We likewise need a better understanding of state certification exams and of the larger issue of whether such grades and exams are associated with the ability to teach. We might investigate to what extent some of the common requirements for admission to education schools, such as recommendations and interviews, help programs select those with teaching potential.

We might look more carefully at selected programs that do and do not attempt to weed out students. Are education professionals skilled at this complex and delicate task? Do the schools that hire education graduates from more selective programs report more successful experiences in the classroom? What do education students themselves think about such questions? There are many reports and dissertations still to be written, perhaps in education schools themselves, which will explicitly address issues of educational quality control.

## CHAPTER 5

# Preparing Tomorrow's Teachers

## An Analysis of Syllabi from a Sample of America's Schools of Education

*David M. Steiner with Susan D. Rozen[1]*

## INTRODUCTION

Concern about the quality of public schooling in America, rarely absent since the mid-nineteenth century, was reignited in the 1980s in the form of the landmark report *A Nation at Risk*. In the 1990s this concern was reinforced by international surveys such as the Third International Math and Science Study (TIMSS) report, which indicated that, relative to students in many other countries, American pupils do steadily worse on math and science tests as they progress through their school years. The results of America's own National Assessment of Educational Progress (NAEP) during that decade suggested that reading proficiency in the United States had barely moved in twenty years, and that while math results had marginally improved, science results had not.[2] The achievement gap between the affluent and the poor, and between white and African American children, remained stubbornly constant.[3]

Many educational policymakers have equated these poor test results with a failed education system. E.D. Hirsch, Chester E. Finn Jr., and Diane Ravitch, among others, have pointed to an educational *gestalt*, or worldview, that to their minds has seriously undermined the effectiveness of U.S.

117

schooling. They argue that America's schools have come to embrace "constructivism," an approach based loosely on the writings of John Dewey that places priority on learning-by-doing and downgrades learning through traditional forms of instruction. Teachers, these critics suggest, are putting less emphasis on teaching content and skills, and more on encouraging children to follow their natural instincts to experiment and to discover. In the current parlance, the American teacher is no longer "the sage on the stage" but the "guide on the side." Pointing to the TIMSS and NAEP results, the critics blame this pedagogical model for contributing to what they see as America's poor educational results.[4]

Are Hirsch, Finn, and Ravitch right about this? Remarkably, there is no good empirical data on what forms of education are being dispensed in America's public schools. Are high school classrooms characterized by a constructivism approach, or is most teaching done more or less traditionally, with a textbook and a lecturing teacher? We just do not know. But advocates of reform insist that schools have to produce demonstrable results based on a detailed curriculum and high-stakes tests, through which and by which children will acquire and demonstrate their knowledge. In the last decade, individual states have responded, taking on the task of setting standards for what students should know, for embedding those standards in assessments, and for using test results to hold schools accountable for their performance.

Recently, the federal government provided the capstone to this effort with the No Child Left Behind Act, which limits federal funds for educational reforms explicitly to states that have accountability programs in place. Preparation of teachers was clearly a critical issue in these efforts at national educational reform. As Secretary of Education Richard Riley put it in 1999, "We can no longer fiddle around the edges of how we recruit, prepare, retain, and regard America's teachers."[5] The tone of impatience is clear. But was he right? This chapter is concerned with the preparation of teachers and offers a fresh perspective on the content of that preparation.

## TEACHING THE TEACHERS: SCHOOLS OF EDUCATION IN CONTEXT

The process by which the majority of U.S. schoolteachers enter the classroom is neither simple nor uniform.[6] Some schools of education require all entering students to have passed an introductory-level academic skills test before they can be admitted, while in others students take that test during or at the end of their programs. In certain cases students who want to become teachers start educational coursework in a school of education as soon as they enter an undergraduate institution; in others they complete up to two years of general or liberal arts coursework, then apply for admission into the teacher-education program, often with the condition that they have achieved a certain GPA. In either case, students may be able to complete their baccalaureate degree in education in four years. In other schools, students enroll in a full four-year degree program and then complete a fifth year of a master's in teaching program in education studies, or qualify for the teacher certification credential without fulfilling all requirements for the master's. Alternatively, students with bachelor's degrees who later decide they would like to become teachers enter one- or two-year master's programs, whose entry requirements vary from program to program. The last few years have seen the steady growth of the numbers of aspiring teachers who enter the profession through alternative routes to certification.

How might one examine the quality of that process of preparing America's teachers? The great majority of public school teachers either pass though a school of education, or through alternative certification programs, most of which involve coursework taught by school of education faculty. Most states now rely on the National Council for the Accreditation of Teacher Education (NCATE), a private organization, to evaluate and accredit their schools of education, and require the graduates to take such tests as the Praxis before they are certified to teach.[7]

If we could determine which schools of education are most effective in producing good teachers, we could perhaps model programs after those, and put pressure on the weaker ones to improve. Has NCATE done this work for us?[8] They currently accredit some 500 out of the 1,500 schools of education: are these 500 the good ones? NCATE emphasizes that its review and accreditation process now embraces the language of research-based, accountable education reform:

- "NCATE is working ... to ensure that accreditation, licensing, and advanced certification standards are compatible, and together form a coherent system."[9] Furthermore, NCATE-certified programs ensure the "alignment of instruction and curriculum with professional, state, and institutional standards."[10]
- NCATE embraces the use of evidenced-based knowledge about pedagogy: NCATE- certified schools require teachers to "understand the importance of using research in teaching and other professional roles."[11]
- NCATE calls for measurable results. In its assessment of schools of education it asks; "Have the candidates . . . demonstrated their knowledge and skills in measurable ways?"[12]

- NCATE claims that "the profession has reached a consensus about the knowledge and skills a teacher needs to help P-12 students learn. That consensus forms the basis for NCATE standards."[13]
- NCATE points to a major study suggesting that teachers who graduate from NCATE- certified schools of education become more effective teachers—measured by student NAEP results—than their peers from noncertified institutions.[14]

However, there are questions about how effective NCATE certification is as a guarantor of effective teacher-preparation programs. In 1998, the state of Massachusetts first administered its test of teacher competence. The pass rate of the graduates of NCATE- certified schools of education varied from 35 percent to well over 70 percent. A close review of the most current NCATE regulations suggests that the organization still continues to resist efforts to bring measurable results to the education of teachers. To give one example: "If a program does not meet the state cut-off score on licensing examinations, the unit must provide other convincing evidence that the unit meets the standard."[15] In the words of one critic, "NCATE considers teachers to be well prepared when they understand, use, and believe in the pedagogical concepts that the teacher-training program has been prescribing for years."[16] Some of the most competitive and influential schools of education in the United States, including those at Harvard, the University of Michigan at Ann Arbor, the University of Texas at Austin, the University of Wisconsin-Madison, and Indiana University, are by choice not NCATE certified. In short, the question of whether NCATE approval of a school of education is an adequate measure of performance is unresolved.

## REVIEW AND ASSESSMENT OF SCHOOLS OF EDUCATION

Data collected about teacher preparation should describe specific features of the content and quality, not merely counts of courses and vague terms.... We need better analytic and descriptive tools for characterizing teacher preparation programs.[17]

How might one distinguish a strong school of education from a weak one? At first glance, the answer might seem obvious: a good education school produces a higher proportion of good teachers in its graduating class than a poor one. The problem is that we know very little about which programs are good ones, to say nothing about why one school is stronger or weaker than the next.[18] A review of the available research shows that we lack studies that track the relationship between the school of education a teacher attends and how well their students perform on achievement measures when these measures are carefully controlled for the variety of conditions in which teachers work.[19]

## How Did We Conduct the Research?

In preparation for this study, we first reviewed major research papers on teacher preparation in the United States. Such papers either embody original research or are review papers that gather together the evidence from multiple original studies. The research reviews are themselves subject to rejoinders from scholars who do not accept the author's interpretations and/or selection of original studies. Given the scope of our work, we reviewed the major research review papers and their rejoinders of the last four years that were known to us: Allen (2000), Darling-Hammond (1999, 2001), Goldfaber and Brewer (2001), Walsh (2001, 2001a), Wenglinsky (2000), Whitehurst (2002), Wilson, Floden and Ferrini-Mundy (2001), and Wilson and Floden (2002).[20] Where we judged the original research studies to be immediately relevant to our study, we went back to review them ourselves (Goldfaber & Brewer, 2000; Koppich & Merseth, 2000).[21] Because we were about to examine school of education course syllabi, we also reviewed studies that had attempted to examine what was being taught in schools of education (Darling-Hammond et al., 2002;[22] Howey & Zimpher, 1989; Smagorinsky & Whiting, 1995; Grossman & Richert, 1988).[23] Of these studies, only Smagorinsky and Whiting actually reviewed a collection of syllabi, all in the field of teaching English.

We undertook a cross-analysis of this research, noting the conclusions that were most commonly shared between them. Our review suggests strong evidence that teachers who graduate from more selective schools and/or have higher verbal ability have the greatest positive impact on student achievement. Subject-matter competence is also important. Unfortunately, little else can be reliably concluded from the research.[24]

Our second step was to focus on the evidence generated by national (NAEP) and international (PISA) assessments about teaching methods that have a track record of raising student performance.[25] Our consideration of how to teach reading is also based on a number of research findings referenced in that section of our paper. Finally, we took into account research about particular teaching methods and curricula, such as Direct Instruction, which have produced evidence of strongly positive effects on student learning.[26]

From this literature review, we infer some useful information about what schools of education could do to prepare effective teachers. We note, however, that relying on evidence from national and international assessments will not satisfy teacher educators who are skeptical of using standardized student achievement measures as evidence of teaching effectiveness.

As our third step, we conducted a review of syllabi and program descriptions from a sample of sixteen schools of education across the United States to examine what professors in these schools were teaching. There are many potentially informative ways to analyze schools of education: one could employ videotaping, interviews, and longitudinal analysis of the student teachers' future teaching records. The difficulties with these approaches is that often they rest on small samples, that they involve the large-scale aggregation of data with all the possibility for error that such a methodology can produce, or that they depend on data about value added by teachers to their students' learning that is still rare and hard to access. We were seeking a systematic and detailed view of what future teachers are being taught as part of their preparation for initial certification. Focusing on syllabi gave us a window into this domain. When professors select the books and articles they will require their students to read, write course requirements, and outline their assessments, we believe they are engaged in a serious effort to structure the learning experience of their students. Syllabi vary in their level of detail, but we believe they embody important evidence about what will be taught.[27]

We employed a three-step methodology. First, we selected our sample of education schools. Next, we defined our focus on crucial domains of teacher preparation. Finally, we analyzed the required course syllabi within those programs.

We reviewed syllabi from schools we selected from the top-rated institutions in the 2004 edition of *U.S. News & World Report*. We chose those institutions that had one or more top-15 ratings in three categories: elementary, secondary, and overall. Then we selected from this group a geographically diverse set of schools. We focused on programs in "elite" schools of education, not only because of their ratings, but also because we wanted to start our research in this area with professionally well-regarded institutions where professors conduct research that influences the profession as a whole (thus the inclusion of the Harvard undergraduate program, despite the fact that it prepares only a few elementary and secondary classroom teachers). We also selected a sample group that varied in program size: the student enrollments in the schools of education we selected range from more than 5,000 to fewer than 400. We then expanded our study to include two schools that were not ranked highly by *U.S. News & World Report* to examine, even in a very small sample, whether the coursework and readings were markedly different from those of elite schools. We selected the universities of Georgia, Illinois at Urbana-Champaign, Indiana, Maryland, Michigan, Texas, Virginia, and Wisconsin, together with Columbia University, Eastern Michigan University, Harvard University, Michigan State University, Penn State University, Sonoma State University, Stanford University, and UCLA. (Details of the schools and programs we reviewed are to be found in Appendix A.)

Within the teacher-preparation programs these schools offer, we focused our attention on initial certification programs and, within those programs, on the professional sequence required for certification. As a result, we concentrated on undergraduate programs, with the exception of those universities in states (e.g., California) that require certification programs to be completed at the postbaccalaureate level. In certain universities where the traditional four-year undergraduate certification program has been expanded to a five-year program, it was the five-year program that we reviewed (e.g., Michigan State University). Where a program offered both graduate and undergraduate certification programs, we chose the undergraduate program. We chose courses that were part of the professional sequence because these courses are specifically designed to prepare prospective teachers for teaching. We did not include in our review courses that were part of the general education requirements or courses that were specific to majors (content courses).

We analyzed syllabi in the domains of Educational Foundations, Reading, and General Methods that, as we will describe below, typically include a practicum teaching experience. We chose these domains because they form the heart of the educational mission.[28] If proponents of schools of education are right about the crucial importance of such schools, we would expect to find evidence here of the unique and essential pedagogical and professional skills that such schools provide.

Analyzing the course catalog from each university, we determined which courses in the professional sequence were required within the domains we were reviewing. Then we conducted an analysis of the syllabi for those courses. For example, at Eastern Michigan we found that students who were majoring in either elementary or secondary education had to take the same foundation courses that fell within the areas we were analyzing: Schools in a Multicultural Society and Human Development and Learning. In reading, students were required to take two courses at the elementary level or one at the secondary level; in methods, they were required to take one elementary methods course or one secondary methods course, and both elementary and secondary majors took the same assessment course and three field-placement courses. Thus, in our judgment, a full review of Eastern Michigan's program required us to review eleven syllabi for the required pedagogical courses in Foundations, Reading, and Methods that all elementary or secondary education majors had to take to become certified.

We employed the same approach to each of the schools we analyzed. Because in some cases we could not acquire a full set of the course syllabi in the domain under analysis, we did not include those syllabi or that domain in our formal findings.[29]

We gathered syllabi from a number of sources, including professors, education school administrators, and the Internet. In total, we reviewed 165 course syllabi that fell within our chosen criteria. Of these, forty-five were in the area of foundations of education, sixty-one in reading, and fifty-nine in general methods and/or practicum. For each of the three domains, we detail below how many university programs we reviewed and the graduate-undergraduate program breakdown.[30]

Our reviews took place in two stages. First, we set forth standards for what would, in our judgment, constitute a strong program. (That judgment and the bases for it are discussed in the relevant sections below.) To summarize, there are no empirical data to support any particular choice of readings in the foundations of education courses, little data on what makes an effective practicum, and considerable data on what makes for the effective teaching of reading. In these circumstances, our judgment with regard to the foundations courses was to ask for a balanced approach in which students would be exposed to different and opposing arguments drawn from the strongest texts.[31] Our approach to evaluating the general methods and practicum experience was to ask that schools of education gather the most data possible on how student teachers were faring in their teaching experiences, and expose them to information about different teaching models for which empirical data were available. Finally, our standards for reading instruction were based on the empirical research that we cite in that section.

In the second stage of our research, we analyzed what we found in the collected syllabi. In no sense did our search for evidence of good practices restrict this part of our analysis. So long as we had identified a syllabus as falling under the broad domains of foundations, reading methods, or general methods/practicum, we included that syllabus in our descriptions of what we found. Readers who take issue with our earlier judgments about ideal course coverage and content may be encouraged by what we actually discovered.

In this chapter, our intention is not to offer the last word, but to raise some pertinent questions, set out a prima facie case for certain answers, and thereby invite further re-examination of the preparation of American teachers.

## Foundations of Education

*What We Looked For*

Just as we cannot prove that studying the liberal arts makes one a better person, so there is no clear empirical data that a particular foundations course will produce an effective teacher.[32] Nevertheless, because education is a complex and contested endeavor, common sense suggests that good foundation courses will expose students to texts and ideas that embrace a variety of judgments, that have stood the test of time, and/or that have influenced our current educational debates. We take a broad approach. Foundation courses should introduce the prospective teacher to the domain of education, including its philosophy and its connection to human psychology, history, and contemporary issues and controversies. Though such courses may not teach specific teaching skills, they play a vital role in forming the general outlook and beliefs of future teachers about their craft. Without a carefully designed exposure to the fundamental issues of education, students will have no way of making informed judgments about the information they are given in their methods courses. The combination of such methods courses with a weak foundation program can leave future teachers at the mercy of fads and fashion in their professional work. A strong foundations course, by contrast, will include:

- A modest number of readings drawn from the classics of the philosophy of education, including Plato, Aristotle, Confucius, Jean-Jacques Rousseau, and John Dewey. Through such study, future teachers learn to reflect on the fundamental purposes of their craft. We are looking for both rigor and ideological balance: the readings should be substantive (longer than two- or three-page excerpts, taken from original sources) and drawn largely from works that have stood the test of time. They should not embody only one point of view: reading only Plato's *Republic* with its endorsement of a natural meritocracy would be as inadequate as reading only Dewey's celebration of participatory democracy.
- A critical introduction to the relationship between psychology and education. Jean Piaget and Lev Vigotsky have clearly had an impact on the preparation of American teachers. But contemporary authors in this field, such as John Bransford and David Elkind, should also be part of the reading. Once again, we would hope to find readings from original

sources and an exposure to research-based findings that link teaching practices grounded in psychological findings to learning outcomes.

- An exposure to the history of education in the United States. Students should become acquainted with this history in order to contextualize current educational issues and to understand how education is entwined with the story of American democracy. A number of excellent studies, such as Larry Cuban and David Tyack's *Tinkering Towards Utopia*,[33] are available. Students can certainly be introduced to different historical narratives about U.S. education, and they should be informed about the extraordinary heterogeneity of contemporary America.

- An introduction to the major debates in contemporary educational policy. Student teachers need to think critically about a variety of key issues, including the ethnic test-score gaps, high-stakes testing, religion and education, vouchers and charter schools, together with the debate between contemporary constructivists and those who advocate a more traditional approach to teaching. The choice of texts should convey to students the best research available and present the complexity of these issues. Texts such as J. Noll's *Taking Sides*[34] that offer two-page summaries of essential topics often trivialize crucial educational disputes.

*What We Found*

We reviewed forty-five foundations courses for elementary and secondary schoolteachers drawn from fifteen schools of education. Of these fifteen, nine offer a four-year undergraduate program, one a five-year program, and five offer master's programs to those who already have an undergraduate degree. In three cases, the schools we reviewed combine their primary and secondary school teacher-preparation foundations courses, and in nine cases the differences between the two are limited to the educational psychology courses. Students preparing to teach older children take courses focused less on child development and more on adolescent behavior or general psychology. In the text below, we count each of these nine as single programs. In three schools, the preparation programs for primary and secondary student teachers are quite different. In total, then, we looked at eighteen substantively different programs in fifteen schools of education.

No program we reviewed in any school gave student teachers an introduction to each of the four domains we reviewed. One program offered none of them. In seven schools, students were required to study psychology and the challenges presented by a diverse and multicultural student population, but nothing else. Just three programs (one available only to graduate students) gave even cursory attention to the philosophy of education, and in the case of one of these three universities, this was offered only in the secondary education program. Five programs offered some material on the history of education, but in one of the undergraduate programs students had the option to take an alternative course without history, and in the same university those in the primary education program did not have to take either course. Seven of the eighteen programs we reviewed offered some introduction to current issues in education policy. However, in one university that teaches this material, only those in the secondary education program take the course. In all but three programs, students are offered some form of an introduction to psychology. Finally, in all but three schools of education, all student teachers are taught a course focused on cultural diversity or multiculturalism.[35]

An overview of the required and recommended readings showed that the most frequently required texts were Anita Woolfolk's *Educational Psychology* and Jonathan Kozol's indictment of inner-city schooling, *Savage Inequalities*. Each one of these texts is used in at least six programs we reviewed. The next most popular authors (each found in at least four programs) were Henry Giroux (a neo-Marxist educational theorist), Paulo Freire (an advocate of using education to achieve political liberation), Joel Spring (an educational historian and author of works on educational multiculturalism), Howard Gardner (a proponent of multiple intelligences and portfolio-based learning and an opponent of standardized high-stakes testing), and Lev Vigotsky (the Russian psychologist who focused on the social/cultural context of children's development and associated learning). Taken as a whole, however, the most frequently used material comes from a group of authors who advocate a form of multiculturalist education. We found that fourteen of the courses in ten different schools that we reviewed used at least one of the following: Gloria Ladson-Billings (*Dream Keepers*), Vivian Paley (*White Teacher*), Sonia Nieto (*Affirming Diversity* and *The Light in Their Eyes*), Jay MacLeod, (*ain't no making it*), L. Olson (*Made in America*), bell hooks (*Teaching to Transgress*), and Joel Spring (*Deculturalization and the Struggle for Equality*). Often powerful, provocative, and rightly disturbing, these texts largely share and promote a particular argument about education: teachers should champion the particular voices and experiences of repressed minorities, engaging in what Ladson-Billings calls "culturally relevant teaching." The alternative viewpoint, that teachers should focus on assuring that all students master universally valuable knowledge, is underrepresented. We found only one course syllabus, in one program, that offered any readings presenting this countervailing view.

*Philosophy of Education*

The names Aristotle and Confucius did not appear in a single foundations course that we reviewed. We found one course that used Plato's *Meno*; otherwise, we found no Plato. We note, however, that two programs used a textbook that included a discussion of classical educational theories. Two syllabi from two different schools made reference to Rousseau, but no specific text was listed. The only major author we found in more than one program was John Dewey, whose works were either required or recommended reading in all syllabi that explicitly addressed education philosophy. In Education and American Culture, the required foundations course at Indiana University, the two set texts were Joel Spring's *The American School* and Robert M. Pirsig's novel *Zen and the Art of Motorcycle Maintenance*.[36]

*Psychology*

Students preparing to teach young children should have some exposure to developmental psychology. The difficulty is that the textbooks that are often used (Woolfolk's,[37] as we indicated above, was the most common) are compendia of information that offer very broad coverage but little guidance to the student who should be trying to select what has proved valuable in the classroom. For example, Woolfolk's book offers summaries of the work of Piaget and Vygotsky, and the student is asked, rightly, to reflect on the differences between the two theories—but to what practical end? Woolfolk writes that theorists who advocate "symbolic processing" believe that "there is an objective reality out there," while those who employ a "cognitive constructivist" perspective deny "that the world is knowable."[38] But the educational consequences of choosing either view are not developed. Moreover, these and other theories of learning are then boiled down to bromides (e.g., "When children begin to have arguments, you can tell that they are listening to each other"[39]).

More importantly, these textbooks are either read as stand-alone works or used with other similar texts. Student teachers need to place theory in the real world of the school, and this was rarely done. We found only one syllabus, for example, that used Laurence Steinberg's book on the contemporary world of the American adolescent, *Beyond the Classroom*. We found only three other syllabi where material of this kind was required reading.

*History of Education*

Among the five programs in four schools that included history of education material, we found two that used Steven Tozer et al.'s *School and Society, His-*

*torical and Contemporary Perspectives*, and two that used texts by Joel Spring. Offering a useful introduction to the field, both these books emphasize the way minorities were excluded for so long from an adequate education. In one graduate and one undergraduate course we found David Tyack and Larry Cuban's *Tinkering Towards Utopia*, a balanced and manageably concise historical survey. While Spring and Tozer offer students a left-liberal reading of U.S. history, we found only a single syllabus that required a text by Diane Ravitch, a historian of U.S. education who has strongly criticized the legacy of constructivist education.

*Education Policy*

Of the eighteen programs we reviewed, seven programs in six schools offered some form of introduction to issues in education policy. In three-quarters of the schools whose course listings we checked, however, there was no indication that future teachers were being taught anything about the major debates (such as high-stakes tests, performance-based accountability, and vouchers) in the profession they hope to join. In three courses from three schools we did find the use of James Noll's *Taking Sides* or M.[NAME?] Williams's *Opposing Viewpoints*. These texts introduce students to policy issues but give them little sustained analysis. In the rare case where a program did try to introduce students to policy debates, we found a one-sided presentation. To give an example, in Stanford's course Equity and Democracy, the final class readings are gathered under the title "Test scores, everywhere test scores. And grade books! Alternatives? Constructive alternatives? Ones that still count?" Given this tone, we wonder if this course includes careful consideration of demands (not only from conservative policy analysts but also from many urban superintendents) to hold schools accountable for measurable results.[40] To give a second example, E.D. Hirsch's advocacy of a core knowledge program grounded in a sequential, content-based curriculum has been influential in recent efforts to establish state curriculum frameworks,[41] yet we found Hirsch on only one recommended reading list and in one other syllabus. Eric Hanushek's work on school funding and other educational policy issues is cited in one syllabus. Despite the fact that almost every program included a course devoted to diversity, we did not find what is arguably the best-researched book on the subject of African American educational performance, Jencks and Phillips' *The Black-White Test Score Gap*, on any syllabus.

Based on the syllabi we reviewed, we conclude that most prospective teachers in these eighteen programs get little or no exposure to any of the texts that have informed and challenged a long history of thinking about teaching and education. Nor are they provided with a balanced or research-based perspective from which to address contemporary debates in U.S. education. Instead, as we have indicated above, they are more frequently exposed to readings that suggest distrust of the "knowledge" offered by the "dominant" culture.

## Reading

According to the Nation's Report Card, 28 percent of all U.S. students in grades four through twelve score below a "basic" level, and about two-thirds of all U.S. students read below the "proficient" level on the same assessment, even when given extra accommodations.[42] The preparation of effective reading teachers is clearly a priority. As Moats and Lyon noted in 1996,[43] teachers of reading should have a sufficient grasp of the structure of spoken and written language to teach it to those with difficulties, and they should be trained or required to demonstrate a competence in this knowledge in order to graduate or be certified.

*What We Were Looking For*

After decades of study by researchers such as Rumelhart, LaBerge and Samuels, Adams, Perfetti, Stanovich, Shaywitz, and Moats,[44] and the work done by the National Reading Panel and the National Research Council,[45] we have solid research on what makes for effective reading instruction. On the basis of this research, we looked for courses that give student teachers the theoretical knowledge and practical ability to provide explicit, systematic, and sequential instruction in reading. For teachers preparing to teach the higher grades, we looked for courses that provide training in the syntactic, semantic, and pragmatic skills that are necessary to understand complex sentences. In both cases we hoped to find the dissemination of knowledge and skills that are transferable to the classroom.

We also considered what teachers tell us they are missing from their programs. Flint et al.[46] reported in their analysis of reading-preparation programs that some teachers believed that their programs should have taught them better integration of whole-language and phonics approaches,[47] while other teachers felt their preparation was too slanted toward whole language and did not give them the skills they needed for proper instruction.[48]

A national debate between proponents of the whole-language and phonics approaches to teaching reading has largely been resolved by adoption of a "balanced" approach that combines an emphasis on literature with sequential skill instruction in phonics and decoding.[49] After initial exposure to letter sounds, students study words with specific sound-spelling patterns. These can be "systematically embedded in connected text"[50] or taught in isolation and reinforced through practice.[51] An alternate approach is to sound words out by applying letter-to-sound relationships (direct-code instruction).[52] While the debate between different approaches to teaching phonics has not been resolved in the literature,[53] we looked for some exposure to the direct-code method because of the similarities it has to successful reading instruction programs, such as Wilson and Orton-Gillingham's. Well-trained teachers need to know about the different approaches to teaching phonics so they can adjust their instruction to meet the individual needs of their students.[54]

As we did the review we looked for:

- Knowledge of how to teach the structure of words, syntax, vocabulary, and fluency with explicit, systematic instruction of phonics, including phonemic awareness, bottom-up and top-down comprehension strategies, and assessments.[55]
- Evidence of course expectations that students would demonstrate competency in the ability to teach specific reading strategies and skills, especially the ability to teach structured, sequential phonics and phonemic awareness and direct instruction of reading-comprehension skills.[56]
- Evidence of secondary-level preparation courses providing age-appropriate study skills, vocabulary skills (including word derivations), and comprehension strategies, together with knowledge of reading problems and how to correct them.[57]
- Courses with challenging assignments and rigorous assessments.
- Extensive practice using a variety of diagnostic assessment tools (including tests of phonemic and phonetic ability) followed by the requirement to determine instructional strategies based on these assessments.
- Explanations of different methodologies for teaching reading, including scripted programs such as Open Court, Orton-Gillingham, Project Read, and Reading Recovery.
- A variety of seminal studies and evidence-based research in reading,[58] such as works by Brown, Chall, Indrisano, LaBerge and Samuels, Perfetti, Pressley, Nagy and Scott, Rumelhart, Stanovich, and others.[59] We also looked for courses that included studies focused on early interventions and targeted instructional strategies: Adams (1990); Adams, Foorman, Lundberg, and Beeler (1997); Moats (1999); Moats and Lyon (1996); Shaywitz (2003); and Torgesen and Mathes (2000).[60] We looked for the

use of the National Research Council's 1998 report on *Preventing Reading Difficulties in Young Children* (Snow, Burns, & Griffin) and the National Reading Panel's *Teaching Children to Read*.[61]A course in each program linking language structure to reading acquisition and development.

*What We Found*

We reviewed syllabi from sixty-one language arts, reading, and reading-related courses in fourteen schools of education. In total we looked at thirty-six elementary/early childhood courses from ten schools,[62] sixteen secondary level courses from nine schools, and nine related courses (six language courses from three schools, one reading disabilities course, and two assessment courses from two schools). We looked at undergraduate certification programs, with the exception of three schools that required a master's degree for certification and one school that offered a five-year certification program. We found:

- Two syllabi in different schools referenced Moats' book, *Speech to Print* (which encourages the use of structured phonics), and one course listed it as required reading. One had students read Hall and Moats.[63] None referenced landmark work done by Jeanne Chall, and four referenced (but did not require reading) Marilyn Adams' work.
- Four schools had students in the elementary program read, as part of their required reading, either from the National Reading Panel's 2000 study, from Snow et al., or from Burns and Snow.[64]
- Ten of thirty-six syllabi at the elementary level in seven schools introduced and had students practice a variety of assessment tools; three of these from three schools used only assessments from the whole-language programs. UCLA, in one course, had students practice with eight literacy assessments, such as comprehension and vocabulary inventories, spelling and phonics assessments.[65]
- We found that three schools required students to take a course in linguistic structure. One of these schools (University of Maryland) had an exemplary course that showed the relationship between spoken language and reading acquisition.[66]

We found, in relationship to the "balanced" approach to reading and to the instruction and assessment of phonics, that:

- Twenty-eight of the thirty-six elementary level syllabi we reviewed offer instruction in the new, balanced approach. These courses used similar texts: twenty-one by such authors as Patricia Cunningham, Lucy Calkins,

Irene Fountas, and Gay Su Pinnell. These authors were originally whole-language advocates, but have since adopted a balanced approach. Seven courses used other popular authors, such as Gail Thompkins. These classes also used similar classroom methodologies, such as shared reading, language experience, literature circles, guided reading, and similar assessments such as the use of Marie Clay's running records (an assessment originally used in whole-language classrooms).[67]

- The review was did of the se four eighty eight courses raised questions about how much practice students get in teaching phonics. Most commonly, discussion of phonics took place in no more than two class sessions. Two schools offered courses with extensive coverage and practice (one syllabus incorporated phonics in six classes). In a third school the instructor offered three classes on phonics, two of which included how-to-teach demonstration. Only two syllabi included testing student teachers' knowledge through a phonics quiz.[68]

- Twelve out of thirty-six elementary school syllabi used Marie Clay's running records. While running records can work well if done carefully, they do not provide a close diagnosis of phonetic ability. We found only three syllabi from three schools that discussed the assessment of phonemic awareness. One additional school, the University of Texas, provided a required course in reading disabilities that included practice on phonics and early intervention assessments.

- Despite much research pointing to the destructive effects of the whole-language approach, we found that a number of the top-rated schools still offered whole language-based courses. We found ten syllabi from four schools that represented many elements of the whole-language ideology (this influence was found in assessment courses, language courses, and reading methods courses).

We also found:

- One syllabus that familiarized student teachers with Open Court and Reading Recovery; another syllabus from a different school introduced students to Reading Recovery.

- Three syllabi from two schools that included the direct code/explicit instruction approach to teaching phonics, as well as the embedded/implicit approach. One referenced explicit instruction of comprehension skills.

- Insufficient rigor in the classroom and homework assignments, projects, and readings.[69] In eighteen elementary courses students were required to write reflection papers, autobiographical pieces, and/or journals, instead of a research paper or an analytic essay. One syllabus requested that students collect poems.

- Future teachers are not being required to demonstrate their knowledge of reading-skill instruction. Only eight of thirty-six courses required that students make a presentation of a skill or strategy.

Little coursework at education schools prepares teachers to confront reading problems among students in their middle and high school years. At the secondary level we looked at sixteen syllabi. We found that:

- Students were not taught the importance of the structure of language in reading for students in grades 4-12. Only one syllabus provided instruction in the importance of teaching syntax and morphology to students beyond the acquisition of phonetic ability. We found no mention in any syllabi of giving older students exposure to reading sentences with complex syntactical structures, or stressing the importance of the grammar of sentence in decoding text.
- Only two strong syllabi in two schools had most of the elements we were looking for: a variety of solid research articles, with three to four to be read each week; tests of students' knowledge; and a broad coverage of topics including how to teach reading skills and strategies, teaching diverse students, and teaching students with learning disabilities.

In general, we are concerned that, in many of the schools of education we reviewed, students are given only cursory knowledge of how to teach reading skills, and given too little instruction in teaching phonics in a sequential systematic manner with requirements that would include demonstrations of competency.

## Methods Courses and the Practicum

*What We Looked For*

Methods courses come in two forms. Either they are integrated with the academic disciplines (e.g., "reading methods," discussed above) or they are not (i.e., offered as generalized introductions to how to teach). These methods courses are linked to or integrated with students' prepracticum or practicum experiences. In the prepracticum, students typically spend one day a week working in a school; the practicum usually involves some weeks of teaching under the joint supervision of a university-appointed supervisor and a teacher at the school.[70]

Do future teachers need general methods courses? Some principals who have produced extraordinary results in their schools stress that the most effective practical training of teachers takes place through immersion in the school culture itself. As Deborah Meier puts it, "When people ask me how we train new teachers, I say that the school itself is an educator for the kids and staff: it's its own staff development project."[71] Much of what a teacher can do effectively in a school depends on the school's culture, as the relative success of urban Catholic schools has demonstrated.

If all of our schools were high-performing, with experienced teachers carefully mentoring newcomers to the teaching profession, there would be far less need for methods courses. However, that is not the case. Beginning teachers may find themselves dropped into a classroom with little or no support: imagine oneself suddenly faced with teaching twenty-five fifteen-year-olds in an inner-city public high school. Such a thought experiment will quickly suggest why a carefully structured methods course closely combined with practicum experience could be valuable. Methods courses are our opportunity to take what we know about quality instruction to model for student teachers what good teachers do. The practicum is the time for a student teacher to begin discovering what can create chaos, indifference, or learning in the classroom. The general methods course or seminar that accompanies that practicum must address those discoveries directly. We looked for methods courses that:

- Help teachers to integrate state curriculum frameworks and tests into lesson plans and assessments.
- Use texts that offer teachers some down-to-earth suggestions. Works like *Tools for Teaching: Discipline, Instruction, Motivation* (Jones, 2000) or *The Skillful Teacher* (Saphier & Gower, 1997) can be useful to the novice teacher in offering a variety of teaching strategies for multiple circumstances. Books such as *Understanding by Design* by [First Name] Wiggins and [First Name] McTighe offer important ideas of how to design curriculum, determine student outcomes based on standards, create an assessment for measuring outcomes, and produce the type of pedagogy or instructional method needed to arrive at those outcomes.
- Include a "how to teach" component that gives students practice writing and implementing well-thought-out weekly and daily lesson plans and curriculum units that are not only presented to other education students, but are also used in the practicum. Specifically, we hoped to find the inclusion in lesson plans of instructional objectives that specify student outcomes, as well as effective assessments of student performance.

- Promote understanding of and practice with effective instructional strategies and different modes or models of instruction. We think methods classes should introduce teachers to the use (and abuse) of curriculum models (e.g., direct instruction, Socratic seminar) as part of the practicum and as demonstrations for their teacher and classmates.
- Teach how to incorporate assessment into learning plans and how to use ongoing assessments to monitor student knowledge and growth. Students should understand the importance of different types of assessments for different purposes, and how to write classroom assessments for students of different ability levels using guidelines such as Bloom's taxonomy.
- Introduce the effective use of educational technology, such as websites and educational software, into the methods courses. Schools have spent billions of dollars on computer hardware and software, and there are good resources available.[72] Schools of education need to teach their students how to use a variety of software programs effectively and how to link technology-based material to state curriculum frameworks.

With regard to the practicum, we looked for evidence that the professor from the school of education, the appointed practicum supervisor (if that is a second person), and the mentoring on-site teacher work in a coordinated way so that the fieldwork is properly assessed. We looked for evidence that all those involved met regularly for evaluation and feedback (at least once every three weeks). Videotaping the student on several occasions and then requiring students to review those tapes with all three teachers would, in our judgment, be an invaluable assessment tool. Ideally, student teachers should spend time in a high-performing school that beats the demographic odds in its test results, has a high retention rate, and engages students in demanding and sustained exercises of intellectual engagement. Where that is impossible, a practicum should present student teachers with a variety of experiences and an opportunity to join teacher-study groups and team with other teachers.

### What We Found

Despite some variation among the general "methods" courses, most had a number of common features. This list of the aims of methods courses is typical in its breadth and ambitious scope:

> Reflective practitioners need to interact with many types of knowledge when they are making decisions in the world of practice. They need to use

their knowledge of subject matter . . . draw frequently upon their knowledge of curriculum...have knowledge of learners . . . need knowledge of educational goals and assessment of student progress . . . need knowledge of social and cultural content to understand how educational goals, learning and their student interact with such social issues as racism and sexism. . . . Finally, reflective practitioners need knowledge of pedagogy.[73]

In reviewing methods courses we looked at the general methods courses in the various schools of education. Within these schools we looked at fifty-nine syllabi, fifty-five of which were taught in conjunction with either a field placement (pre-practicum) or a practicum. We reviewed twenty-nine courses that were part of an elementary (including early childhood) teacher-preparation program and thirty that were geared to secondary teachers. The eleven schools of education included seven undergraduate programs, three that required students do graduate work at the master's level for certification, and one that required that students complete a five-year program. The prepracticums averaged six hours a week, and the practicum involved student teaching for one or two semesters.

Specifically, we found that classes included:

- Lesson planning: twenty syllabi from nine schools (out of fifty-nine methods syllabi) included specific instruction in planning lessons; only four of these incorporated classroom demonstrations.
- Assessment: Eleven syllabi from seven schools included an assessment component. One school, the University of Georgia, included preparing teachers to evaluate their student outcomes with pre- and post-assessments. Stanford's practicum included exposure to different forms of assessments.[74]
- Learning standards: Seven syllabi from four schools linked their instruction to state standards.
- Explicit guidance about teaching strategies: Six syllabi out of fifty-nine included explicit instruction of strategies such as reciprocal teaching, scaffolding instruction, cognitive strategies, and reading strategies. Two syllabi included student demonstration of strategies.
- Curriculum models: Six syllabi from five schools incorporated instruction in curriculum models and modes of instruction. Most syllabi presented one or two models; for example, one syllabus discussed the difference between teaching to large groups, small groups, or to one student; one course at the University of Maryland included presentations of direct instruction, cooperative learning, and problem-based instruction.[75]

- Evidence in four syllabi suggest that professors were teaching students to distrust formal assessments. To cite one example from a program ranked in the top ten by *U.S.. News & World Report*: "Human learning and knowledge can't be partitioned into disjointed components. Why should we pretend it could be? So I propose a more holistic evaluation....If I...ruled the world, there would be no grades."

In addition to these key findings, we also looked at the required readings used in the fifty-nine courses. These fell into four groups: materials on classroom strategies, such as designing heterogeneous classrooms; classroom management and teaching strategies; readings on educational theory; and state standards. A fifth theme in the readings was found in books that represent a particular sociocultural perspective on teaching, learning, and pedagogy. W. Ayers' book *To Teach: The Journey of a Teacher* is the most widely assigned book in the methods courses we reviewed; eight courses in five schools use it. Other texts include Jeanne Oakes and Lipton, *Teaching to Change the World*, [First Name] Bigelow's *Rethinking Our Classrooms Vol. 2*, Vivian Paley's *White Teacher*, and [First Name] Brooks and [First Name] Brooks, *The Case for the Constructivist Classroom.*

- We found almost no evidence that teachers are being prepared to use technology in their methods classes. Only three syllabi explicitly required integration of technology into the course assignments.
- We found no evidence that teachers are being prepared to teach so as to maximize student performance on standardized tests.
- Twenty-nine syllabi from twelve schools used reaction papers, personal journals, and autobiographical reflections; twenty-one syllabi from seven schools used portfolios.[76] One class based 60 percent of the students' grades on the portfolio, the rest on attendance at the course and peer editing.
- We found only two schools that indicated that they used videotaping of student teaching. One school used audiotaping.

## OTHER CRITICAL FACTORS FOR EVALUATING SCHOOLS OF EDUCATION

In addition to a full review of methods courses in academic fields such as history and science that we have not yet analyzed, we wish to stress the need for more research using a larger sample. We know that syllabi can tell us only so much about what is happening in the classrooms in schools of education, and we would like to see the production of statistically robust data about the future teaching records of graduates from the various schools. Evaluators of schools of education today would need to consider several factors that lie outside the scope of this chapter:

- The SAT or GRE scores of the entering student body, together with other relevant demographic information. Is this information publicly available? Do these data indicate that a particular school is becoming more selective?
- Exit evaluations: How are graduating students assessed? If they take newly mandated state content-based tests or Praxis II tests, what are their scores, both in absolute terms and relative to graduates from other schools of education?
- Does the school of education have active partnerships with school districts or individual schools, offering on-site professional development and resources? Is the school providing teachers to high-needs districts? To give an example, in the last decade Boston University's School of Education has taken responsibility for managing the public school district of Chelsea, Massachusetts.
- Are the state curriculum frameworks specific and detailed enough in their content to provide a useful tool for assessing the content of teacher preparation programs? If so, do the programs measure up?
- What is the quality of the principal and/or administrative preparation program? Although this question takes us beyond teacher preparation per se, a school without a first-rate administrative preparation track is not contributing to one of the most crucial aspects of effective school reform.

## EVALUATION MATRIX

We have summarized the findings of our paper in an evaluation matrix (Appendix C). This tool is intended to be a highly condensed set of guidelines for distinguishing the features of a first-rate teacher-preparation program from those that are academically and professionally poor. This matrix should be read in the context of the preceding paper, and is not intended to be used in isolation.

## CONCLUSION

Based on our sampling of the coursework requirements in some of the country's most highly regarded schools of education, we are not convinced that elite education schools are doing an adequate job of conveying fundamental, broad-based knowledge and skills to prospective teachers. The foundations and methods courses we reviewed suggest that faculty at most of these schools are often trying to teach a particular ideology—that traditional knowledge is repressive by its very nature—without directing their students to any substantial readings that question the educational implications of this view.

Instead of focusing on how teachers can best prepare students to learn in the current real world of performance-based assessment and content-rich curricula, a number of syllabi we reviewed suggest that the professors in these schools select readings that teach resistance to that world. It is reasonable for education school faculty to raise questions about the efficacy of high-stakes tests and state-mandated curriculum frameworks, but an unmitigated attack will leave teachers unprepared for these contemporary educational demands.

At their best, some of the programs we reviewed do important work. The national movement toward teaching phonics in reading has had some impact on reading-preparation programs. A very small number of programs offer future teachers solid exposure to the history of education in the United States. We noted above that a modest number of programs provide a practicum structure capable of providing real assessment and timely feedback to student teachers about to enter the profession. We suggest, however, that at the very least all prospective teachers should engage in student teaching under the supervision of experienced and effective teachers. For reasons detailed above, we are not convinced that most of the schools of education we reviewed offer an adequate practicum. Given our state and national educational curriculum and assessment structures, we would argue that student teaching has to be much more rigorously focused on assessments of effectiveness: What did the children learn, and how can the teacher give evidence of that learning? Professors at most of the schools of education we reviewed are not watching their students teach in schools, even on videotape. How, then, can they offer effective and useful instruction on how to teach better?

Given detailed state curriculum frameworks and assessments, teacher preparation can be targeted on achieving academic results. It can be done; arguably, it can be overdone. In England, successive Conservative and Labor party governments in the 1980s and 1990s undertook the wholesale alignment of teacher-preparation programs with a nationally mandated curriculum for schools. At a June 2002 conference hosted by the Federal Reserve Bank of Boston, Michael Barber, who had served as chief advisor to Prime

Minister Tony Blair on education policy, explained that the British government intended to produce "teachers who are driven by data and by what data tells them." The key was to take the best research on what raised student scores and feed it back into the preparation of teachers. Barber argued that teacher-preparation programs had to be pressed into the new reality, one way or another, and that preparing teachers to rely only on their own judgment about how to teach was a mistake. He offered a telling example: "[W]hen we trained teachers to teach literacy, they asked, 'Can we be flexible about this?' We replied, 'Well, this is the model that works. If you are flexible about it, it won't be pure, it won't be based on research, then it won't work, and you'll tell us the program was a bad idea'."[77] Given the close similarities between this British model and the goals of many educational policy leaders in the United States, the results achieved to date in England should be carefully analyzed in terms of both international assessments and national-level testing. Advocates of such reforms can now cite some strong evidence to support their strategies; critics can point to the problems inherent in exaggerating this approach.

Most schools of education we reviewed risk not preparing teachers adequately to use concrete findings of the best education research and not providing their students with a thoughtful and academically rich background in the fundamentals of what it means to be an outstanding educator. In our view, fine teaching must involve more than following a recipe. Locking teachers into a script the way Direct Instruction does for its participating teachers often works better than the status quo in our most underprivileged districts, because those districts often have to hire teachers with very modest content knowledge, then drop them into the most demanding teaching situations. Student teachers should be taught about the methods and successes of such programs precisely because of their track record in raising the performance of disadvantaged children. At the same time, mastery of the art of teaching cannot be reached by rote recitation of packaged scripts. Such scripts may offer extremely important minimal requirements, reminders, suggestions, and examples for use in the classroom, but they cannot adequately define or describe the matter of teaching. As Richard Silberman incisively puts it, "[W]hat is at issue is the quality of the understanding to be engendered in students . . . meaning not only how good an understanding the students acquire, but also what kind of understanding."[78]

A student of the violin reaches for disciplined technique; a mature violinist subsumes that discipline into art. So it should be with teaching. In a recent book devoted to great teachers and their students, George Steiner reminds us what is at stake: "There is no craft more privileged. To awaken in another human being powers, dreams beyond one's own; to induce in others a love for what one loves; to make of one's inward present their future . . . to be the courier of the essential."[79]

Those versed in the history of U.S. educational theory know that it has gyrated between extremes. On the one hand are theorists (often teaching in education schools) who champion forms of constructivism; on the other are parents and policymakers who argue for a return to the basics. The educational results of shifting endlessly from one extreme to the other are, unsurprisingly, mediocre; a fair conclusion might be that the dichotomy itself is damaging. An effective teacher will first prepare students carefully with the content knowledge and skills they will need to master the basics of various academic disciplines, then he or she will deepen students' knowledge and judgment, enabling them to conduct a certain amount of their own thoughtful, imaginative, and probing work. The hope is for teachers who are themselves educated, who have read deeply, and who will hone the discipline and imagination that only real literacy can bring. Each should have dug deeply into his or her chosen discipline, grappling with its language and history. We must try to ensure through better teacher preparation that U.S. education is not about to veer again from one extreme to the other. We need well-educated, thoughtful, and well-mentored new teachers, prepared neither to be arbitrary agents nor puppets on a string.

# APPENDIX A   Profile of Schools of Education

*"Size of school" numbers, italicized below, represent the programs from which we reviewed syllabi.*

| School of education (Public unless indicated) | Loca tion | Size of schools | | NCATE | U.S. News & World Report Rankings** | | |
|---|---|---|---|---|---|---|---|
| | | Under-grad. | Grad. | | Elem entary | Second ary | Overall |
| University of Georgia | South | 2,424 | 2,500 | Yes | 5 | 7 | 27 |
| University of Illinois, Urbana-Champaign | Midwest | N/A | 499* | Applying | 6 | 5 | 24 |
| University of Maryland | East | 1,048 | 1,056 | Yes | 11 | 14 | 21 |
| University of Michigan | Midwest | 1,200 | 923 | No | 10 | | 8 |
| University of Texas | South | 2,029 | 1,334 | No | 16 | 11 | 13 |
| University of Virginia | South | | 124* | Yes | 8 | 8 | 21 |
| University of Wisconsin | Midwest | 2,420 | 1,131 | No | 2 | 2 | 9 |
| Columbia University (Private) | North-east | | 2,959 | Applying | 4 | 5 | 4 |
| Eastern Michigan University | Midwest | 3,812 | 1,771 | Yes | | | |
| Harvard University (Private) | North-east | N/A | 662 | No | | | 1 |
| Indiana University | Midwest | 2,061 | 1,192 | Yes | 8 | 9 | 17 |
| Michigan State University | Midwest | 1,634 | 1,388 | No | 1 | 1 | 15 |
| Penn State University | East | 2,138 | 1,279 | Yes | | 14 | 24 |
| Sonoma State University | West | | 776 & 118*** | Yes | | | |
| Stanford University (Private) | West | | 348 | Yes | NA | 4 | 2 |
| UCLA | West | | 111* | No | 16 | 14 | 3 |

*02 Grad. Licensed to teach, *2004 U.S. News & World Report.***Ratings based on *2004 U.S. News & World Report*; Elementary and Secondary programs rated in top 30; "Overall" category refers to top overall school rating. ***776 enrolled in certification program; 118 in Master's program;

## APPENDIX B   NCATE State Partnership Frameworks

| NCATE-BASED | NCATE STATE-BASED | PERFORMANCE-BASED |
|---|---|---|
| NCATE Program Review<br>NCATE Unit Review | STATE Program Review<br>NCATE Unit Review | STATE Performance Assessment<br>NCATE Unit Review |
| NCATE conducts the review of the unit and content area preparation using national specialized professional association program standards. The state uses evidence from NCATEÆs accreditation findings in making independent state approval decisions for the institution and its content area preparation programs. | NCATE reviews the operation of the unit and the state reviews content preparation programs using its own process and standards. State program standards are subject to NCATE recognition based on program reviews by national specialized professional associations. The results of these reviews and the review of the Process and Evaluation Committee, may require institutions to submit program documents to NCATE if they desire national recognition for programs. | The state establishes a comprehensive performance-based licensing system and/or performance-based program approval system. NCATE conducts the review of the unit and considers the performance of the institution's candidates throughout their preparation and of its graduates on licensing assessments. |
| ALASKA, JOINT team*<br>ARKANSAS, NCATE team*<br>COLORADO, TWO teams<br>CONNECTICUT, JOINT team<br>DELAWARE, TWO teams<br>HAWAII, NCATE team<br>ILLINOIS, JOINT team<br>LOUISIANA, JOINT team<br>MARYLAND, JOINT team*<br>MASSACHUSETTS, JOINT team<br>MISSISSIPPI, JOINT team**<br>NEVADA, JOINT team<br>NEW YORK, JOINT team<br>PENNSYLVANIA, TWO teams<br>PUERTO RICO, JOINT team<br>RHODE ISLAND, TWO teams<br>SO. CAROLINA, JOINT team**<br>TEXAS, JOINT team<br>VIRGINIA, JOINT team<br>WEST VIRGINIA, JOINT team** | ALABAMA, TWO teams<br>DIST. OF COLUMBIA,<br>   TWO teams<br>GEORGIA, Joint team**<br>IDAHO, TWO teams<br>IOWA, TWO teams<br>KANSAS, JOINT team<br>MAINE, JOINT team<br>MICHIGAN, TWO teams<br>MINNESOTA, TWO teams<br>MISSOURI, TWO team<br>MONTANA, TWO teams<br>NEBRASKA, JOINT team<br>NEW MEXICO, JOINT team<br>NO. CAROLINA, TWO teams*<br>NORTH DAKOTA, JOINT teams<br>OHIO, NCATE team<br>OKLAHOMA, JOINT team<br>OREGON, TWO teams<br>SOUTH DAKOTA, TWO teams<br>TENNESSEE, TWO teams, JOINT<br>   team for continuing visits<br>UTAH, TWO teams<br>WASHINGTON, TWO teams<br>WISCONSIN, TWO teams<br>WYOMING, TWO teams | CALIFORNIA, JOINT team<br>INDIANA, JOINT team<br>KENTUCKY, JOINT team<br>FLORIDA, JOINT team<br><br><br><br>———————————————<br>* NCATE Accred. Required of **ALL** institutions (NC requires initial accred. only)<br>** NCATE Accred. Required of **PUBLIC** institutions<br>———————————————<br>NCATE team: Only NCATE Board of Examiners (BOE)<br>JOINT team: BOE and State team<br>TWO teams: Two concurrent teams: NCATE BOE team and separate State team<br>10/28/02 |

www.NCATE.org/partners/chart1.pdf

# APPENDIX C    Evaluations of Selected Coursework: Schools of Education

| | | Readings | Assignments and Assessments | Outcomes |
|---|---|---|---|---|
| **Foundations** | Strong | • Selections from classical texts (Plato, Rousseau)<br>• Introduction to the history of American Education<br>• Overview of principal themes in contemporary education policy<br>• Introduction to the elements of good research | • Substantive reading<br>• Analytical essays<br>• Assessments focused on translation of foundational assumptions into educational practice | • To produce thoughtful and knowledgeable practitioners capable of independent judgments about the fundamental purposes of their craft<br>• Provide educated critics of the latest "professional trends" |
| | Weak | • Snippets of large numbers of texts<br>• Majority of readings in human psychology<br>• Readings focused on a single ideological perspective | • Assessment based on reflection pieces or autobiographical journals<br>• No final content based evaluation<br>• No demand for sustained written analysis | • To create consumers of indifferently researched opinions<br>• Ideological clones<br>• Teachers ready to "blame the system" |
| **Reading** | Strong | • Use of multiple research-based articles/texts<br>• Selections of seminal and current studies (e.g. LaBerge and Samuels, Adams, Rumelhart,<br>• Baker & Brown, Chall, Ann Brown, Pressley,<br>• Kirtsch, Stanovich, NRP, Shaywitz, Snow<br>• Overview of historical perspective and research from multiple fields | • Analytical papers<br>• Demonstrate performance competencies in teaching:<br>• Explicit instruction of reading skills: fluency, phonics, phonemic awareness, vocabulary, spelling, syntax (K–12), sentence, paragraph and text comprehension<br>• Using a variety of appropriate assessment tools diagnostically<br>• Writing lesson plans with performance outcomes | • Prepare teachers who can:<br>• Focus on producing measurable competency in reading<br>• Choose effective and timely intervention strategies<br>• Understand the need for teaching reading skills to all students K–12 |

| | | | |
|---|---|---|---|
| | **Weak** | • Use of a single text book<br>• Use of narrative texts in isolation from scientifically<br>• based research<br>• Use of narrative based texts in place of expository textbooks<br>• Heavy emphasis on whole-language materials | • Use of reflection papers/journals without demonstration of integration of theory into observation<br>• Mindless collections of lesson plans and strategies<br>• Free-flowing discussions unsupported by reference to empirical data | • Follows only whole-language strategies:<br>• Teaches comprehension before phonics<br>• Uses three-cueing system as a reading model<br>• Avoids the teaching of targeted skills |
| **Student Teaching: Methods and Practicum** | **Strong** | • Texts that provide rigorous commonsense and practical wisdom; exemplary portraits of effective teaching (Socrates, Helen Keller)<br>• Accounts of different effective instructional models (e.g., Catholic Schools, Core Knowledge, Montessori)<br>• Modeling effective use of web-based materials and other educational technology | • Constructing syllabi with carefully defined performance targets and assessments<br>• Fully supervised practicums with required video-taping<br>• Assessments based on multiple reviews with reference to a measured impact on student performance | • Provide an initial exposure to teaching that will prepare students for the demands of high-stakes assessments, heterogeneous classrooms and school environments<br>• Learn to adapt teaching strategies to feedback from student performance |
| | **Weak** | • Texts claiming an absent scientific rigor<br>• Reliance on student-generated material<br>• Oversold "recipes" for successful teaching | • Poorly monitored practicum<br>• Student teaching unrelated to state frameworks or assessments<br>• Evaluation based on diaries or single-observer reports | • Teachers with a naïve, often utopian vision of their role setting them up for early exit from the profession |

## CHAPTER 6

# The Preparation and Recruitment of Teachers

## A Labor Market Framework

*Donald Boyd, Hamilton Lankford, Susanna Loeb, and James Wyckoff*

A central question facing education policymakers is how to structure entry pathways into teaching. One possibility is to set no requirements, allowing public school administrators to choose their preferred candidates from the pool of individuals interested in a teaching position. An alternative is to require some set of qualifications for those teaching in the public schools. These qualifications could include a high school degree, a bachelor's degree, required courses, specific work experience, and/or minimum performance on an exam or series of exams. There is little solid evidence that requiring qualifications benefits students or, if so, which qualifications are best. In fact, short of understanding the effects of setting requirements, we know little about the direct effects these qualifications have on teaching ability. These are quite different questions, as teachers may perform better with a given qualification, but requiring that qualification may separately influence the overall effectiveness of the teacher work force if it alters who chooses to teach or where teachers choose to teach. For example, college graduates with ample opportunities in other occupations may be less likely to pursue teaching jobs if they are required to complete many additional courses before entering the classroom to teach.

Teachers and prospective teachers appear quite responsive in their career choices to changes in policies and available opportunities. This responsiveness creates labor-market forces that are central to understanding the characteristics of the teachers that populate our classrooms.

This paper focuses on the role of labor-market dynamics in determining the effects of education policy initiatives that address certification and recruitment of teachers. We set a framework for approaching the questions of whether (and, which) qualifications should be mandated for elementary and secondary public school teachers. We start by describing the qualifications of the current teaching force and the distribution of teachers across schools. We ask what factors influence teachers' decisions of whether and where to teach, and describe current teacher wages, the nonwage characteristics of work environments, and the location of available jobs. We conclude with a discussion of the pros and cons of policy approaches for improving the work force.

We know quite a bit about who teachers are and where they teach. However, holes in our knowledge make it difficult to predict the effect of reforms aimed at improving the quality of teaching. We know of a number of job characteristics, such as salary and student body attributes, that influence individuals' decisions whether to enter teaching and teachers' choices of teaching jobs, but we do not have strong evidence on the relative importance of most job characteristics on these career choices. We do not know how much additional salary compensates for increased class size or for working for a first-year principal who is still learning how to lead. We have some evidence on the connection between teacher qualifications and effective teaching, but much of the variation in teacher quality is unexplained. We also do not know which aspects of teacher preparation contribute to teachers' abilities in the classroom. A lack of appropriate data, perhaps combined with a disconnect between researchers who understand institutions of education and those with appropriate data analysis skills, is partly responsible for the scarcity of information about teacher effectiveness. In any event, this scarcity makes it difficult to design with confidence cost-effective policies for improving teaching and, ultimately, student outcomes. We are left to rely on general principles and descriptive information, which may or may not be solid footing for reform.

## WHO TEACHES?

Before addressing the potential labor-market effects of changes in licensure and certification, it is worth considering the characteristics of the current work force, which result, at least in part, from current and past requirements.

## Degrees and Certifications

In 1961, 15 percent of teachers had not completed an undergraduate degree. By the early 1980s, nearly all teachers had a bachelor's degree, and more teachers held a master's degree or higher than held only a bachelor's.[1] The educational attainment of teachers varies by the type of school in which the teacher works. High school teachers are more likely to hold master's degrees than are middle school teachers, who in turn are more likely to hold master's degrees than elementary school teachers. Degree attainment also varies by region of the country. The Northeast has the highest proportion of teachers with master's degrees (60%), followed by the Midwest (51%). A much lower proportion of teachers in the South (39%) and West (38%) have advanced degrees.[2]

Many teachers acquire their master's degree while teaching. Approximately 16 percent of teachers with less than three years' experience have a master's degree, as compared with 62 percent of those with more than 20 years of experience.[3] Teachers obtain these degrees at least in part because of state requirements and/or pay raises. In addition to degree requirements for teaching, states require teachers to have a specialized certification. In the 1999–2000 academic year, 94.4 percent of public elementary and secondary teachers were certified in their main teaching assignment.[4]

Controversy surrounds the evidence for whether certification or degree attainment improves teacher effectiveness, partly because of the inherent difficulties of assessing these effects. The performance of students in two classes, one with a teacher who has a master's degree and one with a teacher who does not, may be very similar. This could be because a master's degree does not help teachers become more effective, or it might be the result of the school hiring the less educated teacher because he or she had some special skill that we, as outsiders, cannot observe. Data have not been available that would allow us to assess teachers before and after their education to ascertain whether obtaining advanced degrees changes the effects that teachers have on their students. The closest evidence comes from assessment of some teacher professional-development programs, where there is weak evidence that high-quality programs can improve student outcomes.[5] However, the potential for advanced education to improve teaching and the effect of average programs may be quite different; some programs and degrees are better than others. And once master's programs are mandated or given substantial returns in teacher contracts, teachers may seek out particularly low-cost (in both time and money) degree programs in order to reap the salary benefits with the least effort. These low-cost programs may not improve teachers' effectiveness, even if other programs might.

Most research finds that teachers with a master's degree do not, on average, contribute more to student learning than teachers without one.[6] Evidence of the effect of certification is more mixed, partly because almost all teachers are certified, and those who are uncertified are far more likely to teach in schools with low-performing students. This selection leads to a strong positive correlation between test scores and the percentage of certified teachers in a school, but makes it difficult to show causation.[7] The problem is compounded by the fact that most uncertified teachers have little teaching experience, and there is convincing evidence that teachers in their first few years of teaching are less able to help students learn and less consistent in their teaching abilities.[8] The lack of data on more experienced teachers without certification and the concentration of uncertified teachers in low-performing schools make it difficult to estimate the causal effect of certification on student outcomes.

### Test Scores and Knowledge

A number of studies have found that student achievement improves more in classes in which the teachers have higher test scores (especially verbal ability scores) or have attended more selective undergraduate institutions (a proxy for higher ability).[9] On average, teachers tend to score below the mean average of all college graduates on standardized aptitude tests.[10] Using data on all graduates of the State University of New York (SUNY), we find that elementary and secondary school teachers are more likely to have scored at the lower end of the distribution than non-teachers and less likely to have scored at the upper end of the distribution. This does not mean that all teachers have low test scores. Of the SUNY graduates who entered teaching, more than one in five scored at least 600 on the verbal SAT, and more than one in five scored at least 600 on the math SAT. High school math and science teachers score higher, on average, on the math SAT than do non-teachers (43% of these teachers *vs.* 32% of non-teachers score above 600 on the math SAT).

Many high-scoring individuals enter teaching, but the percentage of these teachers has decreased significantly over the last forty years. As job opportunities opened up for female college graduates in occupations outside of teaching, the teacher work force lost some of its high-scoring teachers. Almost one in four new teachers in the 1960s scored in the top 10 percent of their high school graduating classes. By 1992 this number had dropped to one in ten.[11] This drop in teachers' qualifications as a result of improved opportunities for women college graduates appears to have adversely affected students.[12]

Ability (as measured by test scores) helps teachers contribute to student learning; greater content knowledge in the area in which high school teachers teach (e.g., greater physics knowledge for those teaching physics) also appears to help teachers contribute to student learning.[13] One way for teachers to obtain content knowledge is to earn a degree in the field in which they teach. Thirty-seven percent of the degrees received by teachers in the late 1990s were in general education, and another quarter were in other areas of education, such as special education or educational administration. Only 38 percent of degrees were in traditional academic specializations.[14]

Teachers' academic majors vary substantially by teaching assignment. High school teachers are far more likely to have degrees in traditional academic fields (6%) than are elementary (22%) or middle school teachers (44%). In the last twenty years, there has been an increased tendency for teachers to major in traditional academic fields. Half of all teachers with three or fewer years of experience have degrees in these academic fields, compared with approximately one-third of highly experienced teachers.[15] Teachers with degrees in education are more likely to enter teaching directly after completing their degree.

It is not clear whether teachers with degrees in education perform better or worse in the classroom. Of the SUNY graduates taking teacher certification exams, the holders of bachelor's degrees in education tend to have scored lower on both the math SAT (about 0.11 standard deviations) and the verbal SAT (about 0.15 standard deviations). However, course work in pedagogy, in addition to content, appears to increase teacher effectiveness at improving student test scores, and education majors are more likely to have taken these courses.[16]

Teachers with a degree in a specific academic field can use their content knowledge to aid their students if they are teaching in their area of expertise. Most teachers have a graduate or undergraduate major or minor in their main teaching field, although the percentage differs by disciplinary area. The percentage of teachers with a major or minor in their primary teaching field is somewhat lower for mathematics teachers than for teachers in other subject areas. It is also lower in the seventh and eighth grades than in the high school grades. Many teachers teach some classes outside of their main teaching assignment and are much less likely to hold a major or minor in these areas. As a result, almost one-quarter of seventh- through twelfth-grade classes in core academic fields are taught by teachers without a major or minor in that field.[17] This phenomenon has been diminishing, however: in 1993–1994, only 77 percent of seventh- through twelfth-grade math teachers had an undergraduate major or minor in math, compared with 82 percent in 1997–1998.

## Summary

Teachers are a diverse group, demonstrating a range of academic performance and preparation. Yet we know little about the implications of this heterogeneity for student outcomes. Though higher test scores, subject-matter knowledge, and course-taking are correlated with effective teaching, research provides little additional insight into how to improve certification and recruitment policies. What characteristics of preservice education are important? What types of general knowledge should teachers have?

The lack of appropriate data for estimating the effectiveness of teachers is partly responsible for this shortfall in evidence. Teachers decide whether and where to teach and what types of training to receive; thus, when estimating the effects of education or certification, it is important to distinguish the teachers who are choosing the program from the effect of the program itself. For example, teachers educated in one program may perform better in the classroom than teachers from another program, but this difference may be due to the characteristics of individuals entering the program, not the contribution of the program. Analyses that distinguish program effects from the selection of teachers into programs require both detailed data and an understanding of the factors affecting teachers' program selection.

Recent efforts to compile state administrative information have produced the most promising results. A few states have administrative data that link teachers to the students in their classrooms, a link that is important for assessing teacher contributions to student learning. Studies with this data tend to show that measured characteristics of teachers explain only a little of the variation in students' test-score gains. However, the measures characterizing teachers are crude; thus, we cannot know whether other measurable (though unmeasured) characteristics such as test scores, coursework, professional development, and prior work experience are important for explaining student learning. Other states collect more information on teacher backgrounds but do not link teacher data to student data, thus precluding us from estimating the effects of teacher characteristics on student learning. Yet administrative data sets from states and some large metropolitan areas are still the most promising source of information on teacher effectiveness and may soon put us in a better position to know what characteristics are important for successful classroom teaching in different environments.

## WHERE TEACHERS TEACH

The average characteristics of teachers differ dramatically across schools. High-poverty, low-performing schools with a high proportion of non-white students consistently have teachers with less experience and lower test scores than other schools. This sorting of teachers is discernable at the state and city level, but it is especially dramatic when broken down by school type. Here we summarize the information available on the distribution of teachers by selected school characteristics.

We begin by looking at the distribution across large metropolitan areas, then focus on the variability of teacher characteristics across individual schools based on minority composition, percentage of students living in poverty, and test-score performance. While we do not have clear estimates of the effect of this sorting, given our lack of knowledge about the impact of teacher qualifications, the differences in characteristics of teachers across schools may have ramifications for the quality of education students receive in different schools.

There are large differences between schools at either end of the distribution of teacher qualifications. For example, in 10 percent of New York schools nearly one in five teachers have no prior teaching experience, nearly one in four are not certified in any of their assignments, and nearly one in four failed the general knowledge certification exam. In contrast, at the other end of the distribution, more than 10 percent of schools have no first-year teachers, no teachers who have failed the general knowledge exam, and no uncertified teachers.[18]

Part of these differences across schools comes from an uneven allocation across metropolitan areas, but more comes from differences across schools within metropolitan areas. Analysis of the Schools and Staffing Surveys shows that far less than a third of the variation in the selectivity of the undergraduate institution attended by the teachers, the average experience for all teachers in the district, the percentage of teachers that were newly hired, the percentage of new hires with emergency certification, and the percentage of teachers with five or fewer years of experience who plan to teach in the district the following year is between metropolitan areas. The rest of the variation is across districts within the same metropolitan area. Thus, much of the inequality across schools is local in nature rather than national. There are, for example, greater differences in the quality of teachers among the school districts in the Phoenix area than there are between the very different metropolitan areas of Phoenix and Detroit. The distribution of teachers appears to be driven by the forces in a local, not national, teacher labor market.

Part of the differences in teacher qualifications across schools within a city corresponds to differences in student populations. Fifteen percent of teachers work in schools with greater than 80 percent minority enrollment. These schools have more teachers in their first three years of teaching, more teachers with less than ten years' experience, and fewer teachers with more than twenty years' experience. They also have the lowest percentage of teachers with certification in their primary or secondary teaching assignment.[19]

Disparities in the distribution of teacher characteristics within some large urban school districts are even greater than these numbers suggest. In New York City, for example, 26 percent of non-white students have teachers who failed the general knowledge certification exam, compared to 16 percent of white students. Twenty-one percent of non-white students have teachers who are not certified in any subject taught, compared to 15 percent of white students.[20]

Similarly, poor students' teachers are less qualified than non-poor students' teachers. In the New York City school district, 22 percent of poor students have teachers who are not certified in any subject they teach, and 30 percent have teachers who failed the certification exam, compared to 17 percent and 21 percent, respectively, of non-poor students.[21] Figure 1 shows that, nationally, only one out of ten teachers in low-poverty schools are in

**FIGURE 1    Percentage of Teachers with Three or Fewer Years of Experience by the Poverty Composition of the Students (Free or Reduced-Price Lunch), 1998**

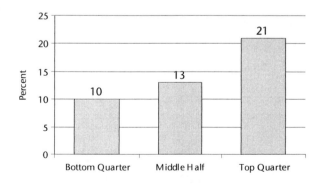

*Source:* Fast Response Survey System, Teacher Survey on Professional Development and Training, 1998. Found in: Monitoring School Quality: An Indicators Report. Dec. 2000. NCES 2001-030 (Fig. 2.3).

**TABLE 1    Average School Attributes of Teachers by Student Test Score**

| Teacher Quality Attributes | Percentage of Students at Level 1 on 4th Grade ELA | | | |
|---|---|---|---|---|
| | 0 | 0% to <5 % | 5 % to <20 % | >20 % |
| % with no teaching experience | 0.06 | 0.07 | 0.09 | 0.14 |
| % cot certified in any assignment | 0.03 | 0.04 | 0.09 | 0.22 |
| % failing NTE gen. now. or NYS lib. Arts Exam | 0.09 | 0.10 | 0.19 | 0.35 |
| % BA from most competitive college | 0.11 | 0.11 | 0.09 | 0.08 |
| % BA from least competitive college | 0.10 | 0.11 | 0.16 | 0.26 |

Source: New York State, fourth grade English Language Arts test. Lankford, Loeb, and Wyckoff, 2002

their first three years of teaching, compared with more than one in five teachers in high-poverty schools. In addition, 91 percent of teachers in low-poverty high schools report having an undergraduate or graduate major or minor in their main teaching assignment field, while just 81 percent of those in higher-poverty schools do.[22]

Similar trends hold for student performance. Table 1 shows that, in New York schools where more than 20 percent of the students performed at the lowest level on the fourth-grade English Language Arts (ELA) exam, 35 percent of the teachers had failed the general-knowledge portion of the certification exam at least once. In comparison, there was just a 9 percent failure rate among teachers in schools where none of the students scored at the lowest level on the state's fourth-grade ELA exam. Statistics on the other teacher attributes are equally dramatic. There are more teachers with no experience, no certification in their assignment areas, and degrees from the least competitive colleges in the lowest performing schools

These national and state-level statistics illustrate the distribution of the least-qualified teachers into schools with the highest minority enrollments, largest low-income enrollments, and the most academically disadvantaged students. This distribution of teachers is the result of forces including the institutional structure of the school systems and administrators' tastes and abilities, but much of it reflects the dynamics of teacher labor markets and teachers' career choices.

### Teacher Preferences

Not all teachers follow the patterns described above. Some high-ability teachers choose to teach in low-performing schools, reflecting unmeasured forces and preferences that differ from the average. In the aggregate, however, potential teachers are more likely to choose teaching and a specific teaching job if conditions are favorable. They are likely to prefer specific types of districts to others and to prefer one school to another within a district if conditions are appealing. This section describes the job attributes that appear important to teachers. In particular, it looks at three powerful predictors of teacher career decisions: wages, nonwage job attributes, and distance from home to available teaching jobs.

*Wages*

A large literature suggests that teachers respond to wages and are more likely to choose to teach when starting teachers' wages are high relative to wages in other occupations.[23] In fact, teachers appear at least as responsive to wages in their decisions to quit teaching as are workers in other occupations.[24] In 1999–2000, the average beginning teacher without a master's degree earned just under $26,000; those with an MA earned just over $28,000.[25] For additional education and years of experience, salaries increase; the top teacher salaries average about $49,000 per year across districts.

Teacher wages are low relative to the wages of full-time college graduates in other occupations. Teachers' salaries are close to those of social workers, ministers, and clerical staff. Lawyers, doctors, scientists, and engineers earn substantially more, as do managers and sales and financial service workers. Fewer workdays may partially compensate for these differences, but teaching is simply not a lucrative option for a college graduate with career opportunities in other occupations.[26] Whether teachers should be paid more is a normative question.[27]

Figure 2 shows that teacher wages have increased dramatically in real terms over the past forty years. There was a large increase in the 1960s as the baby-boom generation entered school, followed by a decrease in the 1970s as the school-age population dropped. In the 1980s, salaries rose again and remained relatively constant through the 1990s. However, when considering whether to enter the teaching profession, individuals are likely to look not only at the salaries they can expect as a teacher, but also at the salaries available in other occupations. Increases in teacher salaries in the 1960s and 1980s corresponded to similar increases in wages for non-teaching college graduates. In fact, as the figure shows, the salaries of teachers have lost

**FIGURE 2    Mean Wage and Salary Income for Women College Graduates (1994 dollars)**

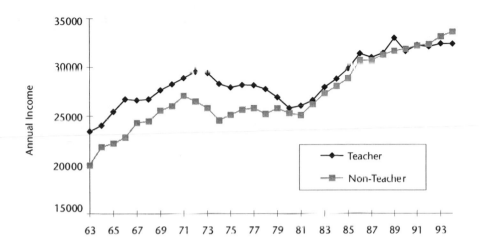

Source: March Current Population Surveys 1964–1995 (Loeb and Page 1999)

ground relative to non-teaching jobs for women college graduates since the 1970s. Although the real wages of teachers grew substantially during the period, the actual opportunity cost associated with teaching (in terms of foregone wages) increased.

Salaries affect not only whether an individual chooses to be a teacher, but also which district he or she chooses to teach in. There is significant wage variation across districts. When assessing whether this variation influences teachers' job choices, it is important to consider the variation among the districts that an individual teacher might choose. Many teachers choose among districts within a relatively small geographic area; thus, differences in salaries among metropolitan areas may be less relevant for teachers' decisions than differences in wages within an area. Most wage variation is across, not within, metropolitan areas in the United States, although some metropolitan areas do have large salary differences across districts. This large interregional wage variation contrasts with variation in the qualifications of teachers, which is largely within, not between, metropolitan areas.

A number of factors may explain the variation in teacher salaries across regions, including differences in tastes for education. The wages available to potential teachers in non-teaching jobs appears particularly important: more than half of the variation in wages across metropolitan areas can be explained solely by differences in the wages of non-teachers.[28] This finding, combined with the difference between the real wages and the opportunity costs of teaching, shows that variation in teacher wages may not reflect differences in the wage benefits of teaching if they are not considered in the context of alternative opportunities.

There is some systematic variation in salaries related to districts' characteristics.[29] The 1993–1994 Schools and Staffing Surveys showed that districts with higher proportions of free-lunch-eligible students tend to pay lower salaries, but the effect is small. There appears to be no evident difference in district wages based on the percentage of Hispanic students in a district, but districts with 30 percent or more black students pay approximately $1,500 per year less for experienced teachers, holding other factors constant. Larger districts tended to pay higher salaries than smaller districts, although this trend does not hold for the very largest districts. Small towns and rural areas within larger metropolitan areas tend to pay lower wages than their urban or suburban counterparts. There is also some evidence that districts in the suburbs of large cities tend to pay higher wages than their urban or rural counterparts, though this is not true in all metropolitan areas (e.g., Rochester, N.Y.).[30]

In summary, teachers appear to respond to wage levels and are likely to look not only at the salaries they can expect as a teacher, but also at the salaries in other available occupations. Teacher salaries are low relative to those of lawyers, doctors, scientists, engineers, managers, and sales and financial service workers, and on a par with those of social workers, ministers, and clerical staff. Much of the variation in teacher wages across districts comes from differences in average wages across metropolitan areas, not from differences within these areas, and can be attributed largely to differences in the wages of other occupations in those areas. Yet there are still some substantial differences in wages across districts within metropolitan areas. Districts with higher proportions of free-lunch-eligible students, for example, paid lower salaries, although the effect is small. Private schools also tend to pay less than public schools.

*Nonwage Job Characteristics*

Salaries are only one element of employment affecting decisions about whether and where to teach. Many nonwage job characteristics likely affect teacher preferences, including attributes of students, class size, school culture, facilities, leadership, and safety. Multiple studies have found indications that teachers prefer to teach in schools with higher-achieving students. For example, when class-size reduction in California resulted in an increase in demand for teachers across the state, teachers in schools with low-achieving students moved to higher-achieving schools.[31] Similarly, studies have found that when teachers switch schools, they are more likely to move to schools with higher-achieving students.[32]

Among the reasons teachers choose schools with more high-achieving and wealthy students is that these schools have other characteristics, such as better facilities or more preparation time, that teachers prefer. A recent survey of California teachers shows that turnover is a greater problem and vacancies harder to fill in schools with larger classes where teachers share classrooms (multitracking), or where teachers perceive the working conditions to be less favorable.[33] Principals also strongly affect the working conditions in a school; some principals are better able to create environments that teachers find favorable.

Working conditions may be more important than salaries in determining the current distribution of teachers across schools.[34] Differences across schools in nonwage attributes of the job will be particularly important when there is little variation in wages, which, as we have shown above, is the case in many metropolitan areas. However, the relative importance of non-wage job attributes does not rule out the possibility that salary differences could be used to compensate teachers for less favorable working conditions and thus provide incentives toward equalizing the distribution of teachers across schools. Working conditions can also act as incentives to attract high-quality teachers. Policies can attract effective administrators, increase preparation time, decrease class size, or provide funds to renovate facilities—all aspects that add to teachers' perceptions of good working conditions.

*Location*

In addition to wages and working conditions, school location has a strong influence on the distribution of teachers, although it has received much less attention in discussions of teacher preferences. Most teachers prefer to teach close to where they grew up and in districts similar to the district where they attended high school. This preference for home is likely true for workers in other professions as well, but it has particular ramifications for elementary and secondary schooling.

Table 2 shows that most public school teachers take their first public school teaching job very close to either their home town or their college. Sixty-one percent of teachers entering public school teaching in New York State from 1999 to 2002 started teaching in a school district located within

**TABLE 2    Distance from Home to Most Recent College, and Home to First Job, 1997–2002**

| Distance (in miles) from home to job | | Distance (in miles) from home to college | | | | |
|---|---|---|---|---|---|---|
| | | 0–15 | 15–40 | 40–100 | ≥100 | All |
| 0–15 | % col total | 75.6 | 55.2 | 49.4 | 48.0 | 61.0 |
| | % row total | 51.0 | 17.8 | 12.3 | 18.8 | 100.0 |
| 15–40 | % col total | 20.1 | 34.2 | 20.8 | 24.0 | 23.9 |
| | % row total | 34.7 | 28.1 | 13.2 | 24.0 | 100.0 |
| 40–100 | % col total | 2.8 | 8.1 | 23.7 | 8.9 | 8.5 |
| | % row total | 13.8 | 18.8 | 42.3 | 25.1 | 100.0 |
| ≥100 | % col total | 1.4 | 2.5 | 6.2 | 19.1 | 6.6 |
| | % row total | 8.9 | 7.6 | 14.2 | 69.4 | 100.0 |
| All | % N | 41.2 | 19.7 | 15.2 | 23.9 | 100.0 |
| | N | 15,891 | 7,598 | 5,861 | 9,238 | 38,588 |

*Source:* Boyd, Lankford, Loeb and Wyckoff, 2003a

fifteen miles of the district from which they graduated high school. Eighty-five percent entered teaching within forty miles of their high school. Even teachers who go far away to college tend to come home to teach: almost half of those who attended college more than 100 miles from where they went to high school returned to within fifteen miles of their high school district for their first teaching job.

These patterns may reflect more than just a preference for proximity. For example, individuals may search for employment in regions where they are comfortable, independent of the distance from their home town. Teachers appear to prefer to teach in regions similar to the one they grew up in, if not the same region. Teachers growing up in an urban area are much more likely to teach in an urban area, and those growing up in a suburban area are more likely to teach in a suburb. More than 90 percent of the teachers whose home town is New York City and who entered public school teaching from 1999 to 2002 first taught in New York City. About 60 percent of those having home towns in the New York City suburbs first taught in those suburbs. Other major urban areas in New York State follow a similar pattern.

Teachers' preferences for teaching close to home or in similar settings pose particular challenges to urban districts, which are net importers of teachers. Urban areas often do not produce as high a proportion of college graduates as suburban areas. Thus, the number of teacher recruits whose home town is urban tends to fall far short of the number of positions that need to be filled in urban districts, so these districts must attract teachers from other regions. Teacher candidates from suburban or rural home towns strongly prefer to remain in those areas. Thus, urban districts must overcome location preferences in addition to addressing the considerations typically identified with recruiting teachers to hard-to-staff urban schools: salary, school conditions, and characteristics of the student population. In general, urban schools must offer salaries, working conditions, or student populations that are more attractive than those of surrounding suburban districts to induce enough qualified candidates from suburban home towns to take jobs farther from home and in a different type of town. To the extent they do not receive these inducements, teachers with suburban home towns who take jobs in urban areas are likely to be less qualified than those who teach in the suburbs.

Urban districts often face a second disadvantage. Historically, the graduates of urban high schools do not receive adequate educations. Preferences for proximity lead to the perpetuation of inequities in the qualifications of teachers, insofar as these preferences present cities with a less qualified pool of potential teachers. The local nature of the teacher labor market increases the difficulty of breaking the cycle of inadequate education.

## USING LABOR MARKETS TO UNDERSTAND TEACHER POLICIES

Two types of policies aim to address teacher supply. One type seeks to influence the supply of teachers through changing recruitment strategies; the other seeks to improve the quality of the supply of teachers by raising standards for entering teachers. Here we address some of the strengths and weaknesses of each approach.

### Improving Recruitment Strategies

Recruiting highly skilled teachers requires a pool of able teachers from which to hire. It also requires the use of effective hiring practices to identify the most capable teachers within that pool. Recruitment policies then seek to increase supply and improve the hiring process.

*Increasing Supply*

A number of policy approaches can increase the quantity and quality of teachers in the hiring pool. Schools can act to improve working conditions through lowering class sizes, providing more mentors and coaches, or providing more material resources. They may also hire strong leaders to help create a positive school climate. Salary increases are a common approach (although perhaps not the most effective) to increasing supply.

An increase in wages increases supply. Similarly, a downturn in job stability or wages in other occupations improves the supply of teachers. Although evidence from the 1980s shows that increases in teacher wages were not accompanied by corresponding increases in the supply of teachers,[35] this was largely because the wages for non-teaching women college graduates outpaced teacher wage gains during this time. An increase in teacher wages that exceeds increases in other fields is likely to improve the supply of teachers.

Despite these basic labor market dynamics, policies that increase wages for all teachers (or decrease wages in other occupations) may not be the most effective means for increasing or improving the supply of teachers, for two reasons. First, since most teachers have been teaching for many years, an across-the-board salary increase will largely benefit those teachers who are already working in the schools. This may not be a bad policy if it improves the efforts of teachers already in the schools or decreases attrition among highly effective teachers, but it isn't the most effective way to direct funds toward individuals who are currently choosing whether to enter teaching. Second, most districts operate under a single salary schedule, paying all teachers with similar education and experience the same salary. Thus, increasing salaries means increasing them for all schools within a district. Many schools do not have difficulty recruiting teachers, and those that do may only have trouble finding teachers for particular fields. The problems with across-the-board salary increases are particularly acute due to the scale of the labor market for teachers. At the turn of the twenty-first century, approximately three million college graduates, representing almost 10 percent of all working college graduates, were teaching in elementary and secondary schools in the United States. Increasing wages for teachers who are not difficult to recruit may be a misallocation of scarce resources.

Schools may be difficult to staff because of their student body characteristics or, as noted above, because they are located in regions that produce few college graduates who are potential teachers for schools there. Policies that do not target the particular schools or subject areas with teacher shortages may increase overall supply, but will only marginally affect either the areas with shortages or the distribution of teachers across schools, because they will not make these traditionally hard-to-staff schools *relatively* more appealing. Targeted wage increases for hard-to-staff schools, especially if they are substantial, are likely to be more effective. Similarly, policies that target potential teachers with needed skills are likely to reduce shortages more effectively than generalized salary increases.

Another aspect of the recruitment debate is whether to increase salaries based on performance. By paying more to teachers who perform better in the classroom, schools may encourage the entry of more skilled teachers and increase the effort of teachers already in the classroom. The difficulty of basing pay on performance is in deciding what constitutes merit. Some policymakers advocate basing teacher pay on the test-score gains of their students, but there are significant difficulties with this. First, most tests do not cover the broad range of skills that teachers cover in the classroom. Second, such a system would encourage teachers to focus instruction on material contained in the test—"teaching to the test"—and neglect other important areas of the curriculum. Third, the policy may encourage cheating and discourage collaboration among teachers. Collaboration and mentoring are particularly important for new teachers. Policies that discourage teacher interaction may increase the time it takes for new teachers to become effective, and it may also contribute to turnover if these new teachers are dissatisfied with their abilities in the classroom.

A second type of merit pay plan would give principals discretion to disperse bonuses. In a system with high-quality administrators, this would have the benefit of rewarding classroom effectiveness while avoiding testing problems. Principals may also be given discretion to target bonuses to teachers in subject areas that are hard to staff. However, many factors that plague the teacher labor market affect the administrator work force as well. In the 1999–2000 academic year, New York City schools were more than 50 percent more likely to have a new principal than were schools in the surrounding suburbs. Inexperienced administrators may not have the skills to use discretionary funds wisely. It is unclear whether principal discretion is the most effective mechanism for increasing the quality of teaching in the schools; with a concerted effort to improve school administration, it may be in the future.[36]

When budget constraints limit the size of across-the-board salary increases, targeting funds to high-needs schools and shortage areas is likely to be more effective than nontargeted reforms, especially at the state level. Yet many recent efforts to increase teacher salaries have not been targeted.

Thirty-five states currently provide retention bonuses for teachers.[37] Five of these states target these bonuses to teachers in high-need schools. Six states have instituted housing incentives, and another five have signing bonuses for new teachers, but only three states target their housing incentives and two target their signing bonuses. Individual districts also use differentiated wage and benefit structures to attract teachers. Out of thirty large school districts, ten give signing bonuses for new teachers and nine give housing incentives. Three of the ten districts that give signing bonuses target them to high-need schools, as do two of the nine districts offering housing incentives.[38]

Wage-based approaches are popular but may not be sufficient or efficient in attracting high-quality teachers or equalizing the distribution of teachers across schools. Improvements in working conditions may be a less costly approach. Capital improvements in schools and better provision of supplies might help attract and retain teachers. Attracting effective leaders is also an important component of a broader policy to improve the quality of teachers' working conditions, and therefore of teachers. Effective leaders often can improve school environments by putting in place support systems for teachers, creating lively learning environments, and allocating resources effectively.

*Improving the Hiring Process*

Teachers' decisions are not the only factors affecting the composition and distribution of the teacher work force. The quality of district hiring and assignment practices is likely to contribute to the disparities in teacher qualifications across schools and districts. Some administrators operate inefficiently and are unable to hire highly qualified individuals who are willing to teach in their schools. Many of the districts with the least qualified teachers hire their new teachers very late in the summer or even in the fall. Districts that hire earlier are able to recruit their top choices; other districts are left with teachers that could not find jobs elsewhere.[39]

Schools with ineffective administration or weak parent participation may be at the whim of district administrators, and their teacher work force may suffer. For example, schools with strong parental input may not accept low-quality teachers. When parents and students complain about poor teachers, the teachers may be transferred to schools with high student transfer rates, large numbers of students receiving free or reduced-price lunches, and large numbers of minority students, where parental pressure may not be as strong.[40] Inefficient hiring procedures and lack of power in the district may be compounded if administrators cannot identify the most qualified teachers from the pool of teacher applicants, or if they do not hire these teachers when they have the opportunity.

It is difficult to tell how pervasive these problems are. Few studies give us an in-depth view of the hiring process, and these studies tend to describe only a small number of districts. One indication that schools are not hiring the best available candidates is that many highly capable individuals (e.g., those who attended selective undergraduate institutions) apply for teaching jobs but don't end up teaching, while many less qualified individuals do end up teaching.[41] There are three possible explanations for this phenomenon. First, districts may not select the most highly qualified individuals available to them. Second, these highly qualified teaching applicants may apply only to the most selective schools, most likely high-achieving suburban schools. If they do not get these jobs, they then seek jobs in other occupations rather than in other schools. Third, schools may choose teachers by other, unmeasured characteristics.[42] We do not yet understand which of these phenomena predominate. A recent study of New York schools and teachers suggests that when given their choice of teachers, schools on average choose teachers with higher test performance, but the study does not address whether this is true specifically in schools serving poor or low-performing students.[43]

In summary, hiring practices in some districts are not efficient and thus these districts are not hiring as highly skilled teachers as they could. It is also clear that the pool of potential teachers differs across districts and that this supply problem is partly to blame for differences in the characteristics of teachers across schools.

## Raising Requirements

Improving recruitment, either through better administration or increasing wage and non-wage benefits, is one approach to improving teaching; changing certification and education requirements is an alternative. Raising requirements for entry into teaching has three potential effects. First, additional education may improve skills and prepare potential teachers for the difficulties of classroom teaching, thus creating a more stable, skilled work force. High teacher turnover, exacerbated by poor preparation, is costly to districts, both because first- and second-year teachers often are less effective with students than more experienced teachers and because there are direct recruitment and hiring costs.

A second potential effect of raising requirements is that potential teachers who do not meet a minimum standard of competency will be barred from the work force. Most states require teachers to pass exams on general knowledge and teaching practice. In 2002, for example, forty-four states required potential teachers to take written tests in order to receive a beginning teacher license.[44]

Although policies that raise requirements have these potentially positive effects, the additional requirements represent barriers to entry that may keep highly skilled individuals away from the classroom. Coursework takes substantial time, a high cost for individuals who could use that time to earn money in other occupations. Increased barriers may be a particular problem for schools that traditionally have had the most difficulty attracting teachers, as well as for the most able individuals interested in teaching. The schools, often with high proportions of poor and low-performing students, face a small pool of possible hires, and increased requirements reduce this pool even more. Insofar as new requirements weed out the worst candidates, provide schools and districts with additional information, and keep them from making poor choices, this may be a beneficial policy. However, to the extent that the new requirements do not accurately identify good teachers and administrators are effectively choosing from the pool of candidates available to them, increased requirements may eliminate some of the better candidates from an already insufficient pool and disadvantage these schools to an even greater extent.[45]

Barriers may also be a particular problem for high-ability teaching candidates, who have ample alternative opportunities. These individuals may be more likely to be on the fence between entering teaching and choosing another career, likely one with higher wages. A test may not present a high barrier to these potential teachers, but additional education requirements that require time investments may. If these potential teachers are unsure of their career choice, they may be unwilling to try teaching if they need to invest substantial time before entering the classroom, especially if that investment has little return in labor markets in other fields.

Sensitivity to barriers may also be particularly strong for individuals who come to teaching from other careers. While many teachers enter the classroom directly from college, more and more enter later in their careers. More than 80 percent of first-year teachers in New York State in 1970 were under twenty-five years of age. By the mid-1980s this number had decreased to roughly 40 percent and has continued to slowly decline ever since. Nationally, approximately one-quarter of first-year teachers are less than twenty-five years of age, but about one-seventh are forty years of age or older. These later entrants may be sensitive to tests if they have been out of school and away from testing (older entrants in New York State tend to score lower on tests than younger entrants), and they may be sensitive to education requirements if they need to continue to support families as they switch careers.

Sensible preparation requirements seek to minimize the costs of entry for teachers while providing the skills they need to be successful in the classroom. Current preparation programs may not be as effective as they should be, especially for low-performing schools. They rarely provide training on the specific issues involved in teaching in these schools, and they do not include mentoring programs that follow new teachers into the classroom and support their development. However, there is virtually no information on what aspects of teacher preparation *would* help teachers—key information for designing requirements that are effective for improving teacher performance but not onerous for individuals considering a teaching career.

Partly because the impact of education and certification requirements on student outcomes is not well understood, as well as the strong belief that these requirements limit the supply of teachers, many states have implemented alternative certification programs aimed at reducing the barriers to entry for college graduates interested in teaching. All but six states have some kind of alternate route program to recruit, train, and certify teachers. Twenty-four states and the District of Columbia have structured alternate route programs with preservice training and mentoring components. Eighteen of the programs require entrants to pass a basic skills or subject-area test. Alternate route programs in twelve states and the District of Columbia also require some classroom training before candidates are assigned to their own classes. These programs mimic teacher-education programs by providing classroom training for teachers, but do not require substantial time investment prior to entering the classroom.[46] They tend to backload the course requirements so that teachers can earn a salary while taking the coursework. To supplement the alternate routes into teaching, more districts are implementing induction programs that help teachers in their first years of teaching. In 1997–1998, 65 percent of teachers in their first three years of teaching had participated in such programs in their first year of teaching, compared with only 14 percent of those with twenty or more years of experience.

As is the case with other important teacher supply policies, we have little evidence regarding the success of alternate route or induction programs in attracting and retaining high-quality teachers. Not all alternate routes are alike; some offer preservice coursework very similar to that provided by traditional routes, while others feature little coursework or exposure to students and schools prior to entry into the classroom.[47]

Attracting more able college graduates into teaching is an important policy goal. The number of teachers needed in our schools is tremendous, and our ability to raise teacher salaries to compete with other professions is limited. Good policies must address the needs and abilities of the individuals interested in teaching within constraints. Areas that have had poor schools in the past and do not produce enough high-scoring college graduates may face a work force without the ideal skills.[48] Education and certification requirements may improve these skills. Similarly, highly skilled candidates from other locations may not have the skills necessary to teach in environments that are very different from the ones in which they grew up. Teacher education may help provide these skills as well. The trick is to understand what types of education are effective, how to create requirements that do not weaken the teacher work force by keeping away high-quality candidates, and how to structure schools to make the best use of the candidates available to them.

## DISCUSSION AND CONCLUSION

Researchers have learned a great deal about what matters in education. For example, demography is not destiny; effective teachers can and do overcome many of the hurdles facing disadvantaged students and can have a great impact on how much students learn. However, a weak research base limits our ability to design cost-effective teacher certification and recruitment policies. We have only rudimentary information on the connection between observable teacher attributes and effective teaching. Similarly, while we know wages, location, and other nonpecuniary aspects of teaching are important for teachers' decisions, we do not know the relative importance of these factors in influencing individuals' decisions to enter teaching or to seek specific teaching jobs. Moreover, though we know that some preparation can improve teaching, we do not know which aspects of preparation are important in preparing effective teachers, nor how much the entry barriers created by additional requirements reduce the entry of highly qualified teachers or unnecessarily reduce the applicant pool for hard-to-staff schools.

Researchers working closely with state and local education agencies have begun to develop databases that will support research to address many of these policy issues. These efforts are characterized by linking student value-added test results to the attributes of the teachers who taught them. A number of policy questions can be informed by examining the variation across teacher attributes that exist within and across districts within a state. For example, the variation in the structure and content of teacher-preparation programs, combined with controls for other relevant factors, can be used to identify the effect of various components of teacher preparation. This research is just beginning.

What advice can researchers offer policymakers amid this uncertainty? First, when trying to solve specific problems such as shortages of math teachers or highly qualified teachers in low-performing schools, don't use the sledgehammer of raising salaries for all. It is extremely expensive and doesn't change relative wages. Rather, adopt policies targeted to the problem at hand, even if it means modifying the usual approach to teacher salary contracts or supplementing uniform local contract wages with more flexible state funds. Reserve general salary increases, where needed, for making the teaching profession more attractive than the alternatives. Second, recognize that salaries are not the only important policy tool. Better working conditions and improved recruitment and hiring practices can help schools and districts attract and retain high-quality teachers. Third, be cautious about imposing new teacher-qualification requirements and teacher-preparation program requirements. Given how little researchers know about what works and what doesn't, there is a danger of imposing new requirements that exclude or discourage potentially capable teachers, while doing little to raise the quality of those included. Requirements should aim to balance the benefits of greater preparation with the possibly dissuading effect of greater time requirements.

# Introduction to Part Two

As we have seen in the preceding chapters, there is reason for serious concern about policymaking, regulatory and legislative enforcement, the limited base of research supporting many current teacher-certification and licensure policies, and the quality and rigor of many teacher-preparation programs. However, these problems are far from overlooked. As Andrew Rotherham and Sara Mead point out in the first chapter, the teacher-certification debate is not a simple contest between defenders of the status quo and proponents of reform. Instead, in a debate where hardly anyone wishes to defend the status quo, the debate rages over competing prescriptions for reform.

But there are widely varying ideas about solution. Major questions that policymakers must consider include: What can and should government regulate in this area? How much training do aspiring teachers need before they can apply for a teaching job, and should these requirements vary by teaching assignment? How can teacher-training institutions be held accountable for the quality of the graduates? Where should they get this training? What formal requirements or tests should aspiring teachers have to complete or pass, and when in their training should they do so? At what point in the training process should such tests be passed? Is there one approach to training or a variety that policymakers should allow?

The final four chapters in this volume delve into solutions and answers to these questions. They can be grouped under two larger rubrics. Policymakers must decide how aggressively the state ought to regulate which individuals are licensed to teach and which programs are approved to provide teacher preparation. Considering these two dimensions of regulation, there are four possible courses that legislatures might take. One path is to strengthen the current system of regulatory and input control in an effort to ensure the quality of both teachers and training programs. A radically different tack is to seek to eliminate measures that regulate teacher entry and teacher-preparation programs. Finally, there are two compromise solutions to consider, one that replaces regulatory and input control with outcome accountability that is focused on *individuals*, and a second that replaces regulatory and input control with outcome accountability focused on *preparation programs*.

Figure 1 illustrates how these options relate to each other.

Individual Centered

| | High institutional requirements/ Low individual requirements | High institutional requirements/ High individual requirements |
|---|---|---|
| | Low institutional requirements/ Low individual requirements | Low institutional requirements/ High individual requirements |

Institution Centered

The chapter by Gary Sykes is likely to be the most familiar to readers. Sykes argues that the existing framework for teacher preparation is not fundamentally flawed but suffers from a lack of rigor and support at the state level. Sykes advocates adding greater rigor to existing requirements for institutions and for individuals, while simultaneously supporting this approach with professional expertise and an investment of new resources. His "professional model" is based on coordinated state-level policies and greater support for aspiring teachers. Sykes sees steps that the state of Connecticut has taken to improve teacher quality as a model for his proposal.

Bryan Hassel and Michele E. Sherburne argue for a more pluralistic version of the approved program route. They propose that state governments charter providers of teacher education for a fixed number of years and certify their graduates as ready to teach in the state's schools. Under their system, entities besides institutions of higher education would be able to train and prepare teachers. Hassel and Sherburne believe that this will create greater diversity and quality in teacher-preparation programs while preserving state oversight and monitoring. While the Hassel and Sherburne proposal is likely to seem novel to many in the world of teacher preparation, it draws heavily on the lessons learned from the experience with charter schooling in K–12 education.

Catherine B. Walsh argues for a strengthened undergraduate program of study to improve the academic skills and knowledge of aspiring teachers. Walsh states that "the importance of teacher's verbal ability has been undersold while the importance of undergraduate education coursework has been oversold." She argues that this misplaced emphasis undermines the academic preparation of teachers, particularly underperforming minority groups. Her proposal would require a well-rounded liberal education for prospective teachers, but the state would no longer prescribe the coursework or credit hours needed to prepare for teaching in order to avoid erecting barriers to the profession to individuals who seek to enter through other routes. The state's assurance of quality would be based entirely on a strong assessment system, not dissimilar to the new American Board certification tests currently under consideration in many states.

Finally, offering a diagnosis and prescription that is opposite to Sykes', Michael Podgursky argues for eliminating most of the bars that now restrict teacher entry or would-be preparation programs. He argues that raising bars for either institutions or individuals will hinder rather than help, because policymakers and researchers know so little about what qualities lead to effective teaching. Podgursky argues instead that policymakers should focus on measuring what they can, educational outputs from schools, and prescribe only minimal requirements for those seeking to teach. Podgursky's proposal is most similar to a loosely regulated alternative certification route.

In relation to the earlier schematic, these four chapters can be roughly viewed as follows:

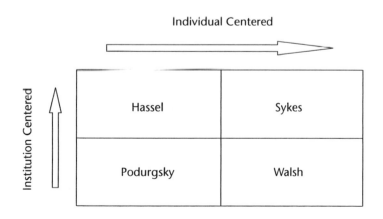

Readers and policymakers will likely find parts of each proposal with which they will be more or less comfortable. Most important here is that each author proposes a concrete answer to important questions about teacher licensure and certification. As they consider these models and their own reforms, policymakers must resist the temptation to simply cobble together various ideas to please multiple constituencies or to split the difference where clear decisionmaking is required. Many of the problems chronicled in this book stem from the accretion of various policies and compromises that over time cloud the original goals policymakers sought to tackle. Clarity about goals, policies, and the benefits and costs of any particular reform is essential to addressing the teacher-quality challenge.

## CHAPTER 7

# Cultivating Quality in Teaching
## A Brief for Professional Standards

*Gary Sykes with Marisa Burian-Fitzgerald*

## Professional Teaching Standards: The Case of Connecticut

"Who is this that darkens counsel by words without knowledge?" Job 38:1

### INTRODUCTION

This paper presents the case for a strong state role in regulating the teaching profession, including a staged system of licensure that extends into the early years of teaching, together with accreditation standards for the programs that prepare teachers. After reviewing the rationale for such a role, policy developments in the state of Connecticut are presented as a case of exemplary state action. Over a fifteen-year span continuing to the present day, Connecticut has developed a comprehensive approach to education reform whose centerpiece has been a combination of state standards and strong incentives for teaching. Evidence suggests that these reforms, taken together, have contributed to a range of positive outcomes in the state. Though the full costs of such a model are high, they may be phased in over time and distributed among the state, local agencies, and individuals. Validation evidence for various aspects of this model has yet to be established, but the case supplies one instance of a strong role for state-professional regulation of teaching.

Once upon a time, the term *professional* was an honorific signifying valued qualities in individuals and occupations so designated. Today the concept of professionalism has come under fire from a variety of quarters,[1] most vehemently in the education field. Under such circumstances, the question arises whether the professional ideal may be made serviceable as an instrument of educational policy and practice.

Professionalism in most fields relies on the authority of the state to sanction standards of various kinds, and education should not be the exception. This analysis begins with the rationale for a strong state role; turns next to a description of one model, established over a period of years in the state of Connecticut, and reviews evidence of its impact; adds an accounting of costs; considers challenges to the model; and concludes with some general observations.

## THE STATE'S INTEREST IN STANDARDS FOR TEACHERS

The foundation of the professional model is the existence of standards of various kinds that represent the knowledge, skills, and dispositions useful to practice. The basic model includes standards for individuals and standards for the programs that prepare them. Both the state and the profession have an interest in these standards. The state's interest is to ensure just that level or amount of competence to protect those whom the profession serves. The profession's interest is to assure that the basic ideals of practice are represented in the standards established by the state in consultation with the profession.

Should the state have a role in regulating the teaching profession? Economists have debated this question, and some have argued in the negative.[2] Their essential argument is that state regulation is neither necessary nor productive when more flexible and performance-based means of controlling teacher quality are potentially available. What do they have in mind? Imagine a hypothetical world where students and their families simply select schools to their liking. With teachers on one- to five-year contracts rather than lifelong tenure, good schools would hire good teachers in order to attract students and families. Poor schools would fail, and schools that failed to attract students would have incentive to replace poor teachers with good ones. In such a world, there would be no need to certify teachers or to accredit programs of teacher preparation. The marketplace would solve the problem of teacher quality.

For three reasons, a solution that looks to the marketplace is inadequate.[3] First, the benefits of schooling are conferred not on individuals alone, but on society as a whole and on its citizenry. These benefits include uniform social goals, such as a common set of values and knowledge for functioning in a democratic society. The precise content of such goals is contestable; the fact that we expect schools to do more than satisfy the private desires of individual students and families is well established. Consequently, the state must have some means of assuring that the social goals of schooling are satisfied. Second, it is not clear that students and their parents are able to appropriately evaluate the quality of teaching. Although the preferences of students and parents surely ought to play some part in the selection of teachers, there also ought to be other objective criteria that enter into decisions about who should teach. For example, at a minimum the state might want to ensure that candidates do not have criminal records or evidence of mental illness. More likely, states also will want to ensure a standard of safe practice in teaching, despite the difficulty in defining such a standard. Consumers of education require such assurances about the competence of teachers because the costs of obtaining these assurances privately are too great.

In other societies, centralized ministries establish common qualifications for all teachers on a national basis. In such systems, parents may have greater confidence that teacher quality from school to school is relatively even. The United States, however, has a system of local control with great variation in the amount and quality of educational inputs from district to district, school to school. The tradition of the neighborhood school prompts parents to enroll their children in the school nearest their residence, heedless of much information about teacher quality. Although some parents take time to assess teachers and to demand the best for their children, others do not. In a school economy of "alert and inert" consumers,[4] too many children, who only go to school once, may lack protections from poor, ill-qualified teachers. With its constitutional responsibility for education, the state must supply the necessary protections.

Finally, unlike the imaginary example, the institution of tenure after three years is well established in the public school system, limiting flexibility in hiring and dismissing teachers based on feedback from parents and students. Whatever the merits of teacher tenure, it is an established feature of the present system of public education, deeply instituted in law, in practice, and in our culture. Because the political costs of abolishing tenure are unacceptably high, any proposal to ensure teacher quality must reckon with this established feature of the educational workplace. As a consequence, guarantees of teacher competence must be relatively strong at the point of entry and throughout evaluation in the pretenure years of teaching.

A middle solution between market control and professional control might be a slender set of state regulations. As one manifesto succinctly puts it, "Every child should be able to count on having a teacher who has a solid general education, who possesses deep subject area knowledge, and who has no record of misbehavior."[5] States might elect standards that include just 1) an undergraduate education with a suitable major and minor; 2) individual qualifications of character and knowledge; 3) assessments of knowledge that individuals must pass in order to teach; and 4) the match or fit between qualifications and teaching assignment. Remarkably, most states do not have even these requirements in place. They have not developed adequate content area tests for teacher licensure,[6] and in many states the distribution of teachers whose disciplinary major or minor fits their teaching assignments is highly uneven and unequal—across teaching areas and across community types—creating serious questions of access to qualified teachers.[7] As a first order of business, then, states should ensure at least these minimal qualifications. Professional standards, as this paper next argues, offer the strongest guarantee of a fully qualified teacher work force.

## Beyond the Middle Solution: The Case for Professional Standards

The primary claim undergirding the professional model is that the additional requirements contained in an accredited course of study and practice, coupled with a staged series of assessments, supply the necessary and sufficient conditions to warrant responsible practice in teaching. In contrast, the middle solution supplies the necessary but not the sufficient conditions for such assurance.

A stepwise progression supplies the logic. First, education, in keeping with other professional fields, must exercise some selectivity on entry to the professional course of study. Consequently, admissions criteria to teacher education that include such indicators as GPA in the liberal arts portion of study, together with preprofessional tests of basic skills in literacy and numeracy, constitute the first line of protection. Then, students should complete an accredited course of study in the education field that is complementary to and integrated with their disciplinary and liberal arts preparation. The accreditation standards supply assurance that the knowledge and skill deemed essential to the practice of teaching are well and fully represented in the coursework and other educational experiences that a teaching candidate undertakes. The logic of program accreditation is straightforward. Candidates for teaching cannot learn what they are not exposed to. Accreditation standards supply the assurance that the appropriate content is offered to teacher candidates. Accreditation, then, may be thought of as an opportunity-to-learn standard applied to all institutions that prepare teachers.

States might stop here, judging that program requirements are sufficient to guarantee competence. For many years this was the policy.[8] More recently, however, states have instituted licensure examinations of various kinds for two reasons. First, examinations provide assurances not simply about opportunities to learn but about actual learning. Second, they constitute an external validation that teaching candidates have acquired the professional knowledge requisite to responsible teaching.

These standards might complete the policy framework, but something vital is still missing. The state must have assurances that teaching candidates are able to put knowledge and skills acquired during preparation into practice, in relation to students from diverse backgrounds. First, institutions must be required to supply opportunity-to-practice standards through an internship or equivalent experience (related terms derived from other fields are induction or residency requirements). Within an internship, teaching candidates on provisional licenses begin to teach under controlled and supervised conditions that typically include a reduced load, access to a mentor teacher, and related features. The intern period combines support with assessment while emphasizing the opportunity to practice, in both senses of the term—to engage in and to try out.

Finally, performance assessments serve as external validation of the intern experience and to ensure that the candidate is able to apply knowledge and skill in the service of competent teaching and student learning. Successful completion of the performance assessment results in a full license to teach, which then is subject to continuing licensure requirements, typically organized around forms of additional study and practice.[9]

In this staged progression, no single piece of evidence testifies alone to the competence of the beginning teacher. Taken alone, each element is an insufficient guarantee. It is the combination of these elements, "the marriage of insufficiencies,"[10] that supplies the full warrant. As one advocate sums up, "A record is built, with evidence accumulated from the beginning of professional study to the final assessment required by the state. It is this aggregation of information that assures the public that a beginning professional is fit to practice, and that provides the basis for public confidence in the quality of beginning professionals."[11]

Beyond these first-line justifications for the professional model there is one additional argument. If research and development continually produce new knowledge about how to teach effectively, then there must be some orderly means for conveying advances in "the art and science of teaching" to practitioners. Professional standards serve as the repository for such advances insofar as they are continuously reviewed and updated by the profession. The improvement of teaching, this argument goes, is substantially tied up in the development of professional standards. As the professional model is elaborated through its programmatic requirements, assessments, procedures, and practices, so it becomes a vehicle through which to disseminate knowledge that underlies effective teaching. The subtitle of a volume written by several prominent advocates for the professional model captures this argument: *Building a Profession for 21st Century Schools*.[12]

## THE PROFESSIONAL MODEL

Lawrence Summers, Harvard's current president, likes to say that one example is worth a thousand theories. The professional model for quality assurance in teaching enjoys such an example in the state of Connecticut. A close examination of this case will reveal the essential elements, which then may be compared with several additional elements that some policy analysts have advocated.

### The Connecticut Example

Phased in over fifteen years, Connecticut has established a substantial pathway to teaching.[13] The current model includes a three-tiered, staged system for beginning, provisional, and professional licensure. Basic elements of the model include:

- A test of basic skills required for entry to a program of teacher education. Connecticut now uses the Praxis I test developed by the Educational Testing Service. Individuals with an SAT score of 1000 or more may waive this examination.
- A subject-matter examination in the candidate's teaching area(s) taken at or toward the end of their college experience. Connecticut now uses the Praxis II tests for this purpose. Completion of this examination results in a beginning license for entry to a teaching position.
- Graduation from a state-approved (recognized by the National Council for the Accreditation of Teacher Education (NCATE)) program of teacher education.
- Provision of a mentor or school-based support team in the first year of teaching together with state-sponsored seminars and clinics that teach-

ers must attend to prepare them for the examination of their teaching in the second year.

- Completion of a highly structured, subject-matter-oriented portfolio in the second year of teaching that is graded on a set of competencies by two trained assessors. Trained mentors and other school-based supports are available to assist teachers in compiling this portfolio. Successful completion of the portfolio results in a provisional license to teach.
- Completion of continuing education for a renewable professional license.

Around these regulations, Connecticut gradually has elaborated a whole system of coordinated polices and supporting elements. Take first the coordinate policies: A rigorous, detailed, extended, and costly system of entry to teaching might produce a number of adverse consequences, including a reduction in the overall supply of teachers, with especially severe shortages in hard-to-staff schools and districts and in such fields as mathematics and the sciences. To overcome these potential problems, the state initiated these additional policies:

- raising and equalizing teacher salaries across districts, providing state salary aid to reach a target minimum for the salaries of fully certified teachers;
- enacting scholarships and forgiveable loans to attract high-ability candidates to teacher education at the undergraduate and graduate levels and to encourage candidates to teach in priority schools and shortage fields;
- facilitating entry to teaching for well-trained teachers from out of state; and,
- authorizing alternate routes into teaching for nontraditional candidates, including examination provisions for such candidates prior to granting provisional licenses.

In addition to these coordinated policies, the state gradually built a system of supports around their state teaching standards. These included:

- training for the assessors and mentors to serve in the new roles that were created within the licensing system;
- feedback and coaching sessions for teachers not meeting the portfolio standard in year two;
- provision of libraries of successful portfolios available for review at regional support centers and online; regional workshops by experienced teachers on the technical aspects of portfolio assembly; and

- integration of portfolio development and content into university teacher education.

## Taking a Closer Look

From a policymaking perspective, Connecticut's is a particularly compelling strategy for educational reform. The most interesting aspect of the case is that the state chose to lead with standards for teaching, then to use these standards as the basis for a comprehensive program of reform. A closer look reveals how the standards evolved in relation to national developments, then gradually became connected to the state's standards for learning and the university programs of teacher education.

First, the state gradually elaborated a core set of standards for teaching, which formed the basis for the assessment system, particularly the portfolio aspects. Appendix I presents Connecticut's Common Core of Teaching, which has been widely disseminated and used throughout the state. These standards were developed gradually in relation to emerging national trends, particularly the work of the Interstate New Teacher Assessment and Support Consortium (INTASC) formed by the Chief State School Officers organization. The INTASC standards in turn were based on the advanced standards established by the National Board for Professional Teaching Standards (NBPTS). The state then relied on the consensus of nationally organized public and professional groups to establish its standards for teaching. These standards represented an advance over their predecessors because they

> recognize the disciplinary base of pedagogical practice and include much greater emphasis on the assessment and diagnosis of student needs and learning as a basis for teaching decisions rather than the implementation of teaching routines. The new standards evaluate teaching in relation to student learning rather than on the basis of teaching behaviors alone, and they do so within specific content fields, drawing on research that points to teaching strategies that are effective for particular purposes (e.g., the teaching of writing, development of mathematical thinking, and the like).[14]

A critical element in this revised conception of teaching has been the portfolio. The state initially established a classroom observation system organized around generic competencies in teaching (the Connecticut Competency Instrument, CCI). With the move toward stronger subject- and student-oriented standards, the state changed its assessment instrument to a year-long portfolio, structured by subject area. Second-year teachers assemble lesson logs, videotapes, teacher commentaries, and student work sam-

## FIGURE 1    Assessments and Supports for Beginning Teachers in Connecticut

| Year One | Year Two | Year Three |
|---|---|---|
| School-Based Support:<br>• By mentor or support team<br>State-Based Support:<br>• Discipline-specific seminars<br>• CCI clinics | School-Based Support:<br>• By mentor or support team<br>State-Based Support:<br>• Discipline-based seminars<br>• Portfolio assessment: submission by May 1 | State-Based support:<br>• Feedback and coaching sessions for beginning teachers not meeting portfolio standard in year two<br>• Portfolio assessment: resubmission of a teaching portfolio |

Source: Adapted from Wilson, Darling-Hammond, & Berry, 2001, p. 17

ples. Two assessors, each certified to teach in the candidate's area, evaluate each portfolio using a common scoring rubric. Teachers who do not meet the passing standard may apply for a third year of teaching, during which they must resubmit their portfolio.[15] As Figure 1 illustrates, the state assessment system is embedded in an elaborate support system that spans up to three years of a new teacher's career.

How, though, do the teaching standards relate to standards for student learning? This is a critical question for states, because standards-based reform is the defining characteristic of the current era. This reform approach seeks to align the critical elements of learning in order to produce a stronger, more coherent set of outcomes. Districts across the country now are busy mapping curriculum materials onto state standards for learning and the content of state assessments. But the theory of standards-based reform also encompasses the content of preservice preparation and ongoing professional development. Achieving alignment with these elements remains problematic. Connecticut approached this issue in distinctive fashion.

Along with the teaching standards, Connecticut also developed and refined standards and assessments for student learning. The state enacted a Common Core of Learning, which sets forth the foundational skills for all students, and then introduced statewide assessments in the core areas of reading, language arts, writing, and listening in grades four, six, and eight, and subsequently in mathematics, science, language arts, and interdisciplinary studies in the tenth grade. The assessments include short-answer and longer essay responses, as well as standardized achievement testing. Connecticut's tests resemble the National Assessments of Educational Progress in many respects, emphasizing higher-order thinking and performance skills. The tests adhere to the professional standards for testing issued by the APA, AERA, and NCME, and they are low-stakes in that no sanctions or rewards are attached to them. The state tracks assessment results and feeds information back to districts and schools on test objectives and results. The state also provides supplemental assessments on request in grades three, five, and seven, and offers additional resources to the neediest districts, including professional development funds, preschool and all-day kindergarten, and smaller pupil teacher ratios.

These developments worked hand in hand with the teacher reforms in two ways. First, strong standards for entry, along with increased recruitment incentives, helped to provide "highly qualified" teachers who were prepared to reach the goals set by the new standards for learning. Second, the state organized significant cross-fertilization in the committees of practitioners, community members, subject-matter experts, and others that developed both sets of standards. Over time, the state elaborated a common vision that united their student assessments, K–12 content standards, Common Core of Learning, Common Core of Teaching, and BEST portfolio standards, creating a coherent set distinguished by a shared philosophical outlook on the learning desired and the teaching necessary to inspire such learning.

An example drawn from the science standards demonstrates how the state pursued the alignment of standards. Connecticut's K–12 content standards for science, together with the Common Core of Learning, specify that students should learn about interactions between elements, recognize the variable and invariant aspects of those interactions, and be able to identify and solve problems through scientific inquiry. To assess students against this benchmark, the CAPT science assessment (required of all tenth-grade students) calls for students to design and carry out an experiment to determine which chemical, when dissolved in water, is best to use in a cold pack. The students must clearly state their research question, complete an experiment of their devising to answer the question, then draw appropriate conclusions from their data. The portfolio assessment mirrors these standards by requiring teachers to organize a set of lessons around an essential question and to provide opportunities for students to engage in scientific inquiry to explore that question.

As in the CAPT, the teacher portfolio assessment divides the inquiry process into pre-activity, activity, and post-activity stages, and evaluates the teacher based on her demonstrated ability to encourage students to explore the validity of scientific data and to promote students' thinking about the science content embedded in inquiry activities. Together, the standards and assessments of students focus on the content of scientific knowledge, the inquiry process used to acquire such knowledge, and applications of the knowledge. In turn, the portfolio assessment evaluates teachers' abilities to design lessons rich in content, to use inquiry-based instruction, and to engage students in the application of scientific knowledge. Furthermore, the portfolio requires teachers to monitor students' progress and adjust their teaching in relation to students' unfolding understanding.

The portfolio assessment represents a vital component of this coherent system of instruction. By outlining expectations for teachers that are aligned with those for students, the state advances a common approach to teaching and learning. The portfolio process serves not only as an assessment for teacher licensure, but also as a capacity-building instrument that focuses teachers' attention on appropriate curriculum content and instructional strategies. This alignment also supplies guidance to teachers on how to evaluate their instruction with respect to the standards students must meet.

Along with articulating the relationship between standards for teaching and for learning, Connecticut also has sought to link their teaching standards and assessments to the programs of teacher preparation in the universities. Several policy initiatives are noteworthy. The state now encourages teacher-preparation institutions to begin using the policy tools established in the licensure system, including the teaching standards, the observation protocol (CCI), and the portfolio requirements. New standards for clinical field experiences also have been enacted. These now focus on competencies rather than course credits and require practice teaching in all areas for which a teacher applies for endorsements. Semester hour and course requirements in teacher education are being replaced with the demonstration of competencies (linked to the teaching standards) through a wider range of means, including use of the state's instruments and procedures.

Connecticut also had state program accreditation processes in place, but in 2003 the state adopted the NCATE standards, which are aligned with the other professional standards (e.g., INTASC, National Board for Professional Teaching Standards (NBPTS)) that guide teaching and learning. The State Board of Education determined that the NCATE program and unit standards fit well with the state's other standards, and so merited adoption. As part of the overall accountability built into this emerging and interlocking set of standards, NCATE recently announced an agreement with ETS to benchmark the Praxis II standards nationwide, then link the pass rate on these examinations to NCATE accreditation. Soon, preparation programs will be required to ensure that their students pass the Praxis II subject area examinations, which will be nationally benchmarked in order to avoid problems with state-established cut scores.[16]

The state also developed an alternate route policy that created access to teaching for nontraditional recruits without lowering entry standards. The Connecticut Department of Higher Education developed a summer-long program (and later, a version that meets throughout the year on weekends) that included stringent entry standards, successful completion of Praxis examinations, and a course of practice teaching before assuming full responsibility for the classroom. This program has been targeted to middle and secondary teachers and to shortage fields. Graduates then must secure a teaching position, which triggers a request to the state for a temporary 90-day certificate. During this trial period, the employing district provides special, intensive supervision of the candidate. At the end of the trial, successful candidates receive their provisional license, then enter the portfolio assessment process. Although the program supplies only a small number of teachers annually (300 in 2003), demand for them is strong, and evidence indicates that they stay in teaching at rates comparable to regular entrants. Along with the recruitment incentives, this program has helped supply urban and rural schools with teachers in traditional shortage areas.

Finally, the state also is taking steps to ensure stronger alignment of continuing education unit (CEU) content with the teaching and learning standards and the teacher evaluation system. The guidelines for issuance of CEUs were rewritten, and the primary focus was that all professional development experiences aim "to enrich or improve the skills, knowledge, and abilities of educators to improve student learning." Gradually, then, the state is extending its standards into continuing professional development for teachers.

## Alternative Elements of the Professional Model

Connecticut offers one approach to professional standards for teachers with a number of noteworthy features. The state played a strong role in creating a common framework of teaching standards, which then anchored coordinated developments. The reform initiative was sustained over an extended period that included turnover in key personnel and fluctuations in the state's economy. Other reforms, particularly salary increases and recruitment incentives, formed necessary accompaniments to the standards. Some evidence, sketched below, suggests that the reforms have begun to have positive effects on student achievement and other outcomes. This case, then, serves as a good example of the professional model, but alternative elements also might be added.

For example, some advocates have proposed adoption of an internship model that would extend teacher preparation into the first year of teaching.[17] Such models might be incorporated into five-year university-based programs, and managed and coordinated with preservice preparation. Another variant conceives the school-based internship, which might include a reduced load and protected teaching assignment, together with active mentoring by expert teachers from the district, as the responsibility of school districts. Though some universities in Connecticut have five-year programs, the state chose to use preparation for the portfolio assessment rather than a required internship as an induction experience for beginning teachers.

A second issue concerns the use of state policy to strengthen the teaching careers and to improve the retention of qualified teachers. An option here is to extend the staged progression of status (e.g., beginning, provisional, professional) into advanced offices for teachers, based on demonstrations of knowledge and skill. Voluntary certification by the NBPTS is one option that may be incorporated into a system of advanced offices that use experienced teachers for mentoring, curriculum development, instructional leadership, and other responsibilities. States and localities are beginning to introduce incentives for board certification, but no state has yet invested in an extensive model of career advancement in teaching, although such models have been proposed.[18] Prior unsatisfactory experience with merit pay and career ladders may give states pause, together with the long-term costs and administrative burdens associated with such plans. While such designs may have merit, analysts also have raised the specter of increased bureaucratization of teaching.

## IMPACT OF THE PROFESSIONAL MODEL

Figure 2 sets forth a set of outcomes against which state regulation of teaching might be judged.

The evidence from Connecticut on all these points is incomplete and inconclusive, but provocative. Consider some findings. Within three years of enacting the first wave of reforms, which included the salary increase and equalization efforts, Connecticut's longstanding teacher shortages in urban areas became surpluses, and the state has maintained steady hiring ever since, despite an increase in the overall poverty levels of students, increases in demand, and downturns in the state economy. Results from the most recent Schools and Staffing Surveys show that Connecticut has reduced its reliance on provisional, temporary, emergency, and uncertified teachers, sig-

## FIGURE 2    Potential Outcomes of State Regulation of Teaching

**Teacher supply.** Do standards restrict supply too much, working particular hardship on communities with hard-to-staff schools? Alternatively, do standards set the foundation for supply, which then must be met via improved recruitment incentives, hiring practices, and other means? Do high entry standards discourage able individuals from entering, or do they signal to able individuals that teaching is a worthy occupation, thereby enhancing supply?

**Teacher retention.** The supply question is heavily influenced by the retention issue because turnover in the early years of teaching is high. How do entry standards affect length of stay in teaching? Do high standards improve or discourage retention?

**Teaching effectiveness.** What is the evidence that teachers who graduate from accredited programs and pass staged licensure examinations teach more effectively than other teachers? How are these teachers more effective? That is, what kinds of practice are associated with high entry standards? Does measurable effectiveness persist over time? How do entry standards and requirements affect teachers' dispositions to continue learning and refining their practice?

**Diversity in the teacher corps.** How do high entry standards affect the demographics of the teacher work force? How do professional standards influence the intentions of minority candidates to become teachers at a time when the student population is growing more diverse?

**Student access to qualified teachers.** How do entry standards influence the distribution of qualified teachers, particularly to hard-to-staff schools and high-demand subject areas? Do professional standards improve or worsen inequities in access to good teachers?

**Student achievement and attainment outcomes.** Do teachers prepared in accordance with professional standards produce better student achievement and attainment than teachers entering via alternate routes or emergency permits, in private schools, etc.? Are there qualitative as well as quantitative differences in the learning of students who are taught by teachers who are prepared professionally?

**Development of the profession.** Does the fully implemented professional model create conditions favorable to the steady, orderly improvement of standards based on the accumulation of new knowledge? Does the professional model produce other benefits for society?

nificantly reducing their numbers in urban schools and for both poor and minority children. Likewise, teacher attrition has been stemmed, most significantly at urban schools and among teachers of poor and minority students.[19] The combination of high standards with competitive salaries produced the desired effects, such that Connecticut now boasts one of the best-qualified work forces in the country, including enhanced supply for the neediest districts due to targeted incentive policies coupled with the standards.

Connecticut also has been working to recruit minorities to the teaching ranks, but here the results have not been encouraging. It has had some success in attracting out-of-state recruits, but the problem of minority recruitment may be traced to the "pipeline" that extends from high schools to college and into the teaching ranks. In Connecticut, as elsewhere, not enough minority students attend college in the first place, so the recruitment pool is still too shallow, and the state cannot attract enough applicants. This problem is not the result of professional standards, however, but of fundamental conditions that produce low college attendance among minority students.

Turning to student achievement, some results have been noteworthy. Connecticut's median household income dropped during the 1990s and its poverty index increased substantially. Proportions of underserved minority groups also grew during this period, along with numbers of new English-language learners due to immigration. During this period, coincident with the enactment of the new state teaching policies, compelling evidence of student achievement began to mount. For example, Connecticut fourth graders outscored all other students in the United States on the 1998 National Assessment of Educational Progress (NAEP) reading test, with trend data showing steady increases; eighth graders also met or surpassed student performance in all other states. These results also held for NAEP mathematics scores, with scores both high and rising over the decade. Growth on Connecticut's challenging Academic Performance Tests has also been substantial, including upward trends in reading, mathematics, and writing. Furthermore, local studies ruled out such alternative explanations for these results as class-size reductions and increases in instructional time.

Achievement gaps remain, however, between minority and white populations, and the correlation between poverty and achievement has not been broken. But in top-performing districts that include concentrations of poor and minority children, the gaps have been narrowing, and educators in those districts tend to regard the state reforms as playing a significant role in the improvements. Furthermore, Connecticut's minority student population scores as well as or better than minority populations in other states on most of the NAEP tests, so by this comparison the state is managing average to slightly above-average performance.

Clearly, however, the teacher policies alone did not produce these results. Rather, the gains seemed to be associated primarily with a combination of 1) the teacher policies, which elevated the overall quality of the workforce while equalizing access to good teachers; 2) "Connecticut's particular brand of low-stakes, standards-based reform [that] tie(s) increasingly authentic, information-rich assessments to analytic supports for districts and schools seeking to understand their achievement patterns as well as to curriculum improvements targeted to those needs and to professional development;"[20] and 3) consistent funding for statewide education reforms, targeting in particular professional development for reading and math, categorical grants to the state's neediest districts, and teacher training in bilingual and special education.

Finally, the reforms have been notable for the scope of their impact. By 2010, 80 percent of all Connecticut's elementary teachers and nearly all secondary teachers will have participated in the new subject-matter-specific portfolio assessment system as candidates for licensing, mentors, or assessors. Substandard permits have been eliminated so that even entrants from alternate routes must have completed a rigorous program of preparation. Most impressive, however, has been the impact of the statewide reforms on the teaching profession in Connecticut.

Connecticut's Beginning Educator Support and Training Program (BEST) has reached deeply into the state's schools and districts, creating a new infrastructure for the improvement of teaching. Through its policies the state has created a community of practice with a shared language of discourse about teaching, a set of common purposes and tasks, a collection of tools (e.g., teaching and learning standards, observation instrument, portfolio system), and a new set of boundary-spanning roles (e.g., assessor, mentor) that now serve as the anchor for the analysis and improvement of teaching. Participating in this community are beginning and veteran teachers, university teacher educators, school administrators, state-level officials, and representatives of the public. This is a remarkable, even unique accomplishment that illustrates how a strong state-led reform can have powerful, enduring effects. The key has been a capacity-building effort that combined mandates with incentives to advance the teaching profession statewide. In sum, while "[s]cholars have noted the weak theoretical link between any one of these policies and quality teaching, . . . the 'package' of policies—any one of which is insufficient when used in isolation—helped create a culture that valued teachers and teaching, enabled the acquisition and ongoing development of professional knowledge among educators, and held those educators to high standards."[21]

## COSTS OF THE PROFESSIONAL MODEL

States wishing to adopt an approach to teacher quality modeled on the Connecticut case must reckon a set of costs that may be broken into the following categories: 1) developmental versus operational costs; 2) direct versus associated costs; and 3) costs borne by the state, by educational institutions, or by individuals.

### Developmental and Operational Costs

Over the span of fifteen years, Connecticut had to invest in the development of the various components of the model. To do so, it relied on a combination of home-grown and adopted features. Where policy tools existed that fit with the overall vision, these elements were adopted. Examples include the use of ETS's Praxis I and II examinations and the eventual adoption of the NCATE accreditation standards. In other cases, the state invested in the development of its own approaches, but drew on work that was underway in other venues. For example, Connecticut took note of the standards for teaching that the INTASC group had developed, but invested in substantial committee work to develop its own standards for teaching and for learning. Likewise, the portfolio content and process was essentially developed for Connecticut with some reliance on parallel work sponsored by the NBPTS and by INTASC.

These costs may be considered as nonrecurring, but the Connecticut system involved continuous revision of its elements so that developmental costs extended over time. For example, while the initial requirement for the provisional license involved classroom observation, the state eventually replaced it with a portfolio system. As the technology for teacher assessment continues to evolve, state assessment systems may be expected to require occasional new development costs.

Operational (i.e., recurring) costs in Connecticut borne by the state include funding for assessor and mentor training, regional support centers, portfolio administration, and state-sponsored clinics and seminars. Operational costs also include personnel in state and regional agencies allocated in whole or in part to development and maintenance of the system of teaching standards. An similar state system will incur similar administrative and operational costs.

## Direct and Associated Costs

A second cost element takes into account not only the costs directly obligated by state regulation of teaching, but also those costs that are associated with professional standards for teaching. Strong state regulation of teaching entails added costs of other kinds. In particular, considerations of teacher supply and distribution and unequal district-to-district funding require policies to enhance recruitment and to ensure equitable access to qualified teachers. Accompanying the evolution of professional standards in Connecticut were policies that raised overall salaries significantly; equalized salaries across districts; provided scholarship and forgiveable loans to high-need areas; offered class-size reductions for high-need schools; and introduced ancillary programs such as extended preschooling. Other policies closed quality-depressing loopholes (e.g., recourse to emergency credentials), while opening up access to qualified out-of-state teachers. The state also created an alternate route to entry, but included regulatory controls over it.

State reliance on a system of professional standards cannot alone raise the quality of teaching. Professional standards must be joined with other policies that enhance the attractiveness of teaching generally and in specific locales and assignments. Connecticut invested in a human resource strategy that includes standards and inducements aimed at long-term, statewide cultivation of the teaching profession. The result is an authentic example of professional standards in action.

## State, Institutional, and Individual Costs

A final reckoning of costs apportions them among three sources. First, the state itself must bear a range of direct and associated costs. Then, institutions including school districts and universities also have costs to share in this model. Districts, for example, must mobilize capacity to support beginning teachers and mentors, construct evaluation systems compatible with the state's standards for teaching and learning, and provide continuing professional development that reinforces the state's standards. The state's universities also have had to revise aspects of their teacher-preparation programs to incorporate the state's standards, and they must absorb the cost of NCATE accreditation as well, which typically occurs on a five-year schedule. Finally, the state's regulatory framework imposes costs on individuals. These include costs associated with additional coursework or programs to meet state standards; (opportunity) costs of deferred entry in order to meet preservice program requirements; and costs of examinations and assessments.

Other costs associated with the professional model (but not included in the Connecticut case) might include new salary schedules differentiated according to skill levels and advanced positions in teaching. Such models have been proposed, and they may incorporate voluntary certification by the NBPTS. Many states and some districts now offer incentives for NBPTS certification, so the full professional model extends into career incentives and advanced positions buttressed by state and local policies and investments.

## CHALLENGES TO THE PROFESSIONAL MODEL

Connecticut's experience demonstrates that the professional model may be implemented in a state at an acceptable, if high, cost to the public. Citizens of the state apparently accepted the view that a compact relying extensively on state-sanctioned professional controls for teaching would be the best guarantor of high quality, and the state invested heavily in both assessment and support of its teacher corps. This case, however, does not conclusively cement an argument for reliance on both state program accreditation and licensure as the best route to teacher quality. A counterargument might be fashioned along the following lines.

First, Connecticut's licensure standards have not been validated carefully, nor does available evidence strongly support the relationship between licensure standards and student achievement.[22] Only recently did the state adopt NCATE standards, so they cannot have played a role in the achievement results reported throughout the 1990s. Connecticut constitutes a stronger demonstration for the positive benefits of a staged licensure system than for a system that relies on a combination of program and individual standards. Then, too, even if the staged licensure system did improve the overall quality of entrants to teaching, the state might have achieved roughly comparable results had it relied solely on salary increases and incentives with very minimal licensure standards. Connecticut also ended the entry of substandard candidates when it mandated the new licensure process, and this development may have had an effect independent of the state licensing system. So it cannot be demonstrated that the state standards, taken singly or together, unequivocally produced or even contributed to the results that Connecticut has achieved. Certainly, many educators in the state believe the standards have played a significant role, but their testimony, while appealing, cannot be considered conclusive. A hard-headed policy analyst has room for skepticism concerning claims about the state's regulatory role.

Connecticut still faces the pandemic problems of urban education. Significant gaps persist between the achievement of middle-class white students and their poor and minority counterparts. Some urban districts in Connecticut have made progress, but others have not. Whether state regulation of teacher quality contributes to the improvement of urban education is still an open question. Even if better qualified teachers are available in applicant pools for urban districts, the districts must still manage and make use of good teachers, and many districts still do not. On at least several of the impact indicators in Figure 2, then, the evidence is not conclusive. Minority recruitment to teaching remains a challenge, as does the achievement of poor and minority students.

Finally, questions arise concerning the benefits and cost-effectiveness of the Connecticut model. Might the same results have been achieved at substantially lower cost, particularly for regulatory aspects of the state role? Were all the costs of licensure and accreditation necessary to ensure the quality of the entrant pool? If the state had adopted more aggressive alternate route policies, perhaps encouraging local districts to develop training programs similar to those operating in Houston, Los Angeles, or other urban locales, might such programs have proven to be more effective at a lower cost in recruiting and retaining new teachers for Connecticut's urban districts?[23] The available evidence does not speak to these issues that are of interest to policymakers in other states.

The remaining, intriguing element in this story is the indirect effects of the state's activism on the culture of teaching. A statewide community of practice was forged around teaching. Policy tools that the state developed (including the standards for teaching and learning, the classroom observation process, and the portfolio); the new roles it created that brought together teachers, teacher educators, and administrators to assess and support beginning teachers; and the many opportunities that the new regulations created for substantive discussions about teaching may have had an impact over and above the regulatory effects. This aspect of the case is the most elusive of proof, but it may be the most important effect in the long run. Ultimately, the state's activism may have created a common definition of good teaching that anchored a host of related, positive developments that continue to unfold to this day. As an intended outgrowth of Connecticut's capacity-building approach, this outcome is worth further study.

## CONCLUSION

This analysis suggests that education requires a human resource strategy initiated at the state level. A strong state regulatory role clearly requires significant investment. Costs, however, can be phased in over time, and states can re-allocate existing funds to meet them. The Connecticut case is instructive in revealing the elements needed for a human resource strategy predicated on professional standards for teaching. Connecticut has emerged as one of the nation's reform leaders based on overall improvement in statewide academic achievement, together with modest progress in narrowing achievement gaps among racial and socioeconomic groups. Although we cannot attribute Connecticut's success solely to its statewide professionalization strategy, the evidence suggests that their comprehensive approach, including the state's standards for teachers, was at least a significant contributing factor.

Complicating assessment of this model is its unfolding, interactive character. Its impact is not strictly dependent on any single element but on the combined, interactive effects of multiple policies. Still, responsible stewardship calls for better validation evidence associated with such regulatory elements as the Praxis examinations, the portfolio, graduation from NCATE-accredited institutions, and CEU-related learning for license renewal. Despite Connecticut's promising results, a recently rendered judgment probably still holds true in many locales: "The current weak validity of formal qualifications [for teachers] is an artifact of existing professional education, in which intending teachers are not well educated in conformance with sound standards of academic performance. Instead, they are sketchily educated in conformance with very general standards that are weakly related to student performance and academic learning. If teachers were better educated in conformance with academic performance standards, formal certification would be more tightly related to performance, and qualifications would be better proxies for teaching proficiency."[24] Nevertheless, the Connecticut case is an intriguing example of how a system of assessment and supports created a statewide environment of continuous learning for teachers and for the public they serve. Such a system may stand the best chance, in the long run, of overcoming the historic weaknesses of teacher preparation—and the key to such a development is a strong state role.

## APPENDIX I   Connecticut's Common Core of Teaching (CCT)

*Foundational Skills and Competencies*

### I. Teachers have knowledge of:

*Students*
1. Teachers understand how students learn and develop.
2. Teachers understand how students differ in their approaches to learning.

*Content*
3. Teachers are proficient in reading, writing, and mathematics.
4. Teachers understand the central concepts and skills, tools of inquiry, and structures of the disciplines they teach.

*Pedagogy*
5. Teachers know how to design and deliver instruction.
6. Teachers recognize the need to vary their instructional methods.

### II. Teachers apply this knowledge by:

*Planning*
1. Teachers plan instruction based upon knowledge of subject matter, students, the curriculum, and the community.
2. Teachers select and/or create learning tasks that make subject matter meaningful to students.

*Instructing*
3. Teachers establish and maintain appropriate standards of behavior and create a positive learning environment that shows commitment to students and their successes.
4. Teachers create instructional opportunities that support students' academic, social, and personal development.
5. Teachers use effective verbal, nonverbal, and media communications techniques that foster individual and collaborative inquiry.
6. Teachers employ a variety of instructional strategies that enable students to think critically, solve problems, and demonstrate skills.

*Assessing and Adjusting*
7. Teachers use various assessment techniques to evaluate student learning and modify instruction as appropriate.

### III. Teachers demonstrate professional responsibility through:

*Professional and ethical practice*

1. Teachers conduct themselves as professionals in accordance with the Code of Professional Responsibility for Teachers (Section 10-145d-400a of the Connecticut Certification Regulations).
2. Teachers share responsibility for student achievement and well being.

*Reflection and continuous learning*

3. Teachers continually engage in self-evaluation of the effects of their choices and actions on students and the school community.
4. Teachers seek out opportunities to grow professionally.

*Leadership and collaboration*

5. Teachers serve as leaders in the school community.
6. Teachers demonstrate a commitment to their students and a passion for improving their profession.

*Source:* Wilson, Darling-Hammond, & Berry, 23.

## CHAPTER 8

# Cultivating Success through Multiple Providers

## A New State Strategy for Improving the Quality of Teacher Preparation

*Bryan C. Hassel and Michele Sherburne*

This chapter explores a new state strategy for improving the quality of teacher preparation: authorizing a portfolio of providers. Under this strategy a state would cultivate a robust portfolio of providers of teacher preparation. These providers would include traditional purveyors of teacher education, as well as other entities such as nonprofit organizations and school districts. Presumably they would vary substantially in their approaches to teacher preparation, making it possible for them to meet the differing needs of candidates (prospective teachers) and to serve as laboratories for diverse approaches to teacher education.

The state would authorize providers that meet certain criteria, giving them a time-limited stamp of approval. During that time, any teaching candidate meeting the requirements of the provider's program would be deemed qualified or certified to teach in the state's public schools. The state would review the performance of authorized providers and make its performance reviews public in order to offer information to prospective teachers and their potential employers. Reviews would also be the basis for decisions about whether to extend authorization for an additional period of time.

The chapter explains the rationale for the portfolio model and discusses a range of challenging design issues that would confront any state seeking to authorize a portfolio of providers.

## INTRODUCTION

Education reformers across the political spectrum recognize the need to improve the quality of teaching. There is also consensus that a central dimension of teaching quality is the caliber of people who enter the teaching profession. Other factors affect teacher quality, including ongoing professional development, evaluation, tenure and dismissal policies, compensation systems, and administrative leadership. However, this chapter will address only state policies relating to the entry of individuals into a state's teaching force. As school districts will hire millions of teachers in the next ten years, almost all observers of education agree on the need to ensure that new entrants are highly capable individuals well prepared for teaching.

But consensus ends when it comes to the question of how to achieve this goal. Broadly, one camp aims to improve the quality of entrants by tightening states' regulation of the entry process: raising licensing standards for candidates, imposing more requirements on teacher preparation programs, or both.[1] A second camp urges less regulation—a market approach in which school districts have great freedom to hire whom they want, with few restrictions imposed by formal certification and preparation requirements.[2]

The different approach proposed here is intended to tap the energy and dynamism of the market while maintaining a vital state role in promoting teaching quality. Rather than dictate strict requirements for certification, this approach delegates the authority to license teachers to a diverse portfolio of approved providers of teacher preparation. Any candidate who meets one of these providers' requirements is deemed certified to teach in the state's public schools. Rather than strictly regulating these providers, the state using the portfolio approach pursues quality by 1) authorizing only providers with high potential to succeed; 2) measuring providers' performance regularly and publicly; 3) revoking the authorization of providers that fail to deliver quality; and 4) encouraging expansion and replication of the best programs.

In this chapter we also examine a range of challenging design issues that would confront any state seeking to authorize a portfolio of providers.

- *Governance*: What agency would make decisions about authorization, an existing agency of the state or a new special-purpose entity?
- *Criteria*: What types of organizations would be eligible? What criteria would the agency apply to prospective providers?
- *Review*: By what measures would the agency judge the performance of providers over time?

- *Transparency*: How would the agency disseminate information about providers?
- *Reauthorization*: How often would the agency reauthorize providers? How high would the agency set the bar for renewing approval? What factors would it consider?
- *Funding*: How would providers be funded? How would state financing systems need to change to accommodate this model?

## RATIONALE

The portfolio strategy represents a departure from the prevailing approach to improving the quality of teachers entering the work force. It contrasts especially with the regulatory approach of setting strict requirements at the state level, both for individuals seeking a teaching license and for institutions running a teacher-preparation program. The regulatory approach rests on some heroic assumptions: that we know fairly precisely what makes a candidate qualified to teach; that we know what makes teacher-preparation programs effective; and that the needs of candidates and of the organizations that hire teachers are similar enough that a standardized program of preparation and licensure will meet all of them.

In fact, none of these assumptions stands up to scrutiny. First, despite numerous claims on all sides of the debate, we know very little about the pre-employment characteristics of teaching candidates that predict good teaching. Research by Goldhaber found that "[o]nly about 3 percent of the contribution teachers made to student learning was associated with teacher experience, degree attained, and other readily observable characteristics. The remaining 97 percent of their contribution was associated with qualities or behaviors that could not be isolated and identified."[3] In that context, it seems doubtful that a state can reasonably establish a set of requirements for becoming a teacher that will serve any meaningful quality-control purpose.

In any case, the quest to define a single set of teacher characteristics that predicts classroom performance rests on the shaky assumption that there is one kind of good teaching for which all teaching candidates need to be qualified. In fact, employers have a diverse range of needs. Schools that use an Expeditionary Learning/Outward Bound experiential approach to education probably want teachers who have different competencies than schools using the highly structured Direct Instruction program. More commonly, schools serving vastly different student populations may have very different needs for teaching. Though there are probably some common elements, it is hard to imagine anything but a minimal list of state requirements working for all employers' situations.

The research into what makes a teacher-preparation program effective is equally inconclusive. Most writing about how to prepare teachers is based more on the authors' experience and craft knowledge than on any solid research findings. A recent Education Commission on the States (ECS) study, "Eight Questions on Teacher Preparation: What Does the Research Say?" concludes: "On the whole, the research lends limited support to the conclusion that coursework in education can contribute to effective teaching, but precisely what coursework and how much is [sic] uncertain."[4] Furthermore, even the findings on coursework don't actually tell us very much. For instance, knowing that coursework is associated with performance doesn't tell us whether it was material actually learned in class, the associated exposure to educational conversations, or anything else that made the difference. Research, it seems, does not provide a great deal of guidance about how to prepare teachers for the classroom. The quest for a research-based list of what makes teacher preparation "work" is probably futile in any case. Candidates have diverse academic backgrounds, preparation needs, and time constraints.

Given the uncertainty and the need for diversity that characterize teacher preparation, a one-size-fits-all regulatory system is not optimal. Instead, what is needed is a more dynamic system in which multiple approaches are offered. Candidates can choose programs that meet their particular needs; employers can decide which preparation programs seem to produce graduates who meet *their* needs. Programs that work can grow and be copied over time; programs that do not can be closed. Moreover, rather than forcibly pushing and pulling whole systems in one reform direction, this approach creates an evolutionary opportunity that allows new programs to adopt new approaches and old programs to stand pat or refine their approach as they see fit.

Such a system's dynamism stems in part from the entry of new providers. Today, nearly 90 percent of teaching candidates graduate from traditional teacher-training programs. These programs are based in schools or departments of education, as are about three-fourths of the existing alternative programs. With this kind of institutional dominance, it is difficult for new approaches to emerge. The portfolio approach makes it possible for school districts, private ventures, unions, community groups, and any other interested party to design a training program and have it considered on its merits.

A varied, dynamic system under which a state authorizes and holds accountable a set of providers of teacher preparation is the ideal response to the degree of uncertainty and diversity that characterizes teachers and teacher preparation today. But why stop there? Wouldn't the most dynamic and varied system be one in which market forces are allowed to determine the landscape? Why impose the intermediate step of state authorization and oversight of providers?

In this respect, the proposed system bumps up against the other major school of thought about how entry to the teaching profession should be structured, the market approach. Allowing schools and districts to hire whom they want, without any formal requirements for candidates or their preparation, would certainly be dynamic, but it also poses significant risks for states in the era of the No Child Left Behind Act of 2001 (NCLB), which requires *states* to ensure that there is a highly qualified teacher in every classroom. The approach proposed here offers a way for the state to play a role that is critical but not regulatory and controlling, which harnesses private initiative and market dynamics within a framework of state-based quality assurance.

Is there enough quality assurance in the portfolio model to satisfy states and their federal regulators? Why not take the added step of imposing requirements on candidates above and beyond graduation from an approved program? Wouldn't that give state leaders more comfort? State leaders pursuing such an approach might find themselves on the horns of a dilemma. If they keep requirements minimal (e.g., requiring a college degree and coursework in the subject matter one wants to teach), they do little to assure quality. If they begin to layer on additional mandates (e.g., certain kinds of teacher training and field experience), they force providers into exactly the sort of mold the portfolio system is designed to avoid.

No state has enacted a strategy exactly like the one we outline in this chapter. Forty-eight states, in partnership with the National Council for Accreditation of Teacher Education (NCATE) use an accreditation or "program approval" process in evaluating their schools of education. These accreditation processes differ from what is proposed in this model because they do not typically extend to authorizing new or unconventional programs. They also tend to stress inputs over the outcomes stressed in this proposal. Two states, however, have enacted aspects of the strategy outlined in this chapter.

### Texas: Authorizing and Holding Accountable Multiple Providers

In 1995, the Texas legislature mandated a performance-based accountability system called the Accountability System for Educator Preparation (ASEP). Under ASEP, the State Board for Educator Certification (SBEC) holds educa-

FIGURE 1    Teachers Obtaining Initial Certification from Educator
Preparation Programs in Texas, 2002

| Types of Programs | Number of Authorized Programs | Number of Teachers Trained |
|---|---|---|
| College or University | 69 | 13,920 |
| School Districts | 4 | 751 |
| Private Entities | 2 | 597 |
| Regional Education Service Centers | 16 | 2,633 |
| Community Colleges | 3 | 26 |
| TOTAL | 94 | 17,927 |

Source: Certification Records, SBEC, October 1, 2002.

tor preparation programs accountable for the quality of their training based on the success rate of education candidates on state certification exams.

The Texas Education Code allows preparation for certification of educators to be provided by "institutions of higher education, regional education service centers, public school districts, or other entities approved by the Board" on the basis of applications they submit. For purposes of ensuring enough providers per community, the SBEC divides the state into twenty geographic regions and requires that each region have at least one provider. Once an entity is approved, it is reviewed at least once every five years. Figure 1 shows what types of entities are approved in Texas.

Each approved entity is required to file an annual report of performance indicators and receives a rating of "Accredited," "Accredited–Under Review," or "Not Accredited." An entity's status is determined by one measure alone: the "pass" rates of their students on the state's certification exams. To be accredited a program must achieve a 70 percent first-year pass rate or an 80 percent cumulative (two-year) pass rate. If a program is under review, a committee comes in to provide guidance. Ten to twelve programs are currently under review.

### Louisiana: RFP Process

In 1999, the governor of Louisiana convened a Blue Ribbon Commission on Teacher Quality, an ad hoc group of thirty-one state, university, district, school, and community leaders, to address education reform issues. One of the outcomes of the Commission was the idea of encouraging both private and public providers to offer a fast-track, rigorous Practitioner Teacher (PT) program.

Since 2001, the state has issued Requests for Proposals (RFPs) for the PT program with stipulations regarding program admission and completion requirements, curriculum, program delivery, evaluation and ongoing support. The proposals are evaluated by a team of experts outside the state of Louisiana. As of fall 2003, the state had approved three non-university providers through this process: one parish (school district) and two nonprofit organizations, one of which focuses on an urban area, the other on several rural communities.[5]

These programs share elements of the strategy proposed in this paper, but neither of them is a fully developed version of the portfolio model. Texas' program permits multiple providers, but measures their results using the single indicator of percentage of teachers passing the state teaching exam. Louisiana throws the system open to nontraditional providers of teaching candidates, but only at the margins.

## THE MODEL IN FULL

A state using the portfolio provider model authorizes multiple providers of teacher preparation in the state. Any teaching candidate who meets the requirements of an authorized provider is deemed certified to teach in the state's schools; there is no separate state licensing process. The state reviews the performance of providers over time, reauthorizing successful programs and deauthorizing less successful ones.

The model has several components that a state would need to design: governance of the authorization system; the authorization process (eligibility, criteria, and application process); ongoing monitoring and evaluation; the reauthorization process; communication and transparency; and attending to the supply of good programs. The following subsections discuss each component, explaining the need for the component, outlining options for states to consider, and setting forth our recommended approach. The additional issue of funding is treated in Section VI below.

### Governance of the Authorization System

States adopting the portfolio-of-providers approach need to give some entity the power to authorize and regulate providers. Most states have a state board of education that could serve this purpose; some have state boards that oversee licensure or higher-education-based teacher-preparation programs.

We recommend, however, that a state pursuing the portfolio approach create an entirely new board whose only purpose is to authorize and monitor teacher-preparation programs. The members of this board should be appointed by the state's governor. Terms of members should be lengthy (e.g., five years) and staggered for continuity, ensuring that the board cannot be transformed immediately by a new governor. The board should adhere to a strict conflict-of-interest policy: no board member should have any affiliation with a current or prospective provider of teacher preparation in the state. The appointment process must be as transparent as possible, with full disclosure by candidates of all relevant affiliations and connections with the appointing governor.

Our aim in proposing this structure is to minimize opportunities for manipulation or capture of the board by special interests. Placing the authority in an existing board or a subsidiary of an existing board would make it too likely that the board would more or less preserve the status quo with its existing supply of teacher-preparation programs. Even appointing a new board, however, would not completely eliminate the possibility of capture by powerful interests. In fact, some analysts have argued that such capture is inevitable in any public body overseeing a public education function.[6] It becomes essential, then, for state legislation authorizing this new board to include strong provisions for transparency with respect to the release of information about applicants for authorization, the process used to accept or reject applications, and performance data on approved providers. Requiring transparency does not directly prevent capture by special interests, but makes it easier for outside watchdogs to spot misdeeds and lay them bare.

The board would meet several times a year and carry out several important functions, each of which is described more fully later in this section. First, the board would establish the specific criteria it would use to review applications from prospective providers, within legislative parameters. Second, the board would have the final word on approval or rejection of such applications. Third, the board would review data on the performance of providers and, if necessary, terminate the authorization of providers that did not measure up. Finally, the board would take responsibility for ensuring that the supply of qualified teachers meets demand. If supply fell short, the board would need to take action to find and authorize new providers with the capacity to fill the teacher gap.

The board would need a small staff to manage the authorization and oversight process. The staff would carry out three critical functions: overall management of the authorization process; data gathering and evaluation; and communication to relevant constituencies, including teaching candidates, employers, providers, state policymakers, and the public. Staffing needs will vary with the size of the state's teaching population and the intricacy of the state's authorization and reporting systems. We estimate that a medium-sized state would need an agency with fifteen to twenty staff members to carry out these functions. See the "Costs" section below for more on the financial implications of this staffing.

## The Authorization Process

### Eligibility

The state must determine the types of organizations eligible to be providers in the state. At one extreme, a state could limit eligibility to traditional providers of teacher preparation. At the other, it could open the application process to any entity, including not only traditional purveyors but also nonprofit organizations, school districts, unions, schools, regional service agencies, and even profit-seeking corporations.

We recommend that states open the process as much as possible. Since a central aim of this model is to encourage diversity of supply and innovation, it makes sense to keep restrictions on eligibility to a minimum. The decision whether to authorize a provider should be based on criteria linked to the likely quality of the proposed program rather than the corporate form of the applicant.

We also recommend that states require preexisting providers of preparation programs to go through the authorization process. They would not be "grandfathered in." However, a state might consider a brief grace period in which graduates of existing programs are deemed certified to teach, to allow individuals who had entered these programs with the expectation of earning a license to complete their programs under the original terms.

### Criteria

The state, by either legislation or board action, needs to specify the criteria it will use when deciding whether to authorize a proposed provider of teacher preparation. It then needs to develop an application process through which the board gathers the information it needs to judge each applicant against the criteria.

We recommend that a state avoid a prescriptive or process-oriented approach that specifies in detail how providers must carry out teacher preparation. Since the aim of this strategy is to encourage diversity and innovation, the state's criteria should impose minimal constraints on the approach to teacher preparation a program may offer. It should be possible to authorize programs that look traditional (e.g., coursework plus field experience), as well as promising programs that look decidedly unconventional (e.g., minimal or no coursework combined with on-the-job training and evaluation).

This point is one critical difference between the approach proposed here and more conventional processes, such as NCATE accreditation. Though NCATE standards allow for some variation among accredited schools, many of its standards are based on very specific normative prescriptions about what good teaching or good teacher preparation looks like, and many focus on inputs such as facilities or the formal credentials of instructors. Taken together, these standards narrow the band within which teacher preparation can operate and still gain accreditation. This narrowing can stifle creativity, making it difficult for providers to step outside the box by, for example, using new technology rather than (or in addition to) more conventional classroom-based instruction.[7]

In our view, it should even be possible to authorize programs that do not offer "preparation" at all. For example, we can envision a program that is highly selective in its admissions, putting candidates through a battery of pencil-and-paper and classroom-performance assessments and applying a high bar for admission based on these assessments. Such a program would, in effect, warrant to employers that its "graduates" were ready to teach and would serve as a monitor and guarantor of their ability, but would not itself have devoted much time or many resources to instructing its "graduates." Such a program would appeal to aspiring public school teachers coming from other professions, states, or countries, or private or charter school teachers who have not been required to be licensed.[8]

But if there are no detailed program requirements, what criteria would the board apply when making decisions? Would anything go? No. We recommend that states impose a high bar for authorization focused on two sets of criteria. First, does the organization proposing the program have the organizational capacity needed to carry out its plan? The board would review the organization's history of implementing programs (teacher preparation and other kinds); the capabilities and qualifications of its leaders and staff; its financial records; its plan for managing the proposed program; and any other data available about the organization's ability to deliver on its promises.

Second, does the organization present a plausible, research-based plan for providing qualified teachers for the state's public schools? Though the board would not prescribe how much and what type of coursework to provide, it would require an applicant program to submit a detailed explanation of the type of preparation it would offer and the rationale for its approach. An applicant would have to make a convincing case that, upon completion of its program's requirements, a graduate would be prepared to teach in the state's schools. Requirements and routes might vary from applicant to applicant, but the board would not approve any application that did not have a plausible route, clearly mapped.[9]

The case for the applicant's proposed approach would need to be made in the context of its intended target population and the state's need for new teachers as identified by the board. Does the applicant propose to prepare teachers with a certain background, candidates from certain parts of the state, or any other specific group? Is its program designed to produce teachers skilled in particular approaches to teaching, or particularly able to work with specific populations of students? The applicant would need to make a convincing case that the proposed approach matched these emphases. One strength of the portfolio-of-providers approach is that it gives a state the means to authorize niche providers serving a particular slice of the educational community. Some programs might specialize in training bilingual, minority, or rural teachers, for instance, without being subjected to the statutory and administrative requirements intended to hold all programs to procedural standards appropriate for larger, less focused programs.

These criteria indicate the issues the board should consider when rating an application. Another critical issue, though, is how high the state should set the bar for approval. How strong must the organizational capacity be in order to merit approval? How strong must the proposed program plan be? There are no easy answers to these questions. The short-term reality is that most states would need to set the bar at whatever level is necessary to ensure an adequate supply of teaching candidates for the state. To use a simple numerical example, if the state projects that its public schools will need to hire 6,000 new teachers a year for the next five years, it must approve enough programs to provide the requisite number of candidates, accounting for some expected attrition. Under this scenario, a state's best strategy is to rank prospective providers and draw a cutoff line wherever necessary to ensure an adequate supply.

This approach could lead to approval of low-quality programs, but this is not a problem unique to the portfolio-of-providers approach. The status quo tolerates low-quality programs as well. The portfolio strategy contains many hedges against low-quality programs. Making information about programs' effectiveness widely available helps drive candidates and employers to better programs and away from worse ones. The board's ability to shut down poorly performing programs adds another layer of protection that is not often implemented in the current system.

But, perhaps most important, the board can act under these circumstances to increase the supply of high-quality offerings and programs that attract more highly qualified individuals into the profession through its control of the authorization of providers. This power gives the state leverage on the teacher supply problem that it generally lacks now. See the "Encouraging Supply" subsection below for a discussion.

*Application Review Process*

Based on its criteria, the state must issue a Request for Proposals that asks applicants to provide information that the board would need to determine the applicant's organizational capacity and the feasibility of its proposed plan. Below is a list of possible elements for an RFP that states may consult in developing their own model.

- Need/Population to Be Served
  - > Describe the teaching candidates your organization intends to serve.
  - > Describe, if applicable, the specific needs in the educational system your organization aims to meet (e.g., demand for skills in particular subjects, using particular teaching methods, or targeting specific kinds of students).
  - > Demonstrate how your organization will meet specific needs in the state/region.
- Goals
  - > Demonstrate a commitment to accountability for results and evidence of the competence to achieve those goals.
  - > Provide goals that are clear and measurable.
- Institution's Leadership and Staffing
  - > Identify key project personnel, the role of each, and the experience or expertise they bring to the program.
  - > Explain how the program will recruit faculty and the criteria used for hiring and assessing them.
  - > Demonstrate the organization's capacity to implement complex programs, in teacher preparation or otherwise.
- Admission to the Program
  - > Identify the procedures and guidelines for admission and selection of candidates.
  - > Describe your recruitment strategies to inform potential applicants about the program.
  - > Project the number of candidates to be served over each of the next three years.

> Identify the skills and traits, if any, applicants must have to enter the program.
- Completion Requirements
  > Provide your program graduation requirements.
  > Describe how your program will measure whether candidates have achieved those standards.
- Curriculum and Program Delivery
  > Describe the structure of the program to be delivered to candidates. Explain in detail any methods the program will use to prepare candidates for teaching (e.g., required coursework, field experiences, follow-up mentoring, use of technology). Explain the research base that supports these approaches.
  > Provide details of partnerships with any school districts, schools, or other organizations and documentation (e.g., letters of support) of the partnerships.
  > Describe a clearly defined implementation plan with projected timeline.
- Program Evaluation
  > Provide an evaluation plan that includes data to be collected to measure the effectiveness of the program and to guide program improvement.
  > Provide evidence of past success if applicant is a preexisting teacher-preparation program. To the extent possible, provide evidence of outcomes of graduates, such as success obtaining positions, scores on licensure examinations, and success with students in their classrooms.
- Financial Information
  > If the applicant is an existing organization, provide two to three years of financial statements (audited if possible).
  > Describe other funding sources (local, state, federal, private, etc.) that will support the program.
  > Describe the costs to the individual participants and procedures to handle tuition/fees.

The process by which the board approves or rejects applications could include such elements as review of applications by professional staff and outside experts; interviews with the leadership of prospective providers; requests for additional detail and/or amended applications; and public hearings. As part of this process, the board would need to apply its criteria explicitly, perhaps using a point system that reflects the importance of each element. Elements may include the organization's history of implementing complex programs; financial information such as operating budget, funding sources to support the program, and the cost to the individual participants; the need for this type of program among targeted candidates or districts; program management plan; preparation model and rationale, including research support for the model; clarity and ambitiousness of program goals; evaluation plan; and relevance of program graduation requirements to state's needs for highly qualified teachers.

### Ongoing Monitoring and Data Gathering

The state's involvement in this process would not stop with authorization. Without regulating providers in the sense of dictating how they go about preparing teachers, it would gather information about the performance of authorized programs and their graduates for two purposes. First, performance information would be useful in its own right to teaching candidates, employers, and providers themselves. Second, the state would ultimately be able to use performance information to make decisions about reauthorization.

A state using this model must decide what data to collect on programs. Broadly, there are two types of data the state could seek: outcomes data, showing programs' success with their graduates, and process data, providing insight into how well programs function internally.

We recommend that states focus their monitoring on outcomes, for two reasons. First, outcomes are what states should care about most in this process. Do teachers who graduate from a given program meet high standards, obtain jobs, and succeed with their students? How a program gets graduates to that point is of less importance. Second, process information is much more difficult and expensive to gather, requiring ongoing visitation to observe programs in action. For states authorizing many programs, the cost of such visits and observations might become prohibitive.[10]

We also recommend that states gather a broad array of outcomes data in order to provide all constituents with a well-rounded picture of each program's performance:

- scores of program graduates on any state teacher examinations
- value added by program graduates as measured by the gains in their students' test scores
- achievement of customized, internal goals set by programs
- results of surveys of graduates (satisfaction with program, how prepared they believe they were for the employment)

- results of surveys of employers
  - > percentage of employers (principals, superintendents) satisfied with teachers in programs
  - > reasons for hiring from a given program
- placement and retention rates
  - > percentage of a program's candidates taking teaching jobs in the state
  - > percentage of a program's graduates still teaching in the state five years out and ten years out

Implementing a data system like this could be quite costly for states that do not already track employment in this way. All entrants to an approved program, including teachers transferring from other states, would need a state-maintained identification number that would stay with the teacher throughout his or her teaching career in the state. Preparation programs would be required to submit data to the state on the completion status of all enrolled candidates by ID number. Employers would be required to report to the state all hirings and departures by ID number. The resulting database would allow the board to do all of the analyses recommended above.

### Reauthorization

A key element of this model is that no provider is guaranteed permanent authorization. The state must reauthorize programs periodically for them to maintain their status. A state adopting this model would need to establish the length of a provider's term of authorization, reauthorization criteria, and a decisionmaking process. In order to give programs time to establish a track record while still holding them accountable for performance, we recommend an initial term of five years.[11]

All of the data elements listed in the previous section could be used as criteria for reauthorization, but we recommend having fewer criteria so the board can focus on what matters most when it is time to consider reauthorization. Our limited list includes 1) progress toward customized, agreed-upon internal goals; 2) satisfaction of graduates; 3) satisfaction of employers; 4) placement rates (in effect, is the program producing candidates who end up teaching in the state?); and 5) value added by graduates, as measured by student test-score gains.

The final item—value added to student test scores—would undoubtedly be the most controversial element. It would also likely be unfeasible unless the state's broader data analysis capacity already includes teacher-level value added; it would be too expensive, and perhaps impossible, for the board to develop such a methodology independently. As of this writing, few states have teacher-level value-added systems. However, we caution against using most other test-score analysis methods for this evaluation because of the potential for perverse incentives. For example, rewarding programs based on the percentage of their graduates' students who achieve grade-level standards creates an incentive for programs to place their graduates in high-scoring schools, not to encourage good teachers to take tougher assignments.

The reauthorization process could involve any number of procedural steps, including submission by the program of an application for reauthorization; staff review of the application and performance data; outside review of the application and performance data; site visits and observations of program (perhaps only for programs "on the bubble"); interviews or public hearings; and the like.

What should a state do if a program is lagging? First and foremost, it is critical for a state to provide a clear process for reauthorization and to state the steps failing programs must take to improve. States could take a more proactive approach, providing technical assistance to struggling programs as they now do to struggling schools. This approach, however, would be expensive, complex, and not very likely to succeed. We would recommend this approach only in states that are having trouble cultivating a new supply of teacher-preparation programs to replace failing ones.

### Communication and Transparency

Strong communication systems and a transparent process are critical to the success of the portfolio model. In particular, teaching candidates and employers need comprehensive, easy-to-use information about all authorized providers. This information facilitates good decisions by candidates about which programs to consider and helps employers in their recruitment and hiring.

The core of the information system would be the outcomes data described above. In addition, it could provide more descriptive information about the programs and their participants. Candidates would be especially interested in program requirements, schedules, and locations. Employers would be especially interested in what graduates are expected to know and be able to do when they graduate.[12]

## Encouraging Supply

If a state opens up the opportunity to provide teacher preparation, will there be any takers? More to the point, will there be enough high-quality programs to meet the state's needs for highly qualified new teachers? What if a state finds, as states do now, that it has to dip deep into the applicant pool to scoop up enough supply?

In such a situation, the board may see fit to encourage more quality supply to emerge. One approach would be to urge districts with very specific needs to serve as providers themselves or to work directly with providers to meet the needs of their schools. Another would be to reach out to highly successful preparation programs and urge them to expand the number of candidates they prepare. It is often well known among professional educators in a given state which preparation programs are top-notch and which are less effective. Yet rarely does state leadership induce the top-notch programs to do more, whether by increasing the number of candidates they train, setting up satellite programs, using Internet technology to reach more people, partnering with school districts or other institutions, or other means. It may be that such expansions (or the startup of new preparation ventures) require too much up-front investment. Without access to "venture" funds, supply does not expand sufficiently. Another state role, then, could be to provide (and/or rally philanthropists to provide) the needed investment funds.

## IMPACT

There are three ways this new system could improve student achievement. First, if the quality of preparation improves, new teachers will be better equipped for the job of teaching. Second, if the composition of new corps of entering teachers improves, the average new teacher will be more capable. Third, if the differentiation among programs leads to better matches between candidates and programs and between graduates and employers, more teachers may end up in settings where they can truly thrive.

### Quality of Preparation

The portfolio approach has many components that encourage program quality. The up-front authorization process screens providers before they begin offering preparation. Transparent access to information about programs' success rates can help teaching candidates choose high-quality programs. Reauthorization and deauthorization processes can weed out poorly performing programs. Potential for innovation and the use of new technologies increase as oversight moves from regulation of inputs to measurement of outcomes. Programs will grow or decline based on how well they do. Over time, teacher preparation should get better and better under this model.

At the same time, because of the diversity of entry points for new teachers, the model should improve the composition of the entering teaching force. Many individuals who would be excellent teachers currently choose other professions. They do so for a variety of reasons, but the hoops one must jump through to obtain a teaching certificate in most states is arguably one important reason. The portfolio model fosters a true diversity of routes into the profession, not just a narrow alternative route on the margins of the mainstream approach.

Nontraditional providers may create niches, pulling into the profession candidates who previously had not seriously contemplated teaching. Moreover, firms like Sylvan or groups like the Urban League may be able to use their existing outreach or marketing heft to connect with potential candidates in ways that current teacher-training programs do not. School districts themselves may be vital players, insofar as they know and can address the specific needs of their systems while avoiding duplication of teacher-training efforts.

Finally, the system will improve matching between candidates and programs, and between program graduates and employers. Using data produced by the system, both candidates and employers will be able to make more informed choices. If there is differentiation across programs, districts and candidates will learn what kinds of preparation different programs offer and what kinds fit their needs. As a result, teaching candidates will be more likely to end up teaching in a setting that suits their capabilities and preparation.

## COSTS

Implementing a portfolio-of-providers system would not necessarily involve new costs for a state, provided that the system replaces existing systems for teacher licensure and regulation of teacher preparation. With a replacement strategy, most states would find that they could simply reallocate resources now devoted to licensure and oversight of teacher-preparation institutions into these new functions. In North Carolina, for example, the Department of Public Instruction lists twenty-seven staff assigned to licensure and teacher education.[13] A staff of that size would be ample to carry out the functions described above.

There are two possible exceptions to this general rule. First, while the ongoing need for funds could be covered by reallocation, the early years of operation could be more expensive due to the need to develop all systems from scratch and to review applications for all established providers of teacher education, as well as new entrants. A state could address this in one of two ways. One would be a small appropriation, perhaps $2 million to $3 million over two to three years, to fund the agency's start-up. A second would be to spread out approvals of existing programs over a period of time, perhaps five years, during which these programs would have provisional approval and could continue preparing and graduating candidates. This approach would give the board a steadier workload.

A state could also face excess costs if it needed to invest public funds in increasing supply. If a state found that approved programs were not producing enough highly qualified graduates, it would need to stimulate more supply. It is possible that providers would have adequate incentives to invest the necessary resources in this expansion without a public subsidy. But if they did not, a state would need to consider investing state funds and/or encouraging private philanthropy.

## IMPLEMENTATION

### Changes In the Law

Multiple changes in statutes would likely be required to effect this model in most states. State licensure requirements, generally codified in law, would need to be replaced with the provisions described above. Legislation would need to establish the new oversight board and set at least the basic parameters for authorization and reauthorization of providers.

### Incremental Steps to Implement the Model

What if a state cannot muster the political support to implement the model in full? Are there incremental steps a state could take that would begin to achieve some of the models' benefits? Two seem most promising. First, like Louisiana, a state could begin to authorize new providers on the margins. This would not be wholesale conversion to the portfolio-of-providers model; existing providers would continue to operate and be regulated as before. But the state would begin to encourage new supply, and it could experiment with the authorization, monitoring, and reauthorization processes described here, expanding them to mainstream institutions later.

Second, a state could implement the monitoring and data gathering system without (at first) the authorization and reauthorization processes. In fact, states have begun to do this with "report cards" on their teacher-preparation programs. By launching such systems and tinkering with them over time, states could build confidence in the indicators it uses to judge quality.

With that confidence, it would be easier to raise the stakes by tying re-authorization to the same indicators.

## What Could Go Wrong?

There are a number of potential pitfalls in implementing this plan. First, the governor could re-create the existing system by appointing to the board the same individuals who have served on statewide education boards, making it virtually impossible to create a true portfolio-of-providers model. Ideally, appointees should come from a variety of institutions and sectors. They should have demonstrated that they can see beyond the status quo in teacher education and share the vision of a multiple-provider model.

There is also the potential for "capture" of the new agency by providers. In one variant of this pitfall, traditional providers could do the capturing, inducing a reversion to the status quo. A state's board could essentially re-create the existing system by establishing criteria for authorization that favor status quo providers. In another scenario, new entities, perhaps those who see potential profit in teacher preparation, use money and influence to tip the scales in their favor regardless of the quality of their offerings. Given this potential, it is critical to ensure the board's independence, though years of experience in public administration have shown there is no absolute defense against capture of regulatory agencies by the regulated.

Even without capture, there is related risk that the market will maintain the status quo. School districts have been hiring graduates of teacher-preparation programs for years. Will they continue to do so, going with the tried and true, even as new providers emerge? If so, it will be difficult for new providers to gain a foothold even if the board is open to approving new entrants?

There is also the potential for chaos. This model is not well organized and neat. Candidates and employers would have to become shrewder "shoppers" among the wider variety of providers from which they choose. The status quo is far from being clear and user friendly. It is simpler, but the cost of simplicity is a lack of clear information for candidates and employers about how programs and their performance differ.

If districts do not discriminate between high- and low-quality preparation and candidates in their hiring, then the potential market dynamics of the portfolio system are undermined. Candidates will realize that it does not matter which program they attend; accordingly, they will tend to seek out programs with the least burdensome graduation requirements. Providers will compete for candidates on the basis of ease of completion, not quality. The board could mitigate this through its authorization and deauthorization processes, but the risk of a "race to the bottom" is real. The only hedge against it is a robust overall school accountability system that provides strong incentives for districts to hire high-quality teachers.

Finally, there is a risk that the state would not, in the end, find itself able to deauthorize poor-quality providers. Deauthorization sounds good in theory: if providers fail to perform, they lose their approval. In practice, closing a program means putting people out of their jobs. Where there are teacher shortages, it may also mean narrowing the pipeline for "qualified" teaching candidates, something no state will want to do under the threat of NCLB. For all these reasons, state boards may have trouble deauthorizing all but the most egregious failures, an outcome that would temper many of the potential advantages of the model.

States could minimize the risk of this final pitfall by taking a page from the experience of charter school authorizers, which face a similar challenge when it comes to low-performing charter schools.[14] The most important safeguards are already built into our recommendations above: an open, staggered appointment process for board members; clear reauthorization criteria; and a transparent process for sharing information with the public about providers' performance. None of these is a complete antidote against inability to shut down a failing provider, but all make it more difficult to allow a laggard to carry on. In this context, the board's efforts to encourage the supply of high-quality providers become especially important. It will be easier to deauthorize a demonstrably poor provider if new teacher-training capacity is ready to replace it.

## CONCLUSION

In matters of public policy, it is often tempting to think that if we could just get the rules right, the game would end well. So we tinker and alter and accumulate, responding to this or that concern from this or that interest group, and soon we have the sort of bureaucratic system that characterizes much of the public's machinery. The system protects against various potential harms but doesn't support the potential for dynamism and continuous improvement.

Arguably, we have such a system in our current approach to teacher preparation and certification. Proposals to raise standards for programs and candidates mean well, but they risk locking in a new status quo with little potential for ongoing improvement.

To avoid that fate, states should create more dynamic systems that can change over time in response to changing needs and to improvements in our knowledge about what works. Markets, with their built-in mechanisms for customer feedback and supply response, offer that kind of dynamism. But in the NCLB era, when states are facing a federal mandate to place a highly qualified teacher in each classroom, a pure market approach to teacher supply seems unlikely to fly.

The model proposed here is our effort to claim many of the benefits of the market's dynamism within a framework of state influences that allows a state to say credibly: "We are ensuring that every child has a highly qualified teacher."

## CHAPTER 9

# A Candidate-Centered Model for Teacher Preparation and Licensure

*Catherine B. Walsh*

## INTRODUCTION

In the United States, few high school graduates who aspire to teach are likely to be turned away. Someone who wants to be a teacher may not always be able to gain admission into certain colleges or get a job in some of the more selective school districts, but there are institutions and school districts in every state that exercise no selectivity. Unlike our European and Asian counterparts, the American system of teacher preparation is inordinately accommodating.[1] Although many higher education institutions and schools districts do a commendable job of screening candidates, many do not.

Unrestricted access to higher education is a particularly American ideal, an extension of our commitment to education for all, but its implications for teacher quality ought to be fully understood. About half of the nearly 2,400 four-year colleges and universities in the United States have an open admission policy or accept individuals with less than a C average from high school.[2] Many of the same colleges and universities that lack stringent admissions standards house the nation's 1,354 teacher-preparation programs[3] and will generally accept anyone with an interest in a teaching career and not much else to recommend them. Some programs do not accept teaching-program applicants who do not test at an eighth-grade level of skills, but others do. The leniency does not end after admission. While the teacher candidate must take the course of study required by the institution and the state, the coursework tends to be aimed at a low academic level because of the low academic levels of most students in the program.

After a college diploma is conferred, most (but not all) states then require that the newly minted college graduate cross a single hurdle—a state licensure exam—but this exam eliminates only those who have achieved the subject-matter knowledge that is equivalent to a tenth-grade education. With license in hand, finding a job in a willing school district poses few challenges, provided the individual is willing to teach in a district that primarily serves poor and minority children. Though many school districts exercise considerable judgment and high standards, there also are many that judge a state license to be a full and adequate measure of a teacher's quality.

It is not the relatively small number of alternative certification programs that run the danger of "letting anyone off the street teach," a charge often made by opponents of alternative routes. Instead it is the nation's traditional teacher-preparation program, girded by an ineffective regulatory system, that can and does let just about anyone teach—provided the individual is willing to participate in a training process that expects little more of them than clocking a certain amount of seat time. Faced with the failure of a highly regulated system to do what it was charged to do—bar people from the profession who should not be teaching and provide sufficient preparation to those who should—we need to find alternative ways to nurture and produce great teachers.

A new model for teacher preparation and licensure is needed that builds upon the commendable, even inspirational, motivation that all aspiring teachers have, but which cannot be judged sufficient for the job that lies ahead. States should enlist this motivation to direct aspiring teachers to earn a truly legitimate place in the classroom and help achieve the nation's goal for improving the quality of all teachers. The candidate-centered model explicated here is characterized by a *low* level of regulatory oversight of the institutions that prepare teachers in concert with a *high* bar for entry into the profession. I have interpreted this high bar as a set of state standards with accompanying assessments in three measurable arenas: broad subject-matter knowledge, specific subject-matter knowledge, and professional teaching knowledge.

The candidate-centered model targets the academic shortcomings of many aspiring teachers, most of whom enter the pipeline for the profession during college. Other worthwhile efforts, such as recruiting talented candidates for alternative certification programs, cannot begin to satisfy the nation's high demand for teachers. The real work lies in improving the caliber of the average college freshman who wants to go into teaching.

By means of a diagnostic assessment early on in the college career, the proposed model would provide candidates with a better understanding of their own academic strengths and weaknesses, the relevance of their academic standing to the job of teaching, and what they must do to improve. More than remedial coursework in reading, writing, and arithmetic is required to improve the quality of many teachers and meet the academic demands of the profession. States would develop a new set of standards that articulate the broader *world knowledge* that teachers at any grade level should have, not just because the notion of a well-educated teacher seems to make sense, but because research shows that well-educated teachers offer the surest path to higher student achievement. When looking at which teachers are most likely to raise student achievement, no other measurable attribute of a teacher has been found to be more important than a teacher's verbal ability, far surpassing any measurable effects found from a teacher's certification status or preservice education coursework.[4] Knowledge and vocabulary, which is really all that "verbal ability" measures, highly correlate: the more a teacher knows, the higher their verbal ability will be.

The conclusiveness of these relationships, largely overlooked by colleges, universities, and states, supports a view of teacher preparation that is broader than can be accommodated in education coursework requirements or even most majors, which often restrict students to an inappropriately narrow scope of study. Policy that is founded on what we know about effective teaching should place high value on the importance of the world knowledge acquired by a liberal arts education geared to be relevant to K–12 teaching.

This model asserts that states should not regulate what they cannot objectively measure. While states can measure knowledge, they cannot measure skills or attitude. This observation is not meant to imply that skills or attitude are less important. College faculty, student-teaching supervisors, school principals, master teachers, and department heads routinely evaluate skills and " teaching disposition" and, when done with a modicum of care, with a fair degree of reliability. This model makes a clear distinction between meeting the academic requirements for state licensure and getting a teaching job in a school. Earning a license to teach represents only that a candidate has acquire the knowledge needed. Getting a job at a school would require that the candidate has been able to demonstrate to someone, probably a school principal, that he or she possess sufficient teaching skills and a disposition for teaching. While observations are not foolproof, schools in an era of accountability are more likely to make a better judgment about a candidate than any other alternative that states could consider.

## RATIONALE

In large part, regulations are a response to human failure. If we did not keep "messing up," the need for regulation would not exist. Regulations make us fix a dangerous step in the workplace before someone has a chance to get hurt or fix our car exhaust systems so we don't pollute. Regulations can ensure a level playing field or increase fairness, as when they prevent us from telling our shareholding friends that our company is about to go bankrupt. We design regulations to keep people from hiring their incompetent uncle or cousin. However, the cost of regulations can be quite high, and not just because they require large bureaucracies to enforce them. Regulations are often counterproductive—outliving their intended purpose, enforced by government officials without thought or understanding of their purpose, ultimately slowing growth and impeding quality.[5] As new issues, questions, and needs arise, people tend to pile on new regulations while failing to discard the old ones. Particularly perilous is the fact that many regulations are wrongheaded from the start, enacted without proper consideration of the facts, or absent any means to measure their effectiveness as officials respond hurriedly to a particular event or scandal.

Education, and specifically teacher preparation, offers many examples of the pitfalls of regulation. For instance, since the 1930s states have been establishing teaching "endorsements" to define each teaching niche by grade level and subject matter and prescribe what preparation is needed. Each of these endorsements has its own set of college coursework requirements, with the result that the regulations confuse rather than clarify what teacher candidates must do to qualify for licensure. Michigan lists at least eighty-nine separate teaching endorsements.[6] Nevada offers three different physical education licenses: Physical Education, Physical Education and Health, and Recreational Physical Education.[7] Three states offer endorsements in Cooperative Education.[8] The proliferation of these endorsements over the years has nearly obliterated their relevance for judging who is an "out-of-field" teacher and has made it inordinately difficult for any district to be in complete compliance.[9]

Groups differ on the benefits of regulations governing teacher licensure, making them the subject of heated policy debates. On one side are many professional educators and organizations that believe there is a right way and a wrong way to prepare teachers and that a strong regulatory policy must be in place to enforce this view. Teacher preparation should, they argue, be offered in a carefully planned program of study that occurs on a college or university campus. This model is commonly referred to as "campus-based" teacher preparation. Even individuals seeking to enter the profession through an alternate route are usually required to have attended a state-approved, campus-based teacher-preparation program before becoming licensed.

Much of the criticism directed at this view over the last century has been based on the low rigor of education coursework and the belief of some that there is an insufficient body of knowledge to justify a professional track for teaching. Evidence for this view has come from economists who study the impact of teachers on student achievement. Economists have studied the particular attributes of teachers that lead to greater student achievement, asking such questions as, "Are veteran teachers more effective than relatively newer teachers?" (it's not clear that they are)[10] and "Are teachers who have a master's degrees more effective than teachers who have only a bachelor's degree?"(generally not).[11] These researchers contend that there is insufficient evidence to support a regulatory policy restricting teacher preparation to state-approved, campus-based programs. Many have concluded that evidence of a correlation between preservice education coursework and student achievement, if any, is so thin that states cannot justify rejecting candidates simply for lack of such coursework.[12] The cost of these regulations is too high, they argue: even if they do keep out some unqualified candidates, there is more evidence that they keep out a greater numbers of high-caliber candidates. In short, the regulations do more harm than good.[13]

In the middle of this debate stands an uncertain public, including many policymakers. While they may know that education schools and coursework are held in low regard, they like the idea of the assurances that a state license implies. The nation's elite private schools are quite willing to hire teachers with no formal training or license, yet much of the public is aghast at the notion that public school children might be assigned one. If this system is found to be as flawed as some critics of certification suggest, then public sentiment might favor revising the regulations over discarding them.

The nation's tendency to tinker with the teacher-preparation system without discarding its basic structure is not new. Ever since states started regulating the teaching profession at the turn of the last century there has been no shortage of criticism of the system's failings, but history shows that successive reform efforts were eventually captured by the educational establishment, making it less likely for real reform to occur.[14] The solutions inevitably give education schools more, not less, control over teacher preparation; many alternative certification programs require nearly as much education coursework as a traditional undergraduate preparation program. In some respects, the No Child Left Behind Act (NCLB) is the latest example of an attempt to retrofit the system to fix its failings. But NCLB bears a critical distinction from previous reform efforts with its clear indictment of teacher licensure, which is embodied in its declaration that more is expected of a highly qualified teacher than the mere possession of a state license. NCLB adds the requirement that teachers prove they know their subject matter. The rather astounding implication of this new requirement is that the certification process is incapable of fixing itself, at least in this particular area. Since the inception of teacher certification at the beginning of the twentieth century, it may be the first time that a federal or state statute so clearly declared that teacher certification is an insufficient measure of a person's qualification to teach.

## WHY THE SYSTEM ISN'T WORTH TWEAKING ONE MORE TIME

The current regulatory system is characterized by four major deficiencies, providing substantial evidence that our faith in a regulatory system has been misplaced:

*1. States base their approvals of teacher-preparation programs on program compliance with regulations, not on the quality of their graduates or on the responsiveness of these programs to the marketplace.*

By and large, states do not approve their teacher-preparation programs based on what should be their most important indication of success: the effectiveness of their graduates in the classroom. Not surprisingly, this problem has been observed by both critics and defenders of regulatory policies, including, for instance, the Interstate New Teacher Assessment and Support Consortium (INTASC). In its policy document, *Next Steps: Moving toward Performance-Based Licensing in Teaching* (1995), INTASC advocates for a shift to performance-based licensing standards to "enable state[s] to permit greater innovation and diversity in how teacher education programs operate by assessing their outcomes rather than merely regulating their inputs or procedures."

Other than the reputations these programs earn by word of mouth, states do not know whether approved teacher-preparation programs add any measurable value, which features of a program add value and which do not, or how programs within the state compare with one another in terms of their value. Measuring student achievement gains fairly is a difficult task, but states have not elected to use other more readily collected objective data as the basis for approving programs. Such measures might include the average score of graduates on the state teacher exam, numbers of teachers prepared in high-shortage areas, or placement and retention rates.

Lately, federal lawmakers have shown more willingness than state officials to hold teacher-preparation programs accountable. The 1998 reauthorization of the federal Higher Education Act was designed to make these programs more accountable. The law requires states to collect data reporting the percentage of graduates in each teacher-preparation program passing the state teacher exam. However, this law has proven largely ineffectual, as states have stalled on compliance and programs mask their true failure rates.[15] Only one teacher-preparation program in the country was classified as low performing in 2002. Programs escape state scrutiny by, for example, not counting an individual as a "program completer" until he or she has passed the state exam, even if he or she has completed the coursework required by the program. The result is that states know nothing about how many students fail the exam and, most importantly, cannot gauge a program's value. It was the intent of the law to encourage states to withdraw program approval from programs with consistently low pass rates. Yet a program that has 100 students of whom only forty pass can still report a 100 percent pass rate, disregarding the sixty students who did not pass as "non program completers."

Though a tightened version of the Higher Education Act may prompt the upheaval that federal lawmakers sought, the relationship between many states and their teacher programs is generally like that of an old married couple—comfortable and accepting of one another's flaws, and not very interested in doing things differently. All but a few states continue to approve programs based on their adherence to coursework requirements and numbers of credit hours, even as many states have espoused a commitment to a performance-based system of licensure intended to do away with such requirements. Many states have delegated their oversight functions to a private accrediting body, the National Council on Accreditation of Teacher Education (NCATE), avoiding unfiltered public accountability. Many NCATE critics argue that the organization has a vested interest in protecting the financial interests of its member schools, making it less likely that they will insist on difficult reforms that carry fiscal implications.

Certainly the fact that many states have chosen to link their own approval process to NCATE's accreditation process sharply limits the possibility of a state expanding the routes to teacher licensure beyond the college campus. Alternative certification programs originally represented a mutiny of sorts against the tight control of schools of education over access to the profession, but many states now require alternate-route candidates to take education coursework at these same institutions. For instance, Maryland's alternative certification program started in 1990 with a requirement of six credit hours of preparation; ten years, later the state had tripled the credit hours needed.[16] The state school board in New Jersey recently added new coursework requirements to its alternative certification program.[17] The American Association of Colleges of Teachers of Education (AACTE) claims that 70 percent of all alternative certification programs in the country are now housed in schools of education.[18] It seems the fox has been welcomed into the henhouse.

Apart from the delegation of oversight to NCATE, states may not feel compelled to hold their teacher programs more accountable if they feel their licensure exams provide sufficient quality control. In only a few instances have states taken schools of education to task. In 2001, the Louisiana Board of Education and Board of Regents, alarmed over the low quality of the state's teachers, withdrew all state approval of teacher-preparation programs, forcing them to reapply under more rigorous guidelines. Louisiana's move was exceptional; overall support for these programs appears to have been institutionalized and protected from painful reform.

Absent state regulatory policy and the persistent support from state education departments that protect teacher-preparation programs from failure, many of these programs might not survive the unforgiving pressures of a free market. Unencumbered by the current program-approval regime, school districts might feel free to recruit individuals for their high-shortage areas from other sources and to develop their own training programs. School districts are much less enamored than state departments of education of the current licensure process. According to a Public Agenda study, only 10 percent of school administrators think certification is an adequate indication that an individual has what it takes to succeed as a teacher.[19]

A district-based preparation model holds at least two distinct advantages that could prove daunting to a campus-based program. First, training can be targeted to the district's curriculum, something schools of education generally refuse to do. Second, training can be provided at a fraction of the price of a campus-based program. To operate without state protection, the campus-based programs would have to add value that is measurable and evident to school districts and aspiring teachers, a far cry from the perception that many aspiring teachers and school districts hold now. By contrast, in teacher-entry pipelines that at least appear to bypass schools of education, there are an enviable number of job candidates in school districts with the worst working conditions. Teach For America turned away six candidates for every one hired in 2003;[20] New York City's alternative program, New Teaching Fellows, turned away eleven applicants for every one hired in 2003.[21]

Campus-based teacher-preparation programs will certainly face challenges under a deregulated system that encourages district-based preparation models or a national route such as the American Board for the Certification of Teaching Excellence (American Board) certification tests, but traditional campus-based programs are still likely to train most of the nation's teachers for the simple reason that the college campus is where most people begin training for any profession.

*2. Using regulatory levers to control quality is ineffective and heavy-handed, and leads to hiring protocols that rely far too much on licensure.*

Policymakers may not appreciate how even their most sensible regulations are enforced, defeating the very teacher-quality goals that led to their creation. When a prospective teacher applies to a school district, evidence must be provided to a state official that the individual has completed an approved teacher-preparation program. States employ certification specialists to review the candidate's transcript and licensure information, allowing or disallowing further consideration of that candidate. If a candidate does not have a teaching license, the specialist provides him or her with a list of coursework needed before licensure will be considered.

In theory, carefully drafted regulations governing the work of these specialists will prevent schools from hiring unqualified teachers. But the expertise of these specialists consists of their knowledge of the state's certification regulations and their ability to analyze a college transcript, *not* their knowledge of good teaching or how to run a school. If their role were purely advisory, their lack of school management experience would not matter so much. However, these specialists are often the first and last arbiters of who is allowed to teach in a state's schools; principals are not free to override their decisions.

The fallout from this process is that the caliber of teacher candidates has become irrelevant to states and school districts. For instance, one study of the hiring experiences of 500 new teachers found that almost three-fourths did not have to submit any standardized test scores as part of the hiring process.[22] Another found that school districts pay surprisingly little attention to the selectivity of applicants' undergraduate institutions.[23] The rigor of the coursework, grades, and even attendance are irrelevant in determining whether a candidate is to be permitted to teach. The candidate's knowledge and skills about subject matter and teaching that he or she may have acquired in a formal program has no bearing. When eligibility to teach is being determined, the only factor of any consequence is a title of each course on the college transcript.

Some observers argue that licensure exacerbates teacher shortages by barring qualified individuals who lack certification credentials, creating shortages that force schools to hire whomever they can find at the last minute to teach. Emergency permits, waivers, and other loopholes allow individuals to enter the classroom who sometimes have not met even the most basic qualifications. One recent analysis found that 35 percent of new teachers in Houston did not possess even a bachelor's degree.[24] Nationally, more than one in twenty teachers teaches under emergency certification or a waiver; this figure disguises the disproportionately high numbers teaching children who are poor.[25] Certification regulations do not prevent high rates of out-of-field teaching.[26]

One can make a reasonable argument that licensure is not about specifying *how* qualified a candidate is, that it can only insure that teachers have met a minimum standard of quality. The license, under this argument, signals to the public that the state is not allowing people capable of educational malpractice in the classroom. But even that expectation is not actually met. The quality of licensed teachers employed in the nation's more affluent school districts appears to provide evidence that some minimum standard is at play and functioning well. The quality of many *licensed* teachers in the nation's needier school districts is a different story. For instance, a *Chicago Sun-Times* investigation revealed that teachers in schools with the fewest white students and who worked in the poorest schools were five times more likely to have failed a certification test at least once, sometimes several times, before passing.[27] Clearly, it is not licensure but selectivity on the part of school districts that contributes some measure of quality.

Many school districts put blind faith in a teaching license, accepting it as all the evidence they need of a teacher's quality. Liu (2003) found that principals hired one out of five teachers sight unseen, passing on the opportunity to conduct an interview. In Florida, one of out five teachers was not interviewed by anyone in the district.[28] Teacher candidates appear rarely to be asked to demonstrate their skills. Only 7.5 percent of candidates were observed teaching a sample lesson. Fewer than one in five candidates was asked to produce a written lesson plan or a writing sample.

Most states do little to persuade districts that licensure has its limitations and actively discourage their districts from broadening their applicant pools by allowing alternate route programs. States impose requirements on alternate certification programs that are nearly as cumbersome as the requirements of an undergraduate program. State officials frequently admonish their poorest school districts, often publicly, for not making enough effort to hire certified candidates. Wealthier school districts with high student achievement are generally free to do as they please; even when they hire uncertified teachers they escape the usual state reprimands. For instance, one of the nation's wealthiest school districts, Scarsdale, New York, which pays an average teacher salary of $92,000 a year, still chooses to employ a considerable number of noncertified teachers.[29]

In many of the nation's neediest school districts, a certified applicant is generally guaranteed a job, no matter how poorly he or she might compare to a noncertified candidate. The most extreme example of some districts' blind faith in certification is the teacher job fair. In these one-day events, district personnel officers offer teaching contracts to any certified applicant who shows up, conditioned only on a successful background check, and even this basic requirement is often violated. Flaws in fingerprinting and background checking procedures mean that criminals—even pedophiles—are not always barred from teaching.[30] In effect, candidates often receive no more scrutiny than day laborers. There may be some school principals from the district present, but candidates generally do not get to decide for whom they want to work. Some districts hire hundreds of teachers in one day at these job fairs.

*3. Teacher candidates can and should bear more responsibility for their preparation.*

States have focused all their attention on their regulatory requirements for training programs while disregarding the player who is in the best position to remedy the teacher-quality problem: the teaching candidate. In effect, the state and the teaching candidate intersect at only one juncture, the state teacher exam, which is administered at the completion of the preparation program. For two reasons, this exam has limited use as a teacher-quality assurance tool: the timing of the exam makes it a poor lever for controlling teacher quality, and the content that is tested does not reflect the work required for a college degree.

In 2003, nearly half of the states required candidates to pass a basic skills test, most commonly the Praxis I, before they could be admitted to a teacher-preparation program.[31] This test ensures that the candidate possesses minimum knowledge at the eighth-grade level, such as the need for a verb to agree with its subject and a basic understanding of fractions. From 1994 to 1997, the test's developer, the Educational Testing Service (ETS), reported that the pass rate on the Praxis I basic skills test was 77 percent. One can assume that, generally speaking, 23 percent of the test-takers either are barred from admission into a school of education or enter remediation so that they are able to pass the test later.[32]

There seems little justification for not significantly raising the pass rate on the Praxis I basic skills test as an immediate move to improve teacher quality. The difference in expectations between this basic skills test and the demanding tests required of aspiring teachers in Europe and Asia at this juncture puts the United States in quite an unflattering light. Nations that score particularly well on the Third International Math and Science Study (TIMSS), such as Japan, Korea, Singapore, and the Netherlands, all use high-stakes tests to select candidates for entry into their teacher-preparation program.[33]

At the next stage, more (but not all) states require a candidate to pass a state teacher test at the end of college, most commonly some version of the Praxis II. The U.S. Department of Education's *The Secretary's Second Annual Report on Teacher Quality* identifies eight states that do not require any sort of licensure test and nineteen states that do not require a content-area test.[34] From 1994 to 1997, ETS reported that 87 percent of all test-takers passed the Praxis II. This statistic suggests that the 13 percent of failing test-takers were then barred from entering the profession, or that the candidates simply kept retaking the test until they passed (since there is no limit on the number of tries that are allowed). In states where no test is required, no objective criteria are used to screen out candidates who may have completed the coursework requirements of a teacher-preparation program but who still should not be teaching.

Though many critics of state teaching tests point to the need to raise the state pass rates, the pass rates for the Praxis II—an amalgam of tests that are typically given at the end of college—appear to be about right for a professional licensure exam. It is not unreasonable for a candidate to expect to do well on a licensure test after completing several years of study to that end. In the medical profession, 92 percent of all medical school graduates pass the licensing examinations on their first try,[35] and 80 percent of all law school graduates pass the bar exam on their first try.[36] What sets the teacher tests apart from these other licensure tests is not their pass rates but their lack of rigor; they are aimed at roughly the tenth- grade level.[37] It seems likely, then, that the pass rate would be just as high if the test were taken by a selection of college-bound high school juniors.

These tests also call into question the breadth and depth of professional teaching knowledge, especially since states generally require teacher candidates to devote about a third of their college career to education coursework. Unlike any licensure exam in the medical, legal, and accounting professions, it is quite possible to pass the professional teaching knowledge tests without ever having taken an education course. In 2003, 100 percent of Teach For America candidates, few of whom have ever taken an education course in college, passed the Praxis II "Principles of Learning and Teaching" for either grades K-6 or 5-9 on their first attempt. The first-time pass rate for Teach For America candidates on the "Elementary Education: Curriculum, Instruction and Assessment, K-5" was considerably lower (59%), but these pass rates must call into question the value added by many teacher-preparation programs.[38]

No one pretends that the state teacher tests are difficult to pass, but states are reluctant to raise their passing score for a couple of reasons. First, classrooms have to be filled, even if the person at the head of the room is only a warm body. States and school districts do not feel they have the luxury of turning the standards up a notch if it means classrooms might stand empty. However, Massachusetts' laudable commitment to raise the standards on its own state test has proven this worry to be largely unfounded. After the state introduced a more rigorous state test in 1998, the number of candidates who took and passed the test quadrupled in four years. Enrollment in education programs has increased, not decreased.[39]

The second reason states do not want to raise the passing score on the state tests is the fact that minorities historically do less well than whites on these tests. States are reluctant to do anything that will make it less likely that minorities will enter teaching. Most recently, minority teachers in California and New York have gone to court, charging that state tests discriminate against minorities and are not relevant to teaching assignments. Both cases were decided in favor of the states, allowing the tests to stand.[40] Nevertheless, the threat of court battles makes states leery about raising the standards. Their inaction may solve some immediate problems, but it is a disservice to the nation's goal of producing more qualified teachers. Meanwhile, teacher preparation programs continue to churn out ill-prepared teachers, a proportion of whom are minorities, without resolving the root causes of poor performance.

*4. To accommodate teacher quality goals, teacher preparation programs must attend to the low literacy rate of a significant portion of the nation's aspiring teachers, particularly minorities.*

The college education of too many aspiring teachers consists of a heavy dose of skills remediation, with far less attention given to developing the broad knowledge that candidates lack. Coursework is too narrowly confined to one of two areas: the teacher's chosen subject matter and education coursework. The state teacher tests send all the wrong signals about the academic demands of the profession. As noted, a disproportionately high number of minorities who try to become teachers are not always able to do so because they are unable to pass these tests. The response by some groups has been to charge that teacher tests are biased against minorities; the mere threat of this charge makes some states fearful of trying to require a test or raising their passing scores to a sufficiently rigorous level. The state of Texas, for instance, implemented a literacy test for its practicing teachers that it withdrew because of the disproportionately poor performance of minorities after only one year (long enough for researcher Ronald Ferguson to demonstrate that teachers with higher scores produced higher student achievement gains).[41]

The need for remedial coursework in reading and mathematics is often used as ammunition by proponents of K–12 reform. Nearly a third of all college students now have to take remedial coursework.[42] But the problem of minority performance disparities is unlikely to be alleviated fully by remedial coursework, either because of the nature of such coursework or because of the dispiriting message that it sends. It brings to mind U.S. Education Secretary Paige's statement on the "soft bigotry of low expectations." These charges and remedies neglect the simple observable fact that many minorities, more of whom have grown up in poverty, need much more than skills remediation; they suffer from enormous disparities in language and world knowledge that can be traced to infancy.[43] They need to participate in a well-planned course of study to acquire the knowledge that characterizes well-educated, quality teachers.

The most authoritative voice on this issue belongs to E.D. Hirsch, who has eloquently articulated the inequities of the U.S. K–12 education system. His strategy for narrowing the nation's persistent achievement gap is premised on the logical (but controversial) connection between a person's level of literacy, as measured by reading comprehension skills, and broad knowledge of the world.[44] This relationship between reading comprehension and knowledge is overlooked in the skills-based curriculum that dominates U.S. schooling. Hirsch's criticism of the focus of U.S. schooling extends to teacher preparation, which does not adequately prepare teachers to deliver a knowledge-based curriculum. In response, Hirsch's Core Knowledge Foundation has developed outlines for sixteen college courses suitable for an aspiring elementary teacher that would require broad reading across many subject areas.[45] However, it seems unlikely that most schools of education will embrace Hirsch's solution. Most faculties in schools of education are openly derisive of Hirsch's views on schooling, and Hirsch of them. Hirsch's solutions are viewed as too prescriptive, and his belief that there should be any one common curriculum for all to learn as too presumptuous. Political battles aside, the scientific underpinning of his position that a person's literacy is a measure of his or her own world knowledge has not been disproved. Aspiring teachers, especially those who are themselves victims of an inadequate K–12 education, need full engagement in an intellectually rigorous education.

## THE MODEL

These are the issues that a new model of teacher licensure needs to address:

- A good proportion of aspiring teachers arrives at college undereducated; a disproportionate number of these are minorities. School districts want to hire qualified minorities and are reluctant to implement policies that would reduce the number of minority applicants.
- Many teacher-preparation programs confer meaningless diplomas that signify no measurable academic achievement by the graduate. Many of these programs enroll high numbers of minorities.
- Most of the nation's teachers (72%) begin their teacher preparation in undergraduate programs, as opposed to master's programs or alternate certification routes.[46]
- Research on the relationship between teacher attributes and student achievement gains provide little indication that education coursework makes a teacher more effective in the classroom.[47] Yet teacher candidates devote about one-third of their 120 college credits to education coursework and student teaching.[48]
- Many states require teaching candidates to complete a subject-matter major in addition to their education coursework. Though this requirement seems to make sense, in practice it poses problems that regulatory enforcers do not seem able to overcome. First, the requirement lends itself to inappropriately narrow interpretations. An engineering or physics major may be barred from teaching mathematics, even though all three majors clearly require extensive knowledge and coursework in mathematics. Second, it is not at all clear what major best prepares elementary teachers. No published studies report a correlation between an elementary teacher's subject-matter coursework and student achievement gains. Third, there is some evidence that neither prospective elementary teach-

ers' choice of major nor the specific coursework taken to satisfy the requirements of the major are sufficiently relevant to the knowledge requirements of K–12 teachers.[49]

• Many individuals who want to teach in even the most challenging school districts are dissuaded by regulatory requirements and hiring protocols that treat licensure as the gold standard of quality.[50]

Much of this suggests that current systems squander an enormous opportunity to improve the caliber of traditional teaching candidates and increase the number of qualified minorities in the process. The challenge before us is how to improve the caliber of teaching candidates, using the college experience more effectively, and ensure that high-caliber people who choose to enter teaching at a later point are also accommodated.

## Giving Teachers' Verbal Ability its Due

Since the 1960s, when James Coleman produced his famous study on school effects and student achievement, researchers have known that verbal ability is a critically important teacher attribute. Research continues to confirm that verbal ability is more significant than any other measurable teacher attribute, including a teacher's subject-matter knowledge and certification status, for raising student achievement.[51] The meaning of the term *verbal ability* may not be immediately obvious. In fact, its meaning has been loosely defined in some teacher policy writing. Stanford education professor Linda Darling-Hammond suggests that verbal ability may be a "more sensitive measure of teachers' abilities to convey ideas in clear and convincing ways."[52] More succinctly and precisely, verbal ability is vocabulary knowledge.

The various instruments used by researchers that yielded the verbal ability findings have all been written multiple-choice vocabulary tests. The fact that the instruments varied adds to the robustness of this finding. Researchers have used the verbal portions of the SAT and ACT, but also several shorter and simpler tests such as the Quick Word Test, used by Hanushek in a 1971 study and by McLaughlin and Marsh in 1978.[53] In addition to the verbal-ability finding, researchers have found that teachers who attend more selective colleges are more likely to raise student achievement, a finding that seems to be a reasonable proxy for verbal ability. One significant study found that selectivity of college was especially beneficial for the student achievement gains of African American students who were poor.[54]

This research indicates that the more effective strategy for raising the academic achievement of minorities and all teachers would be to institute measures that raise their verbal ability. Suggesting a strategy to improve the word knowledge of teachers runs the risk of appearing to advocate that teacher candidates memorize random lists of words for weekly "vocab quizzes." This view of vocabulary acquisition undersells its importance and represents a serious misunderstanding of how most word meanings are acquired.

Though the process of how we acquire word meanings is a subject worthy of books, the basic tenets can be quickly summarized for our purposes here. The most rapid growth in vocabulary occurs in the toddler years; young adults continue to acquire new words at a rate estimated between 1,000 to 3,000 words a year (the higher figure is probably more accurate).[55] Most of these words are learned gradually and subconsciously, primarily via written text, since we use many more words in writing than we use to speak.

Our knowledge of vocabulary represents our knowledge of subject matter.[56] If we know a lot about baseball, we know a lot of words associated with baseball. We can't know a lot about baseball and remain ignorant of terms like *home run* and *double play*. It follows that the more a teacher knows about many subjects, the more words the teacher knows, and vice versa. The bottom line is that people with high verbal ability have not achieved their vocabulary knowledge by memorizing word meanings, but by doing a lot of reading, writing, and speaking about many subjects. This is the stuff of a good college program of study. Verbal ability is, in essence, a measure of what a person knows.

Meeting this need may or may not result in devoting fewer clock hours to education coursework, but it does mean that a substantial portion of teacher preparation should focus on improving a teacher's world knowledge by requiring study of many subject areas.

### The Steps to Licensure

The candidate-centered model consists of the following components, only some of which are required by the state (marked by an *) in granting a license:

- A diagnostic tool administered at the start of college that identifies the academic strengths and weaknesses of candidates.*
- A basic skills test in reading, writing, and mathematics.*
- Liberal arts coursework, typically undertaken in the first four semesters of college (approximately 60 credits).
- A state assessment of verbal ability, administered midway through college.*

- Subject-area specialty coursework in the teacher candidate's intended subject area, typically accommodated in the coursework requirements of a college major (approximately 30 credits).
- Education coursework in a teacher candidate's chosen field, including student teaching (30 credits).
- A state assessment of a teacher's subject-area mastery and professional teaching knowledge.*
- An interview process by a school that adheres to a good hiring protocol for professionals.
- A teaching license after one year of successful teaching.

*Diagnostic Tool*

The intent of the diagnostic tool is to start aspiring teachers on a path that improves their general knowledge as will be measured by a test of verbal ability. The diagnostic would be administered when an aspiring teacher enters college or first indicates an interest in becoming a teacher. It would provide each candidate with information and guidance about their own academic strengths and weaknesses from the perspective of what a future teacher should know and what any well-educated person generally does know. It would measure rudimentary knowledge of such things as, for example, how electricity works, how the sun and the planets are arranged, what the Renaissance was, the origins of jazz, and who Lewis and Clark were. Importantly, it would not be a "high-stakes test" designed to screen out undereducated teachers.

Beginning teacher preparation with a proper diagnosis of an aspiring teacher's level of world knowledge and then following it with a substantial body of liberal arts coursework should improve teacher quality, particularly the academic weaknesses of the undereducated, and increase the numbers of minorities who are genuinely qualified to teach. Historian and college professor Sandra Stotsky recently led an effort in Massachusetts to revamp the state licensure system. The new system includes a much greater emphasis on the liberal arts preparation of teachers. In reviewing the college coursework typically taken by aspiring teachers in the state, Stotsky and her colleagues found that the courses generally bore little relevance to the knowledge needed by K–12 teachers. The disconnect between teacher candidates' preparation and their ultimate career aspirations was especially striking in the typical choices of a major. Stotsky observed three general deficiencies in typical college majors: 1) the irrelevant major, which consists of respectable but irrelevant coursework for the K–12 teacher, such as sociology, psychology, religious studies, and marketing; 2) the grievance major, which too often lacks academic depth or breadth, excessively focusing on victimization issues; and 3) the composite major, which is cobbled together from education coursework and a smattering of arts and sciences courses. The composite major consists of a little of everything but not enough of any one thing, and almost no upper-level coursework; as a result, such majors provide insufficient intellectual depth.

These observations are helpful because they reveal that requiring a college major outside the school of education is not a panacea, and that teacher candidates need more and better guidance about relevant coursework in subject matter.

States would need to convene a knowledgeable panel of college faculty and K–12 educators to decide what knowledge from broad academic areas are perceived as important for generally well-educated individuals, including teachers, to have acquired. The core of such standards already exists in many of the better state K–12 standards, the standards developed for the American Board certification exams, and the work done by the Core Knowledge Foundation on a course of study for elementary teachers. These standards would be used to develop the diagnostic tool that incoming college students who aspire to be teachers would be required to take. The diagnostic would be administered by the state or by a private testing company the state has selected as a contractor.

Individuals who choose to enter teaching later than at the entry point to college would have the option of trying to pass the midway assessment without taking the diagnostic test or the recommended coursework. If they did not pass the assessment, they could take the diagnostic test and pursue the subject matter indicated by the test results, either formally (in college courses) or informally (through their own directed reading).

*Basic Skills Test*

Though the basic-skills test already appears to eliminate 23 percent of the aspiring teachers in the states that require it, the candidate-centered model would make this test more rigorous by establishing a single national pass rate. This rate would be adopted by setting a recommended score, followed by efforts to set the rate in state statutes over time. Currently, each state sets its own passing score, producing an enormous range from state to state but an average pass rate of 77 percent (with 46% of African Americans passing). If all the states adopted the lowest pass rate set by any state, 91 percent of all test-takers would pass, but only 67 percent of African Americans. If all of the states adopted the highest pas rate set by any state, only 47 percent of all test takers and only 17 percent of African Americans would pass. Absent a national standard for the minimum skill competencies expected of all teachers, too many states have proven unwilling to make the painful but necessary decision that will lead to higher teacher-quality goals.

In lieu of a consensus for a national pass rate on the basic-skills test, a consortium of states could be organized and agree to a single standard, in effect shaming those states that continue to adhere to unacceptably low standards. Alternatively, NCATE and/or the Teacher Education Accreditation Council (TEAC, the newest accrediting body) could require that its member schools adopt one pass rate to maintain their accreditation. To date, NCATE has strongly resisted that move, though it has indicated that it will recommend that its member schools accept a national passing score. A third alternative is to implement a relatively low passing score to start, with a commitment to raise the passing score each year over a period of years.

*Liberal Arts Coursework*

Higher education institutions may need to align their existing coursework and possibly develop additional coursework to respond effectively to the results of the diagnostic tool. Though colleges and universities offer coursework in all subject areas, they often do not place sufficient emphasis on the need for survey coursework that imparts a broader perspective. For example, there is nothing inherently wrong with taking a course on the social upheaval in the 1960s to satisfy a college's history requirement, but it may not be the most appropriate choice for the future teacher whose knowledge of American history is typically spotty. At some point, a future teacher needs to have acquired knowledge of the scope of American history from European exploration to recent times.

A potential problem in accommodating the number of liberal arts courses that many aspiring teachers will need is the number of institutional course requirements for both teaching candidates and other students. Teaching candidates, because they often are completing a content major as well as taking courses in education, are not able to sign up for much elective coursework. The coursework for a college major generally takes up at least one-third of the required credits, with education coursework taking up at least another third.[57] In the candidate-centered model, the liberal arts and core institutional requirements would roughly comprise one-half of all college coursework, the major one-quarter and education coursework about one-quarter. To accommodate the expanding role of liberal arts coursework, institutions may need to reexamine the number of credit hours required in education coursework.

The role of the higher education commission or regents board will be integral to the implementation of this or any new model. Given the economics of higher education, it is improbable that a school of education would volunteer to reduce its coursework requirements. The decisionmaking authority must be placed at a higher level where the interests in the quality of the future teacher, not institutional self-interests, are paramount.

## Midway Assessment

The proposed midway assessment would give aspiring teachers a useful measure of their standing. States would require aspiring teachers to achieve a passing score on the midway assessment before institutions would be allowed to admit candidates into a formal teacher-preparation program. Coursework in the college major, often delayed by institutional core requirements, might not begin until after this midway assessment has been taken.

Insertion of the midway assessment is intended to improve the quality of aspiring teachers who arrive at college undereducated, and particularly to improve the outcomes for minority candidates. Two years of broad liberal arts coursework allows these students to address the academic weaknesses that their K–12 education did not, or, if they are not particularly weak, to expand their understanding and perspective. The midway inserts a quality-control lever at an earlier point in the preparation pipeline, though still not as early or unforgiving as the European and Asian tracks, where undereducated students have no hope of attending a college or university. Some benchmark of quality is needed before the candidate or the institution invests four years' time and tuition into achieving licensure, if only for psychological reasons. Denying licensure to candidates after they have finished four years of preparation when they have been led to believe they are doing all that is expected of them seems almost like a breaking a promise. The situation is not unlike that which led many states to make their high school exams end-of-course exams, not actual exit exams. Too many unqualified candidates take the test repeatedly until they achieve a passing score.[58] Mindful of their commitment to candidates, states keep the score low so that they are not in the position of denying what had seemed largely inevitable.

The midway exam is intended to be a test of verbal ability or vocabulary, not a test of subject-matter knowledge. A state might choose to administer a test of general subject-matter knowledge at this point, especially if it has the standards on which to base such a test from the development of the diagnostic tool, but there are good reasons not to do so. First, the purposes of the diagnostic test and the midway test are separate: the first is intended to guide the candidate to better coursework selections relevant to teaching and improving verbal ability. The midway assessment's function as a quality-control lever is served if it measures vocabulary knowledge. Second, a subject-matter test may erect an artificial barrier to entry into the profession, yet there is no direct evidence that a test of this nature will yield more effective teachers than a considerably less complex vocabulary test. After all, it is not as clear that a high school mathematics teacher needs to pass a multiple-choice exam that tests his broad knowledge of ancient Egypt, though it would be a good idea for him to know what a pyramid is. Third, a specific subject-matter test may also undermine some of the flexibility that this model intends to give candidates who consider teaching at a later point in life, long after they have completed their college coursework. Fourth, given the sheer breadth of knowledge that could be included on such a test, states would run the risk of placing too much emphasis on a candidate's recall of facts, some of which may not be at all important to a general understanding of the particular subject matter. Better that the state implement a vocabulary test than be accused of emulating a game of Trivial Pursuit.

It is entirely likely, given the current numbers of aspiring teachers with poor academic credentials, that many candidates will not do as well on the midway exam as states might like. Candidates would then either have to take more liberal arts coursework with the intention of retaking the exam or choose another career. Colleges and universities that chronically produced high numbers of students who failed the exam would have to reassess the rigor of their coursework leading up to this exam, or risk losing students to institutions that report higher passing rates. Undoubtedly, private companies would offer services similar to SAT prep courses to help teacher candidates pass this exam.

The midway exam should have a single passing score for the same reasons that the basic-skills exam should implement a single national passing score.

### Specialization and the Specialty Exam

Candidates who pass the midway exam could then apply for admission into a formal teacher-preparation program, in effect pursuing a dual major: education and a subject-matter major. Typically about half of the remaining coursework (roughly 30 to 36 credits) would be dedicated to a major or coursework in a specialty area. It is most likely that teacher candidates will choose a subject-matter major due to the requirements of the institution and the candidate's own need to master a subject area, but state regulations would not require a candidate to have majored in a subject area in order to teach it. The only regulatory policy would be that the teacher candidate demonstrate mastery by passing a rigorous subject-matter exam in the specialty area.

Although requiring a college major makes sense on many levels, its insertion into regulatory policy is problematic. Too often, teacher candidates possess the knowledge required to teach a subject but not the credential of a major. For instance, physics or engineering majors invariably know enough mathematics to teach the subject. In fact, the case for an academic major is not as obvious for elementary teachers. There is almost no research offering insight into which major an elementary teacher should pursue to be most effective in the classroom. The language in NCLB attempts a reasonable solution, differentiating between what is expected of secondary teachers (a college major or a subject-matter test) and elementary teachers (passing a relevant test that assesses content knowledge in all relevant subject areas.)

If current state teacher exams are any indication, the most likely design flaw in the model's new subject specialty tests will be that they reflect coursework at the high school, not college, level. The content of existing tests does not adequately measure the knowledge, analytical skills, and perception that are acquired at the college level, most likely because the range in academic expectations in U.S. colleges and universities is too extreme. The task of agreeing on a sufficiently challenging set of standards achievable by the nation's three million teachers is daunting. Some states are trying. Illinois and Massachusetts are requiring more difficult teacher tests than are now commercially available. Though the test is more difficult than the Praxis II, Massachusetts was still not able to make its test as hard it would have liked because too many teachers would have failed.[59] The new American Board teacher exams also appear to be extremely difficult to pass, but this alternate route to certification has the luxury of not having to serve as the nation's primary source of teachers; as an alternate route, the American Board can afford to set the bar quite high.

The challenge for states will be to develop a set of subject-area exams that are sufficiently difficult and that a reasonable number of teachers can pass. Until higher education commissions and boards of regents agree on what level of knowledge a mathematics major or an American history major must have, these state exams will continue to be absurdly easy for many to pass, reinforcing the notion that the profession is not intellectually demanding.

*Education Coursework and Student Teaching*

Concurrent with the academic major coursework, a teacher candidate would also typically devote roughly twenty-four to thirty credit hours in the last two years of college to professional education coursework and complete a practicum or student-teaching experience. The outcome would be a dual major in some education field of study (e.g., special education, preschool, primary, intermediate, secondary, ESOL) and a subject area. The state would not specify the coursework or credit hours necessary; the state's expectation is that the candidate will take the coursework necessary to pass a professional teaching knowledge exam in a person's field of study. It is the duty of the program to arrive at an optimum combination of coursework and student teaching to ensure success on the state exam.

Could someone choose not to take some or all of the education coursework and still take the professional teacher exam? From the state's perspective, absolutely. From the institution's perspective, the candidate would not be eligible for a dual degree. From the candidate's perspective, bypassing education coursework would be an option, but it might not be advisable. For one thing, the candidate may not gain the knowledge needed to pass the state exam.

For another, by not entering a formal teacher-preparation program, the candidate would not be eligible for a student-teaching experience. A school district may not want to hire someone who has not had a student-teaching experience or a particular reading course.

Some proponents of teacher-education programs argue that no aspiring teacher should be able to opt out of education coursework. However, there simply is no evidence to suggest that a person cannot become a highly effective teacher without first completing a formal teacher preparation program. It may be *advisable* to complete a program in that the preparation may make someone a good teacher who would otherwise be only adequate, but we do not know this to be uniformly or even mostly true. Comparisons with the medical profession are incongruous. It is the rare person indeed who could practice medicine without going to medical school; the requisite knowledge cannot be acquired by any other practical means. In contrast, there are large numbers of effective teachers who never took an education course, many of whom are employed in the nation's most sought-after private schools, as well as charter schools. There are few examples of individuals passing the medical boards without first going to medical school, yet Teach For America candidates routinely pass teacher-licensure exams with no education coursework.[60]

An aspiring teacher may decide that other pursuits will make him or her a more desirable candidate, such as taking more courses in a subject specialty area, spending a year abroad seeing the world, or gaining teaching skills outside a formal program. In the end, most aspiring teachers are likely to choose the route of formal teacher preparation, but the candidate-centered model would not restrict other considerations provided the standards are met.

*Getting a Job*

To a large extent, earning a license and getting a teaching job require that the candidate demonstrate almost wholly separate competencies. Earning a license requires a candidate to acquire a body of knowledge that the state can objectively assess. Getting a job requires the candidate to demonstrate the teaching skills and disposition that can be properly judged only by a person or team of people. Such observations are never foolproof, but they are much more likely to be accurate than a determination by a state certification specialist limited to a transcript review. Schools in an era of accountability are more likely to make better judgments about a candidate's subjective qualities than any other alternative that states might consider.

Unlike the state, schools have the capacity and the opportunity to observe teacher candidates, and thus to make reasonably sound judgments about their skills and disposition. Schools can interview candidates extensively, ask them to submit a sample lesson plan, or demonstrate how one would be taught. Qualities such as organizational skills, attitude toward children, and good classroom management all can be assessed by a school team headed by the principal during a rigorous interview process, reference check, and thorough screening. The fact that schools do not routinely engage in such practices poses a significant hurdle to teacher quality, but this problem is not solved by stricter regulatory policies. The notion of licensure as a proxy for quality has contributed to schools engaging in unacceptable hiring practices that in any other industry would be considered self-defeating.

Some might contend that the faculty of a teacher-preparation program has already made a judgment about a teacher's qualifications on behalf of the state and a future employer's interests. In effect, program faculty vouch for a candidate having obtained the requisite knowledge and skills. They argue that a teacher candidate's successful completion of a formal teacher-preparation program to earn a license is a sufficient indicator of quality. There is little to no evidence that this is the case; even the staunchest defenders of licensure will acknowledge that the system produces an indefensible range in quality.

Both states and school districts should make every effort to measure what they *can* measure. Most states and few school districts use the available technology to build powerful teacher databases that would link important information on teacher effectiveness. The information that can be obtained from databases linking teacher data with school and student data could help states achieve some of the same goals as a strong regulatory policy with fewer undesirable consequences.

Under any model, many schools need to significantly improve their hiring protocols. Some school principals' sloppy hiring practices (but not all) are attributable to their school districts. For instance, schools need a more reasonable window of time in which to hire teachers, so they are not hiring one out of three teachers after the start of school, as one study found to be the case in California and Florida. On the other hand, principals are known to turn down a district's invitation to interview prospective teachers.[61]

Principals, for their part, need to know good protocol for hiring professional employees and train their senior staff to participate responsibly in this process. Good hiring protocols generally require reviewing the candidate's background and credentials, conducting an extensive interview, involving multiple parties in the interview process, getting a writing sample, reviewing a portfolio, thoroughly checking references, and observing the candidate teach a model lesson.

## Developing the Standards

There are a growing number of efforts to articulate the essential knowledge, skills and disposition needed by a new teacher. Many states, INTASC, NCATE, and, most recently, the American Board have all engaged in efforts to shift teacher preparation to a standards-driven model. Some of these efforts provide a good model for candidate-centered standards; others provide less useful guidance insofar as they are geared to the teacher-preparation program, not the teacher candidate.

### State Standards

Most of the standards being developed by states will not inform better teacher preparation. Their primary audience is the practicing teacher, not the aspiring teacher. Such standards enable a state to claim that its teacher standards are aligned with their K–12 standards, but they do not serve much further practical purpose. Some states make no reference (or at best a vague reference) to the knowledge that teachers need in their subject area. For instance, Indiana's teaching standard for social studies states that a teacher should "[k]now how individuals, groups, and institutions are formed, controlled, and maintained in a society." Arizona teacher standards say that the teacher needs to know "major facts and assumptions that are central to the discipline" but provide no further detail. Idaho lists only five tenets for teacher knowledge of subject matter in mathematics, one of which reads, "The teacher understands the concepts of algebra."

Other states are doing a better job of articulating what teachers need to know, giving teacher candidates a clear idea of what is expected from them. Illinois does a commendable job of specifying the grade-specific knowledge needed by teachers. For example, the state has delineated specific areas of knowledge in mathematics, such as, "The competent teacher of mathematics knows customary, metric, and nonstandard measurement," which is then followed by a standard specifying the knowledge specific to the grade level, for example, "The early childhood or elementary school teacher knows how to measure length, area, volume, capacity, time, temperature, angles, weight and mass." Adoption of these more specific standards make it necessary for a state to design its own state teacher tests, an effort which costs many millions of dollars. Eleven states appear to believe that the investment is worth the expenditure.[62]

### INTASC Model Standards

Since 1994, INTASC, an arm of the Council of Chief State School Officers (CCSSO), has been developing model standards intended to delineate the specific knowledge, skills, and disposition that teacher candidates need to acquire before they begin teaching. INTASC claims to provide standards that are subject specific, but upon examination they appear too vague to provide the teacher candidate much useful guidance. For instance, the INTASC model standards for all the content knowledge that science teachers need to acquire are presented on one page, under a general statement that has more to do with appropriate pedagogy than the science knowledge a teacher needs: "The teacher of science understands the central ideas, tools of inquiry, applications, structure of science and of the science disciplines he or she teachers and can create learning activities that make these aspects of content meaningful to students."[63] The document then refers readers to a set of standards developed by the National Research Council, the National Science Education Standards, for more detail. However, this 272-page document is mainly devoted to student standards, though there is a chapter entitled "Science Teaching Standards." But again, standards like "[i]nquiry into authentic questions generated from student experiences is the central strategy for teaching science" do not delineate the content knowledge needed by a science teacher.[64]

### American Board Standards

In subject-matter and professional teaching knowledge, the new American Board certification exams offer a set of exacting standards in both subject-matter and professional teaching knowledge that, like INTASC's, are specifically targeted to new teachers. Because American Board candidates need not enroll in a formal teacher-preparation program, these standards look quite different from INTASC and NCATE standards geared to the preparation program, not the candidate. American Board standards do not pretend to identify teaching skills and disposition, but are designed to measure a teacher candidate's knowledge. The American Board offers a candidate-centered model that recognizes the inherent limitations of state licensure.

## Who Should Set the Standards?

Two groups are essential to the process of developing standards and test design: the state board of education and the higher education agency (known in some states as the board of regents). There are reasonable arguments for giving either body primary authority over the development of the teacher standards. The state board of education is the more likely entity to represent the interests of K–12 education and has the deeper understanding of its own K–12 standards and teacher-quality goals. The higher education agency will need to implement the standards, ensuring that the necessary courses are offered and that the exams reflect college level work. Under any scenario, both groups must be heavily involved in developing and implementing standards and ensuring that enough teachers are produced to satisfy the needs of the state.

A particular risk in relegating this task to the K–12 state department of education is the pressure to lower standards in response to such likely criticisms as, "A third grade teacher really doesn't need to know this." In the end, the state might find that it had merely reproduced a replica of the K–12 content standards. The authors of these standards must ask themselves continually, "Does this standard require the kind of knowledge, thought, and analysis expected of a college student?" The fact that the knowledge may not be taught in a K–12 classroom is not pertinent to the exercise. K–12 standards can only serve as a foundation for this effort. College-level coursework gives the teacher the necessary perspective and wisdom needed to communicate the fundamental principals of K–12 content. If we do not believe that, then why do we require teachers to attend college at all?

## IMPACT

Apart from colleges, universities, teacher-training programs, school districts, and the candidate, there are actors and organizations that will be affected by implementation of the candidate-centered model.

## Technology Needs

The ability to collect and analyze huge amounts of school data can have a powerful impact on teacher quality. A strong teacher database could help states to achieve some of the goals intended by regulatory policy, without some of the adverse consequences. Information gleaned from increased technological capacity can support much better planning and decision-making.

Unfortunately, the technology capabilities of most states lag far behind their needs. Florida is a notable exception; it has developed the capacity that allows a broad array of data collected by multiple offices of the state department of education to be analyzed from any angle. An effective educator database must be able to compare student achievement and other important school data with such data as teacher performance on the diagnostic tool, the midway assessments, specialty and professional teaching knowledge exams, the status of a teachers' licenses, academic majors, minors, routes to certification, tenure status, turnover and attrition data, evaluation data, postgraduate degrees, years of experience, and school assignments.

At the district level, good hiring protocols are girded by an effective hiring and recruitment tracking system. The New Teacher Project, which recruits teachers for urban school systems across the country, recommends that a system provide the following: contact information; qualifications and certification status of each applicant and hire; wait times between key steps in the hiring process; total number of applicants, offers, and hires; number of and information about withdrawers and declined offers; and results from applicant surveys.[65]

## Nontraditional Candidates

The candidate-centered model would accommodate the many kinds of people who consider teaching: the foreign-born mathematics teacher who may not be proficient in English but who knows mathematics, or the lawyer who decides at age forty to take up teaching, having had no education training.

Currently, teaching candidates coming through an alternate certification program must pass the state teacher tests. The candidate-centered model would not alter the requirement that alternative certification candidates pass the same tests as traditional candidates. Candidates coming in through an alternative route would need to pass three exams: a test of verbal ability (the midway assessment in the traditional route), a subject-area specialty exam in the subject matter that he or she intends to teach, and a professional teaching knowledge exam.

Alternative certification programs as well as the traditional teacher-preparation programs need to anticipate some of the inevitable exemptions and waivers needed to accommodate candidates of high caliber by building some flexibility into the new regulations. For example, evidence of a good score on an SAT or ACT verbal test could substitute for a test of verbal ability, and the regulations ought to say so explicitly. Numerous accommodations are in order for teachers educated in another country. Candidates for whom English is a second language should be exempt from a test of verbal ability if they are teaching a subject in which exceptional knowledge of English is not needed, such as mathematics.

Many states currently impose a variety of requirements on candidates seeking admission into an alternate-route program: a minimum college GPA, a major in the subject matter, an internship in the first year of teaching, and additional education coursework requirements. As practical as some of these requirements may be, none are best enforced by inflexible regulatory policy. A GPA is a highly subjective measure; the state does not and cannot distinguish a high GPA earned from a highly competitive college from one earned at an open-admissions college. Passing scores on the new exams would serve much the same purpose by identifying academically able candidates.

When states do not accept an alternative to a college major, the requirement of a major can erect an unnecessary barrier. For example, under current policy, a sociology major who speaks fluent French but did not earn a major or minor in the language would not be allowed to teach French. Subject-matter tests that reflect college-level mastery of a subject can serve as adequate measures of a person's knowledge. The teacher-quality provisions of NCLB contain a similar allowance.

A mentorship in the first year of teaching is generally perceived as something all new teachers need and few teachers would refuse. The only reason districts might not offer a mentorship is lack of money. States should fund, not regulate, mentorships.

The state's exodus from coursework and credit-hour requirements does not preclude a district or a school from choosing to require new teachers to participate in an induction program or ongoing professional development.

## Postbaccalaureate Programs

The candidate-centered model could reduce the number of persons who need to enroll in a postbaccalaureate teacher-preparation program. If a state is no longer requiring specific education coursework and credit hours, some candidates might look elsewhere to gain the knowledge and experience needed to pass the professional teaching knowledge exam and enter the profession.

On the other hand, given that teachers with master's degrees earn more money and are perceived to add value in any profession, individuals interested in teaching may seek out such programs anyway. Many professions such as business do not require by regulation that an individual obtain an MBA, but many individuals pursue the degree for the value that it adds in terms of both pay and professional prestige.

Another reason that a candidate might elect a master's program is to gain student teaching experience. There may be schools that are less likely to hire teachers who lack such experience, not because they are required to do so but because they believe that the experience is invaluable.

## Private Accrediting Bodies

If private schools offer a reasonable model for education under a deregulated system, accreditation of teacher-preparation programs by private organizations such as NCATE and the newer accrediting body, TEAC, should figure more prominently in a deregulated teacher-preparation system. Private schools and teacher-preparation programs both depend on tuition and, to a large extent, on "happy customers." For years, private schools have successfully used accreditation as to signify quality. A private school that lacks accreditation has a difficult time operating and attracting students. The state's exit from its largely meaningless program-approval process provides an opportunity for private accreditation to assume an even more important role. Unprotected by the state, teacher-preparation programs would need to seek meaningful accreditation to flourish in the marketplace.

It is important to note that NCATE in particular has benefited from state protection that it worked hard to achieve for an accreditation process that is not based on the success of a program's graduates in schools. With states no longer protecting NCATE's dominant role under the new model, this organization will either have to raise its standards to certify for true quality or should expect to become known as the accreditation body for second-tier programs.

## CONCLUSION

The current regulatory structure in the United States fails to provide a meaningful standard of quality to be met by aspiring teachers. What quality there is can be attributed to the institutional selectivity and rigor of many of the nation's colleges and universities, followed by the selective hiring practices of many school districts. A significant number of teachers enter the profession having demonstrated minimal academic competence in an environment of open admissions policies, undemanding coursework, and facile licensure exams. They are nevertheless granted a state license to teach and do not appear to have much difficulty finding teaching positions. Under pressure from their states, districts most in need of talented teachers mistakenly view licensure as an adequate measure of quality.

The candidate-centered model proposed in this paper addresses the urgent need to raise the academic bar for all teacher candidates, while putting in place a structure to improve the academic outcomes of undereducated individuals who aspire to be teachers, particularly minority candidates. It would discard wholesale most current regulatory policies, including state coursework requirements and approval of teacher-preparation programs. The current structure is premised on the ugly supposition that we are doing the right and fair thing by allowing easy access to the profession and demanding so little. We squander the opportunity to use college preparation to advance the quality of all teachers, particularly those who are themselves victims of an inadequate K–12 education. Instead, the right and fair thing to do is to address the root causes of low performance.

States, institutions of higher education, and aspiring teachers would share the responsibility of implementing a strategy, programs of study, and a system of assessments targeted at improving teachers' verbal ability. The importance of a teacher's verbal ability has been undersold, while the importance of undergraduate education coursework has been oversold. States routinely reject teacher applicants with high verbal ability for lack of prescribed coursework, a policy echoed by school districts that do not consider a teacher's verbal ability as even a factor in his or her potential as a good teacher.

Verbal ability may appear to be a nebulous term, but it is not. Our ability to nurture this particular attribute in an individual is well within our reach. Verbal ability is a measure of what a person knows. To improve verbal ability is to broaden one's knowledge of the world. Before teacher preparation became such a political fireball, the notion that teacher preparation should produce a well-rounded, educated individual would have generated no more reaction than some shrugged shoulders. But it is to this principle that we must return: that the first and most important purpose of a teacher's college education is a strong foundational study in the liberal arts.

## CHAPTER 10

# Improving Academic Performance in U.S. Public Schools

## Why Teacher Licensing Is (Almost) Irrelevant

*Michael Podgursky*

## INTRODUCTION: SIX PROPOSITIONS ABOUT TEACHER LABOR MARKETS

The "flexible" regime would call for state education agencies to relax their requirement that teaching candidates graduate from approved teacher-training programs. It is flexible concerning testing, in that it would set relatively low testing requirements for teachers as well. Teachers might need to pass tests of general knowledge and content in areas in which they specialize, but the bar would not be particularly high. Tests would screen out the academically incompetent, and criminal background checks would screen out potentially dangerous teachers. However, the primary focus of state regulation would be on monitoring student learning and educating the public about state education standards and school performance, and not regulating teacher training and licensing. Rather than rely solely, or even primarily, on teacher licensing, state monitoring of student learning and school choice would play a larger role in protecting parents against incompetent teachers. Private associations of teachers and teacher educators would be free to promote whatever models of teacher "professionalization" or accreditation they choose, and districts would be free to hire these candidates as

I would like to thank Youn Soel and Erin Allen for research assistance, and Michael Wolkoff and conference participants for thoughtful comments.

they choose; however, state regulators would not use teacher licensing to impose any particular model of professional training.

The flexible option exists alongside other reform models that are discussed in the companion papers in this book. The alternative models set forth—the "professional," "portfolio," and "candidate-centered" models—all restrict the supply of teachers and teacher-preparation programs in ways that are not likely to produce any significant increase in overall teacher quality.

To lay the groundwork for a discussion of the flexible regime, I begin with some observations concerning research on teachers and on the economics of licensing.

*1. Research Linking Teacher Training or Licensing To Student Achievement is Inconclusive and Provides Little Support for Aggressive Regulation of the Labor Market*

If policymakers choose to raise the bar on teacher licensing, they should have solid evidence that the criteria used to exclude teacher candidates from the market has a demonstrable relationship to student achievement. Otherwise, such policies will simply shrink the size of teacher applicant pools without raising the average quality. How strong is the research base for formulating policy concerning teacher training and licensing? Recent surveys of the scientific research base (including Dan Goldhaber's in this volume) find it is very thin.

Such a claim seems to fly in the face of claims by various education groups about the "knowledge base" for teaching, and certainly seems contradicted by the hundreds of studies published annually in education research journals, many of which are devoted to teacher education.[1] However, there is widespread consensus in the social-science research community that scientific evaluation of social-policy programs (including education) requires either randomized experimental study design or non-experimental longitudinal data on participants.[2] Unfortunately, the little research on teacher testing or licensing that meets either standard is tentative and inconclusive.

Randomized experimental design is the "gold standard" for social-policy research. With respect to teacher quality, this would involve estimating the effect of teachers with different credentials or training on student achievement through random assignment of students to classrooms of variously credentialed but otherwise comparable (in, e.g., experience) teachers within a school. Unfortunately, no existing research on teacher credentials or training meets this standard, although the Institute for Education Sciences of the

U.S. Department of Education is promoting such studies (Moesteller & Boruch, 2002; U.S. Department of Education, n.d.), and some are under way. Thanks to these efforts, it is likely that we will have experimental evidence on teacher licensing and training five years from now.

If randomization is not feasible, and often it is not, then one must rely on non-experimental data to evaluate education policy. If we are to measure the contribution of a classroom teacher to student achievement, it is necessary to control for prior achievement of the student before he or she enters the classroom. Ideally, researchers would pretest the students in the fall and test them again in the spring. The difference in these scores, averaged over the classroom, would be a measure of a teacher's "value added." If students are not pretested in the fall, then it is also possible to use test scores the previous spring, or for more than one previous year (longitudinal achievement data). Large longitudinal data files have formed the basis for the most sophisticated current research on teachers and teacher effects on student achievement (e.g., Aronson, Barnow, & Sanders, 2003; Goldhaber & Brewer, 1997; Rivkin, Hanushek, & Kain, 2000; Sanders & Horn, 1994).

Studies that are not rigorously designed (i.e., do not randomize or control for prior student achievement) are likely to produce seriously biased estimates of the effect of teacher certification or other teacher characteristics on student achievement. The reason is that they do not adequately control for the socioeconomic background of students, which is correlated with teacher credentials and strongly correlated with student achievement. In the language of econometrics, cross-section studies of the effect of teacher credentials on student achievement suffer from "omitted variable bias."[3]

Given the complexities of teacher licensing systems, virtually every school district in the United States has some teachers out of compliance; however, substandard certification tends to be relatively more common in schools with low socioeconomic status (SES) students. Because SES has a powerful effect on student achievement levels and gains, unless the researcher has very good controls for prior achievement and SES in a study of certification and student achievement, the resulting study is likely to yield an upward-biased estimate of the effect of certification.[4]

The number of studies of teacher certification that meet the minimum methodological standards outlined above is very small. A recent survey of the literature by Wayne and Youngs in the Spring 2003 *Review of Education Research* found only two studies of teacher certification that were peer reviewed, used longitudinal student-level achievement data, and controlled for student socioeconomic status. The results of these studies (both by Goldhaber and Brewer, both using the National Longitudinal Educational

Survey of 1988) were mixed. They did find a small positive effect of math teacher certification on math achievement, but no statistically significant effect of science teacher certification on science achievement. Recent surveys of the literature by Hanushek and Rivkin (2003) focusing on "high-quality" studies that meet the standards described above find little evidence linking teacher credentials to student achievement. For example, of nine estimates of the effect of teacher test scores on student achievement, six found no statistically significant effect. Of the three finding a significant effect, two were positive and one was negative.[5]

In short, the research foundation for "raising the bar" with teacher tests or raising standards for schools of education is very weak. The evidence linking any type of teacher training, licensing, or testing to student achievement is mixed at best. Even estimated effects of general academic skills of teachers such as SAT scores, while usually statistically significant, are generally modest in effect.

*2. Teacher Effects on Student Achievement Are Quantitatively Important but Idiosyncratic*

Does this mean teachers do not matter? On the contrary, while the effect of measured teacher characteristics is small, one consistent finding is that there seems to be considerable variation in teacher effectiveness between classrooms. Thus, if comparing the effect on student learning of the top and bottom 20 percent of teachers ranked by classroom value added, the effect is often quite substantial. However, these teacher effects are largely unrelated to traditional measures of teacher quality such as licensing, exam test scores, certification credentials, experience, or graduate degrees, a result highlighted in a survey by Goldhaber (2002). Hanushek and Rivkin (2003), summarizing their own and others' research, come to the same conclusion.[6]

The growing value-added literature suggests that teacher quality, as measured by student achievement gains, is highly idiosyncratic. This does not mean that teacher quality is random or unknowable, but that traditional measures of teacher quality—experience, master's degrees, education coursework—explain virtually none of the variations in teacher effectiveness.[7]

*3. In the Absence of Strong Ex Ante Indicators of Teaching Quality, Raising the Bar in Teacher Licensing Is Likely to Lower Teacher Quality*

Even if the evidence for teacher licensing, testing, or a particular program of pedagogical training is weak, a skeptic might say, Why not raise the entry bar anyway, on the chance that it might work? Many public policies are enacted based on faith and good intentions rather than rigorous scientific research. Why is teacher licensing any different? What harm can come from raising the bar for teachers?

If these reforms were cost free, then one might make the case for their implementation on the chance that some benefits would accrue. However, they are not cost free, and there is a real possibility that schools will find themselves worse off, and student achievement will fall, if such programs are implemented.

First, there are the direct resource costs. To the extent that we raise requirements for education coursework, we incur direct educational costs as candidates take classes, pursue professional development, forgo other employment, etc. Annual costs per student in higher education currently are roughly $27,000 per year, although students on average only pay part of this cost. Tests are less costly, but the fixed costs of updating and validating new teacher tests is considerable. More important are the time costs for teaching candidates spent in pedagogy courses or preparing for and taking exams. If we assume that teaching candidates take a year and a half of teaching courses (including student teaching), this is a costly investment. Even at the minimum wage, this amounts to more than $15,000. One perverse result of conditioning labor market entry on "seat time" in pedagogy courses is that candidates with greater academic skills, who presumably can attract a higher alternative wage, face higher costs in securing a teaching license (Ballou & Podgursky, 1997). These direct costs are resources that might have been put to better use in improving schools or the lives of poor students.

Only about 60 percent of all teacher candidates graduate from teacher-training programs recognized by the National Council for the Accreditation of Teacher Education (NCATE). Closing all teacher-training programs that do not secure NCATE accreditation, as proposed by the National Education Association and the National Commission on Teaching and America's Future (NCTAF), would almost surely restrict the flow of newly trained teaching candidates. So, too, would raising the cutoff score on teacher-licensing exams. If the cutoff is raised from the 20th to the 30th percentile on the elementary education exam, then 10 percent of potential applicants are excluded from the applicant pool.

A common feature of all these policies is that they would reduce the pool of applicants to public schools. Other things being equal, this will tend to lower the average quality of teachers who are hired. Why is this the case? School administrators know many things about teacher candidates that state regulators do not. They conduct job interviews, evaluate student teaching, read letters of recommendation and transcripts, and observe demonstration classes. In fact, school administrators are in a much better position to assess teacher quality than are state regulators, and there is some evidence that their assessments can identify teachers who produce larger student achievement gains.[8] Preventing school administrators from considering any unlicensed applicants, school districts forces them to hire the worst certified candidate even if a superior uncertified candidate is available. "Raising the bar" shrinks the size of the applicant pool. The new pool is better in terms of whatever the regulators specify (e.g., more NCATE graduates, higher Praxis II scores), but school administrators have less ability to select among candidates based on factors that they observe but state regulators do not.

This cost of mandatory certification is illustrated in Figure 1. Here I have presented hypothetical data on the distribution of teacher quality among certified and uncertified applicants. Though these data are hypothetical, I believe they represent the picture emerging in the "teacher effects" literature, namely, that the individual variation in the classroom performance of a teacher is large relative to any measurable teacher characteristic, such as certification. As I indicated above, the evidence concerning teacher certification is mixed at best. However, for the sake of argument, I have assumed a positive effect: the average certified teacher is better than 60 percent of uncertified teachers. Based on the review of the research literature discussed above, I see this as an upper-end estimate for certification effects. However, the conclusions that follow do not hinge on this assumption. If, for example, we assumed that the average certified teachers is better than 80 percent of uncertified teachers, our basic conclusions would not change. The key point is that the research suggests that there is a large dispersion of quality within the certified and uncertified pools.

Suppose Figure 1 represents the population from which a school district recruits teachers, that the school district has a single vacancy, and that it is free to hire the best candidate, certified or not. Imagine that a single candidate applies at random from each pool (certified and uncertified). What is the probability that the certified candidate is the superior teacher? It turns out that 57 percent of the time the certified candidate is better. With two job applicants, the average quality of the best teacher (certified or not) is at the 67th percentile of the certified distribution. Now suppose the school has five random applicants from the certified population, but no uncertified applicants. The quality of the best applicant jumps sharply, from the 67th to the 88th percentile. This illustrates an important point: if teachers are screened well (a point taken up below), a larger applicant pool means better quality hires. Because you are hiring the best applicant from a pool, not the

**FIGURE 1    Overlapping Ability When The Average Certified Applicant Is Better Than 60 Percent of Non-Certified Applicants**

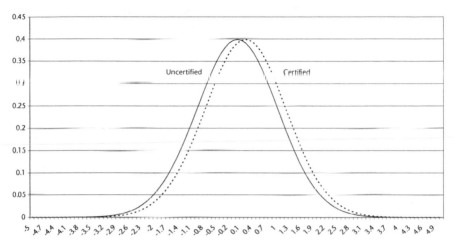

Teacher Quality (Standard Deviations)

average applicant, it is better to have more applicants. This commonsense point is borne out in many other contexts. Other things being equal, the average quality of graduate students will be higher in a program with 200 applicants than one with twenty, even if the average quality of applicants is the same in the two cases. The expected return from twenty lottery tickets is higher than from one.

The example above assumes that we only sample from the certified, "high-quality" applicant pool. Can a district similarly benefit from access to a pool of lower average quality uncertified applicants? The answer is yes. Suppose that five uncertified applicants randomly drawn from the distribution in Figure 1 are allowed to apply for the job, along with five certified applicants. Even though the uncertified applicants are of lower average quality than the certified candidates, 39 percent of the time the uncertified applicant will be the best of the ten applicants. By expanding the applicant pool from five to ten candidates, the mean quality of the best teacher has increased as well. This illustrates the hidden cost of a licensing entry barrier: shrinking the applicant pool gives schools fewer choices and less freedom to pick out talent, and reduces the mean quality of the resulting hires.

Intuitively, if there is a large dispersion in quality within the two groups, sometimes the best candidate will be from the uncertified group. The distributions overlap a great deal. This will also be true even if we make the average certified teacher better than 70 percent or 80 percent of uncertified teachers. Licensing entry barriers, if strictly enforced, tell a school district that they can never hire an uncertified candidate. This makes districts worse off.[9]

### 4. Teaching Is Not Medicine

Whether or not a research base currently exists to support aggressive licensing of teacher labor markets, proponents often argue that teacher "professionalization" is a desirable end in itself. They appeal to a vision of professional self-regulation in education akin to that in medicine. In panel discussions on teacher licensing I am routinely confronted with the question, "Would you send your children to an unlicensed doctor?" I believe the argument implied by the question is this: While it may be true that no rigorous evidence exists for the reforms we have proposed (e.g., tougher teacher testing, accreditation, and more vigorous review of teacher training institutions), they are broadly similar to what is found in medicine. Therefore, if we implement such reforms, teacher quality and the quality of education will improve in the manner seen in medicine.

Argument by analogy is valid only if the analogy is valid. Why teaching is not medicine deserves an entire paper of its own; however, I will briefly explain two important reasons the analogy is inappropriate.

There is a deep body of scientific research in medicine. Commitment to scientific research methods pervades medical schools, professional specialty associations, and the community of medical practitioners generally. The economic case for medical licensing rests on an information *asymmetry* between what these highly trained medical practitioners know and what consumers know about the quality of medical services they are buying. Because of the complexity of the knowledge base in medicine and the high cost of mistakes, it is relatively easy to argue that government licensing is required to screen out incompetent practitioners and protect consumers.[10]

Does this model apply to education? If we replicate the professional self-regulation found in medicine, can we expect qualitatively similar outcomes in education? To be sure, there is scientifically based research on student learning. However, for the most part this research is being produced not in schools of education, but by educational and cognitive psychologists in psychology departments.

Even at leading research universities, most education school faculty do not produce research based on rigorous scientific methodology (certainly nothing akin to what one finds in a medical school). Many education faculty approach research with methods more like those used in the humanities than those in medicine or the sciences. Controlled experiments and randomized studies are rare. Use of large-scale longitudinal data on students is not widespread. However, what education school faculty at leading research universities do or don't do is largely irrelevant since they train relatively few of the nation's classroom teachers. The primary suppliers of classroom teachers (as opposed to doctors) are state colleges, most of which were once teachers' colleges, where much of the teaching is conducted by adjunct faculty not actively engaged in scientific research. To the extent that regular faculty at such institutions do research, it cannot be described as scientifically rigorous and is far removed from the frontiers of scientific research on human learning. The same can be said of other areas of education policy research.

However, even if upper- and lower-tier schools of education were producing scientifically based research, the teachers and their professional associations are in no position to vet this research and incorporate it into their teaching or standards. Professional teacher associations such as the National Council of Teachers of English or the National Council of Social Studies do not base their standards on scientific research. Indeed, most members of these learned societies (practicing teachers) are not trained to evaluate scientific research. I would venture that most practitioners and education school professors in these fields would not even view the scientific method as the most useful method of inquiry in their field. (I do not believe that the medical model is appropriate for departments of history or English, for similar reasons.)

The deep technical and scientific knowledge base in medicine produces well-defined and widely shared agreement on appropriate clinical practice. For the most part this is absent in education. While the judgment of English, mathematics, and elementary school teachers as to the best ways of teaching a subject certainly deserves respect and deference, there is little evidence to suggest that parents cannot make informed choices among practitioners who approach their craft differently.[11] This leads us to the next proposition.

### 5. Unregulated Markets in Education and Training Work Well

The case for the medical analogy would be strengthened if there were pervasive evidence of "market failure" in unregulated markets for education and training. While I am not aware of widespread unlicensed practice of surgery, unlicensed training and schooling is pervasive in our economy. Indeed it is the norm rather than the exception. These markets seem to work quite well with little or no government regulation. A review of the functioning of these labor markets suggests that they operate considerably better than the highly regulated markets in public K–12 education.

Researchers have estimated that American business spends between $18 billion and $43 billion (in 1995 dollars) annually on formal training programs for their workers and an unknown but substantial amount on informal training (Ehrenberg & Smith, 1996, p. 302). Virtually all of this training is delivered by instructors who are not licensed by the state and who have not received specialized pedagogical instruction. Historically, one of the most important sources of high-quality vocational training in our economy has been the U.S. military. The armed services have taken millions of high school dropouts and graduates and given them high-quality training in technical specialty fields, along with basic literacy and numeracy skills, turning millions of young men and women with limited elementary and secondary education into trained aircraft mechanics, radio operators, supply clerks, and the like. Nearly all of this was accomplished by unlicensed instructors.

Approximately six million students are enrolled in two-year community colleges. Much of the coursework offered in these community colleges is remedial, covering material that students should have learned in elementary and secondary schools. States do not require the faculty in community colleges to be licensed, and evidence suggests that most are not certified teachers. Nonetheless, if we judge success by enrollment growth or successful transition to four-year baccalaureate institutions, these community colleges are successfully delivering K–12 educational services.

Many students receive K–12 educational services from private tutoring firms, which range from large multinational educational firms like Sylvan Learning to small independent proprietary firms. Many of these firms specialize in providing remedial help for students in reading and mathematics. Others, like Kaplan, focus on test preparation. In any event, these firms are selling K–12 educational services to the public. There are no state licensing requirements for teachers in these firms (or for the firms themselves), and all indications are that this market is expanding.

Finally, there is a thriving private K–12 school system in the United States that long predates the public school system. Private schools routinely hire unlicensed teachers. Figure 2 provides some data on certification rates of private school teachers. The dependent variable is whether the teacher holds regular or provisional state certification in her primary teaching area. The rate for the public sector is 89.8 percent, whereas the rate for private schools is much lower, particularly in nonreligious schools, where just 48.8

FIGURE 2    Percent of Teachers Holding Regular State Certification in
Primary Teaching Area: Traditional Public, Private, and Charter Schools

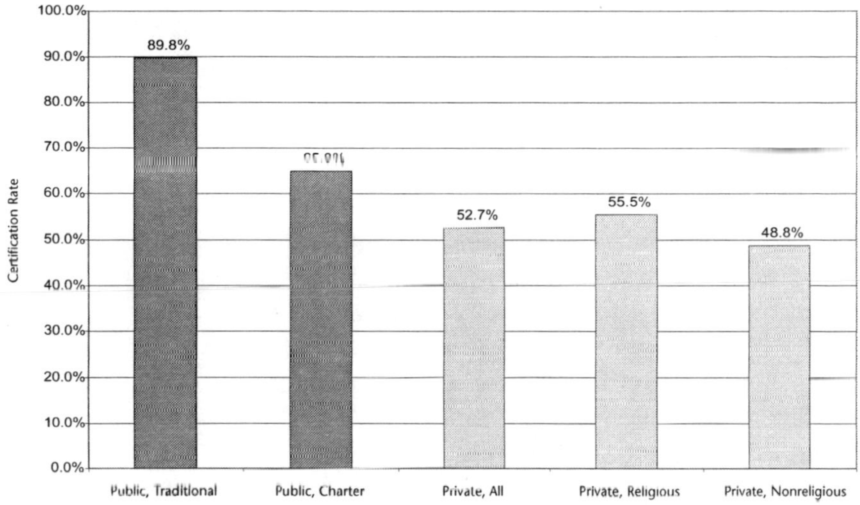

Sources: 1999-00 Schools and Staffing Surveys

percent of teachers are certified. The rates are lower still at the secondary
level. In nonreligious secondary schools the certification rate is just 35.1
percent. Thus, while private schools do hire certified teachers, they also hire
substantial numbers of uncertified teachers. It should also be noted that
charter schools, too, hire large numbers of uncertified teachers.

How does the academic quality of the uncertified teachers compare to
that of certified teachers? One measure of teacher quality is the selectivity of
the college from which the teacher graduated. Several production function
studies find that the selectivity of a teacher's undergraduate college is correlated with student academic achievement (Ehrenberg & Brewer, 1993, 1994;
Summers & Wolfe, 1977; Winkler, 1975). Dale Ballou and I have shown that
private schools use this flexibility to trade off teacher certification to get
higher academic quality for teachers. The share of teachers graduating from
selective institutions, math and science majors, and academic majors is almost consistently higher in the uncertified population (Ballou & Podgursky,
1997). In more recent work, we find a similar pattern in charter schools. In
other words, in terms of Figure 1, charter and private schools benefit from
their ability to hire from beyond the certified candidate pool when an
attractive uncertified applicant appears.

*6. State Teacher Licensing Systems Are So Complex That No One Is in Compliance*

Proponents of raising the bar for teaching licenses assume that such proposals are feasible. However, I find that state licensing systems are already so complex that virtually no school district is in compliance anyway. This raises a serious question of what we accomplish by raising bars.

Like all other states with which I am familiar, Missouri issues a single license to practice medicine, law, dentistry, accounting, nursing, and veterinary medicine. However, in K–12 education, the Missouri Department of Elementary and Secondary Education currently issues 260 certificates and endorsements (171 vocational, 89 nonvocational). However, that is only part of the story. There are levels of certification (permanent, provisional) for all of these and a host of "grandmothered" codes. As a consequence, there are 781 valid certification codes in the master teacher certification file. There is nothing unique about Missouri. Most other states have equally Byzantine systems for teacher licensing.

How is it that the public is protected by a single license in other professions, yet K–12 education requires more than 100? Is teaching a more complex endeavor? I believe part of the answer is that, in the other professions, licensing is used simply to screen out incompetent practitioners, not to control how labor is utilized in the sector. After a practitioner enters the profession, he is free to specialize in any field he chooses. Most doctors do proceed to earn certification in one of the twenty-four recognized medical specialties, but there is no state requirement that they do so. If a medical clinic wants to use a neurosurgeon to treat walk-in family practice patients, it can. Once licensed, lawyers are free to practice any type of law they choose. One does not read about a crisis of lawyers "practicing law out of field," nurses "nursing out of field," or dentists engaged in "dentistry out of field." If states issued a single license in teaching as in other professions, the "out of field" teaching that is the subject of so much hand-wringing would disappear.

In K–12 education, state regulators attempt to use the licensing system to control how teacher labor is allocated. The presumption is that local schools cannot be trusted to staff courses appropriately. Thus, the complicated licensing system is the state's clumsy attempt to monitor the performance of local administrators. In Missouri, school districts are routinely audited to determine whether the hundreds of different types of courses they offer match the certificate or endorsements for the teacher of record.

**FIGURE 3    Percent of Courses Taught by Teachers With Inappropriate or No Licenses by Expenditure Per Pupil in Average Daily Attendance: Missouri K-12 Public School Districts, 2001-2002**

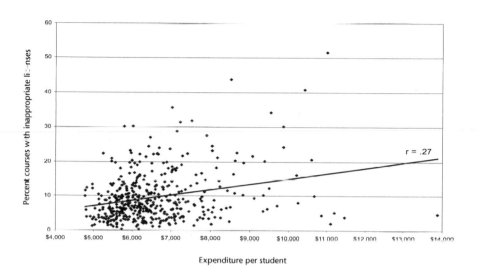

*Source:* Missouri Department of Elementary and Secondary Education

The excessively complex licensing system in K–12 education can also be seen as a tool for what economists call "rent capture" (using government regulation to produce private pecuniary gains) by teachers unions and schools of education. To make the case for higher pay and benefits for their members, any type of supply restriction is desirable from the point of view of teachers unions, so long as the added restrictions apply to new entrants and do not affect dues-paying incumbents. However, high standards for program entry, as in medicine, would invariably drive many schools of education out of business. Thus, teachers unions and schools of education benefit from the proliferation of certifiable areas, generating more demand for education school courses but also restricting supply to school districts.

As a consequence of the complex state licensing systems, virtually no school district in the United States is in full compliance. The complexity of the state licensing systems makes national tabulations of unlicensed, uncertified, or substandard certification difficult. I will illustrate this point with administrative data from two states. Figure 3 presents data for Missouri pub-

**FIGURE 4  Percent of Teachers Not Certified and Median Salaries in Westchester County, NY Public School Districts: 2000–2001**

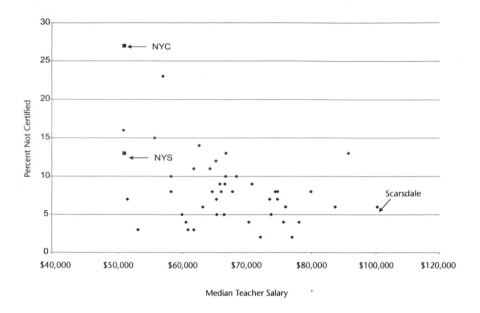

Source: New York Department of Education.

lic K–12 school districts (I have excluded K–8 districts). On the vertical axis we measure the percentage of courses in a district taught by teachers with inappropriate licenses during the 2001–2002 school year. On the horizontal axis we measure spending per student in average daily attendance. Of 447 K–12 school districts, all had at least one course taught by an inappropriately licensed teacher (the average was 9.5%). Moreover, the prevalence of inappropriate licensed practice seems to have little to do with school revenues. The correlation between the rate of unlicensed teaching and spending per student is positive and statistically significant (0.27).

My second example is decidedly nonrandom. Westchester County, New York, is home to some of the wealthiest households and highest paid school teachers in the United States. The schools in these exclusive communities are appropriately compared to the best private day schools. In Figure 4 I have plotted percentage of uncertified teachers and median teacher salaries for school year 2000–2001 from the most recent report of the New York State Department of Education. ("Uncertified" refers to the percentage of classroom teachers who either teach more than 20 percent of their time in a subject or subjects for which they hold no certification or who hold an emergency license.) In spite of very high salaries, no district in Westchester County has fewer than 2 percent of its teaching force uncertified. Note that in Scarsdale, which boasted a 2000–2001 median teacher salary of $90,191, 6 percent of teachers were uncertified. (As a regular reader of the *New York Times*, I have yet to read about Scarsdale parents complaining about the quality of their uncertified teachers.) If not one school district in what may be the highest-spending county in the United States is in compliance with the New York law, this raises serious questions about how we can seriously contemplate raising the bar and further restricting supply.

## THE MODEL

In light of the six propositions laid out above, the case for the "flexible" model is relatively straightforward. State education regulators should protect the public by focusing on what they can measure (student learning, or "education outputs"), and not on what they cannot (teacher quality, or "education inputs"). As noted above, research suggests that teacher quality as measured by student learning is idiosyncratic and not well measured by anything that state regulators are in a position to monitor. Local school administrators, on the other hand, are in a good position to monitor teacher classroom performance. Thus, the model that emerges has several features.[12]

The first, and by far most important, is getting incentives right. Local administrators must be held accountable for student learning, and state regulators need to focus their attention on monitoring student learning. Nearly all states have developed standards for what students should be learning at various grade levels and assessments of the learning that is actually occurring by grade in schools and districts. These data are now routinely provided to parents and to the public at large. Schools that demonstrate persistently poor student learning performance increasingly face administrative sanctions. Another important mechanism for producing accountability is school choice. Indeed, one of the most important protections for parents against incompetent teachers is to give them the option to choose another classroom or school if their assigned teacher fails.

If an accountability regime is in place, with information on performance widely available, state monitoring of school performance, and parental choice of schools, then the role of the state in monitoring "teacher quality" (something they can't measure anyway) should wither away. The guiding principal for the state in issuing teacher licenses should be simply, "Do no harm." Certainly teachers should undergo a careful criminal background check. Bureaucratic impediments to removing teachers who have been convicted or indicted for serious criminal offenses should be removed. It is also reasonable to require that teachers hold a bachelor's degree.

Tests of general academic knowledge and subject-matter knowledge are reasonable. However, as noted above, it is likely to be counterproductive for states to set high cut scores for these exams. A more attractive approach (which is likely to survive legal challenge) is to set relatively low cut scores *and* provide information on the candidate's scores to the school districts. From an economic point of view, the current system makes little sense. Teacher candidates spend hundreds of dollars taking licensing exams. The testing companies then take these test scores and collapse them into a "pass" or "fail" grade, the only test result that school districts ever see. Large testing companies such as the Educational Testing Service will not provide these exam scores to school districts. Indeed, they make the tenuous argument that the scores have "validity" for licensing but not for hiring. Imagine if colleges or professional schools received similar information. Continuous SAT or GRE scores would be collapsed into binary pass/fail measures indicating that a student was "good enough for graduate study" or "not good enough for graduate study." The test scores would have "validity" only for determining who can enter the market for graduate study, but not for the admissions decisions of any graduate program.

Of course, providing flexibility for schools to audition many candidates means that schools must have the ability to act on that information. In fact, in most states, school districts have considerable leeway not to rehire teachers during an initial probationary period of two to five years. After that, once teachers are tenured or enjoy the right of automatic contract renewal, it becomes very costly to dismiss teachers for anything but the most negligent job performance. Sensible reforms would make it easier not to renew the contracts of ineffective senior teachers.

Even if a "magic bullet" for teacher training or testing were found, it would be decades before new, more effective teachers would have diffused through the entire teaching work force. Teacher turnover averages roughly 6 percent to 8 percent annually, and about half of new teacher hires are returning teachers or interdistrict transfers (U.S. Department of Education, 2000). Thus, only a very small share of teachers is affected by licensing reform in any year. However, schools have information on the job performance of the 90 percent of job candidates who do not turn over. They need the flexibility and incentives to use this performance information in personnel matters, including pay and contract renewal.

To summarize, the most efficient flexible regime would have 1) accountability for student learning through testing, sanctions, and parental choice; 2) state regulators who actively promote a competitive market in teacher quality and protect schools from anticompetitive practices on the part of teachers unions, schools of education, or other education producer organizations, 3) minimal state licensing standards for teachers (criminal background check, bachelor's degree, test of general and content knowledge); 4) full information on teacher test results provided to school administrators; and 5) award of a permanent or full license on the basis of successful job performance.

## Statutory Changes

State boards or professional certification boards generally have considerable discretion as to the requirements for teaching licenses. There is ample precedent for a flexible policy. Many states now have created alternative routes to teacher certification that provide a good model for what I have proposed. The Alternative Certification Program in Texas and the Intern program in California are examples. In such programs, prospective teachers must hold a BA, pass exams, and demonstrate content knowledge to receive a probationary license. After a probationary period of two to three years (which in these states includes on- or off-site professional development), mentored practice, and satisfactory evaluations by supervisors, the teachers receive a standard license. Such alternate-route teachers satisfy the "highly qualified teacher" requirement of the No Child Left Behind Act.

I have given examples from only two states. However, Feistrizer, and Chester (2002) note that forty-five states now have such routes, although these programs play a major role only in a handful of states. Nonetheless, the precedent is there for greater flexibility.

In addition to creating more alternate-route programs, states should simplify their licensing systems. As noted above, in professions such as medicine, law, dentistry, accounting, or nursing, the state issues but a single license, whereas in K–12 education, states routinely issue 100 or more. This makes little sense. State regulators should commit themselves to radical simplification of these systems. As a first step in this direction, states should eliminate all vocational licenses and reduce the number of nonvocational licenses to no more than a dozen. If medicine can get by on a single license, K–12 education can manage with twelve.[13]

## The Role of Education Schools and Organizations

Some years ago, Myron Lieberman (1996) perceptively described the K–12 education industry as "producer-dominated." I find this description accurate, particularly in the area of teacher training and licensing, where education school faculty and teacher organizations dominate the regulatory process. Both the teachers unions and the education schools have a common interest in "professionalizing" teaching by restricting supply through proliferation of certificates and suppressing competition in teacher training (e.g., by preventing entry of new institutions). I also find a similar view in state education departments, which embrace "teacher professionalization" as part of their mission, along with raising student achievement.

Moving to the flexible model described above would create strong competitive pressures for teacher-training organizations to improve. Simply put, if education school courses are no longer required to hold a teaching license, then the monopoly power of schools of education largely disappears. If the pedagogical training offered by schools of education does, in fact, raise student achievement, then graduates from such programs will enjoy a competitive edge in the labor market and have more desirable job offers than their untrained peers. In that case, students will flock to such programs. On the other hand, if a teacher-training program cannot attract adequate enrollments in a market, then it will go out of business. Effective programs will thrive; ineffective programs will wither away.

Any institution, public or private, would be free to enter the market and provide teacher training. If a history department at a small liberal arts college wanted to train teachers by offering a course preparing majors to teach in secondary schools and worked out student teaching arrangements with nearby schools, it would be free to do so. Unlike the current system, it would not be required to "partner" with a school of education.

When a major bank comes to a university campus to recruit candidates for management positions, it can interview finance majors in the business school, economics majors in the college of arts and sciences, or operations research or computer science majors from the engineering school. There are no licensing entry barriers creating a monopoly for a particular college. Opening up the teacher-training market to competition is a more effective way to fix the quality problem in schools of education than regulation by state departments of education or mandatory accreditation by NCATE. Many low-quality schools of education (as measured by pass rates on teacher licensing exams) have secured approval from state education agencies, as well as accreditation from NCATE (Ballou & Podgursky, 1996).

Clearly, both of these quality-control systems have failed to weed out programs with academically weak students and low pass rates on state licensing examinations.

Finally, a flexible regime will require a change in gestalt among the regulators in state education agencies. The primary objective of state regulators should be increasing student learning and narrowing achievement gaps. How schools and districts do this—assuming their behavior is ethical and legal—should be of secondary importance. Children are protected from incompetent practice by monitoring learning through regular testing, wide dissemination of the testing results, and school choice.

On the other hand, state education agencies should not be in the business of promoting teacher professionalism. Here is where a new gestalt is required. Promoting teacher professionalism is a role for private organizations. If organizations like teachers unions and schools of education (private or public) choose to promote teacher professionalization by securing NCATE accreditation of teacher-training programs, that is their choice. However, state education agencies should not impose these choices on the entire market through licensing requirements.

Moreover, it should be recognized that in some educational endeavors, the most cost-efficient way to promote student achievement might involve "deprofessionalizing" teaching. In some circumstances, highly scripted curricula, distance learning, or computer-based instructional programs may reduce the need for highly trained teachers. Schools should face incentives to adopt the most cost-efficient approaches to promoting student learning, whether or not they advance teacher "professionalization." If, in the name of teacher professionalization, state education agencies encourage schools to spend additional resources when more cost-effective means for instructional delivery are available, then resources may be diverted from other goals like lowering class size or otherwise enhancing student welfare. In fact, it may be that resources saved on teachers might more effectively promote student learning outside of K–12 schools, for example, in better medical care for poor women, reduction of crime and drugs in low-income communities, or preschool care.

Should states continue to regulate teacher training programs? Since there is virtually no reliable research establishing a causal link between any program of teacher training and student achievement gains, state regulators have little basis for regulating teacher-training programs. Some state and federal legislation (Title 2 of the Higher Education Act) have focused on pass rates on teacher licensing exams as one criterion to judge programs. In my own analysis of Missouri data, I have found that the most important predictor of whether a teacher passes a Praxis II exam is his or her ACT score. Once we control for student ACT scores, there are few significant differences between institutions. In addition, there is wide dispersion of test scores within any institution.

Because there is no reliable research base for approving or denying a teacher-training program and institutional pass rates are largely driven by the quality of program entrants, a reasonable approach would be for regulators to be fairly liberal in program approval. The primary mechanism for raising program quality would be market pressures, not regulation. If a training program does a poor job of preparing teachers to meet state education standards, graduates from such programs will receive fewer job offers in the market and enrollments will decline. Eventually the program may leave the market altogether. By the same token, programs that produce high-quality teachers will attract many applicants and expand. Protection against demonstrably incompetent teachers would come from testing individual candidates, not screening programs.

In sum, state education agencies should create strong incentives for schools and districts to raise student achievement and give them flexibility as to how they get the job done. If one or another model of professionalism promoted by private organizations is a cost-effective way for schools to achieve this end, then professionalization will expand. If it does not, then it will languish. However, this is not a matter for public policy.

## Evaluation

Effective educational policy requires that educational interventions be evaluated. We find ourselves in the current situation precisely because the education research community has for decades failed to conduct research on teacher quality that meets scientific research standards. Relaxing licensing standards will help generate non-experimental data on the causal relationship between teacher credentials and student achievement. Ironically, the current system, by encouraging homogeneity, reduces our ability to assess teacher effects. If all teachers in a school district matriculate from the same teacher-training program or hold the same credentials, then it is impossible to estimate the effect of that program or credential on student achievement. The best way to assess the effect of a treatment variable on an outcome variable is to maximize variation of the treatment variable. Relaxing entry barriers will generate a much more natural variation in the credentials and training of teachers in the work force. This will permit better evaluation of the effects of credentials. Perhaps alternatively certified school administrators will better appreciate the importance of random assignment experiments in schools and help move that project along as well. Certainly charter school operators have shown a willingness to experiment with new approaches in personnel policy and educational practice.

Interestingly, one factor that has often been ignored in the research liter ature on teacher certification has been the effect of the regulatory regime on the distribution of teaching certificates. That is, what was the process that produced the observed distribution of teaching credentials?

Consider the effect of emergency licenses or waivers. In the current regime, school districts are not supposed to hire uncertified teachers if certified teachers are available. Thus, the data we observe on teachers with emergency versus full licenses is generated by a process in which head-to-head competition between certified and uncertified teachers, as depicted in Figure 1, is not permitted. It may be that in a more competitive regime, teachers with emergency licenses would be of higher quality. Why would this be? If schools were free to recruit emergency certified teachers in the same way that they recruit licensed teachers, many who don't currently pursue teaching jobs might be enticed to apply. The result would be a much larger pool of talented emergency candidates. Those hired from a larger applicant pool would presumably be of higher quality. As noted above, on average schools will end up with a better hire if they have fifty applicants for a job than if they have five.

### What Could Go Wrong?

Does this approach involve risk? Yes, it does. Relaxing entry restrictions into teaching will permit greater flexibility for schools to seek out the best teachers and meet the performance targets set by state regulators. Regulators would protect parents and children against incompetent practice by monitoring student learning and making such data widely available. Parents would also be empowered to protect their children from poor teachers by giving them greater choices among schools. Markets and competition are ultimately the best guarantor of quality in the provision of almost any service.

However, would such a system produce greater exposure of children to incompetent teachers? Ultimately, this is an empirical point. However, I do not believe that most objective observers of current licensing system would argue that it is particularly effective in screening out incompetent practitioners. Indeed, as an empirical matter, it is likely that the greatest harm from incompetent teachers comes from experienced, licensed teachers who are protected by tenure statues, not from novices.

## CONCLUSION: THE TAIL IS WAGGING THE DOG

Policy debates about "teacher quality" have tended to dwell on teacher training and licensing. Yet, there is little research indicating that the types of licenses that teachers hold or the type of pedagogical training program they have passed through have a significant relationship to student performance. However, even if effective changes in licensing or training were identified, it would be many years before significant effects on student achievement would obtain. This is because the number of inexperienced teachers hired in any year is very small relative to the stock of incumbent or experienced teachers. In other markets, the best we expect from licensing is to screen out incompetent new practitioners. However, the quality of performance for incumbents is primarily determined by incentives: experienced dentists who do a poor job lose customers; those who perform incompetently get sued.

I have argued that attempts to address the teacher-quality problem by raising bars in teacher licensing are likely to make things worse rather than better. All such an approach is likely to do is reduce the size of the applicant pool with little change in the average productivity of the applicants. In a world of uncertain teacher productivity, it is in the interest of school districts to have more candidates to audition than fewer.

A more productive approach is for state regulators to focus on what they can measure (student achievement), not on what they can't (teacher quality). State regulators should make sure local school administrators have adequate instructional resources and strong incentives for raising school performance. They should use licensing to reduce the likelihood that a demonstrably incompetent teacher is put into the classroom. A prudent standard in this regard is a test of general academic skills, and more specialized tests covering the teaching fields and material to which the teacher is assigned. However, the most important role for teacher licensing reform is permissive or enabling. We need to make sure that these procrustean licensing systems do not stand in the way of school administrators who are responding to the incentives we are creating for improved student performance.

Rather than dwell on the credentials and training of the 3 percent to 4 percent of newly minted teachers hired each year, it is much more important to create strong performance incentives for the other 95 percent of teachers. Performance incentives are absent when pay is set by rigid salary schedules and tenure systems that protect teachers whose poor performance warrants dismissal. Rather than expend further resources seeking indirect measures of job performance, like licensing exam scores or teaching portfolios, it would be far more productive to use available information on teaching performance for the 95 percent of incumbent teachers. Dismissing the least productive 2 percent of teachers based on current job performance is likely to have a much larger effect on student achievement than marginal changes in the training or licensing of 3 percent to 4 percent of newly minted hires. Finally, it is important to address the role that collective bargaining contracts play in stifling efforts to raise teacher quality, particularly in urban school districts.

Teacher quality and effort is a primarily a management problem, not a licensing problem. School principals in most major urban districts often lack the ability to select their teachers, dismiss ineffective teachers, are often severely hampered by collective bargaining agreements (and licensing regulations) in how they can assign their teachers or staff vacant positions, and, with district-wide salary schedules, play no role in setting individual teacher pay. The teacher quality policy debate needs to focus on creating efficient incentive structures and reducing constraints on effective management. Teacher licensing is of secondary importance in that discussion.

# Conclusion

*Frederick M. Hess, Andrew J. Rotherham, and Catherine B. Walsh*

As Andrew J. Rotherham and Sara Mead made abundantly clear in chapter one, there is a lot of disagreement when it comes to teacher quality. There's disagreement about what constitutes a qualified teacher, about how well today's preparation programs are training teachers, and whether we can best improve teaching through new regulations or by relaxing the old ones. There is disagreement about whether good teaching leans heavily on innate skill or is primarily a matter of training and experience.

While policymakers and reformers tend to focus on these and other disagreements, when we convened the authors for a conference in November 2003 it surprised us how much agreement there is, even among people who approach the teacher-quality challenge from very different directions.

We'll begin by noting four major points of agreement that emerged among reformers of all stripes and that we think come through clearly in the papers in this volume. First, the current system is simply not providing enough of the quality teachers we need. Second, current policy is failing to provide the teachers we need particularly in the troubled, high-poverty school districts that need them most. Third, there is real concern that teacher-preparation programs are not teaching important skills or working to weed out unsuitable candidates, and are too often emphasizing a particular normative message in lieu of focused instruction in the skills and content that teachers need.

Finally, there is little prospect that, left to their own devices, either schools of education or school districts will be willing or able to correct these problems anytime soon. This practical challenge has been given a new urgency for public officials and practitioners who are also expected to find a way to comply with the NCLB "qualified teacher" mandate by 2006.

While these points of agreement don't necessarily provide a clear roadmap for reform, together they do suggest the need for an ambitious rethinking of the status quo. Governors and legislators will not meet the teacher-quality challenge by fine-tuning current arrangements or by pushing more funding into teacher preparation or professional development. More creative and far-reaching solutions are required.

The standard approach to teacher licensure has relied on four assumptions in trying to ensure a qualified teacher work force. It has presumed that preparation programs are providing teachers with essential knowledge and skills, are keeping unsuitable individuals from entering the profession, are not deterring too many quality candidates from entering the profession, and are providing an effective pipeline for conveying teachers to schools.

## NEXT STEPS FOR INFORMING POLICY

It seems to us that the broader body of emerging research and some of the new analyses presented in this volume call these assumptions into doubt. In light of that fact, we recommend three courses of action for federal, state, and local officials.

### Collecting Data on Preparation Programs

First, the groundbreaking research by David Leal and David Steiner finds little evidence that teacher-preparation programs are screening out unsuitable teachers or teaching essential knowledge and skills. However, the analyses presented here represent exploratory efforts and should therefore be interpreted with caution. As Leal and Steiner themselves are careful to note, it is imperative that future research examine these questions more systematically and for a more complete sample of institutions. In light of these limitations, there is an obvious role for more extensive reporting on the practices and teaching in these schools.

What kinds of measures would be appropriate? As discussed by Heidi Ramírez in chapter two, the 1998 reauthorization of the Higher Education Act (HEA) requires both teacher-preparation institutions and states to report teacher candidates' pass rates on state teacher licensure exams. However, this reporting has been subject to manipulation at both the state and institutional level, does not support meaningful comparison across states, and provides at best a crude gauge of institutional quality. The federal government should amend the HEA to improve transparency and uniformity, and to call for broader reporting on quality control and professional preparation at the institutional level. As a condition for federal aid, teacher-preparation programs should be required to fill out a standardized form that collects the information assembled by Leal and Steiner relating to program acceptance rates, student performance, the rate of program completion, required courses of study, and to post these data on the Internet and other public formats, along with syllabi of required teacher preparation courses. Such reporting would not be an onerous burden for programs already collecting such data. For programs that don't track these essential data, such a measure would be a firm wake-up call.

The critical role for the U.S. Department of Education would merely be to use its leverage and coordinating role to collect this information in a consistent, reliable, and timely fashion. The analyses of these data can be left to others, available for researchers of all stripes to systematically assess the performance of preparation programs. There are a number of entities that spend tens of millions of dollars annually to support research and analysis in the area of teacher quality and teacher preparation. We can be confident that such information, once collected, would indeed be used. The information will be particularly helpful because, as Dan Goldhaber explained in chapter three, it can now be combined with rich new data on student learning and teacher effectiveness that is being generated by state accountability systems

### Linking Teacher Quality to Accountability Systems

New state accountability systems also offer tremendous new opportunities to assess and regulate the quality of teachers and teacher-preparation programs in new ways. Where we once had to rely upon formal training to gauge the quality of a teacher, we now have data such as annual student assessments at most grade levels that can be used to determine just how well different students are progressing. As states take the step of identifying individual teachers when collecting data on student performance, they gain the ability to monitor how teachers fare in the classroom and need no longer depend so heavily on the signals provided by a teacher's credentials or training. Moreover, if districts include a teacher's preparation institution as part of their routine data collection, it becomes possible to track the student performance of all the teachers who graduated from particular preparation programs. Information of this kind could bring clarity to discussions of teacher quality and teacher preparation that were never previously possible.

### Are We Keeping People Out?

The evidence from programs like Teach For America (TFA) and The New Teacher Project (TNTP) and some public opinion research, makes, as Michael Podgursky notes in chapter ten, a strong circumstantial case that teacher certification is dissuading potentially qualified teachers from considering the profession. Of particular concern is the evidence from alternative certification programs suggesting that traditional barriers may especially deter prospective teachers seeking to work in the inner cities—exactly where the teacher-quality challenge is greatest. However, there is little reliable evidence on any of these questions that stretches beyond the anecdotal or theoretical.

This is a call for systematic efforts on the parts of researchers, philanthropists, and education departments to understand more fully the ways in which certification requirements or state licensing processes are deterring potentially effective teachers from the schools. While we can study the *benefit* of an extra requirement, it is too easy to overlook the *cost* of an otherwise qualified teacher who turns away in the face of procedural barriers or red tape.

### How Do We Get Teachers into the Schools

In chapter six, Susanna Loeb and her colleagues present the surprising fact that the vast majority of teachers wind up teaching fewer than fifty miles from their home. Policymakers will no doubt want to know the degree to which this localized market is the product of state-by-state licensing systems and localized teacher preparation, and to what extent it is a characteristic of teaching more generally. Such an inquiry will require consideration of teachers in alternative licensing programs such as TFA, TNTP, and the American Board, as well as new efforts to understand how teachers are recruited and choose jobs.

For instance, in 2003, The New Teacher Project produced an alarming study showing that 40 percent of applicants to four urban school systems wound up going elsewhere because of delays and frustration with the hiring process. It is not enough to get qualified candidates into the profession; we must also get them into schools, particularly schools where they are most needed. Understanding why teachers take the positions they do is a critical first step toward any comprehensive solution to getting good teachers into the worst-served schools.

### NEW DIRECTIONS FOR POLICY

The analyses presented here are arrayed along a continuum framed by two very different conceptions of how to address the teacher-quality challenge. One approach is the "professionalization" model endorsed by Gary Sykes, which urges us to set new and more demanding standards for teachers and preparation programs, and would thereby seek to "professionalize" teaching. The model Sykes has in mind is that of accounting or medicine. At the opposite extreme is Michael Podgursky's call to eliminate barriers to professional entry and to end the state oversight of teacher preparation, on the grounds that such a model would invite talent into the profession and permit accountable district officials to hire freely on the basis of candidate quality. Podgursky's model brings to mind professions such as journalism or consulting. One of the profound lessons for policymakers is that even these diametrically analyses find common ground in agreeing that there is a need to do something radically different than what we're currently doing.

Between the Podgursky and Sykes models are two distinct visions of reform that provide for more state regulation than Podgurksy's but less than Sykes'. Catherine Walsh envisions a model in which states set clear standards for who may teach, but then remain agnostic about how teachers meet those criteria, ending the privileged position of traditional teacher-preparation programs and creating new room for a market in teacher development. Bryan Hassel would have the states end their regulation of who can enter the profession but would have states adopt a much more hands-on and demanding role in regulating teacher preparation, leaving it to the preparation programs to self-interestedly play an aggressive role in monitoring teacher quality.

We don't find the evidence to clearly dictate that any of these courses is necessarily the "right" one, either nationally or for any given state. We would caution that there is no benefit to mandating any national solution to the teacher-quality challenge. There is no cookie-cutter model that all states would be wise to embrace. Rather, there are probably multiple ways to address the challenge, and the best policy answer depends on the resources, needs, and the popular preferences of a given state.

There are three principles that we believe should guide policymakers as they weigh the merits of the various reforms. First, any certification requirements should be crafted with an eye to the possibility that they will dissuade qualified candidates, which suggests tailoring them as narrowly as possible. Second, if preparation programs are to be a required part of a licensure regime, it is essential that they provide quality control and teach candidates professional skills and knowledge. Third, the case for licensing teachers or regulating teacher-training programs rests on the notion that there is professional body of knowledge and skills that these programs teach and that the trained teachers have mastered. Today, that body of knowledge and skills is too often amorphous, vague, and unsupported by clear research. While clarifying and developing that body of skills and knowledge must be a central goal for those in the worlds of policy and education in the years ahead, today's policies should reflect only what we can reasonably ascertain today, not what we might hope to know tomorrow.

It is clear that the old system isn't working, but not yet apparent exactly what the best course of change will be. As state officials weigh these three considerations and await continued efforts to cultivate and systematize the professional knowledge base of teaching, the appropriate course is one of sensible innovation and experimentation. While each of the editors has their own opinion as to what is likely to be the wisest course of reform, we don't have any pat answers to propose for every state. This book is intended not to provide a roadmap, but, rather, guideposts. We urge new efforts to collect the information that can help states make wise choices, encourage the asking of tough questions relating to how we ought to prepare teachers, and advise policymakers to be bold in rethinking teacher preparation to meet the teacher-quality challenge.

# Notes

## CHAPTER 1

1. In general, information on state teacher certification policies described below comes from state reports on teacher certification required by Title II of the Higher Education Act of 1998, information available at www.title2.org. However, because of differences in state terminology and procedures for teacher certification, this information is sometimes confusing, and apparently contradictory even in reports from the same state. In addition, many states have altered their teacher certification regulations since these reports were made or are in the process of doing so. As a result, we have sought wherever possible to augment these reports with information from a variety of sources, including U.S. Department of Education, Office of Policy Planning and Innovation, *Meeting the Highly Qualified Teacher Challenge: The Secretary's Second Annual Report on Teacher Quality* (Washington, DC: Author, 2003); C. Emily Feistritzer and David T. Chester, *Alternative Teacher Certification: A State by State Analysis, 2002* (Washington, DC: National Center for Education Information, 2002); state departments of education and professional standards board websites; Education Commission of the States, *Recent State Policies/Activities: Teacher Quality* (Denver: Author, July 2003 updates). In a few instances, we have spoken with state department of education staff to clarify the meaning of their requirements.
2. Feistritzer and Chester, *Alternative Teacher Certification*.
3. Feistritzer and Chester, *Alternative Teacher Certification*.
4. Feistritzer and Chester, *Alternative Teacher Certification*.
5. Feistritzer and Chester, *Alternative Teacher Certification*.
6. Five states (Florida, Maine, Maryland, New York, Rhode Island) and the District of Columbia indicate in their Title II reports that they do not require completion of a state-approved program for teacher certification. However, all of these states do have approved teacher-preparation program routes, and in most of these states a majority of teachers prepared in the state go through the approved program route. Florida requires completion of an approved teacher-preparation program, completion of an approved alternative route program, or 20 hours of professional education coursework. In Maine, individuals must meet a combination of academic and professional requirements for each Maine teaching certificate. Maryland has an approved program route and requires all teacher-preparation programs to be NCATE accredited. Individuals can also obtain certification through transcript analysis demonstrating that they have met specific coursework requirements. Individuals in New York who have not completed their approved program but have met all the coursework and other requirements set by the state for licensure can apply to the state on their own. Rhode Island applicants who have not completed an approved program can submit evidence of meeting specific professional and academic coursework requirements.

**283**

7. Under the No Child Left Behind Act of 2001, teachers in all states are required to demonstrate subject-matter mastery and have full certification by 2006. Theoretically, this will result in less variance on several of these measures.

8. Some states make exceptions for individuals holding special certificates as, for example, career education teachers or teachers of Native American language and culture.

9. Alaska, North Carolina, and Vermont indicate in their Title II reports that they do not require coursework in pedagogy. However, all three states require completion of an approved program. Rather than coursework requirements, North Carolina requires approved programs to demonstrate how they will prepare students to meet state professional competencies.

10. However, many states grant additional endorsements based on a minor or passage of subject exam.

11. The exceptions are Florida and South Dakota. Several states also allow substitution of a mentored in-service internship in lieu of student teaching.

12. Iowa, South Dakota, Utah, and Wyoming have no state teacher-testing regimes. Alabama, Delaware, Idaho, Maine, Montana, North Dakota, Washington, and Wyoming require only basic skills tests. Washington is developing content exams for use beginning in 2005.

13. A few make this a condition of employment (rather than certification), for which districts are responsible.

14. National Council for the Accreditation of Teacher Education, available online at www.ncate.org; Frederick M. Hess and Sandra Vergari, "The Accreditation Game," *Education Next* 2, no. 3 (Fall 2002), 48–57.

15. Of the 35 states with such systems, 34 require teachers to progress through two levels of certification (from an initial or provisional to a standard or professional license). Connecticut requires teachers to progress through three levels.

16. See Emily Shartin, "New Rules Test Teachers' Patience," *Boston Globe,* September 25, 2003; Deborah Bach, "Revised Certification Rules Anger Teachers," *Seattle Post-Intelligencer,* August 7, 2003.

17. National Education Association Research, *Status of the American Public School Teacher 2000–01* (Washington, DC: National Education Association, 2003).

18. These figures do not include information for North Carolina or Hawaii, where professional development regulations are currently under revision. Changing professional development requirements for existing teachers is often a highly contentious process.

19. New Jersey and West Virginia also issue lifelong certificates. However, New Jersey still requires life certificate holders to obtain 100 hours of professional development every five years. West Virginia's permanent certificates are issued only after two renewals of a five-year certificate (in practice only, after at least 18 years teaching) and all West Virginia teachers are required to complete 18 clock hours of professional development annually as a condition of employment not related to certification. Many other states also have some individuals still teaching on lifelong certificates that used to be common but which most states no longer issue.

20. A few states prefer coursework but allow individuals who have already attained an advanced degree expanded options to meet renewal requirements. One other state (Nebraska) requires coursework for renewal only for individuals who have not taught in the past three years.

21. Alabama, Indiana, Mississippi, Montana, Virginia, Iowa, Kentucky, Louisiana, Missouri, Nebraska, Nevada, North Dakota, West Virginia.

22. Colorado, Delaware, Illinois, Nebraska, North Dakota, Wisconsin.

23. These terms can be confusing because of the politicized nature of the current debate. At the risk of oversimplifying, we use "progressive" to denote those who are most concerned with

emphasizing how to learn and "liberal/classical" to denote those most concerned with what children learn. To be sure, most educators are not firmly in one camp or the other, so this is something of a false dichotomy. However, we think it captures the macro-contours of this debate, particularly as it relates to what skills teachers should bring to the classroom and how they should acquire them.

24. For more on this group, see David L. Angus, *Professionalism and the Public Good: A Brief History of Teacher Certification*, ed. Jeffrey Mirel (Washington, DC: Thomas B. Fordham Foundation, 2001). See also David B. Tyack and Elisabeth Hansot, *Managers of Virtue: Public School Leadership in America, 1820–1980* (New York: Basic Books, 1982)

25. Sarah Mondale, ed., *School: The Story of American Public Education* (Boston: Beacon Press, 2002).

26. Angus, *Professionalism and the Public Good*.

27. Benjamin Frazier, *Development of State Programs for the Certification of Teachers* (Washington, DC: U.S. Office of Education, 1938), as cited in Angus, *Professionalism and the Public Good*; Raymond J. Kendall, "The Closing Door," *Journal of Higher Education* 9, no. 5 (May 1938), 256–262; David F. Labaree, *The Ed School's Romance with Progressivism*, paper presented at Brookings Institution Conference on Educational Policy, Washington, DC, May 21, 2003.

28. Angus, *Professionalism and the Public Good*; Kendall "The Closing Door."

29. Angus *Professionalism and the Public Good*.

30. Angus *Professionalism and the Public Good*.

31. Angus *Professionalism and the Public Good*.

32. Angus *Professionalism and the Public Good*.

33. Angus *Professionalism and the Public Good*.

34. Angus *Professionalism and the Public Good*.

35. Chester E. Finn, Jr., "High Hurdles," *Education Next* 3, no. 2 (Spring 2003), 62.

36. For examples, see Task Force on Teaching as a Profession, *A Nation Prepared: Teachers for the 21st Century* (New York: Carnegie Corporation, 1986); National Commission on Teaching and America's Future, *What Matters Most: Teaching for America's Future* (New York: Author, 1996).

37. For examples, see Finn, "High Hurdles"; Frederick M. Hess, *Tear Down this Wall: The Case for a Radical Overhaul of Teacher Certification* (Washington, DC: Progressive Policy Institute, 2001); Thomas B. Fordham Foundation, *The Teachers We Need and How to Get More of Them* (Washington, DC: Author, 1999).

38. This is a calculation of the total tuition and fees charges to students over the entire teacher-preparation program for the cohort of students completing teacher preparation programs in a given year. According to the National Center for Education Information, 200,545 students completed teacher-preparation programs in 1998–1999. Of these, approximately 72 percent completed undergraduate programs, and 28 post-baccalaureate teacher-preparation programs. Similarly, roughly 75 percent were in public institutions and about 25 percent private. On average, undergraduate teacher-preparation programs required 125 semester hours or equivalent of coursework, including 51–52 hours general education, 36–39 hours in the major, 24–31 in professional education, and 14–16 hours student teaching. Post-baccalaureate programs averaged 108 semester hours, 42 in general education, 31–33 in a major, 23–28 in professional education, and 12 in student teaching. The average cost of full-time (30 hours a year) undergraduate tuition and fees at public four-year colleges and universities was $4,081 in 2002–2003, and $18,273 at private. Average full-time graduate tuition at public universities was $4,491 in 2001–2002 and $15,233 at private. The above cost was calculated by multiplying the number of students completing each of four types of teacher-preparation programs by the annual cost for that type of school by the number of hours required

for the average teacher-preparation program, divided by 30 (public undergraduate: 108,335 ´ $4081 ´ 125 / 30 = $1,842,146,396; private undergraduate: 34935 ´ $18,273 ´ 125 = $2,659,863,563; public post-baccalaureate: 40,069 ´ $4,491 ´ 108 = $647,819,564; private post-baccalaureate: 17,206 ´ $15,233 ´ 108=943,556,393; Total $6,093,385,916). If one ignores the fact that many elementary and special education teachers and a dwindling number of secondary teachers actually have majors in education, and counts as spending for teacher-preparation and education programs only the cost of hours in professional education and student teaching, this cost would be about $2.2 billion. If, on the other hand, one was interested primarily on the additional costs of certification requirements for prospective teachers, assuming that undergraduate students would complete a bachelor's in some field anyway and only the difference between average hours required by teacher-preparation programs (125+) and average number of hours required for a bachelor's degree (120) (but all costs of postgraduate teacher preparation could presumably be attributed to teacher certification), that cost would be $1.8 billion. All of these figures underestimate the value of expenditures on teacher preparation, possibly dramatically, because they do not account for students who enroll in such programs but do not complete them. Sources: U.S. Department of Education, National Center for Education Statistics, *Digest of Education Statistics 2002* (Washington, DC: Author, 2002); College Board, *Trends in College Costs and Pricing* (New York: Author, 2003); C. Emily Feistritzer, *The Making of a Teacher* (Washington, DC: National Center on Education Information, 1999).

39. Carol E. Cohen, *Issues and Challenges in Financing Professional Development in Education* (Washington, DC: The Finance Project, June 2001), citing Eric Hirsch, Julia E. Koppick, and Michael S. Knapp, *Revisiting What States Are Doing to Improve the Quality of Teaching: An Update on Patters and Trends* (Seattle: Center for the Study of Teaching Policy, February 2001).

40. National Education Association. The National Center for Education Statistics Estimates that there were 2.988 million public school teachers in the United States in 2001. U.S. Department of Education, *Digest of Education Statistics 2002.*

41. National Center for Education Statistics' 1993–1994 Schools and Staffing Survey notes that 22.8 percent of public school teachers responded "yes" to the question, "What types of support have you received during the current school year for in-service education or professional development in your MAIN teaching assignment field? (Tuition and/or fees)" http://nces.ed.gov/surveys/SASS/sassib/article.asp?TxtID=79&Yr=1993.

42. This assumption is likely very low. However, there is no national data available on tuition reimbursement policies, which in most cases are set by school districts, often as part of a collective bargaining agreement. In many cases, these policies are keyed to tuition costs at state universities, and they may cap the dollar amount, number of classes that may be taken for reimbursement, or be set as a percentage of total expenditures on coursework. A few states have unique systems to pay for teacher coursework. In Michigan, for example, when teachers supervise student teachers from one of the state's public colleges or universities, there is an option to be compensated with credit in a "bank" the district has. Credits from this "bank" can then be used by teachers in the district toward tuition payments.

43. National Commission on Teaching and America's Future, *What Matters Most;* Dale Ballou and Michael Podgursky, "Gaining Control of Professional Licensing and Advancement," in *Conflicting Missions? Teachers Unions and Educational Reform,* ed. Tom Loveless (Washington, DC: Brookings Institution Press, 2000); Suzanne B. Clery and John B. Lee, *Faculty Salaries: 2001–02* (Washington, DC: National Education Association, 2003).

44. National Commission on Teaching and America's Future *What Matters Most;* Ballou and Podgursky, "Gaining Control of Professional Licensing and Advancement"; Clery and Lee, *Faculty Salaries: 2001–02.*

45. Angus, *Professionalism and the Public Good;* Labaree, "The Ed School's Romance with Progressivism."
46. These costs are not negligible. The federal government alone spent more than $70 million on alternative routes to certification in 2003, not including financial aid subsidies for which some alternative candidates are eligible as students. States, school districts, and private philanthropies spent far more.
47. For more on teachers unions and teacher certification, see Ballou and Podgursky, "Gaining Control of Professional Licensing and Advancement"; American Federation of Teachers, *Assuring Teacher Quality: It's Union Work* (AFT Convention resolution adopted July 19, 1998) (Washington, DC: American Federation of Teachers).
48. This resolution offers the following recommendations:
    - Work with universities to ensure that pre-service preparation programs for teachers have high standards . . . rigorous preparation in pedagogy and the academic disciplines, and have strong clinical components that involved exemplary teachers both at the field sites and on the clinical faculty of education departments;
    - Work with universities and pre-service institutions and the organizations representing them, such as the National council for Accreditation of Teacher Education, to support the development of a stronger core curriculum in teacher preparation tied to the best research knowledge about effective practice;
    - Work with licensing bodies and professional standards boards to require that entering teachers meet high standards;
    - Work with legislators and local school district policymakers to assure that beginning teachers are given a well-supervised induction period . . . mentored by highly accomplished teachers, and that only teachers who meet professional standards are awarded tenure;
    - Work through collective bargaining to develop programs . . . such as: 1.) peer assistance programs that provide mentoring to new teachers and assistance to tenured teachers whose teaching has been identified as in need of improvement, 2.) internship programs . . . 3.) peer review programs . . .
    - Negotiate contract provisions and advocate state policies that encourage teachers to seek national board for Professional Teaching Standards certification by offering financial incentives and preparation programs, and
    - Support state tenure statutes that provide strong due-process safeguards.
49. A number of private colleges and universities, including several "name" institutions, have faculty collective bargaining, but there is no legal imperative on private higher education to allow faculty to bargain collectively, as there is for public institutions in 24 states. Four southern states prohibit faculty collective bargaining in institutions of higher education, and the remainder allow but do not require it. See Gregory N. Saltzman, "Legal Regulation of Collective Bargaining in Colleges and Universities," in *The NEA 1998 Almanac of Higher Education* (Washington, DC: National Education Association, 1998); Gary Rhoades, "Retrenchment Clauses in Higher Education Contracts," *Journal of Higher Education*, 64 (May/June 1993), 312–347.
50. Letter from Diane Shust, NEA Director of Government Relations and Randall Moody, Manager of Federal Policy and Politics, to Representatives, July 8, 2003. It's worth noting that the NEA's letter is more adamant, and takes a more extreme pro-IHE position on some related administrative issues, than communications to Congress on the same topic from the American Council on Education, the umbrella group of higher education interest organizations that advocates for their interests in Washington, DC.

51. Hess and Vergari, "The Accreditation Game"; Bess Keller, "Popular Exam to Get New Cut-off Score," *Education Week* 22, no. 40 (June 11, 2003).
52. National Commission on Excellence in Education, *A Nation at Risk* (Washington, DC: U.S. Government Printing Office, 1983).
53. Task Force on Teaching as a Profession, *A Nation Prepared.*
54. It's also worth noting that this disenchantment became far more pronounced, and criticism more vocal, following the 1996 National Commission on Teaching and America's Future (NCTAF) report that drew attention to NBPTS by calling for creation of 100,000 NBPTS-certified teachers and President Bill Clinton began to champion the program through budget requests and by publicly calling for 100,000 National Board Certified teachers by 2006.
55. See Hess, *Tear Down this Wall;* Chester E. Finn, Jr., "Teacher Reform Gone Astray," in *Our Schools and Our Future . . . Are We still at Risk?* ed. Paul E. Peterson (Cambridge, MA: Harvard Program on Education Policy and Governance, 2003); Robert Holland, *National Teacher Certification: Advancing Quality or Perpetuating Mediocrity?* (Arlington, VA: Lexington Institute, December 2002). NBPTS recently commissioned several respected researchers to evaluate the impact of NBPTS-certified teachers on student achievement, but those studies are not yet complete.
56. James Salzer, "Teacher Bonuses Strain Budget," *Atlanta-Journal Constitution,* September 9, 2003.
57. Dan Goldhaber, David Perry, and Emily Anthony, *NBPTS Certification: Who Applies and What Factors Are Associated with Success?* (Washington, DC: Urban Institute, March 2003).
58. National Commission on Teaching and America's Future, *What Matters Most.*
59. These states are Alabama, Georgia, Hawaii, Idaho, Illinois, Indiana, Kansas, Kentucky, Louisiana, Maryland, Missouri, Montana, New Mexico, North Carolina, Ohio, Oklahoma, Tennessee, Vermont, Washington, and West Virginia.
60. Alabama, Arkansas, California, Delaware, District of Columbia, Georgia, Hawaii, Illinois, Indiana, Iowa, Kansas, Kentucky, Louisiana, Maine, Maryland, Massachusetts, Minnesota, Nebraska, Nevada, New Jersey, New York, North Carolina, Ohio, Oklahoma, Rhode Island, South Carolina, South Dakota, Tennessee, Texas, Utah, Vermont, Virginia, Washington, and Wisconsin.
61. INTASC "core" teaching standards are subject to the same criticisms as NBPTS standards: they are insufficiently concrete to provide a practical guide for training or assessing the competence of prospective teachers, and they are more focused on broad attitudes and beliefs than specific competencies. Subject-area standards have also been criticized by some observers, who see them as too reflective of a progressive approach to education with too little emphasis on specific content knowledge.
62. The specific number of states varies depending on which sets of standards are considered.
63. Source: NCATE. Bylaws also specify what percentages of seats on various governing boards will be held by various different NCATE member types. For example, 10 of 32 seats on the critical Unit Accreditation board, which determines accreditation status of applicants, are held by teachers unions, and 10 by teacher educator groups (since one seat on this board is held by a student and one by a lay member of the public, unions and teacher educators each effectively control one-third of this board). Specialized professional organizations include subject specific teacher associations (e.g., National Council of Teachers of English), administrator associations (e.g., American Association of School Administrators), child-centered organizations (e.g., National Association for the Education of Young Children), education technology groups, and specialty associations (e.g., American Library Association). Policymaker groups are the Council of Chief State School Officers (CCSSO), National Association of State Boards of Education (NASBE), and National School Boards Association (NSBA).

64. Other organizations endorsing NBPTS include the National Governors' Association, the National Council for Accreditation of Teacher Education, the American Federation of Teachers, the Council for American Private Education, the Council of Great City Schools, the National Alliance of Black School Educators, the National Conference of State Legislatures, the National Education Association, the National School Boards Association,

65. AACTE reserves spaces on its board for representatives from institutions that are members of various teacher education organizations that existed prior to AACTE's creation, and AACTE's Advisory Council of State Representatives, composed of the presidents of its state chapters.

66. Task Force on Teaching as a Profession, *A Nation Prepared;* Finn, "Teacher Reform Gone Astray."

67. Hess and Vergari, "The Accreditation Game"; Michael Poliakoff, "Mastering the Basics," *Philanthropy* (October 2001).

68. Fordham Foundation, *The Teachers We Need and How to Get More of Them,* http://www.edexcellence.net/foundation/publication/publication.cfm?id=16.

69. Hess, *Tear Down this Wall.*

70. Steve Farkas, *Different Drummers: How Teachers of Teachers View Public Education* (New York: Public Agenda Foundation, 1997).

71. Many states also include representatives from private schools, public and private higher education, the liberal arts, school board members, parents, business, the general public, or state departments of education.

72. For example, Delaware, Illinois, and Wisconsin require that teacher members be selected from lists of nominees by teachers associations in the state. Other states specify that recommendations shall be solicited from constituent organizations representing various groups represented on the board. Maryland, Rhode Island, and West Virginia further specify the share of teacher seats that may be held by different teachers unions, state NEA and AFT affiliates.

73. Education Commission of the States, *Professional Standards Boards—State-Level Policies* (Denver: Author, updated November 2002). Autonomous boards make decisions, have the power to set policies, and in some cases carry to them out. Advisory boards make recommendations to state boards or departments of education.

74. For one view of how this applies to education, see Terry M. Moe, *Politics, Control, and the Future of School Accountability,* paper presented at Conference on Taking Account of Accountability, Kennedy School of Government, Harvard University, Cambridge, MA, June 10–11, 2001.

75. The six states that do not have professional standards boards are Arizona, Maine, Michigan, New Mexico, Ohio, and Tennessee, as well as the District of Columbia. In Nebraska, South Dakota, and Utah professional standards boards deal with licensure primarily in disciplinary matters, rather than setting standards for certification.

76. For more on this issue, see Jennifer Loven, "Committee Rejects Board of Ed. Plans," *Grand Rapids Press,* February 20, 1997; Karen Schulz, "Democrats on State Board to Sue Engler," *Grand Rapids Press,* March 1, 1997; Malcolm Johnson, "Judge Blocks State School Board Moves," *Grand Rapids Press,* March 7, 1997.

77. North Carolina SB 931.

78. Rob Christensen, "Teacher Licensing Vetoed," *Charlotte News-Observer,* June 9, 2003; "Easley Vetoes Bill Lessening Authority of State Education Board," Associated Press, June 8, 2003.

79. Education Commission of the States, *Teacher Quality: Governors' 2003 State of the State Addresses* (Denver: Author, 2003).

80. For more on this, see Aims C. McGuinness, *1997 State Postsecondary Structure Sourcebook* (Denver: Education Commission of the States, 1997,) available updated online, along with Postsecondary Governance Structures Database, on the Education Commission of the States website at http://www.ecs.org/clearinghouse/31/02/3102.htm.

81. See Heidi Ramirez, in this volume. See also Sandra Huang, Yun Yi, and Kati Haycock, *Interpret with Caution: The First State Title II Reports on the Quality of Teacher Preparation* (Washington, DC: Education Trust, 2002).

82. Pamela M. Prah, "Teacher Certification Plans Dodge Budget Cuts," *Stateline.org*, July 15, 2003, referencing an unpublished study from the Economic Policy Institute, quoting author Anne Heald.

83. Education Commission of the States, *Recent State Policies/Activities*, retrieved August 2003 from http://www.ecs.org/ecs/ecscat.nsf/WebTopicMonth?OpenView&Start=1&Count=-1.

84. For more on this, see Peggy Fikac, "Board Backs Down on Certification Renewal," Associated Press, January 11, 1998; Suzanne Hoholik, "Recertification Plan Gets Bad Marks from Teachers," *San Antonio Express-News*, November 23, 1997. The State Board for Educator Certification (SBEC) is appointed by the governor and intended to operate, as with professional standards boards in most states, as an independent, practitioner-driven regulator of professional standards. The State Board of Education may veto policies of the (SBEC) with a two-thirds vote, but may not amend them.

85. Alaska and Utah do not.

86. Some states condition bonuses or raises on additional responsibilities, local match, or appropriations. Some states reimburse fees only for teachers who successfully obtain NBPTS certification.

87. National Board for Professional Teaching Standards as of Spring 2003.

88. Hess and Vergari, "The Accreditation Game."

89. According to the teacher recruitment database Recruiting Teachers, http://www.recruiting teachers.org/channels/clearinghouse/becometeacher/126_finaidresources.htm, by 1998 at least 18 states also granted some form of loan forgiveness to students who commit to teaching in the loan-granting state for a certain number of years after they become certified. Missouri and Hawaii have created loan programs since then (Education Commission of the States). Several states have amended their programs since 1998, both to expand them and to cap benefits as a result of recent budget shortfalls.

90. For example, West Virginia's National Institute for Teaching Excellence (HB 3245, 2001).

91. For example, South Carolina, HB 3534, Section 1, 2001.

92. For example, Virginia SB 1304 2001, Hawaii SB 1315 2001.

93. Feistritzer and Chester, *Alternative Teacher Certification*.

94. Andrew J. Rotherham and Sara Mead, "Beyond No Child Left Behind: A Response to Kaplan and Owings (2002)," *NASSP Bulletin* 87, no. 635 (June 2003), 65.

95. See "State Education Board Approves Alternative Teacher Certification," Associated Press, January 2003.

96. For more on this controversy, see John Mooney, "A Rare Political Drama Over the Teacher Code: Ex-Commissioners Lobby to Protect Alternative Route Program," *Newark Star Ledger*, August 20, 2003; Jon Mooney, "Split Board Backs New Teacher Standards," *Newark Star Ledger*, September 4, 2003.

97. The guidance specifies, "Teachers who are not yet fully certified but participate in an alternative route to certification program may be considered to meet the certification requirements of the definition of a highly qualified teacher if they are participating in an alternative route program under which they: (1) receive high-quality professional development that is sustained, intensive, and classroom-focused in order to have a positive and lasting

impact on classroom instruction before and while teaching; (2) participate in a program of intensive supervision that consists of structured guidance and regular ongoing support for teachers, or a teacher mentoring program; (3) assume functions as a teacher only for a specified period of time not to exceed three years; and (4) demonstrate satisfactory progress toward full certification as prescribed by the State." U.S. Department of Education, Office of Elementary and Secondary Education, *Improving Teacher Quality; Non-Regulatory Guidance* (Washington, DC: Author, revised draft September 13, 2002), http://www.ed.gov/programs/teacherqual/guidance.doc. For more discussion of these concerns, see Chester E. Finn, Jr., "Is Alternative Certification Perishing?" *Gadfly* (Thomas B, Fordham Foundation) 3 no 19 (March 13, 2003), http://www.edexcellence.net/foundation/gadfly/issue.cfm?id=14#288.

98. NCLB also defines how this competence may be demonstrated, which differs for teachers of different grade levels and for veteran versus new teachers. Briefly, new secondary teachers must demonstrate subject-matter competence by either passing a rigorous subject exam or possessing an academic major or equivalent coursework, graduate degree, or advanced certification or credentialing in the subject taught. New elementary school teachers must pass a rigorous test of subject matter and teaching skills in reading, writing, math, and other basic areas of the elementary curriculum. Veteran teachers may demonstrate subject competence through these same options or by meeting an objective, uniform standard set by the state to determine subject competency. See U.S. Department of Education (2002); No Child Left Behind Act of 2001 (H.R. 1), 107 Cong. 110 (2002) (enacted).

## CHAPTER 2

1. The 1785 law provided for the disbursement of federal lands in the Western Territory, such that one section in every township was reserved for schools within that township.

2. The 1787 law went so far as to assert that "religion, morality and knowledge being necessary to good government and the happiness of mankind, schools and the means of education shall forever be encouraged."

3. See, for example, the 1917 Smith-Hughes Act, the 1918 Vocational Rehabilitation Act, and the 1920 Smith-Bankhead Act.

4. Preston M. Royster and Gloria J. Chernay, *Teacher Education: The Impact of Federal Policy* (Springfield, VA: Banister Press, 1981), p. 51.

5. In 1953, the NSF sponsored its first summer workshops for the professional development of college science teachers.

6. This included legislation such as the 1950 Financial Assistance for Local Educational Agencies Affected by Federal Activities Act.

7. For example, federal legislation for military education established West Point Military Academy in 1802, the Naval Academy at Annapolis in 1845, Army War College in 1901, Coast Guard Academy in 1915, Armed Forces Institute in 1942, and the Air Force Academy in 1954.

8. Royster and Chernay, *Teacher Education*, p. 58.

9. John F. Jennings, "Federal General Aid—Likely or Illusory?" *Journal of Law and Education* 2, no. 1 (1973, January), p. 89.

10. Royster and Chernay, *Teacher Education*.

11. The common school movement initiated by Horace Mann in 1827 led to dramatic increases in the number of children enrolled in elementary school over the next 100 years.

12. Lucas reports that by 1922 approximately one-fourth of primary school teachers lacked a high school education and approximately 50 percent or less had completed two years of college or less. In 1931, only about one-tenth of elementary school teachers had a bachelor's

degree; a quarter of secondary teachers lacked a four-year degree. Christopher J. Lucas, *Teacher Education in America* (New York: St. Martin's Press, 1997), p. 50.

13. Robert Freeman Butts and Lawrence A. Cremin, "A History of Education in American Culture" (New York: Holt, 1953), p. 606, cited in Lucas, *Teacher Education in America,* p. 51.

14. These included general education, advanced subject-matter knowledge, professional education (e.g., developmental stages, social understanding, creative expression), and hands-on learning through student teaching and observation experiences.

15. Speech delivered by Harold Clapp (then vice president of the Council for Basic Education) at the 1959 annual conference of the National Commission on Teacher Education and Professional Standards held in Kansas, cited by G. K. Hodenfield and Timothy M. Stinnett, *Education of Teachers, Conflict and Consensus* (New Jersey: Prentice Hall, 1961), p. 58.

16. This included, among others, James Bryant Conant's *The Education of American Teachers* (New York: McGraw Hill, 1963); James D. Koerner's *The Miseducation of American Teachers* (Baltimore: Penguin, 1963), Othanel Smith, *Teachers for the Real World* (Washington, DC: American Association for Teacher Education, 1969), Martin Haberman and Timothy M. Stinnett's *Teacher Education and the New Profession of Teaching* (Berkeley, CA: McCutchan, 1973), and Robert B. Howsam et al.'s *Educating a Profession* (Washington, DC: American Association of Colleges for Teacher Education, 1976).

17. Ralph Cyr, "Demographics of Teacher Education Institutions: Implications for Policy Making," in *Policy for the Education of Educators: Issues and Implications,* ed. Georgianna Appignani (Washington, DC: American Association of Colleges of Teacher Education, 1981), pp. 9–26.

18. Holmes Group, *Tomorrow's Teachers: A Report of the Holmes Group* (East Lansing, MI: 1986). Also see Jonas F. Soltis, *Reforming Teacher Education: The Impact of the Holmes Group* (New York, New York: Teachers College Press, 1987) for a series of papers discussing the Holmes Group's recommendations and their implications.

19. Linda Darling-Hammond, "Standard-Setting in Teaching: Changes in Licensing, Certification, and Assessment," in *The Handbook of Research on Teaching,* 4th ed. (Washington, DC: American Educational Research Association, 2001), reports that states' "onsite program reviews by panels of experts almost never occur," and that "in some of these states, colleges have felt quite free to reduce their own standards for and investments in teacher education."

20. In fact, most state departments of education experienced considerable budget cuts during the 1980s, leaving the likelihood of meaningful program review and institutional accountability even more improbable.

21. Darling-Hammond, "Standard-Setting in Teaching."

22. Darling-Hammond, "Standard-Setting in Teaching."

23. Wayne J. Urban, "Historical Studies of Teacher Education," in *Handbook of Research on Teacher Education,* ed. W. Robert Houston (New York: Macmillan, 1990), pp. 59–71, reports, however, that skepticism over teacher qualifications on the part of arts and sciences higher education faculty predated the Sputnik launch.

24. Senate Republicans significantly cut the number of scholarships authorized under the law.

25. National Defense Education Act of 1958, U.S. Statutes at Large, Public Law 85-864 (Sec. 101).

26. It should be noted, though, that grants were awarded to institutions not the individuals, who were made to apply to the institutions.

27. Public Law 85-864 provided assistance to state and local school systems for strengthening instruction in science, mathematics, modern foreign languages, and other critical subjects; improvement of state statistical services; guidance, counseling, and testing services and

training institutes; higher education student loans and fellowships; foreign language study and training provided by colleges and universities; experimentation and dissemination of information on more effective utilization of television, motion pictures, and related media for educational purposes; and vocational education for technical occupations necessary to the national defense.

28. Royster and Chernay, *Teacher Education,* p. 67.

29. http://www.pbs.org/johngardner/chapters/4c.html

30. The 1974 ESEA reauthorization expanded the Bilingual Education Act (Title VII, first authorized in 1968) to include a series of preservice teacher education grants, including the Ca-reer Ladder program to support the training of teacher aides aspiring to the teaching profession. NOTE: #30 IN THE TEXT WILL NEED TO BE MOVED TO THE END OF THE PREVIOUS SENTENCE THAT ENDS ". . . FIRST FEDERAL DOLLARS FOR PRE-COLLEGE EDUCATION."

NOTE: SOMEHOW THE ABOVE WERE SEPARATED INTO THREE SEPARATE ENDNOTES- THEY SHOULD BE TOGETHER. ALSO:

31. Larry Cuban, "The Holmes Group Report: Why Reach Exceeds Grasp, in Reforming Teacher Education," *The Impact of the Holmes Group Report,* ed. Jonas F. Soltis (New York: Teachers College Press, 1987), pp. 38–43.

32. See also the 1963 Vocational Education Act.

33. The COP was first funded at nearly $11 million in 1969 and grew to $24.3 million by the 1970 fiscal year.

34. Royster and Chernay, *Teacher Education,* pp. 99–100.

35. C. Emily Feistrizer and David G. Imig, "Federal Involvement in Educational Personnel Development," in *Policy for the Education of Educators: Issues and Implications,* ed. Georgianna Appignani (Washington, DC: American Association of Colleges of Teacher Education, 1981), pp. 90–114.

36. Marshall (Mike) Smith later served as undersecretary, then Acting Deputy Secretary of Education in the Clinton administration.

37. Smith did voice concerns, however, that such consolidations often have severe implications for their funding, as individual programs tend to garner better support.

38. The legislative language included in P.L. 95-561, ESEA Title IV-C and V-B, was, however, not completely clear about what such plans for coordination, to be submitted to the Department of Education, would include or how they should be reviewed. It did, however, set the tone for future federal policy attention to state planning and program coordination efforts.

39. Feistrizer and Imig, "Federal Involvement in Educational Personnel Development," pp. 93–95.

40. Georgianna Appignani, "Federal Involvement in Educational Personnel Development," p. 1.

41. Francis Keppel, "The Need for Policy Development," in *Policy for the Education of Educators: Issues and Implications,* ed. Georgianna Appignani (Washington, DC: American Association of Colleges of Teacher Education, 1981), pp. 5–8.

42. Senator Stafford, 1984 Congressional Hearings on SJ Res. 138, the establishment of a National Commission on Education.

43. National Commission on Education Act, S.J. Res. 138.

44. Subcommittee on Education, Arts and Humanities of the Committee on Labor and Human Resources, American Defense Education Act, S.Hrg. 99-232, pp. 1–16, Washington, DC, 1985.

45. The proposed America 2000 legislation would have provided discretionary dollars for state development of aligned standards and assessments. The proposal was defeated by Democrats skeptical of standards and testing and Republicans concerned about an expanding fed-

eral role in education. Robert B. Schwartz and Marian A. Robinson, "Goals 2000 and the Standards Movement," in *Brookings Papers on Education Policy, 2000,* ed. Diane Ravitch (Washington, DC: Brookings Institution, 2000), pp. 173–214.

46. Much of Clinton's education leadership team had been involved in the governors' summit. Secretary of Education Richard Riley had, as South Carolina governor, hosted the 1986 National Governors' Association meeting focused entirely on education and leading to the 1989 conference. Deputy Secretary of Education Madeline Kunin had participated in the 1989 summit as governor of Vermont. NOTE: AUTHOR SAYS THAT THIS CITE IN THE TEXT SHOULD COME AT THE END OF THE SENTENCE

47. See the Technology Literacy Challenge Fund and related technology discretionary grants.

48. National Commission on Teaching and America's Future (NCTAF), "What Matters Most: Teaching for America's Future" (New York: National Commission on Teaching and America's Future, 1996), p. 10.

49. The NCTAF was not, however, the first such report. For example, in 1984 the Council of Chief State School Officers released "Staffing the Nation's Schools: A National Emergency," and in 1985 the American Association of Colleges for Teacher Education issued "A Call for Change in Teacher Education."

50. Nancy Kraft, *Standards in Teacher Education: A Critical Analysis of NCATE, INTASC, and NBPTS* (paper presented at annual meeting of the American Educational Research Association, Seattle, 2001).

51. In 1986, the Holmes Group, an ad hoc group of education deans from research universities, collaborated to develop several recommendations for the improved training of teachers for America's schools.

52. For example, 25 percent of each state's Eisenhower allocation was dedicated to the state agency for higher education for higher education-school/district partnerships.

53. "Secretary Riley, President Unveil 4 New Federal Education Initiatives," *Department of Education Reports,* February 2, 1998, p. 2.

54. The President's FY1999 budget request included $1.1 billion for a class-size reduction initiative.

55. The president's early proposal did include provisions requiring that states implement basic skills testing for new teachers, and that participating states and districts would ensure that those hired to fill new positions be either fully certified or making progress toward full certification.

56. "House Advances Legislation to Reauthorize the Higher Education Act," *Department of Education Reports* 19, no. 11 (1998), 2–6.

57. From a speech delivered February 17, 1998, as reported in "In 'State of American Education' Address, Riley Defends Federal Spending & Public Education," *Department of Education Reports* 19, no. 8 (1998), 1–4.

58. H.R. 2228.

59. S. 1484 (the final Senate bill on the 1998 HEA reauthorization was S. 1182).

60. NCTAF advised states to "develop an annual public report on the status of teaching in the state in relation to the issues . . . raised" and find ways to "close all loopholes that allow for lowering teaching standards." National Commission on Teaching and America's Future (NCTAF), *What Matters Most: Teaching for America's Future* (New York: National Commission on Teaching and America's Future, 1996), pp. 126–127. As ESEA debates got underway in 1998, civil rights and child advocacy organizations lobbied for public report cards not only on student performance outcomes, but also on the inputs—including class size, teacher quality, materials, etc.—in public, particularly urban, schools.

61. Jessica L. Sandham, "Focus on Teacher Preparation, Not Numbers, Panel Hears," *Education Week*, March 4, 1998.

62. Jessica L. Sandham, "House Plan Demands More Data on Teacher Training," *Education Week*, May 6, 1998.

63. The House bill also eliminated funding for the National Board for Professional Teaching Standards (NBPTS) that sets rigorous standards for teacher mastery and recognizes and rewards those who meet the standards as observable examples for others in the profession.

64. Ann Bradley, "Test Questions," *Education Week*, November 25, 1998.

65. Among the Clinton administration priorities for HEA reauthorization were the creation of GEAR UP and two new teacher preparation programs, as well as changes to student aid.

66. "In House, Higher Education Act Would Create 2 New Federal Teaching Programs," *Department of Education Reports* 19, no. 14 (1998), 3–5.

67. This argument had particular resonance with institutions whose teacher candidates received their content training at wholly separate institutions, as in graduate level programs and those programs that accept high numbers of transfer students from other institutions.

68. The U.S. Department of Education, based on states' 2002 reports to the secretary, reports that Florida offers 71 different tests, Oregon and Maryland 51 each, and Iowa 43. Alaska leads in the number of different credentials with 229, and most states offer more than 50 different types of licenses.

69. Sandra Huang, Yun Yi, and Kati Haycock, *Interpret with Caution: The First State Title II Reports on the Quality of Teacher Preparation* (Washington, DC: Education Trust, 2002).

70. Standardized tests continue to be critiqued for their failure to fully describe all that teachers know or are able to accomplish within classrooms; as the National Research Council reports, such tests do not adequately predict classroom success. Similarly, Marilyn Cochran-Smith writes, "Unfortunately, as a number of critics . . . have argued, . . . many current policies and policy recommendations share narrow—and some would say impoverished—notions of teaching and learning that do not account for the complexities that are at the heart of the educational enterprise in a democratic society." Marilyn Cochran-Smith, "The Unforgiving Complexity of Teaching: Avoiding Simplicity in the Age of Accountability," *Journal of Teacher Education* 54, no. 1 (2003), 4.

71. U.S. Department of Education, NCES, "Response to Public Comment on the July 1999 Draft System of Accountability for Programs that Prepare Teachers: Section 207 of the Higher Education Act" (submission to the Office of Management and Budget in Compliance with the Paperwork Reduction Act, January 20, 2000).

72. Amy Wilkins (The Education Trust), as reported by Julie Blair, "Ed. Schools Strain to File Report Cards," *Education Week*, April 4, 2001.

73. National Research Council, *Testing Teaching Candidates: The Role of Licensure Tests in Improving Teacher Quality* (Washington, DC: National Research Council, 2001).

74. Such arguments came in large part after the enactment of the 1998 law and were largely directed to the Department of Education, which was impotent to respond. IHEs of all types (including the historically black colleges and universities [HBCUs], Hispanic-serving institutions, and schools serving high numbers of poor, rural and urban, and first-generation college students) that trained teachers would need to report the pass rates of their teacher candidates.

75. Stephanie Soler, *Teacher Quality Is Job One: Why States Need to Revamp Teacher Certification* (Washington, DC: Progressive Policy Institute, 1999).

76. Representatives of the United Negro College Fund, as well as the nation's more than 100 HBCUs, which traditionally trained the majority of non-white teachers argued that some institutions would be punished (through public shame and sanctions for lower initial pass

rates) for their commitment to serving the underserved. Diversity of America's teachers was at risk. See Antoine M. Garibaldi (1989), "The Revitalization of Teacher Education Programs at Historically Black Colleges: Four Case Studies," In *Recruiting People of Color For Teacher Education,* ed. Judith R. James (Bloomington, IN: Center for Evaluation, Development, and Research, and Phi Delta Kappa, 1993), p. 2. (It should be noted that states like Texas and New York, which already had institutional accountability based on minimum pass rates [and in Texas pass rates by subpopulations], scores on state assessments have increased both in general and for minority students.)

77. See Marci Kanstoroom and Chester E. Finn, Jr., "Better Teachers, Better Schools" (Washington, DC: Fordham Foundation, 1999); Caroline M. Hoxby, "Changing the Profession," *Education Matters,* 1, no. 1 (Spring 2001), 57–63; Frederick M. Hess, "Tear Down this Wall: The Case for a Radical Overhaul of Teacher Certification," *Educational Horizons,* 80, o. 4 (Summer 2002), 169–183.

78. Kanstoroom and Finn, "Better Teachers, Better Schools," p. 8; Thomas J. Laseley, William Bainbridge, and Barnett Berry, "Improving Teacher Quality: Ideological Perspective and Policy Prescriptions," *Educational Forum* 67 (Fall 2002), 14–25.

79. See Sec. 207(a) of the HEA law.

79. Pass rates were generally defined in Sec. 207(f)(1)(A).

80. U.S. Department of Education, *Reference & Reporting Guide for Preparing State and Institutional Reports on the Quality of Teacher Preparation: Title II, Higher Education Act* (Washington, DC: National Center for Education Statistics, 2000), p. 5.

82. To deal with the practical challenge of reporting multiple assessments, the 1999 draft federal guidelines proposed a "categorical rate" to track the performance of the individual on all those assessments required for a given license. However, this rate would have counted as failures those who had not yet taken all requisite tests in the battery (though he might have passed all those taken) the same as it would those who completed the full battery, though unsuccessfully. Needless to say, representatives of the schools of education were not pleased with this solution to the multitest problem. But providing only a single summary pass rate was not a viable solution.

83. Huang, Yi, and Haycock, *Interpret with Caution,* p. 6.

84. U.S. Department of Education, *Reference and Reporting Guide for Preparing State and Institutional Reports on the Quality of Teacher Preparation,* p. 8.

85. Linda Darling-Hammond and Deborah Loewenberg-Ball, *What Can Policymakers Do to Support Teaching to High Standards?* CPRE Policy Bulletin (Philadelphia: Consortium for Policy Research in Education, January 1999), pp. 1–6.

86. Craig Jerald, "All Talk, No Action: Putting an End to Out-of-Field Teaching" (Washington, DC: Education Trust, 2002).

87. Linda Darling-Hammond and Eileen Schlan, "Who Teaches and Why: Dilemmas of Building a Profession for Twenty-First Century Schools," in *Handbook of Research on Teacher Education,* 2nd ed., ed. J. Sikula, T. J. Brittery, and E. Guyton (New York: Macmillan, 1996), pp. 61–101.

88. U.S. Department of Education, *Reference and Reporting Guide,* p. 16.

89. In addition, President Clinton's proposed Teacher Quality Awards would not only have provided financial rewards to school districts making progress in reducing the number of uncertified and out-of-field teachers, it also would have required states to ensure that 95 percent of teachers were certified and teaching in their licensed area by 2004 (White House Education Press Release, January 27, 2000).

90. Erik W. Robelen, "Politics Watch 2000: Accountability," *Education Week on the Web,* available online at http://www.edweek.org/context/politics/pol_accountable.htm

91. The law defines the "highly qualified" teacher as one who: "(A)(i) . . . has obtained full State certification . . . or passed the State teacher licensing examination, and holds a license to teach in such State . . . (ii) . . . has not had certification or licensure requirements waived on an emergency, temporary, or provisional basis" (Sec. 9101(23)).

92. NCLB defines a beginning teacher as an educator who has been teaching for no more than three complete school years. Practicing teachers must also meet the state's "highly qualified" standard with emphasis on holding full certification and demonstrating subject matter competency, but these terms are left to the states to define.

93. U.S. Department of Education, OPE, *Meeting the Highly Qualified Teachers Challenge: The Secretary's Annual Report on Teacher Quality* (Washington, DC: U.S. Department of Education, 2002), p. 34.

94. U.S. Department of Education, *Meeting the Highly Qualified Teachers Challenge*, p. 39.

95. Under Secretary Paige's leadership, the Department of Education made a $5 million grant to the ABCTE in 2002.

96. For example, while California did not report to the Department information on the number of "emergency certified" teachers in the State for the *Initial Report of the Secretary on the Quality of Teacher Preparation* (Washington, DC: U.S. Department of Education, 1999), the data were made widely available by newspapers and education research organizations.

97. Data are from U.S. Department of Education, OPE, *Initial Report of the Secretary on the Quality of Teacher Preparation*. They are based on states' own definitions and existing data.

98. Data are from U.S. Department of Education, *Meeting the Highly Qualified Teachers Challenge*.

99. U.S. Department of Education, *Meeting the Highly Qualified Teachers Challenge*.

100. Data are from the National Research Council, Committee on Assessment and Teacher Quality, Board on Testing and Assessment, "Tests and Teaching Quality: Interim Report" (Washington, DC: National Research Council, 2002). Additional reports indicate that 38 states have basic skills tests, 31 have subject-matter assessments, 28 assess pedagogical knowledge, and seven require assessments subject-specific pedagogical knowledge for initial teacher licensure.

101. NASDTEC (1996) reported that 31 states required tests of subject-matter knowledge for initial teacher licensure.

102. The Education Trust reports 41 states.

103. The Education Trust reports 41 states based on their review of the Secretary's 2002 report.

104. Huang, Yi, and Haycock, *Interpret with Caution*.

105. Bess Keller, "States Claim Teachers Are 'Qualified,'" *Education Week*, October 29, 2003.

106. R. Mitchell and P. Barth, *How Teacher Licensure Tests Fall Short* (Washington, DC: Education Trust, 1999), p. 15.

107. U.S. Department of Education, Office of Postsecondary Education, *Meeting the Highly Qualified Teachers Challenge: The Secretary's Annual Report on Teacher Quality*.

108. The NASBE Study Group on Coordination and Accountability in Teacher Education reports that, "In general, high-quality teacher preparation programs are those that link components of teacher candidate experience—across higher education and K–12 clinical experiences and across education and arts and sciences coursework—and that insist upon high standards in knowledge and practice among their graduates." National Association of State Boards of Education (NASBE), *The Full Circle: Building a Coherent Teacher Preparation System* (Alexandria, VA: National Association of State Boards of Education, 2000), p. 6.

109. As Huang et al. write, "Requiring undergraduates to pass these tests prior to program completion is one way to assure that a teaching degree means something." But "reporting pass rates in these circumstances reveal(s) nothing about how many aspiring graduates took the tests but failed. As a result, the burden of accountability shifts away from the institution

and falls completely on the shoulders of the individual." Huang, Yun, and Haycock, *Interpret with Caution*, p. 7.

110. These can be attributed to reform efforts, as well as an economic downturn, which slowed the rate of departure from and brought others back to the profession, and severe budget cuts across states and districts, which have limited the number of available teaching positions.

111. U.S. Department of Education, "Teacher Quality: A Report on the Preparation and Qualifications of Public School Teachers" (Washington, DC: Author, 1999).

## CHAPTER 3

1. The number of states that have instituted some type of alternative program has increased dramatically, only 18 states having formal alternative programs in 1986. Jianping Shen, "Alternative Certification: A Complicated Research Topic," *Educational Evaluation and Policy Analysis* 20, no. 4 (1997); but by 2002, 45 states plus the District of Columbia have such programs. C. Emily Feistritzer and David T. Chester, *Alternative Teacher Certification: A State-by-State Analysis* (Washington, DC: National Center for Education Information, 2002).

2. Some estimates project that the teacher labor force will increase from 3.30 million teachers in 1999 to around 3.65 million in 2011. Debra E. Gerald, "Elementary and Secondary Teachers," in *Projection of Education Statistics to 2011* (Washington, DC: U.S. Department of Education, National Center for Education Statistics, 2002).

3. For more information on alternative licensure requirements, see Feistritzer and Chester, *Alternative Teacher Certification*.

4. Feistritzer and Chester, *Alternative Teacher Certification*.

5. For example, in 2002, 11 states required teachers to have majored in education while 13 other states require non-education degrees. Thirty-three states require that teachers take a subject matter exam to obtain a teaching certificate, only 13 states require teachers to take a general knowledge exam, and 16 states require that teacher candidates have some previous teaching performance of theirs assessed and submitted to state or school officials. *The NASDTEC Manual on the Preparation and Certification of Educational Personnel*, 6th ed. (Sacramento, CA: National Association of State Directors of Teachers Education and Certification, 2002). See Table B-4 and Table B-2.

6. For more on the debate over states' role in licensure, see, for example, *The Teachers We Need and How to Get More of Them: A Manifesto* [website] (Washington, DC: Thomas B. Fordham Foundation, 1999), retrieved September 11, 2003 from http://www.edexcellence.net/library/teacher.html; National Commission on Teaching and America's Future (U.S.), *What Matters Most: Teaching for America's Future—A Report of the National Commission on Teaching and America's Future*, 1st ed. (Woodbridge, VA: Author, 1996); Catherine Walsh, "Teacher Certification Reconsidered: Stumbling for Quality" (Baltimore: Abell Foundation, 2001); and Linda Darling-Hammond, "The Research and Rhetoric on Teacher Certification: A Response to 'Teacher Certification Reconsidered'" (Washington, DC: National Commission on Teaching and America's Future, 2001).

7. For a discussion of licensure, see Stuart Dorsey, "The Occupational Licensing Queue," *Journal of Human Resources* 15, no. 3 (1980); Martin Haberman, "Licensing Teachers: Lessons from Other Professions," *Phi Delta Kappan* 67, no. 10 (1986); Morris M. Kleiner, "Occupational Licensing," *Journal of Economic Perspectives* 14, no. 4 (2000); or M. Stephen Lilly, "Research on Teacher Licensure and State Approval of Teacher Education Programs," *Teacher Education and Special Education* 15, no. 2 (1992). Although licensure and certification are often used interchangeably in discussion of the teacher labor market, these are actually distinct concepts. Licensure refers to a set of standards and a process, defined by some level of government, that governs entry into an occupation, and it is illegal for individuals who do not

hold a license to perform specified tasks in that profession. Certification, by contrast, refers to a set of standards maintained by a profession or government agency that individuals in that profession may or may not choose to meet, and consumers of a product or service can decide whether or not to hire certified individuals to perform a task. Kleiner, "Occupational Licensing."

8. As described below, the hiring preferences of private and charter schools do provide some insight into which teacher characteristics are valued by school officials in a less restrictive regulatory environment.

9. Since individuals must meet some requirements prior to employment in teaching (typically they must hold at least a baccalaureate degree and meet a testing requirement), alternative licensure does not represent the total deregulation of the teacher labor market envisioned by some free market advocates, but it does represent a reduction of state-level regulation.

10.   Feistritzer and Chester, *Alternative Teacher Certification*, p. 9. Chester E. Finn, Jr., and Kathleen Madigan, "Removing the Barriers for Teacher Candidates," *Educational Leadership* 58, no. 8 (2001), for instance, wonder, "How many eager, able, nontraditional teacher candidates . . . do we lose because of our system of hoops and hurdles and red tape? How many gifted teachers do we lose because they throw up their hands in despair at the obstacles, costs, and coursework between them and the classroom?" (p. 29).

11. Linda Darling-Hammond, "Teaching and Knowledge: Policy Issues Posed by Alternate Certification for Teachers," *Peabody Journal of Education* 67, no. 3 (1990); Linda Darling-Hammond, "What Matters Most: A Competent Teacher for Every Child," *Phi Delta Kappan* 78, no. 3 (1996). As an example, Linda Darling-Hammond, "Who Will Speak for the Children? How 'Teach For America' Hurts Urban Schools and Students," *Phi Delta Kappan* 76, no. 1 (1994), argues in the context of Teach For America (TFA), probably the best-known alternative program, that TFA "is bad for the recruits because they are ill-prepared. . . . The schools don't get the help they need, and more lasting solutions are not pursued. It is bad for the children because they are often poorly taught. . . . Finally, TFA is bad for teaching. By clinging to faulty assumptions about what teachers need to know and by producing so many teaching failures, it undermines the profession's efforts to raise standards and create accountability" (p. 33).

12. Since teachers serve many different roles, the term *teacher quality* may mean different things to different people. However, this term can for the moment be left ambiguous, since the analysis presented below is unaffected by the meaning of the term.

13. See Table B-1 in *The NASDTEC Manual on the Preparation and Certification of Educational Personnel*.

14. See Table B-1 in *The NASDTEC Manual on the Preparation and Certification of Educational Personnel*.

15. The more closely the two are related, the narrower the mound will be and it will lie on a diagonal line. If the two have no correlation between them, the mound will be a symmetric cone centered at the origin.

16. Individuals outside of the teacher work force frequently cite licensure requirements as a reason for not seeking a teaching job, and only a minority of Teach For America teachers report that they would have chosen to pursue a job in teaching if they had been required to enter the profession through a traditional route. Dale Ballou and Michael Podgursky, "Gaining Control of Professional Licensing and Advancement," in *Conflicting Missions? Teachers Unions and Educational Reform*, ed. Tom Loveless (Washington, DC: Brookings Institution Press, 2000).

17. Kleiner, "Occupational Licensing."

18. Arthur E. Wise, "We Need More Than a Redesign," *Educational Leadership* 49, no. 3 (1991), for instance, argues that "[t]here can never be a profession of teaching until the public has reason to trust teachers, and that trust will not develop until all teachers are well educated and carefully licensed" (p. 7).

19. Frederick M. Hess, "Tear Down This Wall: The Case for a Radical Overhaul of Teacher Certification" (Washington, DC: Progressive Policy Institute, 2001).

20. See Dan D. Goldhaber and Albert Yung-Hsu Liu, "Occupational Choices and the Academic Proficiency of the Teacher Workforce," in *Developments in School Finance 2001–02*, ed. William J. Fowler, Jr. (Washington, DC: National Center for Education Statistics, 2003), for more discussion of the academic proficiency of teachers versus other college graduates.

21. The case for licensure, in general, is stronger if the consumers of a product lack the knowledge necessary to make informed choices about the product.

22. For more information on occupational licensure, see Kleiner, "Occupational Licensing."

23. For reviews of this literature, see Dan D. Goldhaber, "Teacher Quality and Student Achievement" (New York: Teachers College Institute for Urban and Minority Education ERIC Clearinghouse on Urban Education, 2003); Rob Greenwald, Larry V. Hedges, and Richard Laine, "The Effect of School Resources on Student Achievement," *Review of Educational Research* 66, no. 3 (1996); Erik A. Hanushek, "The Economics of Schooling: Production and Efficiency in Public Schools," *Journal of Economic Literature* 24, no. 3 (1986); and Eric A. Hanushek, "Assessing the Effects of School Resources on Student Performance: An Update," *Educational Evaluation and Policy Analysis* 19, no. 2 (1997).

24. For example, Dan D. Goldhaber, Dominic J. Brewer, and Deborah J. Anderson, "A Three-Way Error Components Analysis of Educational Productivity," *Education Economics* 7, no. 3 (1999), find that teacher effects accounted for approximately 8.5 percent of the variation in students' tenth grade achievement; and Erik A. Hanushek, John F. Kain, and Steven G. Rivkin, "Inferring Program Effects for Special Populations: Does Special Education Raise Achievement for Students with Disabilities?" *Review of Economics and Statistics* 84, no. 4 (2002), estimate that teacher effects account for a minimum of 4 percent of the variation in students' achievement in elementary grades.

25. A meta-analysis is a study that examines whether there are systematic patterns in results from a group of studies conducted on the same topic (that all meet certain criteria defined by those conducting the meta-analysis). For examples of some meta-analyses linking schooling attributes to student achievement, see Rob Greenwald, Larry V. Hedges, and Richard Laine, "Interpreting Research on School Resources and Student Achievement: A Rejoinder to Hanushek," *Review of Educational Research* 66, no. 3 (1996); Hanushek, "The Economics of Schooling"; Hanushek, "Assessing the Effects of School Resources on Student Performance"; Larry V. Hedges, Richard Laine, and Rob Greenwald, "Does Money Matter? A Meta-Analysis of Studies of the Effects of Differential School Inputs on Student Outcomes (an Exchange: Part 1)," *Educational Researcher* 23, no. 3 (1994); and Richard D. Laine, Rob Greenwald, and Larry V. Hedges, "Money Does Matter: A Research Synthesis of a New Universe of Education Production Function Studies," in *Where Does the Money Go? Resource Allocation in Elementary and Secondary Schools*, ed. Lawrence O. Picus and James L. Wattenbarger (Newbury Park, CA: Corwin Press, 1995).

26. Hanushek, "The Economics of Schooling," p. 1162.

27. Rob Greenwald, Larry V. Hedges, and Richard D. Laine, "The Effect of School Resources on Student Achievement," *Review of Educational Research* 66, no. 3 (1996), 384.

28. See, for example, Dan Goldhaber, "The Mystery of Good Teaching," *Education Next* 2, no. 1 (2002), for a review.

29. See, for example, Ronald F. Ferguson, "Paying for Public Education: New Evidence on How and Why Money Matters," *Harvard Journal on Legislation* 28, no. 2 (1991); Ronald F. Ferguson and Helen F. Ladd, "How and Why Money Matters: An Analysis of Alabama Schools," in *Holding Schools Accountable: Performance-Based Reform in Education,* ed. Helen F. Ladd (Washington, DC: Brookings Institution, 1996); Robert P. Strauss and Elizabeth A. Sawyer, "Some New Evidence on Teacher and Student Competencies," *Economics of Education Review* 5, no. 1 (1986); and Robert P. Strauss and William B. Vogt, "It's What You Know, Not How You Learned to Teach It: Evidence from a Study of the Effects of Knowledge and Pedagogy on Student Achievement" (paper presented at the American Educational Finance Association Conference, Cincinnati, 2001).

30. See, for example, Anita A. Summers and Barbara L. Wolfe, "Which School Resources Help Learning? Efficiency and Equality in Philadelphia Public Schools" (Philadelphia: Federal Reserve Bank of Philadelphia, Department of Research, 1975); and Ronald G. Ehrenberg and Dominic J. Brewer, "Do School and Teacher Characteristics Matter? Evidence from High School and Beyond," *Economics of Education Review* 13, no. 1 (1994).

31. Although several studies have been published since their 1996 meta-analysis, Greenwald et al. found a total of only 12 studies that analyzed the effects of teacher academic proficiency on student achievement. Greenwald, Hedges, and Laine, "The Effect of School Resources on Student Achievement." See Table 1.

32. National Research Council (U.S.), *Testing Teacher Candidates: The Role of Licensure Tests in Improving Teacher Quality,* Committee on Assessment and Teacher Quality, Karen J. Mitchell et al., eds., Board on Testing and Assessment, Center for Education, Division on Behavioral and Social Sciences and Education (Washington, DC: National Academy Press, 2001), p. 122.

33. Carolyn M. Evertson, Willis D. Hawley, and Marilyn Zlotnik, "Making a Difference in Educational Quality through Teacher Education," *Journal of Teacher Education* 36, no. 3 (1985), pp. 2, 3, 8.

34. Walsh, "Teacher Certification Reconsidered."

35. For example, Linda Darling-Hammond, Barnett Berry, and Amy Thoreson, "Does Teacher Certification Matter? Evaluating the Evidence," *Educational Evaluation and Policy Analysis* 23, no. 1 (2001), wrote that the Abell report "dismissed or misreported much of the existing evidence in order to argue that teacher education makes no difference to teacher performance or student learning, and that students would be better off without state efforts to regulate entry into teaching or to provide supports for teachers' learning" (p. 60). A rejoinder by the Abell Foundation to Darling-Hammond refutes this assertion. See Catherine Walsh, "Teacher Certification Reconsidered: A Rejoinder" (Baltimore: Abell Foundation, 2001).

36. Andrew J. Wayne and Peter Youngs, "Teacher Characteristics and Student Achievement Gains: A Review," *Review of Educational Research* 73, no. 1 (2003). A related issue is whether graduates who attend an accredited teacher-preparation program, and as a consequence of attending such a program, are more effective teachers. The literature on this question is also sparse, as is pointed out in a recent report by the Education Commission of the States. See Michael B. Allen, "Eight Questions on Teacher Preparation: What Does the Research Say?" (Denver: Education Commission of the States, 2003).

37. Dan Goldhaber and Dominic Brewer, "Does Teacher Certification Matter? High School Teacher Certification Status and Student Achievement," *Educational Evaluation and Policy Analysis* 22, no. 2 (2000).

38. Emergency certification can be issued to teachers who have not satisfied all of the requirements necessary to obtain a standard certificate.

39. Robert P. Strauss et al., "Who Should Teach in Our Public Schools? Implications of Pennsylvania's Teacher Preparation and Selection Experience" (paper presented at the American Education Finance Association Conference, Mobile, AL, 1998).

40. Donald Boyd et al., "Analyzing the Determinants of the Matching of Public School Teachers to Jobs" (Albany: State University of New York, Rockefeller Institute of Government, 2002).

41. The hiring of employees proximate to their hometowns in education may also be consistent with general labor market trends.

42. Dale Ballou, "Do Public Schools Hire the Best Applicants?" *Quarterly Journal of Economics* 111, no. 1 (1996).

43. Edward Liu, "New Teachers' Experiences of Hiring: Preliminary Findings from a Four-State Study" (paper presented at the annual meeting of the American Educational Research Association, Chicago, 2003).

44. Ashindi Maxton, email communication, October 8, 2003.

45. National Research Council (U.S.), *Testing Teacher Candidates*, ch. 5.

46. For more on the "importance" of teacher role models, see Jacqueline Jordan Irvine, "Making Teacher Education Culturally Responsive," in *Diversity in Teacher Education: New Expectations*, ed. Mary E. Dilworth (San Francisco: Jossey-Bass, 1992); Beatrice Chu Clewell and Ana Maria Villegas, "Introduction," *Education and Urban Society* 31, no. 1 (1998); J. T. Zapata, "Early Identification and Recruitment of Hispanic Teacher Candidates," *Journal of Teacher Education* 39, no. 1 (1988); Ronald F. Ferguson, "Can Schools Narrow the Black-White Test Score Gap?" in *The Black-White Test Score Gap*, ed. Meredith Phillips (Washington, DC: Brookings Institution, 1998); or Ronald G. Ehrenberg, Dan D. Goldhaber, and Dominic J. Brewer, "Do Teachers Race, Gender, and Ethnicity Matter? Evidence from the National Educational Longitudinal Study of 1988," *Industrial and Labor Relations Review* 48, no. 3 (1995).

47. Suzanne M. Wilson, Robert E. Floden, and Joan Ferrini-Mundy, "Teacher Preparation Research: Current Knowledge, Gaps, and Recommendations" (Seattle: University of Washington, Center for the Study of Teaching and Policy, 2001).

48. Of course over the long run one would not only want to know how effective alternative and traditionally licensed teachers are, but also how long each tends to remain in the profession (or in a particular school district) and the costs associated with replacing them when they leave.

49. It is important to note, however, that it's quite difficult for researchers to actually access these state data due to restrictions like the Family Educational Rights and Privacy Act.

50. The challenge of accurately defining the relevant alternative is nicely illustrated by a debate over a recent study using data from Houston, Texas, on the relative effectiveness of Teach For America (TFA) teachers, which suggests that TFA teachers are slightly more effective than new non-TFA teachers and about as effective as the average teacher in the district. However, critics have suggested that the "pro-TFA" results stem at least in part from the comparison made between TFA teachers and a mix of licensed and many unlicensed teachers. The implication is that TFA teachers would not look good relative to fully licensed teachers. What then, is the right comparison group? Imagine, for instance, that TFA teachers are found to be more effective than a mix of licensed and unlicensed teachers, but found to be less effective than a comparison group of fully licensed teachers (I don't believe this comparison has been made). The conclusion one draws from these findings depends on what the alternative to hiring a TFA teacher is in Houston. See Margaret E. Raymond and Stephen Fletcher, "Teach for America: An Evaluation of Teacher Differences and Student Outcomes in Houston, Texas," *Education Next* 2, no. 1 (2001). For an example of criticism of the Raymond and Fletcher TFA study, see "Facts to Consider about Teach For America: An Evaluation of Teacher Differences and Student Outcomes in Houston, Texas" [Electronic

Bulletin of National Commission on Teaching and America's Future], *Focus on Teaching Quality*, retrieved October 9, 2003.

51. This is the strategy that is employed in the study, Ballou, "Do Public Schools Hire the Best Applicants?"

52. For more detail on this issue, see Goldhaber, Brewer, and Anderson, "A Three-Way Error Components Analysis of Educational Productivity."

53. Research by Catherine Minter Hoxby, "Would School Choice Change the Teaching Profession?" *Journal of Human Resources* 37, no. 4 (2002), 846–891; and Dale Ballou and Michael Podgursky, *Teacher Pay and Teacher Quality* (Kalamazoo, MI: W. E. Upjohn Institute for Employment Research, 1997), shows that private and charter schools do in fact tend to employ teachers with different characteristics than do public schools.

## CHAPTER 4

1. In addition, schools of education can improve the quality of teachers through the recruitment of qualified candidates to apply for the teacher preparation program. As Gitomer and Latham pointed out, simply raising standards may be counterproductive unless a sufficient number of talented individuals can be convinced to apply. This issue is beyond the scope of the paper, but there is already much discussion in the academic and policy worlds about how to increase the attractions of the education profession. Drew H. Gitomer and Andrew S. Latham, "Generalization in Teacher Education: Seductive and Misleading," *Journal of Teacher Education* 51 (2000), 215–220.

2. The average reported minimum GPA was 2.86, which is almost exactly between a B and B-minus average on most scales. Only one respondent did not report a minimum GPA.

3. The respondents listed a variety of different tests, ranging from national exams (GRE, Praxis) to state-specific exams. Not enough data were received for any category to create meaningful summary statistics.

4. Several respondents wrote in the margins that teachers are not "trained" but "prepared."

5. "The old, old contention that professional education courses are cotton candy. There are many explanations for this frequently observed phenomenon, most of which are never given."

6. Website of the National Conference of Bar Examiners, http://www.ncbex.org/stats/pdf/2002stats.pdf

7. The numbers do not add up to 100 because some respondents did not provide answers that totaled 100 percent.

8. Jianping Shen, *The School of Education: Its Mission, Faculty, and Reward Structure* (New York: Peter Lang, 1999).

9. Several respondents wrote in the margins that the question was not well written. I agree that the "negative" phrasing was not ideal, and I should probably have begun the statement with "We think that test scores . . ." There is, therefore, the possibility that some respondents, if they did not read the question carefully, may have marked answers that did not correspond with their beliefs.

## CHAPTER 5

1. Ms. Rozen provided invaluable research assistance throughout the preparation of this paper. Further, as a scholar of reading instruction and director of reading and literacy for a public school district, Ms. Rozen served as first reviewer and commentator on the syllabi in that field. I would like to thank in addition colleagues from the School of Education at Boston University who gave most generously of their time and expertise. Dean Douglas Sears, who

served as Superintendent of the Chelsea Public School District, offered his own uniquely informed perspective on the failings of schools of education. Professor Stephan Ellenwood very kindly discussed his model of good methods courses. All responsibility for the text remains with me.

2. TIMSS, *Trends in Math and Science Achievement Around the World,* available online at Timss.bc.edu/Timss/1999.html; National Assessment of Educational Progress (NAEP), *The Nation's Report Card* (Washington, DC: U.S. Department of Education, National Center for Education Statistics), available online at http://nces.ed.gov/nationsreportcard/.

3. For an extended presentation and analysis of this data, see Christopher Jencks and Meredith Phillips, eds., *The Black-White Test Score Gap* (Washington, DC: Brookings Institution Press, 1998).

4. E. D. Hirsch, Jr., *The Schools We Need* (New York: Doubleday, 1996); Chester Finn, Jr., *We Must Take Charge: Our Schools and Our Future* (New York: Macmillan, 1991); Diane Ravitch, *Left Back: A Century of Failed School Reforms* (New York: Simon & Schuster, 2000).

5. Richard Riley, *Meeting the Highly Qualified Teachers Challenge: The Secretary's Annual Report on Teacher Quality* (Washington, DC: U.S. Department of Education, Office of Postsecondary Education, 1999).

6. This paragraph paraphrases sections from Aubrey Wang, Ashaki Coleman, Richard Coley, and Richard Phelps, *Preparing Teachers around the World* (Princeton, NJ: Educational Testing Service, 2003). This study offers a fine and concise summary of American teacher preparation.

7. For details of NCATE's involvement at the state level, please see Appendix B.

8. NCATE is one of two national professional accrediting agencies for schools and colleges of education. The other is TEAC (Teacher Education Accreditation Council), which has just received federal approval as an accrediting agency.

9. National Council for Accreditation of Teacher Education (NCATE), *Professional Standards for the Accreditation of Schools, Colleges and Departments of Education* (Washington, DC: Author, 2002), p. 3; available online at http://www.ncate.org/2000/unit_stnds_2002.pdf.

10. NCATE, *Professional Standards for the Accreditation of Schools,* p. 23.

11. NCATE, *Professional Standards for the Accreditation of Schools,* p. 19.

13. NCATE, *Professional Standards for the Accreditation of Schools,* p. 19.

14. Linda Darling-Hammond's 1999 study, *Teacher Quality and Student Achievement: A Review of State Policy Evidence* (Seattle: University of Washington, Center for the Study of Teaching and Policy), is itself the subject of scholarly debate. See, for example, page seven of Grover J. Whitehurst, *Research on Teacher Preparation and Professional Development,* paper presented at the White House Conference on Preparing Tomorrow's Teachers, 2002, p. 7; retrieved July 12, 2003, from http://www.nctq.org/press/whitehurst.html, downloaded 7/12/2003.

15. NCATE, *Professional Standards for the Accreditation of Schools,* note 8.

16. John Stone, "Value-Added Assessment: An Accountability Revolution," in *Better Teachers, Better Schools,* ed. Marci Kanstoroom and Chester E. Finn, Jr. (Washington, DC: Thomas B. Fordham Foundation, 1999).

17. Suzanne Wilson, Robert Floden, and Joan Ferrini-Mundy, *Teacher Preparation Research: Current Knowledge, Gaps, and Recommendations* (Seattle: University of Washington, Center for the Study of Teaching and Policy, in collaboration with Michigan State University, 2001), p. 32.

18. Of the studies on teacher preparation we consulted, the most thorough is Wilson, Floden, and Ferrini-Mundy, *Teacher Preparation Research.* Suzanne Wilson and Robert Floden also wrote a follow-up text, *Creating Effective Teachers: Concise Answers for Hard Questions,* an addendum to the earlier report. We consulted another study cited in this research: Kenneth

Zeichner, Lynne Miller, and David Silvernail, "Preparation in the Undergraduate Years," in *Studies of Excellence in Teacher Education,* ed. Linda Darling-Hammond (New York: AACTE, 2000). Many reports on schools of education are based on the self-reporting of those to be studied, or were focused on too small a sample size to be of use for policy purposes. Wilson, Floden, and Ferrini-Mundy, in *Teacher Preparation Research,* make this point repeatedly.

19. The Tennessee Value-Added Assessment System (TVAAS) has been around since the late 1980s, and since 1995 it has been enlarged to produce value-added teacher effectiveness data for review by principals, and other school system personnel. TVAAS has shown us that it is possible to measure the value that a teacher adds to the performance of his or her students, but many teachers do not accept that test scores represent a fair way to evaluate their teaching. According to Public Agenda polling (www.publicagenda.org), three-quarters of all teachers think it is a bad idea to link their compensation to their students' performance.

20. Michael Allen, *Eight Questions on Teacher Preparation: What Does the Research Say?* (Denver: Education Commission of the States, 2000), available online at http://www.ecs.org/report; Darling-Hammond, *Teacher Quality and Student Achievement;* Linda Darling-Hammond, *The Research and Rhetoric on Teacher Certification: A Response to "Teacher Certification Reconsidered"* (Washington, DC: National Commission on Teaching and America's Future, 2001), available online at http://www.teacherscollege.edu/nctaf/publications; Dan Goldhaber and Dominic Brewer, "Evaluating the Evidence on Teacher Certification: A Rejoinder," *Educational Evaluation and Policy Analysis* 23, no. 1 (Spring, 2001), 76–86; Catherine Walsh, *Teacher Certification Reconsidered: Stumbling for Quality* (Baltimore: Abell Foundation, October 2001); Catherine Walsh, *Teacher Certification Reconsidered: Stumbling for Quality—A Rejoinder* (Baltimore: Abell Foundation, November, 2001), available online at http://www.able.org/pubsitems/ed_cert_rejoinder_1101.pdf; Harold Wenglinsky, *How Teaching Matters* (Princeton, NJ: Educational Testing Service, 2000); Whitehurst, *Research on Teacher Preparation and Professional Development;* Wilson and Floden, *Creating Effective Teachers;* Wilson, Floden, and Ferrini-Mundy, *Teacher Preparation Research.*

21. Goldhaber and Brewer, *Evaluating the Evidence on Teacher Certification;* Dan Goldhaber and Dominic Brewer, "Does Teacher Certification Matter?" *Education Evaluation and Policy Analysis* 22, no. 2 (2000), 129–145; Julia Koppich and Katherine Merseth, "Preparation in a Five-year Program," *Studies of Excellence in Teacher Education,* ed. Linda Darling-Hammond (New York: AACTE, 2000).

22. Linda Darling-Hammond, Ruth Chung, and Fred Frelow (with Heidi Fisher), "Variation in Teacher Preparation: How Well Do Different Pathways Prepare Teachers to Teach?" *Journal of Teacher Education* 53, no. 4 (September/October 2002), available at http://www.nctaf.org/publications/NYC_Teacher_Survey_Study.pdf. It is Linda Darling-Hammond who makes the case for the importance of pedagogical course work (Darling-Hammond, *Teacher Quality*). Interested readers should certainly review her report. Once again, there are a series of exchanges between Darling-Hammond and critics of her work. See, for example, Catherine Walsh, *Stumbling for Quality* and *Stumbling for Quality—A Rejoinder.* Whitehurst writes that "the aggregation bias may account for Darling-Hammond's estimates of the effects of certification being light years out of the range of effects that have been reported by all other studies of the topic"; Whitehurst, *Research on Teacher Preparation,* p. 7.

23. Ken Howey and Nancy Zimpher, *Profiles of Preservice Teacher Education: Inquiry into the Nature of Programs* (Albany: State University of New York Press, 1989); Peter Smagorinsky and Melissa Whiting, *How English Teachers Get Taught: Methods of Teaching the Methods Class* (Urbana, IL: NCTE, 1995); Pamela Grossman and Anna Richert, "Unacknowledged Knowledge Growth: A Re-Examination of the Effects of Teacher Education," *Teachers and Teacher Education* 4 (1988), 53–56.

24. The question of whether teachers who graduate from schools of education are more effective is a highly political one: most of the reports we reviewed indicated very little reliable evidence that attending such a school made a major positive difference. However, specific studies focused on subject matter preparation do offer some important findings.

25. NAEP results for 2002 (U.S. Department of Education, National Center for Education Statistics); PISA, the OECD Programme for International Student Assessment, results from 2000, as analyzed in *Learners for Life: Student Approaches to Learning* (city?: Organisation of Economic Co-operation and Development, 2003), available online at http://www1.oecd.org/publications/e-book/9603101E.PDF.

26. Education Commission of the States, "Comprehensive School Reform: Identifying Effective Models" (ECS document #AN–98–3, 1998).

27. We take issue with critics of this approach who dismiss course syllabi as "ideological portraits." It is enough to secure validity for our approach that professors take trouble over the design of their syllabi, care about which books and articles are to be read, are serious about how the knowledge of their students is to be assessed, and are concerned about how student teachers are supervised and evaluated in their first teaching experience. Would the professors who critique our use of syllabi wish their own students to share their views? The charge that syllabi should not be taken seriously can be found in "Education School Courses Faulted as Intellectually Thin," *Education Week,* November 12, 2003.

28. In the original paper on which this chapter is based, we included a review of Mathematics Methods syllabi. We stand by those findings, but believe that a full account of the preparation of mathematics teachers must include a review of their content courses —work that we intend to complete in the future. We would also like to include preparation in special education and civics, together with the core or general education requirements that all students (including student teachers) are required to take.

29. We have over 50 syllabi that we have read, but did not include. Our broader conclusions about our sample set are informed by the knowledge of these syllabi, and the fact that they do not offer contra-positive evidence to our findings.

30. Issues of confidentiality concerning syllabi not placed on the web limit the degree to which we could report disaggregated data.

31. To the extent that we identify as missing certain texts that come from a "conservative" point of view, this has to do with the fact that we found evidence in the syllabi that texts from a progressive or constructivist viewpoint were already required reading.

32. Those who maintain that a particular educational philosophy or methodology undermines good teaching will certainly want to argue that foundation courses based on the "wrong" approach can do harm. While we do offer evidence in the reading methods section that some teaching methods have strong empirical support, we suggest that students in foundations courses will benefit from exposure to the best thinking from different points of view.

33. David Tyack and Larry Cuban, *Tinkering Towards Utopia: A Century of Public School Reform* (Cambridge, MA: Harvard University Press, 1995).

34. James Noll, *Taking Sides* (Guilford, CT: Dushkin/McGraw-Hill, 2001).

35. In one of these three, the primary teacher program did not include such a course, but the secondary program did so.

36. Available at http://education.indiana.edu/~tep/elemed/theory.html. Available at http://education.indiana.edu/~tep/elemed/theory.html. For three major topics that the course covers—"What is Higher Education?", "Quality and Education," and "Understanding and Engagement"—Pirsig's novel is the only reading.

37. Anita Woolfolk, *Educational Psychology* (Boston: Allyn & Bacon, 2001).

38. Woolfolk, *Educational Psychology,* p. 277.

39. Woolfolk, *Educational Psychology*, p. 57.
40. We reviewed the syllabi in the Stanford preparation program that were relevant to our domains. In our judgment, the suggested readings strongly embody a constructivist methodology and a particular vision of multiculturalism. The books are by Deborah Meier, Howard Gardner, Jeannie Oakes, and Linda Darling-Hammond, Vivian Paley, Guadalupe Valdes and Laurie Olson, Paulo Freire, William Ayers, and John Dewey. The exceptions are works by Stanford professor David Tyack.
41. See, for example, E. D. Hirsch's talk presented to the California State Board of Education, available at http://ourworld.compuserve.com/homepages/mathman/edh?cal.htm
42. NAEP results for 2002, National Center for Educational Statistics, at or above proficient, accommodations permitted: grade 4, 31 percent; grade 8, 33 percent; grade 12, 36 percent.
43. Louisa Cook Moats and G. Reid Lyon, "Wanted: Teachers with Knowledge of Language," *Topics in Language Disorders* 16, 2 (February 1996), 73–86.
44. Marilyn Adams, *Beginning to Read: Thinking and Learning about Print* (Cambridge, MA: MIT Press, 1990); Louisa C. Moats, *Speech to Print* (Baltimore: Brookes, 2000); David Laberge and Jay Samuels, "Toward a Theory of Automatic Information Processing in Reading," in *Theoretical Models and Processes of Reading*, ed. Harry Singer and Robert Ruddell (Newark, DE: International Reading Association, 1976); Louisa Moats, *Teaching Reading Is Rocket Science: What Expert Teachers of Reading Should Know and Be Able to Do* (Washington, DC: American Federation of Teachers, 1999); Charles Perfetti, *Reading Ability* (New York: Oxford University Press, 1985); David Rumelhart, "Toward an Interactive Model of Reading," in *Attention and Performance, VI*, ed. Stanislav Dornic (Hillsdale, NJ: Erlbaum, 1977); Keith Stanovich, *Progress in Understanding Reading: Scientific Foundations and New Frontier* (New York: Guilford Press, 2000); Sally Shaywitz, *Overcoming Dyslexia: A New and Complete Science Based Program for Overcoming Reading Problems at Any Level*, 1st ed. (New York: Knopf, 2003).
45. National Reading Panel, *Teaching Children to Read: An Evidence-Based Assessment of the Scientific Research Literature on Reading and Its Implications for Reading Instruction* (Bethesda, MD: National Institute of Child Health and Human Development, 2000); National Research Council, Catherine Snow, Susan Burns, and Peg Griffin, eds., *Preventing Reading Difficulties in Young Children* (Washington, DC: National Research Council, 1998; hereafter cited as Snow, Burns, and Griffin, *Preventing Reading Difficulties*).
46. Amy Seely Flint, Christine Leland, Beth Patterson, James Hoffman, Misty Sailors, Mary Mast, and Lori Czop Assaf, "'I'm still figuring out how to do this teaching thing': A Cross-Site Analysis of Reading Preparation Programs on Beginning Teachers' Instructional Practices and Decisions," in *Learning to Teach Reading: Setting the Research Agenda*, ed. Cathy M. Roller (Newark, NJ: IRA, 2001), pp. 100–118.
47. Flint et al., *A Cross-Site Analysis*, p. 114.
48. After years of debate, the term *whole language* has come to mean somewhat different things to different scholars. The term is, however, still very much in use. For a definition that offers a useful general definition, see http://www.indiana.edu/~eric_rec/ieo/bibs/whole.html.
49. For a good definition of the balanced approach, see Michael Pressley, *Reading Instruction that Works: The Case for Balanced Teaching* (London: Guilford Press, 1998).
50. Snow, Burns, and Griffin, *Preventing Reading Difficulties*, p. 198.
51. For an example, see Gay Su Pinnell and Irene Fountas, *Phonics Lessons: Letters, Words and How They Work, for Grades K–2* (Portsmouth, NH: Heinemann, 2003).
52. Snow, Burns, and Griffin, *Preventing Reading Difficulties*.
53. See the National Reading Panel, *Teaching Children to Read*, and Sally Shaywitz, *Overcoming Dyslexia*, for a discussion of this research.

54. Reid Lyon, "Reading Development, Difficulties and Intervention," tape #6804, *Learning and the Brain,* presented at the conference entitled Using Brain Research to Reach All Learners, May 9–11, 2002, Fleetwood On Site conference Recording, available at www.Fltwood.com/onsite/brain.

55. Michael Pressley, "What Should Comprehension Instruction Be the Instruction of?" in *Handbook of Reading Research,* vol. 3, ed. Michael Kamil et al. (Mahwah, NJ: Lawrence Erlbaum, 2000), pp. 545–561.

56. Marilyn Adams, Barbara Foorman, Ingvar Lundberg, and Terri Beeler, *Phonemic Awareness in Young Children: A Classroom Curriculum* (Baltimore: Brookes, 1997); National Reading Panel, *Teaching Children to Read;* Snow, Burns, and Griffin, *Preventing Reading Difficulties;* Moats, *Teaching Reading Is Rocket Science;* Benita Blachman, "Phonological Awareness," in *Handbook of Reading Research,* vol. 3, ed. Michael Kamil et al. (Mahwah, NJ: Lawrence Erlbaum, 2000), pp. 483–502.

57. Albert Harris and Edward Sipay, eds., *How to Increase Reading Ability* (London: Longman, 1990); Sherrie Nist and Michele Simpson, "College Studying," in *Handbook of Reading Research,* vol. 3, ed. Michael Kamil et al. (Mahwah, NJ: Lawrence Erlbaum, 2000), pp. 645–666; William Nagy and Judy Scott, "Vocabulary Processes," in *Handbook of Reading Research,* vol. 3, ed. Michael Kamil et al. (Mahwah, NJ: Lawrence Erlbaum, 2000), pp. 269–284; Dorothy Hennings, "Contextually Relevant Word Study: Adolescent Vocabulary Development across the Curriculum," *Journal of Adolescent and Adult Literacy* 44, no. 3 (2000), 268–278.

58. This requires careful selection of pieces that make clear the statistical foundations upon which they are built, and the limits inherent in their design.

59. We recommend any of the work done by Ann Brown and her associates on metacognition, for example, Ann Brown, "Writing and Reading and Metacognition," in *Directions in Reading: Research and Instruction,* ed. Michael Kamil (Washington, DC: National Reading Conference, 1981); Jean Chall, *Stages of Reading Development* (New York: McGraw Hill, 1983); Roselmina Indrisano and Jean Chall, "Literacy Development," *Journal of Education* 177, no. 1 (1995), 63–84; LaBerge and Samuels, *Toward a Theory;* Nagy and Scott, *Vocabulary;* Perfetti, *Reading Ability;* Pressley, *Reading Instruction that Works;* Stanovich, *Progress in Understanding Reading.*

60. Adams, *Beginning to Read;* Adams et al. *Phonemic Awareness;* Moats, *Teaching Reading Is Rocket Science;* Moats and Lyon, *Topics in Language Disorders;* Shaywitz, *Overcoming Dyslexia,* or any of her earlier articles; Joseph Torgesen and Patricia Mathes, *A Basic Guide to Understanding, Assessing, and Teaching Phonological Awareness* (Austin, TX: Pro-Ed, 2000), or other articles by Torgesen.

61. Snow, Burns, and Griffin, *Preventing Reading Difficulties;* National Reading Panel, *Teaching Children.*

62. These 36 syllabi were taken from 10 schools from their Early Childhood and Elementary programs. The other schools reviewed either did not have an elementary program at the time of this review (i.e., Stanford), or did not have a reading course or relevant language arts course as part of their professional sequence for certification.

63. Susan Hall and Louisa Moats, *Straight Talk about Reading: How Parents Can Make a Difference During the Early Years* (Chicago: Contemporary Books, 1999).

64. Snow, Burns, and Griffin, *Preventing Reading Difficulties;* Susan Burns and Catherine Snow, *Starting Out Right: A Guide to Promoting Children's Reading Success* (Washington, DC: National Academy Press, 1999).

65. Available at http://centerx.gseis.ucla.edu/TEP/proginfo/syllabi/fall02/ED315AB_StOk_Rubric.html.

66. Available at http://www.searchum.umd.edu/search?q=EDHD+425&restrict=&btnG=Search +UM&site=UMCP&output=xml_no_dtd&client=UMCP&btnG.y=3&btnG.x=15&proxystyle sheet=UMCP.

67. "Running Records" are an informal assessment in which teachers record the reading behaviors as students reads. Qualitative analysis is made based on observation of how children use the three cueing systems (meaning, structural, visual) to help them read as well. We are concerned about the use of the three cueing system because of its representation of the reading model. Marilyn Adams has criticized this model in "The Three Cueing System," in *Reading for Understanding: Towards and R& D Program in Reading Comprehension*, chair, Catherine Snow (Santa Monica, CA: RAND Reading Study Group, 2001), retrieved August 2003 from http//www.readbygrade3.com/3cue.

68. Surprisingly, even in those syllabi that included teaching phonics in two class sessions, in four syllabi only a small part of the time in those sessions was devoted to phonics. For example, two schools included in their syllabi activities such as reading strategies, lesson planning, assessments (running records), and literature circles within the same classroom session in which they were teaching the students about teaching phonics. In another school (UCLA), one syllabus announced a "balanced approach" to reading, but it included phonics, phonemic awareness, breaking the alphabetic code, and spelling, all of which were concentrated into a single class. However, another syllabus at UCLA included both phonics games and the building of a phonics notebook.

69. We did find one syllabus of a course for secondary teachers that had all of the elements we were looking for: a variety of solid research articles; high demands for performance with from three to four research articles required to be read per class; and a broad coverage of topics, including how to teach reading skills and strategies, teaching diverse students, and teaching students with learning disabilities.

70. A number of schools of education are introducing fieldwork through which students in their initial course work can spend time in a school. Such fieldwork may even be required before enrolling in an education program, serving as a useful reality check for would-be teachers.

71. Deborah Meier, *The Power of Their Ideas* (Boston: Beacon Press, 1995), p. 105.

72. See for example "Commanding Heights," a first-rate set of materials from WGBH public television.

73. Available at www.education.umd.edu/EDCI/info/syllabi/Fall2002/EDCI397_Gourley.pdf.

74. Two schools included full assessment courses; Stanford's included a discussion of formative and standard assessments and a discussion of the standards movement. Students were required to collect and evaluate sample classroom assessments. Eastern Michigan's course incorporated understanding of different types of assessments such as criterion and norm referenced tests and pre-assessments, formative and summative evaluations. It included how to design alternative tests and interpret standardized tests. In addition, Eastern Michigan had students plan a unit of instruction, write assessments, and create scoring systems. The assessments students wrote were based on appropriate benchmarks and standards taken from state frameworks. This type of assignment was unique to Eastern Michigan. UCLA indicated two class sessions in their general methods class for a discussion of assessment, with a very different focus than the course at Eastern Michigan. The first week they asked the guiding question, "How might you structure interactive learning activities and assessment tasks that make learning accessible to a culturally and linguistically diverse group of students? In the second class the guiding question was, "How do classroom teachers measure what matters most?" Readings included chapters from Oakes and Lipton, whose text emphasizes authentic assessments, and has a sociocultural and constructivist perspective on

learning. A second text, Ayers' book, does not advocate for traditional assessments. Jeannie Oakes and Martin Lipton, *Teaching to Change the World,* 2nd ed. (New York: McGraw-Hill, 2002); William Ayer, *To Teach: The Journey of a Teacher,* 2nd ed. (New York: Teachers College Press, 2001). The Stanford syllabi can be found at: http://stanford.edu/group/step/ academics/ED246_Practicum/02-03/practicumwinter.htm; the Eastern Michigan University syllabus can be found at: http://www.emich.edu/coe/NCATE2003/Docs/G-10/standards/ soc_stds/syllabi/CURR305.html; the UCLA syllabus can be found at: http://centerx. gseis.ucla.edu/TEP/Program/syllabi/past.php.

75. www.sis.umd.edu/SOC/0001/EDCI.html

76. Portfolios are a collection of what students did during student teaching "a means to inquire about and reflect on what you are experiencing," a chance to "document your thinking"; see www.ed.psu.edu/pds/03mentor_resources/ci495B_01_02.pdf.

77. Yolanda Kodrycki, ed., *Education in the 21st Century* (Boston: Federal Reserve Bank of Boston, 2002), pp. 187–188.

78. Richard Silberman, "An Art or a Science?" *Journal of Education* 183, no. 2 (2003), 43.

79. George Steiner, *Lessons of the Masters* (Cambridge, MA: Harvard University Press, 2003), pp. 183–184.

## CHAPTER 6 SHEILA—TWO NOTES WILL BE RENUMBERED IN TEXT NEAR THE END—THEY'RE MARKED

1. National Education Association Research, "Status of the American Public School Teacher, 1995–1996" (Washington, DC: National Education Association, July 1997), http://www. nea.org/neatoday/9709/status.html.

2. Laurie Lewis, Basmat Parsad, Nancy Carey, Nicole Bartfai, Elizabeth Farris, and Becky Smerdon, Bernie Greene, project officer, "Teacher Quality: A Report on the Preparation and Qualifications of Public School Teachers," NCES Document No. 1999–080 (Washington, DC: U.S. Department of Education, National Center for Education Statistics, 1999), http:// nces.ed.gov/pubsearch/pubsinfo.asp?pubid=1999080.

3. Lewis et al., "Teacher Quality." While this difference between experienced and new teachers also could occur if newer teachers were less likely to obtain master's degrees than teachers hired long ago, in practice the trend has been toward higher degrees, which teachers often obtain while on the job.

4. Kerry J. Gruber, Susan D. Wiley, Stephen P. Broughman, Gregory A. Strizek, and Marisa Burian-Fitzgerald, *Schools and Staffing Surveys, 1999–2000: Overview of the Data for Public, Private, Public Charter, and Bureau of Indian Affairs Elementary and Secondary Schools,* NCES 2002-313 (Washington, DC: U.S. Department of Education, National Center for Education Statistics, 2002).

5. Joshua D. Angrist and Victor Lavy, "Does Teacher Training Affect Pupil Learning? Evidence from Matched Comparisons in Jerusalem Public Schools," NBER Working Paper No. 6781 (Cambridge, MA: National Bureau of Economic Research, November 1998).

6. Daniel Goldhaber and Dominic Brewer, "Does Teacher Certification Matter? High School Teacher Certification Status and Student Achievement," *Education Evaluation and Policy Analysis* 22, no. 2 (2000), 129–145.

7. Authors' calculations using data on California schools.

8. Steven Rivkin, Eric Hanushek, and John Kain, "Teachers, Schools and Academic Achievement," NBER Working Paper No. w6691 (Cambridge, MA: National Bureau of Economic Research, August 1998).

9. Ferguson and Ladd, for example, find a positive relationship between Alabama teachers' ACT composite scores and student reading score gains from third to fourth grade. Ronald F. Ferguson, *Holding Schools Accountable: Performance-Based Reform in Education*, ed. Helen F. Ladd (Washington, DC: Brookings Institution, 1996).

10. Eric A. Hanushek and Richard R. Pace, "Who Chooses to Teach (and Why)?" *Economics of Education Review* 14, no. 2 (1995), 101–117; Emiliana Vegas, Richard J. Murnane, and John B. Willett, "From High School to Teaching: Many Steps, Who Makes It?" *Teachers College Record* 103, no. 3 (June 2001), 427–449.

11. Sean P. Corcoran, William N. Evans et al. "Changing Labor Market Opportunities for Women and the Quality of Teachers 1957–1992," NBER Working Paper No. w9180 (Cambridge, MA: National Bureau of Economic Research, 2002), http://www.nber.org/papers/w9180.

12. Susanna Loeb and Marianne Page, "Examining the Link between Teacher Wages and Student Outcomes: The Importance of Alternative Labor Market Opportunities and Non-Pecuniary Variation," *Review of Economics and Statistics* 82, no. 3 (2002).

13. Carolyn M. Evertson, Willis D. Hawley, and Marilyn Zlotnik, "Making a Difference in Educational Quality through Teacher Education," *Journal of Teacher Education* (May-June, 1985), 2–12; David H. Monk, "Subject Area Preparation of Secondary Mathematics and Science Teachers and Student Achievement," *Economics of Education Review* 12, no. 2 (1994), 125–145.

14. Lewis et al., "Teacher Quality."

15. This may underestimate changes over time if teachers with degrees in academic fields are more likely to exit teaching early in their careers.

16. Jennifer Rice King, *Teacher Quality: Understanding the Effectiveness of Teacher Attributes* (Washington, DC: Economic Policy Institute, 2003).

17. Richard Ingersoll, *Out-of-Field Teaching and the Limits of Teacher Policy* (Seattle: Center for the Study of Teaching and Policy, 2003), http://depts.washington.edu/ctpmail/Abstract-LTP.html.

18. Hamilton Lankford, Susanna Loeb, and James Wyckoff, "Teacher Sorting and the Plight of Urban Schools: A Descriptive Analysis," *Education Evaluation and Policy Analysis* 24, no. 1 (2002), 37–62.

19. Gruber et al., *Schools and Staffing Surveys, 1999–2000*.

20. Lankford, Loeb, and Wyckoff, "Teacher Sorting and the Plight of Urban Schools."

21. Lankford, Loeb, and Wyckoff, "Teacher Sorting and the Plight of Urban Schools."

22. U.S. Department of Education, National Center for Education Statistics, Fast Response Survey System, NCES Fast Response Survey System, "Teacher Survey on Professional Development and Training," FRSS 65, 1998.

23. William H. Baugh and Joe A. Stone, "Mobility and Wage Equilibration in the Educator Labor Market," *Economics of Education Review* 2, No. 3 (1982), 253–274; Dominic J. Brewer, "Career Paths and Quit Decisions: Evidence from Teaching," *Journal of Labor Economics* 14 no. 2 (1996), 313–339; Peter J. Dolton, "The Economics of UK Teacher Supply: The Graduate's Decision," *Economic Journal* 100, no. 400 (1990), 91–104; Peter J. Dolton and Wilbert van der Klaauw, "The Turnover of Teachers: A Competing Risks Explanation," *Review of Economics and Statistics* 81, no. 3 (1999), 543–552; Peter J. Dolton and Gerald H. Makepeace, "Female Labour Force Participation and the Choice of Occupation," *European Economic Review* 37 (1993), 1393–1411; Hanushek and Pace, "Who Chooses to Teach (and Why)?"; Charles F. Manski, "Academic Ability, Earnings, and the Decision to Become a Teacher: Evidence from the National Longitudinal Study of the High School Class of 1972," in *Public Sector Payrolls*, ed. David A. Wise (Chicago: University of Chicago Press, 1987), pp. 291–312; Daniel Mont

and Daniel I. Rees, "The Influence of Classroom Characteristics on High School Teacher Turnover," *Economic Inquiry* 34 (1996), 152–167; Richard J. Murnane, Judy D. Singer, and John B. Willett, "The Influences of Salaries and 'Opportunity Costs' on Teachers' Career Choices: Evidence from North Carolina," *Harvard Educational Review* 59, no. 3 (1989), 325–346; Bill D. Rickman and Carl D. Parker, "Alternative Wages and Teacher Mobility: A Human Capital Approach," *Economics of Education Review* 9, no. 1 (1990), 73–79; Todd R. Stinebrickner, "An Empirical Investigation of Teacher Attrition," *Economics of Education Review* 17, no. 2 (1998), 127–136; Todd R. Stinebrickner, "Estimation of a Duration Model in the Presence of Missing Data," *Review of Economics and Statistics* 81, no. 3 (1999), 529–542; Todd R. Stinebrickner, "An Analysis of Occupational Change and Departure from the Labor Force: Evidence of the Reasons That Teachers Quit," working paper, 2000; Neil D. Theobald, "An Examination of the Influences of Personal, Professional, and School District Characteristics on Public School Teacher Retention," *Economics of Education Review* 9, no. 3 (1990), 241–250; Neil D. Theobald and R. Mark Gritz, "The Effects of School District Spending Priorities on the Exit Paths of Beginning Teachers Leaving the District," *Economics of Education Review* 15, no. 1 (1996), 11–22.

24. William H. Baugh and Joe A. Stone, "Mobility and Wage Equilibration in the Educator Labor Market," *Economics of Education Review* 2, no. 3 (1982), 253–274.

25. Gruber et al., *Schools and Staffing Surveys, 1999–2000*.

26. Robin R. Henke, Xianglei Chen and Sonya Geis, *Progress through the Teacher Pipeline*, 1993 Baccalaureate and Beyond Longitudinal Study (Washington, DC: U.S. Department of Education, National Center for Education Statistics, 2000).

27. See, for example, *Education Next,* Summer 2003.

28. Susanna Loeb and Marianne Page, "The Role of Compensating Differentials, Alternative Labor Market Opportunities and Endogenous Selection in Teacher Labor Markets," working paper, 2001. Loeb and Page use a regression approach to estimate this, regressing metropolitan area average wages on measures of average earned income, average earned income for male college graduates, and average earned income for female college graduates

29. The starting salaries of private school teachers are approximately $5,500 less than those of public school teachers. Likewise, the highest salary in private school teachers is approximately $14,400 less than is the highest step on the salary schedule for public school teachers. Salaries in charter schools are closer to their public school counterparts than to private schools. Source: NCES 2002–313

30. These estimates are based on regressions of district wage on district characteristics and dummy variables for metropolitan areas. Susanna Loeb and Marianne Page, "The Role of Compensating Differentials, Alternative Labor Market Opportunities and Endogenous Selection in Teacher Labor Markets," final report to the Spencer Foundation, 2001.

31. Julian R. Betts, Kim S. Reuben, and Anne Danenberg, "Equal Resources, Equal Outcomes? The Distribution of School Resources and Student Achievement" (San Francisco: Public Policy Institute of California, 2000); George W. Bohrnstedt and Brian M. Stecher, eds., "Class Size Reduction in California: Early Evaluation Findings, 1996–1998," CSR Research Consortium, Year 1 Evaluation Report (Palo Alto, CA: American Institutes for Research, 1999), p. 9.

32. Rivkin, Hanushek, and Kain, "Teachers, Schools and Academic Achievement."

33. Susanna Loeb, Linda Darling-Hammond, and John Luczak, "How Teaching Conditions Predict Teacher Turnover in California Schools," working paper, 2003.

34. Eric A. Hanushek, John F. Kain, and Steven G. Rivkin, "Do Higher Salaries Buy Better Teachers?" working paper, 1999.

35. Eric Hanushek and Steven Rivkin, "Understanding the 20th Century Growth in U.S. School Spending," *Journal of Human Resources* 32, no. 1 (1997), 35–68.

36. For a useful discussion of these issues, see Bryan Hassel, "Better Pay for Better Teaching: Making Teacher Compensation Pay Off in the Age of Accountability" (Washington, DC: Progressive Policy Institute, 2002).

37. "If I can't learn from you . . .", Ensuring a Highly Qualified Teacher for Every Classroom, *EdWeek* Annual Survey, 2002, using data from National Center for Education Information.

38. *EdWeek* Annual Survey, pp. 10, 56.

39. For a study of four urban districts, see Jessica Levin and Meredith Quinn, *Missed Opportunities: How We Keep High Quality Teachers Out of Urban Classrooms* (New York: New Teacher Project, 2003).

40. Edwin M. Bridges, "Evaluation for Tenure and Dismissal," in *The New Handbook of Teacher Evaluation,* ed. Jason Millman and Linda Darling-Hammond (Newbury Park, NJ: Sage, 1996), pp. 147–157.

41. Dale Ballou, "Do Public Schools Hire the Best Applicants?" *Quarterly Journal of Economics* 111, no. 1 (1996), 97–133.

42. Dale Ballou, "Do Public Schools Hire the Best Applicants," *Quarterly Journal of Economic Research* 111, no. 1 (1996), 97–133.

43. Donald Boyd, Hamilton Lankford, Susanna Loeb, and James Wyckoff, "Analyzing Determinants of the Matching of Public School Teachers to Jobs: Estimating Compensating Differentials in Imperfect Labor Markets," National Bureau of Economic Research working paper 9878, 2003.

44. *EdWeek,* "If I can't learn from you . . ."

45. *Ed Week,* 2003 [7, p.36] Data: EdWeek annual survey 200.

46. Lewis, Parsad, Carey, Bartfal, Farris, and Smerdon, Greene, project officer, "Teacher Quality: A Report on the Preparation and Qualifications of Public School Teachers."

## CHAPTER 7 SHEILA—SEE NOTE 19

1. For a broad overview on this question, see William M. Sullivan, *Work and Integrity: The Crisis and Promise of Professionalism in America* (New York: HarperCollins Books, 1995); for a short, pungent critique of the professionalism agenda in education, see Chester E. Finn, Jr., "High Hurdles," *Education Next* (Spring 2003), 62–67.

2. Milton Friedman, *Capitalism and Freedom* (Chicago: University of Chicago Press, 1962).

3. Henry Levin, "Teacher Certification and the Economics of Information," *Educational Evaluation and Policy Analysis* 2, no. 4 (1980), 5–18. Another frequently referenced study of the teacher labor market ultimately reaches a similar conclusion. Murnane and colleagues note that traditional economic assumptions about consumer competence, priorities, knowledge, and information do not always hold with respect to teacher hiring because "some local districts (the purchasers of teacher services) are underfunded, incompetent, or have priorities that the state finds unacceptable" (p. 94). They continue, "States are concerned because equal opportunity is threatened when incompetent teachers are hired, and the costs of inadequate education are borne not only by the children themselves, but also by the larger society. Dimensions of these costs include a lower rate of economic growth, higher incidence of welfare, greater crime rates, and higher unemployment rates" (p. 95). See Richard Murnane, Judy Singer, John Willett, James Kemple, and Randall Olsen, *Who Will Teach? Policies That Matter* (Cambridge, MA: Harvard University Press, 1991).

4. This phrase comes from Albert Hirschman, *Exit, Voice, and Loyalty* (Cambridge, MA: Harvard University Press, 1970).

5. Marci Kanstoroom and Chester E. Finn, Jr., eds., *Better Teachers, Better Schools* (Washington, DC: Thomas B. Fordham Foundation, 1999), p. 11.

6. For a review of recent state licensure requirements, see Peter Youngs, Allan Odden, and Andrew C. Porter, "State Policy Related to Teacher Licensure," *Educational Policy* 17, no. 2 (2003), 217–236. They report that, in 2001–2002, 33 of the 50 states were assessing new teachers' knowledge of subject matter. The majority relied on the Praxis II tests, while other states used the NES tests or others. There has been little effort to align these or other tests with the standards for learning that most states have adopted. The authors conclude that, "[t]here has been little research from individual states on the consequences for student achievement of adopting these policies, but a growing body of research indicates that teachers' performances on tests of literacy and their knowledge of content and pedagogy are related to student achievement" (p. 233).

7. The incidence—and measure—of out-of-field teaching is open to debate, but recent work on the subject indicates that the practice occurs in over one-half of all secondary schools in the United States, and that about one-quarter of all secondary teachers are assigned to teach one or more classes outside their area of preparation. For analysis of this issue, see Richard Ingersoll, "The Problem of Underqualified Teachers in American Secondary Schools," *Educational Researcher* 28, no. 2 (1999), 26–37; Richard Ingersoll, "Misunderstanding the Problem of Out-of-Field Teaching," *Educational Researcher* 30, no. 1 (2001), 21–22. For a more extended treatment of these and related issues, see Richard Ingersoll, *Who Controls Teachers' Work? Power and Accountability in America's Schools* (Cambridge, MA: Harvard University Press, 2003). How much mis-assignment is tolerable, given a standard of safe practice? Surely all mis-assignment cannot be eliminated; just as surely, if the incidence of mis-assignment passes some tipping point and/or is patterned—concentrated for example in poor schools serving poor students—then there is a problem for public policy.

8. For one history of teacher licensure, see David Angus, *Professionalism and the Common Good: A Brief History of Teacher Certification* (Washington, DC: Thomas B. Fordham Foundation, 2001); for another view, see Michael Sedlak, "'Let Us Go and Buy a School Master': Historical Perspectives on the Hiring of Teachers in the United States, 1750–1980," in *American Teacher: Histories of a Profession at Work,* ed. D. Warren (New York: American Educational Research Association, Macmillan, 1989), pp. 257–290.

9. The use of performance assessments to evaluate teaching competence is in its infancy, but the issues in developing a system of performance assessments for use in licensure decisions are complex. For recent reviews, see Robert L. Linn, "Performance Standards: Utility for Different Uses of Assessment," *Educational Policy Analysis Archives* 11, no. 31, retrieved September 6, 2003, from http://epaa.asu.edu/epaa/v11n31/; Anne Marie Uhlenbeck, Nico Verloop, Douwe Beijaard, "Requirements for an Assessment Procedure for Beginning Teachers: Implications from Recent Theories on Teaching and Assessment," *Teachers College Record* 104, no. 2 (2002), 242–272.

10. Lee Shulman, "A Union of Insufficiencies: Strategies for Teacher Assessment in a Period of Educational Reform," *Educational Leadership* 46, no. 3 (1988), 36–41.

11. Arthur Wise, "What's Wrong with Teacher Certification? Making the Case for a 'Professional Beginning Teacher' Licensing Process," *Education Week,* April 9, 2003, p. 56.

12. Arthur Wise, Linda Darling-Hammond, and Stephen P. Klein, *A License to Teach: Building a Profession for 21st-Century Schools* (Boulder, CO: Westview Press, 1995).

13. Details of this case are based on the monograph by Suzanne Wilson, Linda Darling-Hammond, and Barnett Berry, *A Case of Successful Teaching Policy: Connecticut's Long-Term Efforts to Improve Teaching and Learning* (Seattle: University of Washington, Center for the Study of Teaching and Policy, 2001).

14. Wilson, Darling-Hammond, and Berry, *A Case of Successful Teaching Policy,* pp. 23–24.

15. Connecticut has worked on streamlining and simplifying its portfolio system. In 1999–2000, the state streamlined the process, reducing the time and effort to prepare the portfolio. The state now distributes bound handbooks to all first-year teachers with clear instructions on how to complete the requirements.

16. This new NCATE policy is aimed at reducing state-to-state variability in pass rates on the Praxis II examination. Still, many observers regard these examinations as relatively weak assessments of content knowledge, which could be strengthened considerably. This an area for improvement that states should undertake in consultation with the Educational Testing Service.

17. See Arthur Wise and Jane Leibbrand, *A Professional Model of Accountability for Teaching* (Denver: Education Commission of the States, 2003). This paper supplies an excellent rationale and extended model for professional standards in teaching, including comparisons with other nations and with other professions.

18. Allan Odden and Carolyn Kelly, *Paying Teachers for What They Know and Do: New and Smarter Compensation Strategies to Improve Schools* (Thousand Oaks, CA: Corwin Press, 1997).

19. 2000 Schools and Staffing Surveys reveal the following:

*Percentage of teachers with provisional, temporary, or emergency certification or uncertified:*

|  | Connecticut | | Other 49 states | |
|---|---|---|---|---|
|  | 1987–88 | 1999–00 | 1987–88 | 1999–00 |
| Total | 14.8 | 10.8 | 7.7 | 10.7 |
| Central City | 14.2 | 7.6 |  |  |
| FRL | >70% | 7.1 |  |  |
| Minority Students | >70% | 8.5 |  |  |

*Attrition From Teaching, 1999–2000*

|  | Connecticut | | Other 49 states | |
|---|---|---|---|---|
| Total | 12.0% | 15.2% |  |  |
| Central City | 7.6% | 6.0% |  |  |
| FRL | >70% | 0.3% | 19.5% |  |
| Minority Students | >70% | 6.4 % | 18.2% |  |

20. Wilson, Darling-Hammond, and Berry, *A Case of Successful Teaching Policy*, p. 31.

21. Wilson, Darling-Hammond, and Berry, *A Case of Successful Teaching Policy*, p. 32.

22. See, for example, Yanxuan Qu and Betsy Becker, "Does Traditional Teacher Certification Imply Quality? A Meta-analysis," paper presented at the annual meeting of the American Educational Research Association, Chicago, 2003.

23. In fact, Connecticut experimented with several district-sponsored alternate route programs, but found that they performed poorly, failing to recruit and retain effective teachers. These programs were discontinued. In consequence, the state determined that centrally operated alternate route programs were superior to local provision, and this should give pause to such options in other locales.

24. David K. Cohen, Stephen Raudenbush, and Deborah Loewenberg Ball, "Resources, Instruction, and Research," *Educational Evaluation and Policy Analysis* 25, no. 2 (2003), 125.

## CHAPTER 8

1. See Gary Sykes, in this volume; Catherine Walsh, in this volume; see also National Commission on Teaching and America's Future, "What Matters Most: Teaching for America's Future" (New York: Author, 1996).

2. Michael Podgursky, in this volume; Frederick M. Hess, "Tear Down This Wall: The Case for a Radical Overhaul of Teacher Certification" (Washington, DC: Progressive Policy Institute, November 2001); Michael Podgursky and Dale Ballou, "The Case against Teacher Certification," *Public Interest* 132 (1998), 17–29.

3. Dan Goldhaber, "The Mystery of Good Teaching," *Education Next* (Spring 2002).

4. Michael Allen, "Eight Questions on Teacher Preparation: What Does the Research Say?" (Denver: Education Commission of the States, August 2003).

5. Through its Teacher Training Agency (TTA), England authorizes entities such as schools themselves to run programs that lead to teacher certification. School Centered Initial Teacher Training (SCITT) is based in schools and run by staff in partnership with local universities. Candidates have the benefit of starting day one in a classroom environment, acquiring knowledge and skills required for effective teaching. Groups of schools take the lead in designing the program and may choose to work with a range of partners, including higher education institutions, local education agencies, and others. In order to be accredited by the TTA, a potential new provider must design training that meets the requirements set by the Secretary of State and leads trainees to receive Qualified Teacher Status. Accreditation can be withdrawn where there is evidence of noncompliance with the Secretary of State's criteria and requirements.

6. See Terry M. Moe, "The Politics of the Status Quo," in *Our Schools and Our Future: Are We Still at Risk?* ed. Paul E. Peterson (Palo Alto, CA: Hoover Institution Press, 2003).

7. Sandra Vergari and Frederick M. Hess, "The Accreditation Game," *Education Next* 2 (2002), 48–57.

8. One existing example of such a "provider" is the American Board for Certification of Teacher Excellence, http://www.abcte.org/.

9. The inclusion of "research-based" in criteria is almost obligatory now in any discussion of an education policy proposal. One challenge for a state adopting this model, however, is that the research base under girding the preparation of teachers is exceedingly weak. It is unlikely that most prospective providers, including existing university-based programs, will be able to make a strong case that research clearly shows their program will work. In addition, the state wants to encourage new approaches, including approaches that may never have been tried in full. The research-based standard needs to focus on the applicant's ability to cite research that supports elements of its proposed program, rather than proof of success.

10. One approach would be for states to triage their process monitoring. As programs approach reauthorization, some will have achieved sufficiently high or low outcomes that their reauthorization prospects will be clear. For programs on the bubble, process information gathered via site visits and observations could be critical to determining whether the programs are on the right track.

11. In addition to opting not to reauthorize a program, a state could also deauthorize a program mid-term in extreme cases of misconduct, such as fraudulent use of public funds, sexual harassment of teaching candidates, or chronic failure to provide required data.

12. The UK's Teacher Training Agency (TTA) website provides a starting model for such efforts. The site offers performance profiles of each program provider that provide candidates and employers with much needed information about each program. Upon entering the performance profile section of the site, a map of the country appears, making it easy to click on the area of the country where one lives. Then a candidate or employer accesses a pull-down menu of providers in that region. With one more click it is easy to access the performance profiles of the providers in that region. For example, candidates can search program performance profiles by subject area, region, new providers, and its TTA Quality Category. Each

program receives a rating on a scale of A (very satisfactory) to E (unsatisfactory/non-compliant).

13. Public Schools of North Carolina, *Education Directory 2002–2003* (Raleigh: Public Schools of North Carolina, 2002), pp. 25–26.

14. Frederick M. Hess, "Whaddya Mean You Want To Close My School? The Politics of Regulatory Accountability in Charter Schooling," *Education and Urban Society* 33 (2001), 141–156.

## CHAPTER 9

1. Audrey Wang, Ashaki B. Coleman, Richard J. Coley, and Richard B. Phelps, *Preparing Teachers around the World* (Princeton, NJ: Educational Testing Service, 2003).

2. J. Fredericks Volkwein and Stephen Grunig, "Double, Double, Toil and Trouble: Reputation Ratings in Higher Education," in *The Many Faces of Accountability*, ed. Joseph Burke (San Francisco: Jossey-Bass, forthcoming). NOTE: THE TEXT ACCOMPANYING THIS NOTE IS GOING TO BE CHANGED SLIGHTLY.

3. C. Emily Feistritzer, *The Making of a Teacher: A Report on Teacher Preparation in the U.S.* (Washington, DC: National Center for Education Information, 1999).

4. The evidence on the importance of verbal ability, also measured as general academic ability and by proxy, selectivity of college is extensive. See Samuel Bowles and Henry Levin, "The Determinants of Scholastic Achievement: An Appraisal of Some Recent Evidence," *Journal of Human Resources* 3 (1968), 3–24; James Coleman et al., *Equality of Educational Opportunity* (Washington, DC: Government Printing Office, 1966), Ronald Ehrenberg and Dominic Brewer, "Did Teachers' Verbal Ability and Race Matter in the 1950s? Coleman Revisited," *Economics of Education Review* 14 (1995), 1–21; Ronald Ferguson, "Paying for Public Education: New Evidence on How and Why Money Matters," *Harvard Journal on Legislation* 28 (1991), 465–498; Ronald Ferguson and Helen Ladd, "How and Why Money Matters: An Analysis of Alabama Schools," in *Holding Schools Accountable*, ed. Helen Ladd (Washington, DC: Brookings Institution, 1996), pp. 265–298; Rob Greenwald, Larry Hedges, and Richard Laine, "Does Money Matter? A Meta-Analysis of Studies of the Effects of Differential School Inputs on Students' Outcomes," *Educational Researcher* 23, no. 3 (1994), 5–14; Rob Greenwald, Larry Hedges, and Richard Laine, "The Effect of School Resources on Student Achievement," and "Interpreting Research on School Resources and Student Achievement: A Rejoinder to Hanushek," *Review of Educational Research* 66, no. 3 (1996), 361–396; Eric Hanushek, "Teacher Characteristics and Gains in Student Achievement: Estimation Using Micro-Data," *American Economic Review* 61, no. 2 (1971), 280–288; Eric Hanushek, *Education and Race: An Analysis of the Educational Production Process* (Lexington, MA: D. C. Heath, 1972); Eric Hanushek, "A More Complete Picture of School Resource Policies," *Review of Educational Research* 66 (1996), 397–409; John Kain and Kraig Singleton, "Equality of Educational Opportunity Revisited," *New England Economic Review* (May/June 1996), 87–111; Henry Levin, "Concepts of Economic Efficiency and Educational Production," in *Education as an Industry*, ed. Joseph Froomkin, Dean Jamison, and Roy Radner (Cambridge, MA: Ballinger, 1976); David Monk and Jennifer Rice King, "Subject Area Preparation of Secondary Mathematics and Science Teachers and Student Achievement," *Economics of Education Review* 12, no. 2 (1994), 125–145; Richard Murnane, The *Impact of School Resources on the Learning of Inner City Children* (Cambridge, MA: Ballinger, 1975); Richard Murnane, "Understanding the Sources of Teaching' Competence: Choices, Skills and the Limits of Training," *Teachers College Record* 84, no. 3 (1983); Richard Murnane and Barbara Phillips, *Effective Teachers of Inner City Children: Who They Are and What Are They?* (Princeton, NJ: Mathematica Policy Research, 1978); Richard Murnane and Barbara Phillips, "What Do Effective Teachers of Inner City Children Have in Common?" *Social Science Research* 10 (1981),

83–100; Milbrey McLaughlin and David Marsh, "Staff Development and School Change," *Teachers College Record* 80, no. 1 (1978), 69–94; Robert, Strauss and Elizabeth Sawyer, "Some New Evidence on Teacher and Student Competencies," *Economics of Education Review* 5 (1986), 41; Anita A. Summers and Barbara L. Wolfe, "Which School Resources Help Learning? Efficiency and Equity in Philadelphia Public Schools," *Business Review* (Federal Reserve Bank of Philadelphia, February 1975); Anita Summers and Barbara Wolfe, "Do Schools Make a Difference?" *American Economic Review* 67, no. 4 (1977), 639–652; Donald Winkler, "Educational Achievement and School Peer Composition," *Journal of Human Resources* 10 (1975), 189–204.

5. Economist Morris Kleiner notes the evidence of consumer benefits from most licensing requirements is thin or nonexistent. Mandatory licensing requirements impose a barrier to occupational entry that is likely to increase wages in the licensed occupation. Morris M. Kleiner, "Occupational Licensing," *Journal of Economic Perspectives* 14 (2000), 189–202.

6. U.S. Department of Education, *Meeting the Highly Qualified Teacher Challenge: The Secretary's Second Annual Report on Teacher Quality* (Washington, DC: Author, 2003).

7. Example found on the Nevada State Department of Education website, http://www.nde.state.nv.us/licensure/moreinfo/secacademic.htm.

8. NASDTEC, *The NASDTEC Manual on the Preparation and Certification of Educational Personnel* (Dubuque, IA: Kendall/Hunt, 2001), p. B44.

9. Dale Ballou and Michael Podgursky, "Teacher Training and Licensure," in *Better Teachers, Better Schools*, ed. Marcia Kanstoroom and Chester E. Finn, Jr. (Washington, DC: Fordham Foundation, 1999).

10. There is a great deal of conflicting research on teacher experience, making it difficult to state firm and specific conclusions about its importance. Much research has found that teachers get better with a few years of experience, but at some point their effectiveness drops, viewed as an inverted U-shaped pattern of effectiveness and perhaps caused by "burnout" or the promotion of better teachers out of the classroom. The effect of experience can be distorted or obscured because teachers who enter the profession at the same time tend to share certain common attributes having nothing to do with experience. However, these attributes may be mistakenly interpreted as the effect of experience rather than other traits of a particular cohort of teachers. Another reason the effect of experience is so hard to measure is that teachers who have seniority can choose to teach in the better schools.

11. Ronald G. Ehrenberg and Dominic J. Brewer, "Do School and Teacher Characteristics Matter? Evidence from High School and Beyond," *Economics of Education Review* 13, no. 1 (1994), 1–17; Rob Greenwald, Larry Hedges, and Richard Laine, "The Effect of School Resources on Student Achievement," *Review of Educational Research* 66, no. 3 (Fall 1996), 361–396; Dan Goldhaber and Dominic Brewer, "When Should We Reward Degrees for Teachers?" *Phi Delta Kappan* 80, no. 2 (October 1998), 134; Dan D. Goldhaber and Dominic J. Brewer (1997), "Evaluating the Effect of Teacher Degree Level on Educational Performance," in *Developments in School Finance,* ed. William J. Fowler (Washington, DC: U.S. Department of Education, National Center for Education Statistics, 1996), pp. 197–210; Delwyn L. Harnisch, "Characteristics Associated with Effective Public High Schools," *Journal of Educational Research* 80, no. 4 (1987), 233–241; Eric Hanushek, "Teacher Characteristics and Gains in Student Achievement: Estimation Using Micro-Data," *American Economic Review* 61, no. 2(1971), 280–288; Eric A. Hanushek, "The Impact of Differential Expenditures on School Performance," *Educational Researcher* 18, no. 4 (May 1989), 45–51, 62; Eric A. Hanushek, "The Trade-off between Child Quantity and Quality," *Journal of Political Economy* 100, no. 1 (1992), 85–117; Delwyn Harnisch, "Characteristics Associated with Effective Public High Schools," *Journal of Educational Research* 80, no. 4 (1987), 233–241; Herbet J. Kiesling, "As-

signment Practices and the Relationship of Instructional Time to the Reading Performance of Elementary School Children," *Economics of Education Review* 3, (1984), 341–350; Charles R. Link and Edward Charles Ratledge, Student Perceptions, IQ and Achievement," *Journal of Human Resources* 14, no. 1 (1979), 98–111; Milbrey McLaughlin and David Marsh, "Staff Development and School Change," *Teachers College Record* 80, no. 1 (1978), 69–94; David H. Monk, "Subject Area Preparation of Secondary Math and Science Teachers and Student Achievement," *Economics of Education Review* 13, no. 2 (1994), 125–145; Richard Murnane, "Understanding the Sources of Teaching Competence: Skills, Choices, and the Limits of Training," *Teachers College Record* (Spring 1982); Steven G. Rivkin, Eric A. Hanushek, and John F. Kain, "Teachers, Schools, and Academic Achievement," National Bureau of Economic Research, NBER working paper w6691 (Cambridge, MA: National Bureau of Economic Research, August 1998), available at http://dsl.nber.org/papers/w6691.pdf; Anita A., Summers and Barabra L. Wolfe, "Do Schools Make a Difference?" *American Economic Review* 67, (1977), 639–652; contrasted with small effects shown by Ronald F. Ferguson and Helen F. Ladd, "How and Why Money Matters: An Analysis of Alabama Schools," in *Holding Schools Accountable: Performance-based Reform in Education*, ed. Helen F. Ladd (Washington, DC: Brookings Institution, 1996), pp. 265–298; Ronald F. Ferguson, "Paying for Public Education: New Evidence of How and Why Money Matters," *Harvard Journal on Legislation* 28 (1991), 465–498.

12. Eric Hanushek, "The Economics of Schooling: Production and Efficiency in the Public Schools," *Journal of Economic Literature* 24 (1986), 1141–1178; Daniel Goldhaber and Dominic Brewer, "The Effect of School Resources on Student Achievement," *Review of Educational Research* 66, (1998), 361–396.

13. Daniel Goldhaber, and Dominic Brewer, "Does Teacher Certification Matter? High School Teacher Certification Status and Student Achievement" (2000); Morris M. Kleiner, and Daniel L. Petree, "Unionism and Licensing of Public School Teachers: Impact on Wages and Educational Output," in *When Public Sector Works Unionize*, ed. Richard B. Freeman and Casey Ichniowski (Chicago: University of Chicago Press, 1988); Eric Hanushek and Richard R. Pace, "Who Chooses to Teach (and Why)?" *Economics of Education Review* 14, no. 2 (1995), 101–117.

14. David Angus, *Professionalism and the Public Good: A Brief History of Teacher Certification*, ed. Jeffrey Mirel (Washington, DC: Thomas B. Fordham Foundation, 2001). Angus describes two such efforts: the Carnegie Taskforce on Teaching as a Profession and the Holmes Group.

15. Education Trust, *Interpret with Caution: The First State Title II Reports on the Quality of Teacher Preparation* (Washington, DC: Author, 2002).

16. Catherine Walsh, *Teacher Certification Reconsidered: Stumbling for Quality* (Baltimore: Abell Foundation, 2001).

17. National Council on Teacher Quality, *Teacher Quality Bulletin* 4, no. 31 (September 12, 2003), available online at www.nctq.org.

18. Email correspondence from David Imig, President of AACTE to Chester Finn, Jr., president of the Thomas B. Fordham Foundation, April 2003.

19. Steve Farkas, Jean Johnson, and Anthony Folena, *A Sense of Calling: Who Teaches and Why* (New York: Public Agenda, 2000).

20. Author email correspondence with Abigail Smith (October 14, 2003), vice-president for research and public policy, Teach For America.

21. Author email correspondence with Vicki Bernstein (October 16, 2003), director of the New Teaching Fellows program in New York City.

22. Edward Liu, *New Teachers' Experiences of Hiring: Preliminary Findings from a Four-State Study* (Cambridge, MA: Harvard Graduate School of Education, Project on the Next Generation of

Teachers, 2003), available online at http://www.gse.harvard.edu/~ngt/aera_conference. htm.

23. Dale Ballou, "Do Public Schools Hire the Best Applicants?" *Quarterly Journal of Economics* 111 (1996), 97–133.

24. Margaret Raymond, Stephen H. Fletcher, and Javier Luque, *Teach For America: An Evaluation of Teacher Differences and Student Outcomes in Houston, Texas* (Palo Alto, CA: Stanford University, CREDO, 2001).

25. U.S. Department of Education, *Meeting the Highly Qualified Teacher Challenge: The Secretary's Second Annual Report on Teacher Quality* (Washington, DC: Author, 2003).

26. Craig D. Jerald, with data analysis by Richard M. Ingersoll, *All Talk, No Action: Putting an End to Out of Field Teaching* (Washington, DC: Education Trust, 2002), available online at http://www.edtrust.org/main/documents/AllTalk.pdf.

27. Available at http://www.suntimes.com/sepcial_sections/failing_teacher/part2educ4.html.

28. Liu, *New Teachers' Experiences of Hiring.*

29. "New York, the State of Learning: Statistical Profiles of Public School Districts," a Report to the Governor and the Legislature on the Educational Status of the State's Schools, submitted June 2002, page 79, available online at http://www.emsc.nysed.gov/irts/ch655_2002/RptTable03_2002.pdf.

30. National Council on Teacher Quality, "Highly Qualified Teacher Roundup," *Teacher Quality Bulletin* 4, no. 22 (July 2003), available online at www nctq.org.

31. See, for example, Stephen A. Newman, "The Teacher Who Advocated Pedophilia," 230 *New York Law Journal,* 2 (August 7, 2003).

32. NASDTEC, *The NASDTEC Manual on the Preparation and Certification of Educational Personnel,* p. B–44.

33. Drew Gitomer and Andrew Latham, *The Academic Quality of Prospective Teachers: The Impact of Admissions and Licensure Testing* (Princeton, NJ: Educational Testing Service, 1999).

34. Audrey Wang, Ashaki B. Coleman, Richard J. Coley, and Richard B. Phelps, *Preparing Teachers around the World* (Princeton, NJ: Educational Testing Service, 2003).

35. U.S. Department of Education, *Meeting the Highly Qualified Teacher Challenge: The Secretary's Second Annual Report on Teacher QualityPUB INFO?.*

36. 2002 data from the United States medical licensing examination website, available at wwww.usmle.org/news/2002perf.htm.

37. *R. David Stramm and Beverly Tarpley,* "A Look Forward—and Back: Predictions for Bar Admissions in the 21st Century," *Bar Examiner* 69, no. 2 (May 2000).

38. Education Trust, *Not Good Enough: A Content Analysis of Teacher Licensing Examinations* (Washington, DC: Author, 1999).

39. Data supplied by Teach For America includes all 328 corps members who took the Praxis II exam during the summer institute in 2003.

40. Sandra Stotsky and Lisa Haverty, "Can a State Department of Education Increase Teacher Quality? Lessons Learned in Massachusetts," Brookings Papers on Educational Policy, ed. Diane Ravitch (Washington, DC: Brookings Institution Press, forthcoming).

41. National Council on Teacher Quality, "Hiring, Firing and Licensing in New York," *Teacher Quality Bulletin* 4, no. 30(September 2003), available online at www.nctq.org.

42. Ferguson, "Paying for Public Education."

43. Laurie Lewis and Elizabeth Farris, *Remedial Education at Higher Education Institutions in Fall 1995,* NCES 97-584 (Washington, DC: U.S. Department of Education, National Center for Education Statistics, 1996).

44. Betty Hart and Todd R. Risley, *Meaningful Differences in the Everyday Experience of Young American Children* (Baltimore: Paul H. Brookes, 1995); Jeanne Chall, Vicki Jacobs, and Luke

Baldwin, "The Reading Crisis: Why Poor Children Fall Behind," in *The Reading, Writing and Language Connection,* ed. J. Shimron (Cresskill, NJ: Hampton Press, 1996).

45. E. D. Hirsch, Jr., "Reading Comprehension Requires Knowledge—of Words and the World," *American Educator* (Spring 2003), available at http://www.coreknowledge.org/CKproto2/about/CommonKnowledge/V16iiJune2003/AE_SPRNG.pdf.

46. Available at http://www.coreknowledge.org/CKproto2/rcsrcs/syllabi/PDF/About%20this%20Project.pdf

47. Feistritzer, *The Making of a Teacher.*

48. Michael Allen, *Eight Questions on Teacher Preparation: What Does the Research Say?* (Denver, Education Commission of the States, 2003); Catherine Walsh, *Teacher Certification Reconsidered: Stumbling for Quality* (Baltimore: Abell Foundation, 2001); Andrew Wayne and Peter Youngs "Teacher Characteristics and Student Achievement Gains: A Review," *Review of Educational Research* 73, no. 1 (Spring 2003), 89-122; Grover Whitehurst, "Research on Teacher Preparation and Professional Development," paper presented at White House Conference on Preparing Tomorrow's Teachers on March 5, 2002, available at www.whitehouse.gov/firstlady/initiatives/education/teachingconference.html.

49. NASDTEC, *The NASDTEC Manual on the Preparation and Certification of Educational Personnel,* pp. B15–B24.

50. Stotsky and Haverty, "Can a State Department of Education Increase Teacher Quality?" 51. Jessica Levin and Meredith Quinn, *Missed Opportunities: How We Keep High Quality Teachers Out of Urban Classrooms* (New York: New Teacher Project, 2003), available online at www.tntp.org.

52. See endnote 4.

53. Linda Darling-Hammond, *Teacher Quality and Student Achievement: A Review of State Policy Evidence* (Seattle: University of Washington, Center for the Study of Teaching and Policy, 1999), p. 8.

54. Eric Hanushek, "Teacher Characteristics and Gains in Student Achievement: Estimation Using Micro-Data," *American Economic Review* 61, no. 2 (1971), 280–288; McLaughlin and Marsh, "Staff Development and School Change."

55. Anita A. Summers and Barbara L. Wolfe, "Do Schools Make a Difference?" *American Economic Review* 67 (1977), 639–652.

56. Steven Stahl, *Vocabulary Development* (Cambridge, MA: Brookline Books, 1999).

57. Steven Stahl and Marilyn Fairbanks, "The Effects of Vocabulary Instruction: A Model-Based Meta-Analysis," *Review of Educational Research* 56, no. 1 (1987), 72–110.

58. Approximations derived from TQSource, Education Commission for the States. Requirements vary from state to state.

59. See discussion and reference for endnote 27.

60. Stotsky and Haverty, "Can a State Department of Education Increase Teacher Quality?"

61. See endnote 37.

62. 2003 Public Agenda survey (forthcoming).

63. Liu, *New Teachers' Experiences of Hiring.*

64. Education Commission for the States, TQ Source.

65. INTASC, *Model Standards in Science for Beginning Teacher Licensing and Development: A Resource for State Dialogue* (Washington, DC: Council of Chief State School Officers, April 2002), p. 4, available at http://ccsso.org.red.doceus.com/content/pdfs/ScienceStandards.pdf.

66. National Committee on Science Education Standards and Assessment, National Research Council, *National Science Education Standards* (Washington, DC: National Academy Press, 1996), available at http://www.nap.edu/readingroom/books/nses/html/.

67. Levin and Quinn, *Missed Opportunities*, p. 45.

## CHAPTER 10

1. For example, a 1996 report of the National Commission on Teaching and America's Future, a self-appointed commission including the president of National Council for the Accreditation of Teacher Education (NCATE) and the National Board for Professional Teaching Standards (NBPTS) stated: "Although hundreds of studies have shown that fully prepared teachers are more effective than those who are unqualified, the practice of hiring untrained teachers continues. . . . Teachers who know how to do these things [pedagogy] make a substantial difference in what children learn. Furthermore, a large body of evidence shows that the preparation teachers receive influences their ability to teach in these ways" (National Commission on Teaching and America's Future, 1996, pp. 15, 27).

2. A third model, most frequently used by economists, is the "natural experiment" (Heckman, Lalonde, and Smith, 1999). This has not been widely employed in the teacher literature. An exception is Jacob and Lefgren (2002), who use longitudinal student-level achievement data for Chicago public school students and exploit a quirk in the administrative regulation to create a "quasi-experiment" to examine the effect of teacher training on student achievement. However, even with "natural experiments" longitudinal data is highly desirable.

3. A recent study by Hoxby (2001) highlights the importance of these socioeconomic variables and their potential for producing bias in studies of teachers and student achievement. Hoxby analyzed the effect of family, neighborhood, and school input variables on student achievement and educational attainment using two large nationally representative longitudinal studies of students (the National Educational Longitudinal Survey, NELS88, and the National Longitudinal Survey of Youth, which began in 1979). Hoxby compared the percent of the variation in student achievement on various field tests (math, reading) explained by school, family, and community factors. For every test, the percent of the variation explained by the family variables far exceeded the school input variables. The family variables explained from 34 to 105 times as much variation in student achievement test scores as the school input variables. She also examined years of schooling completed at age 33. Family variables explained 19 times as much variation in student educational attainment as did school inputs

4. Moreover, this is not a problem that is "fixed" by meta-analyzing large numbers of flawed cross-section studies, since all of these studies are biased in the same direction. Meta-analyzing 200 such studies simply produces a more accurate estimate of a biased coefficient. A target shooting analogy can illustrate this point. If the scope on a rifle is off or out of adjustment (biased) then the rifle shots will cluster around a point that is away from the target bull's eye (the true effect). Firing more shots will simply do a better job of identifying the point around which the sight is targeted but will not help determine where the bull's eye is. That requires that the bias or error in the rifle scope be fixed.

5. A recent survey of teacher quality research by the Education Commission of the States (Allen, 2003) sets a lower standard for inclusion of studies. Allen considers cross-section as well as descriptive studies. Nonetheless, he finds at best tepid research support for aggressive regulation of the teacher labor market. On the question of whether pedagogical training contributes to teacher effectiveness, he finds only "limited" support in the research, and adds: "It is not clear from the research reviewed for this report, however, whether such knowledge and skills are best acquired through coursework, field experience (especially student teaching) or on the job" (Allen, 2003, p. 29). On the question of whether more stringent screening for teacher training program entrants pays off in terms of student achievement, he finds the literature "inconclusive." A new study by Betts, Zau, and Rice (2003)

examines student achievement gains in the San Diego school district. They find mixed results for teacher credentials. In some cases, students of emergency certified teachers have higher gains than those of experienced fully credentialed teachers. At the upper grade levels, full certification in math has a significant positive effect at in high schools, but a negative effect in middle schools.

6.  A recent study of Chicago public teachers by Aaronson, Barrow, and Sander (2003) illustrates this point well. Like other such studies, this work is based on a very longitudinal file of linked student achievement scores. What makes this study unique is that the authors also have very extensive administrative data on teacher characteristics that are unavailable in other studies, including education, experience, types of teaching licenses, and selectivity of the teacher's undergraduate college. They find that over ninety percent of teacher effects are not explained by any measured teacher characteristics.

7.  It may be that other potential measures, involving direct observation of classroom practice or psychological assessments of teacher attitudes toward students and teaching may do a better job of explaining classroom effectiveness. Indeed, many school districts use the latter types of assessments in their hiring decisions.

8.  Studies using student longitudinal data by Armor et al. (1976) and Murnane (1975) find large effects of principal evaluations on student achievement gains. More recently, Sanders and Horn report: "There is a very strong correlation between teacher effects as determined by the data and subjective evaluations by supervisors" (1994, p. 2000).

9.  A skeptic might argue that I have "stacked the deck" in this simple simulation by assuming that in hiring, the school district screens perfectly and always hires the best candidate. However, in a more elaborate simulation, Ballou (2000) assumes that school administrators have imperfect, but independent, information about the quality of job applicants, that is, over and above certification or a test score—things like direct observation of teaching performance, recommendation letters, psychological assessments. Ballou also shows that the cost of the reduced supply tends to be larger for low SES districts, which tend to draw relatively more applicants around the cut scores.

10. However, for a vigorous counterargument, see Friedman (1962, ch. 9).

11. Another subtle difference between teaching and medicine (as well as other professions) deserves mention. In medicine, the primary desire of a patient is simply to be made well. When we go to a doctor with a ruptured appendix, a dentist with a toothache, or a lawyer for legal representation, we want a "sage on the stage," not a "guide at the side." That is, we want their profession expertise put to work solving our problem. Usually, the process is a secondary concern to the end and we usually defer to the judgment of the expert professional on the best course of "treatment." Of course, if there are several ways to achieve the same end, the consumer will need to make a choice. However, more often than not, the treatment protocols are standard, and the consumer follows the advice of the doctor to achieve the desired end (a cure). However, in education, for many parents, the process is as important as the end result. Indeed, the two can be hard to separate. When parents choose a Montessori or a Waldorf school for their children, they clearly expect their children to learn basic literacy and numeracy skills, but they are also expressing a preference over a mode of inquiry and learning as well. Similarly, when parents object to the use of calculators by young children as in the initial NCTM standards or to whole-language reading instruction, they are expressing a preference for a type of instruction as well as an outcome. In fact, the experience in the private K–12 education marketplace suggests that parents are perfectly capable of making informed choices among vendors who offer a wide range of instructional strategies (e.g., from constructivist, to traditional, to military schools) and can select a

school that meets their preferences. We see little evidence of market failure or calls for government regulation coming from private school consumers.

12. The model proposed here is similar that in Hess (2001), which he describes as "competitive certification."

13. A critic might respond that for doctors licensing is merely the first step. Doctors then proceed to earn certification from one of 24 medical specialty boards. However, this certification is voluntary and not required by states. By the same token, teachers could proceed to earn certification (provided by private vendors) beyond the requirements for a state license. School districts could use information about advanced certification in hiring or promotion decisions. Of course, this is similar to the model of advanced certification provided by the National Board for Professional Teaching Standards.

## References

Allen, M. B. (2003). *Eight questions on teacher pay: What does the research say?* Denver: Education Commission of the States.

Armor, D., Conry-Osenguera, P., Cox, M., King, N., McDonnell, L., Pascal, A., Pauly, E., & Zellma, G. (1976). *Analysis of the School Preferred Reading Program in selected Los Angeles minority schools*. Santa Monica, CA: RAND .

Aaronson, D., Barrow, L., & Sander, W. (2003). "Teachers and student achievement in the Chicago Public High Schools." Working paper, Federal Reserve Bank of Chicago Research Department.

Ballou, D. (1999). "Recruiting smarter teachers: Is testing the answer?" Vanderbilt University. **need full pub info**

Ballou, D., & Podgursky, M. (1999). "Teacher training and licensing: A layman's guide." In C. Finn, Jr., & M. Kanstoroom (Eds.), *Better teachers, better schools* (pp. 31–82). Washington, DC: Fordham Foundation.

Ballou, D., & Podgursky, M. (1997). *Teacher pay and teacher quality*. Kalamazoo, MI: W. E. Upjohn Institute for Employment Research.

Ballou, D., & Podgursky, M. (1998). "Teacher recruitment and retention in public and private schools." *Journal of Policy Analysis and Management, 17,* 393–418.

Betts, J. R., Zau, A. C., & Rice, L. A. (2003). *Determinants of student achievement: New evidence from San Diego*. San Francisco: Public Policy Institute of California. http://www.ppic.org/content/pubs/R_803JBR.pdf

Darling-Hammond, L. (2003). "Access to quality teaching: An analysis of inequality in California Public Schools." Available online at http://www.mofo.com/decentschools/expert_reports/darling-hammond_report.pdf

Ehrenberg, R. C., & Brewer, D. J. (1993). "Did teachers' race and verbal ability matter in the 1960's? Coleman revised" *Economics of Education Review, 14,* 1–23.

Ehrenberg, R. C., & Brewer, D. J. (1994). "Do school and teacher characteristics matter? Evidence from high school and beyond." *Economics of Education Review, 13,* 1–17.

Ehrenberg, R. C., & Smith, R. S. (1996). *Modern labor economics* (6th ed.). Reading MA: Addison-Wesley.

Ferguson, R. F., & Ladd, H. (1996). "How and why money matters: An analysis of Alabama schools." In H. Ladd (Ed.), *Holding schools accountable: Performance-based reform in education*. Washington, DC: Brookings Institution.

Feistritzer, E. C., & Chester, D. C. (2002). *Alternative teacher certification: A state-by-state analysis: 2002*. Washington, DC: National Center for Education Information.

Friedman, M. (1962). *Capitalism and freedom*. Chicago: University of Chicago Press.

Goldhaber, D. D., & Brewer, D. J. (1997). "Why don't schools and teacher's seem to matter?" *Journal of Human Resources, 32,* 505–523.

Goldhaber, D. (2002). "The mystery of good teaching." *Education Next, 2,* 50–55.

Hanushek, E. A. (2003). "The failure of input-based resource policies." *Economic Journal, 113*(485), F64–F98.

Hanushek, E. A., & Rivkin, S. G. (2004). "How to improve the supply of high quality teachers" (Brookings Papers in Education Policy, 2004). Washington, DC: Brookings Institution.

Heckman, J. J., LaLonde, R. J., & Smith, J. A. (1999). "The economics and econometrics of active labor market programs." In O. Ashenfelter & D. Card (Eds.), *Handbook of labor economics* (pp. 1865–2097). town?Netherlands: Elsevier Science.

Hess, F. M. (2001). *Tear down this wall: The case for radical overhaul of teacher certification.* Washington, DC: Progressive Policy Institute.

Hoxby, C. (2001). "If families matter most, where do schools come in?" In T. M. Moe (Ed.), *A primer on America's schools.* Palo Alto, CA: Stanford University, Hoover Institute Press.

Lieberman, M. (1995). *Public education: An autopsy.* Cambridge, MA: Harvard University Press.

Mosteller, F., & Boruch, R. (Eds.). (2002). *Randomized trials in education research.* Washington, DC: Brookings Institution.

Murnane, R. (1975). *The impact of school resources on the learning of inner city children.* Cambridge, MA: Ballinger.

National Commission on Teaching and America's Future. (1996). *What matters most.* New York: Teachers College Press.

Rivkin, S. G., Hanushek, E. A., & Kain, J. F. (2000). "Teachers, schools, and academic achievement." Unpublished manuscript.

Sanders, W. L., & Horn, S. P. (1994). "The Tennessee Value-Added Assessment System (TVAAS): Mixed model methodology in educational assessment." *Journal of Personnel Evaluation in Education, 8,* 299–311.

Summers, A. M., & Wolfe, B. L. (1977). "Do schools make a difference?" *American Economic Review, 67,* 639–652.

U.S. Department of Education, Institute of Education Sciences. (n.d.). *Random assignment in program evaluation and intervention research: questions and answers.* Available online at http://www.mathematica-mpr.com/PDFs/randomassign.pdf

U.S. Department of Education, National Center for Education Statistics. (2000). "Teacher supply in the U.S.: Sources of newly hired teachers in public and private schools, 1987–88 to 1993–94." Washington, DC: Author.

Winkler, D. R. (1975). "Educational achievement and school peer group composition." *Journal of Human Resources, 10,* 189–204.